LUTHERAN SERVICE BOOK

Pastoral Care Companion

Prepared by
The Commission on Worship
of
The Lutheran Church—Missouri Synod

CONCORDIA PUBLISHING HOUSE · SAINT LOUIS

LUTHERAN SERVICE BOOK
Pastoral Care Companion (03-1178)

ALSO AVAILABLE:
Altar Book (03-1176)
Agenda (03-1177)

Copyright © 2007 Concordia Publishing House
3558 S. Jefferson Ave., St. Louis, MO 63118-3968
1-800-325-3040 • www.cph.org

Unless otherwise indicated, the Scripture readings used in *Lutheran Service Book* are from The Holy Bible, English Standard Version. Copyright © 2001 by Crossway Bibles, a publishing ministry of Good News Publishers, Wheaton, Illinois. Used by permission. All rights reserved.

The Holy Bible, English Standard Version (ESV) is adapted from the Revised Standard Version of the Bible, copyright Division of Christian Education of the National Council of the Churches of Christ in the U.S.A. All rights reserved.

A few alternative readings of the English Standard Version have been used in *Lutheran Service Book* by permission of the publisher and in accordance with the translation principles of the English Standard Version.

Manufactured in China

ISBN 0-7586-1225-7
ISBN 978-0-7586-1225-0

Cataloging-in-Publication Data can be found on page 708.

6 7 8 9 10 11 12 13 14   25 24 23 22 21 20 19 18

CONTENTS

RESOURCES FOR PASTORAL CARE

At the Time of Birth

Ministering to the Sick

At the Time of Death

Times of Spiritual Distress

Home and Family

Vocation

Times of Celebration

CONTENTS

INTRODUCTION
Lutheran Service Book: Agenda

General Introduction

The *Lutheran Service Book: Agenda*, containing the occasional rites and services for congregations of the Evangelical Lutheran Church, is a companion volume to the *Lutheran Service Book*. The *Lutheran Service Book* project was begun by The Lutheran Church—Missouri Synod in 1998 and, after extensive field-testing, received final approval by the Synod in 2004. The rites in this volume are built upon the confessional and theological foundation of the Holy Scriptures and the Lutheran Confessions and draw upon the history and practice of both the Evangelical Lutheran Church and the Church catholic. Overviews preceding each section of rites carefully articulate the rich Biblical theology and confession of faith that undergird the language and structure of the rites and explain how each fits into the overall tapestry of the Church's liturgy and practice of pastoral care.

The Agenda as Handbook for Pastoral Theology

Pastoral care is the spiritual care given by those placed into the pastoral office who use the means that God has given in order for sinners to hear the Gospel (AC V). The primary handbook for pastoral care is the agenda, which contains the rites that the pastor uses in his work. The rite of Ordination makes explicit what it is that the pastor is to do. The candidate pledges faithfulness to the Scriptures as the inspired Word of God and declares that the teachings confessed in the Lutheran Confessions are his own "because they are in accord with the Word of

God." He promises to perform all the duties of his office "in accordance with these Confessions." Inquiry is made of the ordinand: "Will you faithfully instruct both young and old in the chief articles of Christian doctrine? Will you forgive the sins of those who repent, and will you promise never to divulge the sins confessed to you? Will you minister faithfully to the sick and dying, and will you demonstrate to the Church a constant and ready ministry centered in the Gospel? Will you admonish and encourage the people to a lively confidence in Christ and in holy living?" The agenda provides the rites that are vehicles for this faithful ministry in various stages and situations of life.

The agenda rites are best seen in light of the Divine Service, which stands at the center of the Church's life. The liturgy itself is the primary place of ongoing pastoral care as week after week Christians are called together in the name of the triune God to receive His gifts in sermon and Sacrament and are enlivened to live in Christ by faith and in love toward the neighbor. All pastoral care radiates from the preaching of the Gospel and the administration of the Sacraments and ultimately culminates in the reception of the Lord's gifts proclaimed and distributed in the liturgy. Just as the planets are in orbit around the sun, so the rites of pastoral care revolve around the Divine Service, reflecting the light of Christ's gifts on our living and dying, hallowing grief and pain with His promises.

Agenda Rites and the Liturgy

The liturgy extends itself into the hospital room and cemetery, to the home and the prison cell, and to all the places where the pastor goes to speak as the "bodily voice" of the Good Shepherd (Martin Luther, *Sermon on the Sacrament, Against the Fanatics,* AE 36:340). As God visits His people to redeem them (Luke 1:68), so the pastor visits those committed to his care, bringing Christ and His gifts into the pit of sin and sickness, despair and death. The agenda provides the pastor with words to speak, blessings to bestow, and prayers to utter that are grounded in the Word of God. The agenda serves as a guard against abstractions in pastoral speaking and praying, such as superficial talk about the love of God. Instead, the agenda guides the pastor to speak concretely of the mercy of Christ for sinners. It binds the pastor to the task entrusted to him in ordination so that he speaks the word of forgiveness in the midst of the chaos created by our sin. It ties him to the table that Christ has prepared in the presence of His enemies—sin, death, and hell—so that the homebound, the sick, and the dying are fed with Christ's body and given to drink of the blood of His new testament.

Ordinary and Extraordinary Pastoral Care

It is helpful to distinguish between the ordinary and extraordinary means of pastoral care. The ordinary means include preaching, catechization, confession/absolution, prayer, and the liturgy itself. Extraordinary means of pastoral care are just that—they are out of the ordinary. Counseling, intervention, and referral are examples of the extraordinary. While recognizing the place of the extraordinary forms of pastoral care, the agenda attends to the ordinary. The wise pastor will know when others must be summoned to care for physical or psychological maladies. As others may render helpful service in caring for bodily and mental affliction, the pastor will devote himself to spiritual care—the care of the soul.

The liturgy has a cumulative effect in the care of the soul. Sure and certain gifts are going into people, strengthening and building them up for the long haul of life under the cross. Our Lord's words are implanted in the heart, taking root to bear fruit in faithful confession with the lips. Baptized into the death and resurrection of Christ, the Christian lives in the perpetual promise of baptism by repentance and faith. Fed with the body and blood of Christ, the believer is strengthened in faith toward Christ and in fervent love toward others.

Language of Pastoral Care

The liturgy itself provides the language for pastoral care. We are not left with the poverty of our own words or with the grammar of self-righteousness. The stability of the liturgy both in terms of form and text gives both pastor and people a common language. In times of crisis, people do not need creativity or novelty but forms and words that are well known and reliable. This accounts for the frequent use of the Apostles' Creed, the Lord's Prayer, familiar psalms and hymns, well-known biblical texts, and catechetical phrases in prayers in the rites for individual pastoral care. The language of the agenda is the language of the liturgy and as such it draws upon resources that are embedded in the life of the Christian. We may observe, by way of example, how the Commendation of the Dying reflects the language of Compline as well as that of many evening hymns. The Funeral Service is rich in baptismal imagery, since the death of a Christian is the culmination of his Baptism.

Agenda as Ritual

"Every pastor is either a witting or an unwitting ritualist," as John Kleinig has observed ("Witting or Unwitting Ritualists," *Lutheran Theological Journal* 22, no. 1 (1988): 20). It is not a question of whether or not ritual will be used but, rather, *how* ritual will be used. The agenda provides for rites and ceremonies that are characterized by theological integrity and pastoral sensitivity. Rather than relying on self-constructed forms, the pastor is furnished with a "pattern of sound words" (2 Tim. 1:13) consisting of biblical texts, psalms, hymns, and collects to use in ministering to people in a variety of circumstances. While the agenda cannot cover every conceivable crisis that may arise in the course of life in a fallen world, it does provide material for circumstances related to birth, marriage, family, vocation, transitions in life, sickness, accident, addiction, death, and grief.

Public Rites of the Agenda

Some of the rites of the agenda are primarily directed toward individuals; others are especially communal in nature. Marriage and burial are, perhaps, the most public of the Church's rites, since these services are typically attended by both Christians and non-Christians. Here it is essential that the pastor remember that these rites confess the Christian faith to the world. The marriage service holds up the biblical truth that marriage is an estate ordained by God for the faithful and lifelong union of one man and one woman. The Christian funeral does not eulogize the deceased on the basis of his or her virtues but confesses hope that is grounded in the God who justifies the ungodly. As such, it is a testimony to the forgiveness of sins, the resurrection of the body, and life everlasting. These rites are therefore centered in the triune God and His Word.

The Twofold Word of Law and Gospel

The terrain of pastoral care encompasses faith and love. Luther's description of the Christian reminds us that the believer lives outside of himself. He lives in Christ by faith and in the neighbor by love (see *On the Freedom of the Christian*, AE 31:371). The diagnosis of the Law uncovers that which blocks faith in Christ and therefore diminishes love for the neighbor. The speaking of the Gospel creates and sustains faith in the face of all that seems to contradict the promises of God. Here the pastor tutors his people in repentance, faith, and holy living. Pastoral care arms the Christian with God's Word so that he may lay hold of Christ's promises and take comfort in Baptism when assaulted by sin, death, and the devil.

In contrast to the counselor, the pastor's work is primarily kerygmatic rather than therapeutic. The basis of pastoral care is grounded in the first commandment itself, namely, that "we should fear, love, and trust in God above all things" (Small Catechism). The goal of pastoral care is nothing less than the faith confessed in the conclusion of the Apostles' Creed: "I believe in the forgiveness of sins, the resurrection of the body, and the life everlasting." This guides the agenda's use of scriptural readings, psalmody, and hymnody in addressing faith and love in life and in death. These texts function not as spiritual or moral principles to enable the Christian to attend to a disordered life, but as words from God that kill and make alive, convict of sin and console with our Lord's own absolution. Contained in that word of pardon is the promise of resurrection for "where there is forgiveness of sins, there is also life, and salvation" (Small Catechism).

Christ locates Himself in the Gospel and Sacraments for our consolation. "If you want to have God, then mark where He resides and where He wants to be found" (*Sermons on John 6—8, Luther's Works* 23:121). These are the only instruments that the pastor is given to bring Christ and His gifts to sinners. The agenda guides the pastor as he serves the means of grace so that, in the midst of the changes and chances of this life, hearts may be fixed in Christ, the place of everlasting joy.

Key to Terminology

Notes—Statements that precede each rite, directing how the rite is to be used and, in some cases, how the rite is to be understood in the overall context of the Church's worship life and pastoral practice.

Rubrics—Rubrics are italicized directions in red that are used throughout the services to describe how the rite is to be conducted. Rubrics using simple, declarative sentences identify what is ordinarily done in the service (e.g., "one or more of the following are read," "during Advent and Lent, the Hymn of Praise is omitted").

"May" rubrics—Rubrics that contain the word "may" are optional and may or may not be followed according to the needs of the particular circumstance or according to pastoral judgment.

P   Presiding minister (ordained)

A   Assisting minister (ordained or lay)

L   Liturgist or leader (ordained or lay)

C   Congregation

R   Response of individuals or group, but not the entire congregation

✝   the sign of the cross may be made by the presiding minister and/or the congregation

INTRODUCTION
Pastoral Care Companion

The *Pastoral Care Companion* contains all the rites and blessings from the *Lutheran Service Book: Agenda* that the pastor will need for pastoral care outside of the chancel and nave. Overviews and extensive notes on each of these rites are provided in the main *Agenda*. In addition to these "traveling rites," the *Pastoral Care Companion* also contains Resources for Pastoral Care that cover a wide range of issues that a pastor may encounter in ministering to individual members of his congregation. Each section of resources includes an introductory paragraph that gives the pastor suggestions on how to minister Law and Gospel to the people or person in that particular crisis or need. There is also resource material that assists the pastor in leading his members through various occasions of celebrations or difficult challenges. Each section includes psalms, readings, hymn stanzas, and prayers appropriate to the particular topic. The principal psalms and readings are printed out for easy reference. Additional psalms and readings are listed with short sentences describing their content. These resources are not intended to be exhaustive, nor are they intended to be used in a wooden or artificial way. Rather, they are intended, as their name suggests, to be resources for the pastor in caring for his flock.

The Pastor's Preparation for Pastoral Care

The best preparation for pastoral care is the pastor's own faithful hearing of the Word of God and praying of the Psalter. The discipline

Pastor's prayer on Saturday evening

O God, Father, Son, and Holy Spirit, my Lord and my God, I humbly pray You to pardon all my sins. Look not upon my unworthiness but upon Your great mercy, by which You have appointed me to be Your ambassador in Christ's stead. Put Your Word in my mouth and tomorrow speak with my tongue. Bring forth fruit through me, Your unworthy servant, and let not the preaching of Your Word be without effect among us. May all that I utter be in accord with Your Word and the confession of Your Church, that Your name may be glorified, Your congregation truly awakened, and thus, through me, Your unworthy servant, Your Church be edified.

As You inhabited the praises of Israel, dwell in the praises of this our Church. Let the sacrifice of our praise be acceptable to You, and preserve us from insincerity and thoughtless worship.

Incline Your ear to our prayer, O God of Jacob; hear the voice of our supplications and help us.

Preserve unto us Your holy Word that it may be joyfully and boldly proclaimed in its purity, and guard us in the right use of the Sacrament in accord with the institution of Jesus Christ, our Savior. Restrain all who would destroy us and turn them to Yourself.

Be our God and our children's God, now and henceforth, and hear my prayer, O Father, for the sake of Your dear Son, Jesus Christ, our blessed Savior, in the unity of the Holy Spirit, the Comforter divine. Amen. (703)

Kyrie Eleison

LORD, HAVE MERCY

SPECIFIC PASTORAL ACTS

Before a Baptism

Lord, I thank You that You are willing to receive this child through Holy Baptism as Your child. Be in our midst according to Your promise. Grant that this child may learn to grasp Your great gift in faith and live as a thankful and joyful child of God. Grant this each day also to me and to all the congregation of the baptized, that Your name may be glorified and Your kingdom come; through Jesus Christ, our Lord. Amen. (704)

Before instructing children

Lord Jesus Christ, our Savior, I give You thanks that You called the children unto Yourself and blessed them. I pray that You would bless these children also. Put Your saving Word into their hearts, and grant them the power gladly to live in accord with it, that when You call them they may come to You in heaven. Grant to us who proclaim Your Word to Your children joy and wisdom that Your Church may be built and bring forth the fruit of everlasting life; in Your holy name. Amen. (705)

Before visiting the sick

Lord Jesus, our Savior, You have compassion upon all the sick and afflicted. Be with me, Your servant, in this hour that I may rightly comfort, strengthen, encourage, admonish, and prepare the sick for a blessed death. Grant me Your Holy Spirit that all I say may be blessed and my prayers and supplications be pleasing to You. Into Your hands I commend myself; at Your bidding I go. You will preserve me, for I trust in You. Blessed be Your holy name. Amen. (706)

Before administering the Lord's Supper
to the sick and homebound

Lord Jesus Christ, in the solemn night of Your betrayal You established the holy meal of Your body and blood for us Christians to eat and to drink. Look in mercy on those who will receive the holy Sacrament this day. Grant that they come to Your table in true repentance and faith, that the gift of Your body and blood will sustain them in their afflictions, strengthen them in the communion of Your holy people, and be a pledge of the resurrection of their bodies to life everlasting; for You live and reign with the Father and the Holy Spirit, one God, now and forever. Amen. (707)

Before ministering to the dying

Lord God, I am called to the side of one who is about to die. In _his/her_ last bitter conflict, I am to stand by _name_ in the hour of utmost need and bring _him/her_ comfort. I acknowledge before You that of myself I have no ability or sufficiency. I come before You in deepest humility and pray that You would send from heaven all necessary courage and joy, faith and wisdom, power and strength. O God of all mercy, be gracious to Your child and make _his/her_ faith strong that _his/her_ trust may not waver or fail. Forgive _his/her_ sins and be _his/her_ helper in every need. Be pleased to come with Your comfort in these last hours when all human power has failed and there is no other help. Equip _him/her_ with the shield of faith and the whole armor of God that _he/she_ may fight the good fight, staunchly resist every temptation of Satan, and through death come to life in Your heavenly kingdom. Shorten for _him/her_ the agony, the labor, the fear, and the pain of death, and receive _him/her_ into Your eternal glory that You have prepared for _him/her_ through the blood of Your Son and firmly promised by Your Spirit in Your Word. Hear me for the sake of Jesus. Amen. (708)

Before calling on the bereaved

O Lord, in whose house are many mansions, speak through me to these whose loved one has gone from their sight, but not from Yours. There is nothing in me to heal the wounded heart or fill the aching void. Let Your words of comfort and truth be given me to speak that these sorrowing ones may find their peace in You. Amen. (709)

Before a funeral

O Lord, grant me a full awareness of the powerful reality of death. Help me in this hour to speak the right word concerning the pilgrimage of _ name _ and to bear witness to Your power over life and death, the severity of Your judgment, and the abundance of Your mercy in our crucified and risen Lord Jesus. Unite us with all those who have gone before us in the fellowship of faith, hope, and love. The world passes away; may Your kingdom come. Amen. (710)

Before a marriage

O Lord, You promised Your blessing upon marriage. Grant that I may so proclaim Your commands and promises to this couple that, being forgiven by You, they may live together in love and peace and serve You in gratitude and joy. Give them day by day the strength to bear each other's burden that they may grow together in every need and joy and become a blessing one to the other. Be a strong helper in every marriage in our congregation; through Jesus Christ, our Lord. Amen. (711)

Before hearing confession

Father of mercies and God of all consolation, before You all hearts are laid bare and no secrets are concealed. Open the lips of Your children that they may not hide their iniquity and so waste away in deceit, but in truth acknowledge their sin and receive Your word of absolution. Guide me, Your servant, by Your Word and Spirit, that I may rightly discharge this holy office with faithfulness and mercy, wisdom and compassion. Guard the door of my lips that I never utter what is divulged in confession and, by the word of pardon that You have placed on my lips, grant that those whose bones have been crushed by the weight of Your wrath might be restored with the forgiveness purchased by the blood of Your Son. Protect them from the accusation of the evil one as he strives to rob them of Your peace. Save them from temptation and keep them in the company of Your holy Church to sing of Your saving righteousness forever; through Jesus Christ, our Lord. Amen. (712)

Before ministering to those in conflict

God and Father of my Lord Jesus Christ, give to me the spirit of wisdom and understanding, of patience and compassion, that I may rightly speak Your words of judgment and mercy to _names_, that by the power of Your Gospel they may repent of their sin, trust in Your pardon, and be reconciled to live in the unity of the Spirit in the bond of peace; through Jesus Christ, our Lord. Amen. (713)

Lord God, You raise up faithful pastors to seek out those who stray and to speak the Gospel of peace to those who live in alienation. Strengthen me with Your Spirit that, clothed with humility and courage, I might minister to _names_ with the word of Your truth. Use me as an instrument of Your peace and healing so that they may be restored to life with You and one another; through Jesus Christ, our Lord. Amen. (714)

Pastor's confession of sin

O almighty God, merciful Father, I, a poor, miserable sinner, confess unto You all my sins and iniquities. Especially do I acknowledge my neglect of prayer, my indifference to Your Word, and my seeking after worldly luxury and self-promotion. I am heartily sorry for them and sincerely repent of them; and I pray, of Your boundless mercy and for the sake of the holy, innocent, bitter sufferings and death of Your beloved Son, forgive me all my sins, and be gracious and merciful to me. Cleanse me through Your Spirit by the blood of Jesus Christ, and give me more and more power and willingness to strive after holiness, for You have called me to be holy and blameless before You in love; through Jesus Christ, our Lord. Amen. (715)

For the pastor's family

O faithful God and Lord, I thank You for my family—my wife and children—and for all my relatives. You have given them to me purely out of fatherly, divine goodness and mercy, without any merit or worthiness in me. Preserve them in good health, and give them their daily bread. But above all keep them in Your grace and in the true confession of Your name to the end. For those among my relatives who do not know You, bring them to repentance and faith in Your Son, Jesus Christ, our Lord, who lives and reigns with You and the Holy Spirit, one God, now and forever. Amen. (716)

Prayer for strength and help in the ministry

O God of all grace and mercy, You have called me, a poor, unworthy sinner, to be a servant of Your Word. You have placed me into the office that preaches reconciliation and given me this flock to feed. In and of myself, I am wholly incompetent to perform the work of this great office. Therefore, by Your grace make me an able minister of Your Church. Give me Your Holy Spirit, the Spirit of wisdom and knowledge, of grace and prayer, of power and strength, of sanctification and the fear of God. Fill me with the right knowledge of Your Word, and open my lips that my mouth may proclaim the honor of Your name. Fill my heart with a passion for seeking the lost and with skillfulness to give to the lambs and sheep entrusted to my care what each one needs at the proper time. Give me at all times sound words, and empower me to perform just works. Whenever I overlook something or, in the weakness of my flesh, speak or act wrongly, O Lord, set it aright, and grant that no one may suffer eternal harm through me. All this I ask of You through the merits of Jesus Christ, Your Son, our Lord, who lives and reigns with You and the Holy Spirit, one God, now and forever. Amen. (717)

Prayer of thanksgiving for the congregation committed to the pastor's care

Glory and honor, praise and thanks be to You, God, Father, Son, and Holy Spirit, for all the mercy and faithfulness You have shown to this congregation. Your Word has not returned to You void, but You have here gathered a people that knows You and fears Your name. Give me Your Holy Spirit that I may at all times see the good things in this congregation and praise and thank You for them. Bless Your Word in times to come that it may preserve the faithful in Your grace, convert those who do not yet belong to You, and bring back the erring and straying. Gather Your people as a hen gathers her chicks under her wings, and shelter Your congregation with Your love; for You live and reign, one God, now and forever. Amen. (718)

Prayer for all the sick and distressed of the congregation

Merciful God, graciously take into Your fatherly care the sick and needy, those who are widowed and orphaned, the homeless and homebound, the lonely and forgotten, and all who are in any trouble, temptation, anguish of labor, peril of death, or any other adversity (especially _name(s)_). Comfort them, O God, with Your Holy Spirit that they may patiently endure their afflictions and acknowledge them as a manifestation of Your fatherly will. Preserve them from faintheartedness and despondency, and help them to seek You, the great physician of their souls. If any pass through the valley of the shadow of death, do not allow them in the last hour, for any pain or fear of death, to fall away from You, but let Your everlasting arms be underneath them, and grant them a peaceful departure and a joyful entrance into Your eternal kingdom in the resurrection of all flesh; through Jesus Christ, our Lord. Amen. (719)

Prayer for the leadership of the congregation

Lord God, heavenly Father, I pray that You would at all times fill the offices of this congregation and its societies with upright, honest, and sincere men and women who have the welfare of their congregation at heart and are able to help me in my office with their counsel and their deeds. Unite their hearts with me in love for the truth, and give them the spirit of prayer for me and for this congregation so that we may in unity and harmony hallow Your name and further Your kingdom in this place and to the ends of the earth; through Jesus Christ, our Lord. Amen. (720)

Prayer for reconciliation in the congregation

Almighty God, merciful Father, since hypocrites and ungodly people are found among the faithful within the Church, do not permit Satan to disrupt this congregation through such persons or to hinder the carrying out of the duties of my office. If there are such in our midst, grant that Your Word may bring them to repentance and faith. Grant me patience and kindness and a forgiving heart toward all. Help me, for the sake of all in the congregation, to speak the truth in love; through Jesus Christ, our Lord. Amen. (721)

Prayer for the youth of the congregation

Heavenly Father, preserve and keep the youth of our congregation from falling away from the faith and conforming to the world. Keep them from the many temptations of youth that lead to sin. Give me wisdom and skill to be inspiring, faithful, and charitable as I minister among them; through Jesus Christ, our Lord. Amen. (722)

Prayer for parents, Sunday School, and catechesis of the congregation

Lord God, heavenly Father, Your Son gathered the little children to Himself that He might bless them. Strengthen the parents of our congregation that they may faithfully bring up their children in the nurture and instruction of the Lord by a life of prayer and devotion to You and Your Word. Bless the work of our Sunday School teachers and all who assist our parents in teaching the faith to children, that all might be led into the Savior's loving arms and grow to lead godly lives to the praise and honor of Christ's holy name; through Jesus Christ, our Lord. Amen. (723)

Prayer for the Christian Day School

Heavenly Father, mercifully bless the Christian education of Your children in our parish that they may grow up in Your fear to the praise of Your holy name. Bless our Christian Day School and all other settings in which our children are brought closer to You. Restrain the activities of the evil one who would seek to undermine these efforts to provide for the spiritual growth of Your children. Help me to regard these children and our educational ministries as gifts from You. Encourage the members of our congregation to support those who teach and those who learn. Give joy to all who serve as teachers, and give them the privilege of seeing the fruits of their labors; through Jesus Christ, our Lord. Amen. (724)

Prayer for brother pastors and all fellow servants in the Church

O Lord, to Your grace and mercy I commend all my fellow pastors and every brother and sister who holds an office in Your Church. Remove any discord and dissension from among us. Give me a brotherly heart toward all in true humility, and help me to bear with compassion the burdens of others. Grant that we may act as true brothers and sisters in all circumstances; through Jesus Christ, our Lord. Amen. (725)

Prayer for the Synod

Almighty God, merciful Father, keep and preserve our whole Synod, its teachers and officers, true to Your Word. Cause the work of our Synod to grow and flourish. Guard and protect all members of our Synod against the danger of sinful ambitions, the love of dissension, and the spirit of indifference in doctrine and practice. Preserve us from all heresy and false belief. Bless and defend the seminaries, colleges, and universities of our Synod. Give us faithful pastors and teachers of Your Word. Accompany all missionaries on their perilous ways, and help them to perform their work faithfully. Gather the elect from every nation into Your holy Christian Church, and bring them at last into Your Church triumphant; through Jesus Christ, our Lord. Amen. (726)

Prayer for the civil authorities

Almighty God, grant integrity and well-being to all who are in authority in our nation and this community (especially _name(s)_). Grant them grace and wisdom to rule according to Your good pleasure, to the maintenance of justice and to the hindrance and punishment of wickedness, that we may lead quiet and peaceable lives in all godliness and honesty; through Jesus Christ, our Lord. Amen. (727)

SERVICES
AND
RITES

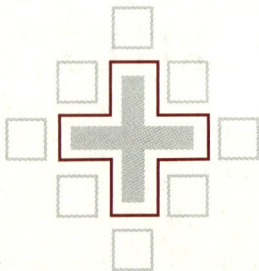

HOLY BAPTISM

General Notes

1. The rite of Holy Baptism is for use with candidates of all ages. Candidates are infants born to members of the congregation or those for whom members assume the responsibility of nurture, and older persons who, after adequate instruction in the Christian faith, declare their faith in Jesus Christ and their desire for Baptism.

2. When the candidate is unable to speak, sponsors may be appointed to speak in his or her stead. Sponsors should be chosen with great care. They are practicing Christians and should be members in good standing of an Evangelical Lutheran congregation.

3. The rite of Holy Baptism is a public rite of the Church that is usually administered in the presence of the congregation. The rite may be conducted apart from the Divine Service or Daily Office.

4. When extraordinary circumstances require that Holy Baptism be administered privately, public announcement of the Baptism shall be made to the congregation at the service the Sunday following.

5. In the case of an emergency Baptism, the rite of Public Recognition of Holy Baptism (*LSB Agenda,* page 18) is used at a later time.

6. This rite is a more complete version of the corresponding rite in *Lutheran Service Book,* pages 268–271.

The Rite in Detail

1. In the Divine Service this rite may occur in place of the Service of Confession and Absolution or the Creed. When it occurs in the Daily Office, it may precede the opening versicles.

2. When this rite occurs at the beginning of the Divine Service, the

3

Creed may be omitted from its normal place; the Lord's Prayer, however, is not omitted later during the celebration of the Lord's Supper.

3. The font should be filled with warm water before the rite begins. Baptismal napkins or small towels, together with other items, should be placed nearby. A baptismal shell may be used for pouring water on the candidate's head.

4. The paschal candle is lighted for all baptisms. It remains lighted for the entire service or office. The paschal candle is ordinarily placed next to the font for all baptisms.

5. The first part of the rite may take place at the entrance to the nave, with the baptismal party processing to the font for the second part (immediately following the Lord's Prayer). Or the entire rite may take place at the font.

6. The enrollment of sponsors may occur in one of several ways. The "address to sponsors" included in the rite of Holy Baptism may be used at the appointed time, or the rite for the Enrollment of Sponsors (page 23) may be used instead, either in a private setting with family and sponsors or immediately prior to the rite of Holy Baptism.

7. When the pastor asks the name of the candidate, the parents or the candidate give the Christian name, i.e., first and middle names.

8. The pastor pours or sprinkles water three times on the head of the candidate while naming the persons of the Holy Trinity. If Baptism is by immersion, the candidate is immersed three times as the pastor names the persons of the Trinity.

9. While making the sign of the cross during the blessing after the Baptism, olive oil may be used to symbolize the sealing with the Holy Spirit for salvation (Eph. 1:13–14). This oil is applied with the thumb.

10. The baptismal candle is lighted from the paschal candle.

An appropriate baptismal hymn may be sung.

The candidate(s), sponsors, and family gather with the pastor at the entrance of the nave or at the font.

When candidates are unable to speak for themselves, the sponsors answer the questions on their behalf.

Stand

P In the name of the Father and of the ✝ Son and of the Holy Spirit. *Matthew 28:19b*

C **Amen.**

P Dearly beloved, Christ our Lord says in the last chapter of Matthew, "All authority in heaven and on earth has been given to Me. Therefore go and make disciples of all nations, baptizing them in the name of the Father and of the Son and of the Holy Spirit." In the last chapter of Mark our Lord promises, "Whoever believes and is baptized will be saved." And the apostle Peter has written, "Baptism now saves you."

Matthew 28:18b–19; Mark 16:16a; 1 Peter 3:21

The Word of God also teaches that we are all conceived and born sinful and are under the power of the devil until Christ claims us as His own. We would be lost forever unless delivered from sin, death, and everlasting condemnation. But the Father of all mercy and grace has sent His Son Jesus Christ, who atoned for the sin of the whole world, that whoever believes in Him should not perish but have eternal life.

5

The pastor addresses each candidate:

P How are you named?

R ___Name___

The pastor makes the sign of the holy cross upon the forehead and heart of each candidate while saying:

P ___Name___, receive the sign of the holy cross both upon your ✠ forehead and upon your ✠ heart to mark you as one redeemed by Christ the crucified.

P Let us pray.
Almighty and eternal God,
according to Your strict judgment You condemned the unbelieving world through the flood,
yet according to Your great mercy You preserved believing Noah and his family,
eight souls in all.
You drowned hard-hearted Pharaoh and all his host in the Red Sea,
yet led Your people Israel through the water on dry ground,
foreshadowing this washing of Your Holy Baptism.
Through the Baptism in the Jordan of Your beloved Son,
our Lord Jesus Christ,
You sanctified and instituted all waters to be a blessed flood
and a lavish washing away of sin.
We pray that You would behold ___name(s)___ according to Your boundless mercy
and bless ___him/her/them___ with true faith by the Holy Spirit,
that through this saving flood all sin in ___him/her/them___,
which has been inherited from Adam
and which ___he himself / she herself / they themselves has/have___ committed since,
would be drowned and die.

Grant that _*he/she/they*_ be kept safe and secure in the holy ark
    of the Christian Church,
    being separated from the multitude of unbelievers
    and serving Your name at all times with a fervent spirit and
      a joyful hope,
so that, with all believers in Your promise,
    *he/she/they* would be declared worthy of eternal life;
through Jesus Christ, our Lord. (501)

C **Amen.**

*If the sponsors were previously enrolled, the service continues below
with the Holy Gospel.*

P From ancient times the Church has observed the custom of appointing sponsors for baptismal candidates and catechumens. In
the Evangelical Lutheran Church sponsors are to confess the faith
expressed in the Apostles' Creed and taught in the Small Catechism. They are, whenever possible, to witness the Baptism of
those they sponsor. They are to pray for them, support them in
their ongoing instruction and nurture in the Christian faith, and
encourage them toward the faithful reception of the Lord's Supper. They are at all times to be examples to them of the holy life
of faith in Christ and love for the neighbor.

The pastor addresses the sponsors.

P Is it your intention to serve _*name of candidate(s)*_ as sponsors
in the Christian faith?

R *Yes, with the help of God.*

P God enable you both to will and to do this faithful and loving
work and with His grace fulfill what we are unable to do.

C **Amen.**

P Hear the Holy Gospel according to St. Mark.

They brought young children to [Jesus] that He might touch them; but the disciples rebuked those who brought them. But when Jesus saw it, He was greatly displeased and said to them, "Let the little children come to Me, and do not forbid them; for of such is the kingdom of God. Assuredly, I say to you, whoever does not receive the kingdom of God as a little child will by no means enter it." And He took them up in His arms, put His hands on them, and blessed them. *Mark 10:13–16 NKJV*

P This is the Word of the Lord.
C **Thanks be to God.**

The pastor places his hands on the head(s) of the candidate(s), and the congregation joins in praying:

C **Our Father who art in heaven,**
    hallowed be Thy name,
    Thy kingdom come,
    Thy will be done on earth as it is in heaven;
    give us this day our daily bread;
    and forgive us our trespasses
      as we forgive those who trespass against us;
    and lead us not into temptation,
    but deliver us from evil.
  For Thine is the kingdom and the power and the glory
    forever and ever. Amen. *Matthew 6:9–13*

If the baptismal party has stood at the entrance of the nave to this point, they now move to the font. A hymn may be sung during the procession. Then the pastor says:

P The Lord preserve your coming in and your going out from this time forth and even ✛ forevermore.
C **Amen.**

Sit

The pastor addresses the candidate(s) and asks the following questions:

P   *Name(s)* , do you renounce the devil?
R *Yes, I renounce him.*

P Do you renounce all his works?
R *Yes, I renounce them.*

P Do you renounce all his ways?
R *Yes, I renounce them.*

P Do you believe in God, the Father Almighty, maker of heaven and earth?
R *Yes, I believe.*

P Do you believe in Jesus Christ, His only Son, our Lord, who was conceived by the Holy Spirit, born of the virgin Mary, suffered under Pontius Pilate, was crucified, died and was buried; He descended into hell; the third day He rose again from the dead; He ascended into heaven and sits at the right hand of God the Father Almighty; from thence He will come to judge the living and the dead?
R *Yes, I believe.*

P Do you believe in the Holy Spirit, the holy Christian Church, the communion of saints, the forgiveness of sins, the resurrection of the body, and the life everlasting?
R *Yes, I believe.*

P   *Name* , do you desire to be baptized?
R *Yes, I do.*

The pastor pours water three times on the head of each candidate while saying:

P   _Name_ , I baptize you in the name of the Father and of the Son and of the Holy Spirit.

C **Amen.**

The pastor places his hands on the head of the newly baptized while saying:

P The almighty God and Father of our Lord Jesus Christ, who has given you the new birth of water and of the Spirit and has forgiven you all your sins, strengthen you with His grace to life ✠ everlasting.

C **Amen.**

The pastor may place a white garment on the newly baptized while saying:

P Receive this white garment to show that you have been clothed with the robe of Christ's righteousness that covers all your sin. So shall you stand without fear before the judgment seat of Christ to receive the inheritance prepared for you from the foundation of the world.

The pastor may light a baptismal candle from the paschal candle and give it to the newly baptized while saying:

P Receive this burning light to show that you have received Christ who is the Light of the world. Live always in the light of Christ, and be ever watchful for His coming, that you may meet Him with joy and enter with Him into the marriage feast of the Lamb in His kingdom, which shall have no end.

The newly baptized may be welcomed with the following:

[A] In Holy Baptism God the Father has made you __*a member /*__ __*members*__ of His Son, our Lord Jesus Christ, and __*an heir /*__ __*heirs*__ with us of all the treasures of heaven in the one holy Christian and apostolic Church. We receive you in Jesus' name as our __*brother(s)/sister(s)*__ in Christ, that together we might hear His Word, receive His gifts, and proclaim the praises of Him who called us out of darkness into His marvelous light.

[C] **Amen. We welcome you in the name of the Lord.**

Stand

While remaining at the font, the pastor prays the following:

[P] Let us pray.

Almighty and most merciful God and Father, we thank and praise You that You graciously preserve and enlarge Your family and have granted __*name(s)*__ the new birth in Holy Baptism and made __*him/her/them*__ __*a member / members*__ of Your Son, our Lord Jesus Christ, and __*an heir / heirs*__ of Your heavenly kingdom. We humbly implore You that, as __*he/she/they*__ __*has/have*__ now become Your __*child/children*__, You would keep __*him/her/them*__ in __*his/her/their*__ baptismal grace, that according to Your good pleasure __*he/she/they*__ may faithfully grow to lead a godly life to the praise and honor of Your holy name and finally, with all Your saints, obtain the promised inheritance in heaven; through Jesus Christ, our Lord. (503)

[C] **Amen.**

One or more of the following collects may also be prayed.

Thanksgiving for the gift of a child

P Heavenly Father, You sent Your own Son into this world as the child of the virgin Mary. We thank You for the life of this child entrusted to our care. Help us remember that we are all Your children and so love and nurture __*him/her*__ that __*he/she*__ may attain to the full stature intended for __*him/her*__ in Your eternal kingdom, for the sake of Jesus Christ, our Lord. (504)

C **Amen.**

For an adopted child

P Merciful Father, in Holy Baptism You grant us the adoption as sons through Your Son, our Lord Jesus Christ, and claim us as Your own from the kingdom of Satan, rescuing us from sin and everlasting condemnation. We give thanks to You that __*name(s)*__ __*has/have*__ been made Your own dear __*child/children*__ in Holy Baptism and that __*name of parents*__ have also adopted __*him/her/them*__ . Grant Your blessing to these parents that, being strengthened in the grace of their own Baptism, they may faithfully nurture their __*child/children*__ in the knowledge and love of the Lord Jesus Christ, who lives and reigns with You and the Holy Spirit, one God, now and forever. (505)

C **Amen.**

For parents

P Lord and Giver of life, look with kindness upon the father(s) and mother(s) of __*this child / these children*__ and upon all our parents. Let them ever rejoice in the gift You have given them. Enable them to be teachers and examples of righteousness for their children. Strengthen them in their own Baptism that they may share eternally with their children the salvation You have given them; through Jesus Christ, our Lord. (506)

C **Amen.**

For the Church and her members

P Almighty and everlasting God, since You govern and sanctify the whole Christian Church by Your Holy Spirit, hear our prayers for all her members, and mercifully grant that by Your grace we may serve You in true faith; through Jesus Christ, our Lord. (507)

C **Amen.**

The rite concludes:

P Peace ✛ be with you.
C **Amen.**

All return to their places.

HOLY BAPTISM
Alternate Form Based on Luther's Baptism Rite

General Notes

1. The rite of Holy Baptism is for use with candidates of all ages. Candidates are infants born to members of the congregation or those for whom members assume the responsibility of nurture, and older persons who, after adequate instruction in the Christian faith, declare their faith in Jesus Christ and their desire for Baptism.

2. When the candidate is unable to speak, sponsors may be appointed to speak in his or her stead. Sponsors should be chosen with great care. They are practicing Christians and should be members in good standing of an Evangelical Lutheran congregation.

3. The rite of Holy Baptism is a public rite of the Church that is usually administered in the presence of the congregation. The rite may be conducted apart from the Divine Service or Daily Office.

4. When extraordinary circumstances require that Holy Baptism be administered privately, public announcement of the Baptism shall be made to the congregation at the service the Sunday following.

5. In the case of an emergency Baptism, the rite of Public Recognition of Holy Baptism (*LSB Agenda*, page 18) is used at a later time.

6. This rite is based on the form found in the Baptismal Booklet as appended to Luther's Small Catechism (*The Book of Concord,* Kolb-Wengert, pages 371–375).

The Rite in Detail

1. In the Divine Service this rite may occur in place of the Service of Confession and Absolution or the Creed. When it occurs in the Daily Office, it may precede the opening versicles.

2. When this rite occurs at the beginning of the Divine Service, the Creed may be omitted from its normal place; the Lord's Prayer, however, is not omitted later during the celebration of the Lord's Supper.
3. The font should be filled with warm water before the rite begins. Baptismal napkins or small towels, together with other items, should be placed nearby. A baptismal shell may be used for pouring water on the candidate's head.
4. The paschal candle is lighted for all baptisms. It remains lighted for the entire service or office. The paschal candle is ordinarily placed next to the font for all baptisms.
5. The first part of the rite may take place at the entrance to the nave, with the baptismal party processing to the font for the second part (immediately following the Lord's Prayer). Or the entire rite may take place at the font.
6. The enrollment of sponsors may occur either in a private setting with family and sponsors or immediately prior to the rite of Holy Baptism. The rite for the Enrollment of Sponsors (page 23) is used.
7. When the pastor asks the name of the candidate, the parents or the candidate give the Christian name, i.e., first and middle names.
8. The pastor pours or sprinkles water three times on the head of the candidate while naming the persons of the Holy Trinity. If Baptism is by immersion, the candidate is immersed three times as the pastor names the persons of the Trinity.
9. The white garment symbolizes being clothed with Christ and His righteousness (Gal. 3:26–27).

———————

An appropriate baptismal hymn may be sung.

The candidate(s), sponsors, and family gather with the pastor at the entrance of the nave or at the font.

When candidates are unable to speak for themselves, the sponsors answer the questions on their behalf.

Stand

P Dearly beloved, Christ our Lord says in the last chapter of Matthew, "All authority in heaven and on earth has been given to Me. Therefore go and make disciples of all nations, baptizing them in the name of the Father and of the Son and of the Holy Spirit." In the last chapter of Mark our Lord promises, "Whoever believes and is baptized will be saved." And the apostle Peter has written, "Baptism now saves you."

Matthew 28:18b–19; Mark 16:16a; 1 Peter 3:21

The Word of God also teaches that we are all conceived and born sinful and are under the power of the devil until Christ claims us as His own.

Therefore, depart, you unclean spirit, and make room for the Holy Spirit in the name of the Father and of the ✛ Son and of the Holy Spirit.

The pastor makes the sign of the holy cross upon the forehead and heart of the candidate while saying:

P Receive the sign of the holy cross both upon your ✛ forehead and upon your ✛ heart to mark you as one redeemed by Christ the crucified.

One or both of the following may be prayed. When only one is prayed, the second is the preferred choice.

P Let us pray.
O almighty and eternal God, Father of our Lord Jesus Christ, we pray on behalf of Your servant(s) *name(s)*, who ask(s) for the gift of Your Baptism and desire(s) Your eternal grace through spiritual rebirth. Receive *him/her/them*, Lord, according to Your promise: "Ask, and it will be given to you; seek, and

16

you will find; knock, and it will be opened to you." Now give
Your blessing to ___him/her/them___ who ask(s) and open the door to
___him/her/them___ who knock(s), so that ___he/she/they___ may obtain the eternal blessing of this heavenly bath and receive the
promised kingdom that You give; through Jesus Christ, our
Lord. (502)   *Matthew 7:7*

C **Amen.**

P Almighty and eternal God,
according to Your strict judgment You condemned the unbeliev-
    ing world through the flood,
yet according to Your great mercy You preserved believing Noah
    and his family,
        eight souls in all.
You drowned hard-hearted Pharaoh and all his host in the Red Sea,
yet led Your people Israel through the water on dry ground,
    foreshadowing this washing of Your Holy Baptism.
Through the Baptism in the Jordan of Your beloved Son,
    our Lord Jesus Christ,
You sanctified and instituted all waters to be a blessed flood
    and a lavish washing away of sin.
We pray that You would behold ___name(s)___ according to Your
    boundless mercy
and bless ___him/her/them___ with true faith by the Holy Spirit,
that through this saving flood all sin in ___him/her/them___,
        which has been inherited from Adam
        and which ___he himself / she herself / they themselves___
            ___has/have___ committed since,
    would be drowned and die.
Grant that ___he/she/they___ be kept safe and secure in the holy ark
    of the Christian Church,
    being separated from the multitude of unbelievers   ▶

17

and serving Your name at all times with a fervent spirit and
a joyful hope,
so that, with all believers in Your promise,
　　he/she/they　 would be declared worthy of eternal life;
through Jesus Christ, our Lord. (501)

C **Amen.**

P Hear the Holy Gospel according to St. Mark.

They brought young children to [Jesus] that He might touch
them; but the disciples rebuked those who brought them. But
when Jesus saw it, He was greatly displeased and said to them,
"Let the little children come to Me, and do not forbid them; for
of such is the kingdom of God. Assuredly, I say to you, whoever
does not receive the kingdom of God as a little child will by no
means enter it." And He took them up in His arms, put His hands
on them, and blessed them.　　　　　　　　*Mark 10:13–16 NKJV*

*The pastor places his hands on the head of the candidate, and the
congregation joins in praying:*

C **Our Father who art in heaven,**
　　　　hallowed be Thy name,
　　　　Thy kingdom come,
　　　　Thy will be done on earth as it is in heaven;
　　　　give us this day our daily bread;
　　　　and forgive us our trespasses
　　　　　　as we forgive those who trespass against us;
　　　　and lead us not into temptation,
　　　　but deliver us from evil.
　　For Thine is the kingdom and the power and the glory
　　　　forever and ever. Amen.　　　　　　*Matthew 6:9–13*

If the baptismal party has stood at the entrance of the nave to this point, they now move to the font. A hymn may be sung during the procession. Then the pastor says:

P The Lord preserve your coming in and your going out from this time forth and even ✠ forevermore.

C **Amen.**

Sit

The pastor addresses the candidate(s) and asks the following questions:

P ___Name(s)___ , do you renounce the devil?

R *Yes, I renounce him.*

P Do you renounce all his works?

R *Yes, I renounce them.*

P Do you renounce all his ways?

R *Yes, I renounce them.*

P Do you believe in God, the Father Almighty, maker of heaven and earth?

R *Yes, I believe.*

P Do you believe in Jesus Christ, His only Son, our Lord, who was conceived by the Holy Spirit, born of the virgin Mary, suffered under Pontius Pilate, was crucified, died and was buried; He descended into hell; the third day He rose again from the dead; He ascended into heaven and sits at the right hand of God the Father Almighty; from thence He will come to judge the living and the dead?

R *Yes, I believe.*

P Do you believe in the Holy Spirit, the holy Christian Church, the communion of saints, the forgiveness of sins, the resurrection of the body, and the life everlasting?

R *Yes, I believe.*

P   _Name_ , do you desire to be baptized?

R *Yes, I do.*

The pastor pours water three times on the head of each candidate while saying:

P   _Name_ , I baptize you in the name of the Father and of the Son and of the Holy Spirit.

C **Amen.**

A white garment may be placed on the newly baptized.

The pastor places his hands on the head of the newly baptized while saying:

P The almighty God and Father of our Lord Jesus Christ, who has given you the new birth of water and of the Spirit and has forgiven you all your sins, strengthen you with His grace to life ✝ everlasting.

C **Amen.**

P Peace ✝ be with you.

C **Amen.**

All return to their places.

HOLY BAPTISM
In Cases of Emergency

In urgent situations, in the absence of the pastor, any Christian may administer Holy Baptism.

If time permits, the following may precede the Baptism.

Jesus said, "Assuredly, I say to you, whoever does not receive the kingdom of God as a little child will by no means enter it." And He took them up in His arms, put His hands on them, and blessed them. *Mark 10:15–16 NKJV*

Eternal God, Father of our Lord Jesus Christ, give ___name(s)___ Your grace through rebirth by the Holy Spirit. Receive ___him/her/them___ according to Your promise: "Ask, and it will be given to you; seek, and you will find; knock, and it will be opened to you," that through this heavenly washing ___he/she/they___ may receive the gift of the Holy Spirit and the forgiveness of all ___his/her/their___ sins and come to the eternal kingdom which You have prepared for ___him/her/them___; through Jesus Christ, our Lord. Amen. (508) *Matthew 7:7*

Lord's Prayer

Apostles' Creed

Take water, call the child or adult by name, and pour or sprinkle the water on the head of the candidate while saying:

    <u> Name </u>, I baptize you in the name of the Father and of the Son and of the Holy Spirit. Amen.

Holy Baptism administered by a layperson shall immediately be reported to the pastor for its recognition by the congregation.

Holy Baptism administered by the pastor in cases of emergency shall also be recognized by the congregation. See LSB Agenda, *pages 18–21.*

ENROLLMENT OF SPONSORS

1. This rite is used to enroll members of the Evangelical Lutheran Church as baptismal and catechetical sponsors. It is most appropriate that baptismal candidates have at least two sponsors who also serve as witnesses to the candidate's Baptism. Adult catechumens who are being enrolled in the congregation's catechumenate and have already been baptized may be assigned one sponsor. When there is only one sponsor (or only one parent of a child), the wording of the rite will need to be adjusted accordingly.

2. Prior to their enrollment and the Baptism of those they sponsor, it is appropriate for the pastor to instruct sponsors concerning the Sacrament of Holy Baptism and the catechetical life of the congregation in which the sponsored children or adults will be involved.

3. This rite may take place in a variety of settings, especially in the home, in the pastor's study, or publicly in the Divine Service before the rite of Holy Baptism or the rite of Public Recognition of Holy Baptism.

4. This rite may be used before the Prayer of the Church when enrolling sponsors for those entering the catechumenate. Catechumens join their sponsors at the entrance to the chancel.

P In the name of the Father and of the ☩ Son and of the Holy Spirit. *Matthew 28:19b*

C Amen.

℘ Beloved in the Lord, from ancient times the Church has observed the custom of appointing sponsors for baptismal candidates and catechumens. In the Evangelical Lutheran Church sponsors are to confess the faith expressed in the Apostles' Creed and taught in the Small Catechism. They are, whenever possible, to witness the Baptism of those they sponsor. They are to pray for them, support them in their ongoing instruction and nurture in the Christian faith, and encourage them toward the faithful reception of the Lord's Supper. They are at all times to be examples to them of the holy life of faith in Christ and love for the neighbor.

At this time the pastor may give further instruction to the sponsors concerning the sacrament of Holy Baptism and the catechetical life of the congregation.

A copy of the Small Catechism may also be given to sponsors to be used by them with those they sponsor.

The pastor addresses the sponsors of each candidate or catechumen with the following question:

℘   *Names of the sponsors* , is it your intention to serve   *name of candidate*   as sponsors in the Christian faith?

℞ *Yes, with the help of God.*

After all sponsors have been addressed, the pastor continues with the following:

℘ God enable you both to will and to do this faithful and loving work and with His grace fulfill what we are unable to do.

C **Amen.**

℘ Let us pray.

24

For the sponsors

P Heavenly Father, grant Your blessing upon these faithful Christians, __*names of sponsors*__, who have pledged themselves to __*this/these*__ catechumen(s) as sponsors in Holy Baptism and catechesis. Pour upon them Your Word and Spirit that they may faithfully confess the faith to __*him/her/them*__, support and encourage __*him/her/them*__ in __*his/her/their*__ instruction and nurture, and pray for __*him/her/them*__ that __*he/she/they*__ might not fall away from Christ. Enable these sponsors to be examples of prayer and faithfulness in hearing the Word of God, receiving the Sacraments, confessing sin, and living by faith in Christ's forgiveness with love toward others. Grant that their catechumen(s) might learn from them to suffer under the cross of persecution and affliction with steadfastness, patience, and joy, to the glory of the only true God; through Jesus Christ, our Lord. (509)

C **Amen.**

One or more of the following collects may also be prayed. If no additional prayers are offered, the rite concludes with the blessing on page 27.

Thanksgiving at the birth of a child

P O God, giver of all blessings, we praise You for this gift of a new life granted to these parents in the birth of a __*son/daughter*__. Protect mother(s) and __*child/children*__ and shield them from anything harmful in body or soul. Give joy to these parents as they bring __*this child / these children*__ for reception into Your kingdom through the water of Holy Baptism, and grant __*this child / these children*__ Your continued blessing; through Jesus Christ, our Lord. (510)

C **Amen.**

At the adoption of a child who is to be baptized

P Merciful Father, in Holy Baptism You grant us the adoption as sons through Your Son, our Lord Jesus Christ, and claim us as Your own from the kingdom of Satan, rescuing us from sin and everlasting condemnation. We give thanks to You that ___name of parents___ have adopted ___this child / these children___ , ___name(s)___ . Grant Your blessing to these parents as they bring ___him/her/them___ to the waters of Holy Baptism that, being strengthened in the grace of their own Baptism, they may faithfully nurture their ___child/ children___ in the knowledge and love of the Lord Jesus Christ, who lives and reigns with You and the Holy Spirit, one God, now and forever. (511)

C **Amen.**

At the adoption of a child who was previously baptized

P Merciful Father, in Holy Baptism You grant us the adoption as sons through Your Son, our Lord Jesus Christ, and claim us as Your own from the kingdom of Satan, rescuing us from sin and everlasting condemnation. We give thanks to You that ___name(s)___ ___has/have___ been made Your own dear ___child/children___ in Holy Baptism and that ___name of parents___ have also adopted ___him/her/them___ . Grant Your blessing to these parents that, being strengthened in the grace of their own Baptism, they may faithfully nurture their ___child/children___ in the knowledge and love of the Lord Jesus Christ, who lives and reigns with You and the Holy Spirit, one God, now and forever. (505)

C **Amen.**

For parents

P Lord and Giver of life, look with kindness upon the father(s) and mother(s) of __*this child / these children*__ and upon all our parents. Let them ever rejoice in the gift You have given them. Enable them to be teachers and examples of righteousness for their children. Strengthen them in their own Baptism so that they may share eternally with their children the salvation You have given them; through Jesus Christ, our Lord. (506)

C **Amen.**

For the Church and her members

P Almighty and everlasting God, since You govern and sanctify the whole Christian Church by Your Holy Spirit, hear our prayers for all her members, and mercifully grant that by Your grace we may serve You in true faith; through Jesus Christ, our Lord. (507)

C **Amen.**

For the catechumens

P Almighty God and Father, because You always grant growth to Your Church, increase the faith and understanding of our catechumens that, recalling the new birth by the water of Holy Baptism, they may forever continue in the family of those whom You adopt as Your sons and daughters; through Jesus Christ, our Lord. (430)

C **Amen.**

The rite concludes:

P Peace ✠ be with you.

C **Amen.**

All return to their places.

27

INDIVIDUAL CONFESSION AND ABSOLUTION

Based on the Rite in Luther's Small Catechism

1. This rite is identical to the rite found in *Lutheran Service Book*, pages 292–293.
2. Upon arriving at the church, the penitent may be instructed to prepare for confession by turning to the rite in *Lutheran Service Book* and using the recommended resources.

You may prepare yourself by meditating on the Ten Commandments (LSB pages 321–322). You may also pray the penitential psalms (6, 32, 38, 51, 102, 130, or 143).

If you are not burdened with particular sins, do not trouble yourself or search for or invent other sins, thereby turning confession into a torture. Instead, mention one or two sins that you know and let that be enough.

When you are ready, kneel and say:

Pastor, please hear my confession and pronounce forgiveness in order to fulfill God's will.
Proceed.

I, a poor sinner, plead guilty before God of all sins.
I have lived as if God did not matter and as if I mattered most.
My Lord's name I have not honored as I should;
     my worship and prayers have faltered.
I have not let His love have its way with me, and so my love for
     others has failed.
There are those whom I have hurt, and those whom I have failed
     to help.
My thoughts and desires have been soiled with sin.

If you wish to confess specific sins that trouble you, continue as follows:

What troubles me particularly is that . . .

Confess whatever you have done against the commandments of God, according to your own place in life.

The pastor may gently question or instruct you—not to pry or judge—but to assist in self-examination.

Then conclude by saying:

I am sorry for all of this and ask for grace. I want to do better.

God be merciful to you and strengthen your faith.
Amen.

Do you believe that my forgiveness is God's forgiveness?
Yes.

Let it be done for you as you believe.

The pastor places his hands on the head of the penitent and says:

In the stead and by the command of my Lord Jesus Christ I forgive you all your sins in the name of the Father and of the ✛ Son and of the Holy Spirit.
Amen.

The pastor may speak additional Scripture passages to comfort and strengthen the faith of those who have great burdens of conscience or are sorrowful and distressed.

The pastor concludes:

Go in peace.
Amen.

You may remain to say a prayer of thanksgiving. Psalms 30, 31, 32, 34, 103, or 118 are also appropriate.

VISITING THE SICK AND DISTRESSED

1. This rite is for use with baptized Christians who are sick or infirm.
2. An option for receiving Holy Communion is provided in the rite. For repeated visits to the sick and homebound, the Communion of the Sick and Homebound (page 39) may be used.
3. According to apostolic custom (Mark 6:13; James 5:14), a sick person may be anointed with oil as a reminder of the grace of God given by the Holy Spirit in Holy Baptism. Olive oil is used when anointing the sick.
4. If Individual Confession and Absolution is desired, the penitent may follow along in the pew edition of *Lutheran Service Book* (pages 292–293). If a pew book is not available, the pastor may share his copy with the penitent.
5. See pages 195–233 for appropriate Scripture resources.

As he enters the house or room, the pastor speaks this greeting:

Peace be to this house (place). *Luke 10:5*

Amen.

The pastor may read an appropriate portion of Holy Scripture according to the circumstance. He will then instruct the person patiently to trust God's holy will, confident that, according to His gracious promise, in all things He works for the good of those who love Him. The pastor may also sing an appropriate hymn.

The confession of sins may follow one of the forms below. In the case of individual confession, the pastor assures the confidentiality of the confession by requesting others present to leave the room or by taking other appropriate measures.

General Confession

O almighty God, merciful Father, I, a poor, miserable sinner, confess unto You all my sins and iniquities with which I have ever offended You and justly deserved Your temporal and eternal punishment. But I am heartily sorry for them and sincerely repent of them, and I pray You of Your boundless mercy and for the sake of the holy, innocent, bitter sufferings and death of Your beloved Son, Jesus Christ, to be gracious and merciful to me, a poor, sinful being.

OR

Individual Confession

Pastor, please hear my confession and pronounce forgiveness in order to fulfill God's will. Proceed.

I, a poor sinner, plead guilty before God of all sins. I have lived as if God did not matter and as if I mattered most. My Lord's name I have not honored as I should; my worship and prayers have faltered. I have not let His love have its way with me, and so my love for others has failed. There

Question Form

Do you confess to almighty God that you are a poor, miserable sinner?
Yes.

Do you confess to our merciful Father that you have sinned against Him in thought, word, and deed?
Yes.

Do you confess that you justly deserve His temporal and eternal punishment?
Yes.

are those whom I have hurt, and those whom I have failed to help. My thoughts and desires have been soiled with sin.

What troubles me particularly is that . . .

The penitent confesses whatever he has done against the commandments of God, according to his place in life. Then he concludes by saying:

I am sorry for all of this and ask for grace. I want to do better.

God be merciful to you and strengthen your faith.
Amen.

Do you believe that my forgiveness is God's forgiveness?
Yes.

Do you believe that our Lord Jesus Christ died for you and shed His blood for you on the cross for the forgiveness of all your sins?
Yes.

Do you pray God, for the sake of the holy, innocent, bitter sufferings and death of His beloved Son, to be gracious and merciful to you?
Yes.

Finally, do you believe that my forgiveness is God's forgiveness?
Yes.

Let it be done for you as you believe.

The pastor places his hands on the head of the penitent and says:

In the stead and by the command of my Lord Jesus Christ I forgive you all your sins in the name of the Father and of the ✝ Son and of the Holy Spirit.
Amen.

When Individual Confession and Absolution is concluded, the pastor invites the family and loved ones to return.

> *When a sick person is to be anointed with oil, the following passage from Holy Scripture is read:*

Is anyone among you sick? Let him call for the elders[1] of the church, and let them pray over him, anointing him with oil in the name of the Lord. And the prayer of faith will save the one who is sick, and the Lord will raise him up. And if he has committed sins, he will be forgiven. Therefore, confess your sins to one another and pray for one another, that you may be healed. The effective prayer of a righteous person has great power.

James 5:14–16

[1]The Greek word for "elders," *presbyteroi*, in the reading from James refers to pastors and not lay elders.

___Name___, you have confessed your sins and received Holy Absolution. In remembrance of the grace of God given by the Holy Spirit in the waters of Holy Baptism, I will anoint you with oil. Confident in our Lord and in love for you, we also pray for you that you will not lose faith. Know that in godly patience the Church endures with you and supports you during this affliction. We firmly believe that this illness is for the glory of God and that the Lord will both hear our prayer and work according to His good and gracious will. *[John 11:4]*

Using his right thumb, the pastor anoints the sick person on the forehead while saying:

Almighty God, the Father of our Lord Jesus Christ, who has given you the new birth of water and the Spirit and has forgiven you all your sins, strengthen you with His grace to life ✠ everlasting.
Amen.

The pastor leads those gathered in the following prayers.

Lord, have mercy upon us.
Christ, have mercy upon us.
Lord, have mercy upon us.

Our Father who art in heaven,
 hallowed be Thy name,
 Thy kingdom come,
 Thy will be done on earth as it is in heaven;
 give us this day our daily bread;
 and forgive us our trespasses
  as we forgive those who trespass against us;
 and lead us not into temptation,
 but deliver us from evil.
For Thine is the kingdom and the power and the glory
 forever and ever. Amen.   *Matthew 6:9–13*

The pastor and those gathered pray the Prayer Sentences (Preces).
Circumstances may require that the pastor read them by himself.

O Lord, save your servant __*name*__ ,
who trusts in You.   *Psalm 86:2*

Send __*him/her*__ help from the sanctuary
and strength from Your holy dwelling.   *Psalm 20:2*

Look upon __*his/her*__ affliction and pain,
and forgive all __*his/her*__ sins.   *Psalm 25:18*

O Lord, hear our prayer,
and let our cry come to You.   *Psalm 39:12*

The Lord be with you.   *2 Timothy 4:22*
And also with you.

Let us pray.

O Lord, look down from heaven; behold, visit, and relieve Your servant _ name _, for whom we pray. Look upon _ him/her _ with the eyes of Your mercy, and give _ him/her _ comfort and sure confidence in You. Defend _ him/her _ from every danger to body and soul, and keep _ him/her _ in peace and safety; through Jesus Christ, Your Son, our Lord, who lives and reigns with You and the Holy Spirit, one God, now and forever. (518)

Father of all mercy, You never fail to help those who call upon You in faith. Give strength and confidence to Your servant _ name _ in _ his/her _ time of affliction. Grant that _ he/she _ may know that You are near, and that underneath _ him/her _ are Your everlasting arms. Grant that _ he/she _, resting on Your protection, may fear no evil, for You are with _ him/her _ to comfort and deliver _ him/her _; through Jesus Christ, Your Son, our Lord, who lives and reigns with You and the Holy Spirit, one God, now and forever. (519)

Amen.

If the Lord's Supper is not to be received, the service concludes with the Blessing on page 38.

It is truly good, right, and salutary that we should at all times and in all places give thanks to You, O Lord, holy Father, almighty and everlasting God, for the countless blessings You so freely bestow on us and all creation. Above all, we give thanks for Your boundless love shown to us when You sent Your only-begotten Son, Jesus Christ, into our flesh and laid on Him our sin, giving Him into death that we might not die eternally. Because He is now risen from the dead and lives and reigns to all eternity, all who believe in Him will overcome sin and death and will rise again to new life.

Our Lord Jesus Christ, on the night when He was betrayed, took bread, and when He had given thanks, He broke it and gave it to the disciples and said: "Take, eat; this is My ✝ body, which is given for you. This do in remembrance of Me."

In the same way also He took the cup after supper, and when He had given thanks, He gave it to them, saying: "Drink of it, all of you; this cup is the new testament in My ✝ blood, which is shed for you for the forgiveness of sins. This do, as often as you drink it, in remembrance of Me."

Matthew 26:26–28; Mark 14:22–24
Luke 22:19–20; 1 Corinthians 11:23–25

It is appropriate that the pastor receive the body and blood of the Lord with the sick or distressed person, together with those present who have previously been admitted to the Lord's Table. During the DISTRIBUTION, *the pastor says:*

Take, eat; this is the true body of our Lord and Savior Jesus
　　Christ, given into death for your sins.
Take, drink; this is the true blood of our Lord and Savior Jesus
　　Christ, shed for the forgiveness of your sins.

After all have communed, the pastor says:

The body and blood of our Lord Jesus Christ strengthen and preserve you in body and soul to life everlasting. Depart in peace. **Amen.**

O God the Father, the fountain and source of all goodness, who in loving-kindness sent Your only-begotten Son into the flesh, we thank You that for His sake You have given us pardon and peace in this Sacrament, and we ask You not to forsake Your children but always to rule our hearts and minds by Your Holy Spirit that we may be enabled constantly to serve You; ▶

through Jesus Christ, Your Son, our Lord, who lives and reigns with You and the Holy Spirit, one God, now and forever. (403) **Amen.**

The pastor speaks one of the following blessings:

God our Father grant you His wholeness and peace so that you may remain constant in faith and call upon His holy name. The Lord Jesus Christ grant you the joy of His countenance and a new, steadfast spirit. The Holy Spirit generously pour upon you His mercy and grace, that He would fill you inwardly and outwardly, surround you, and be with you always. The blessing of almighty God, the Father, the ✝ Son, and the Holy Spirit, be and remain with you now and forever. **Amen.**

The Lord bless you and keep you.
The Lord make His face shine upon you and be gracious unto you.
The Lord lift up His countenance upon you and ✝ give you peace.
Amen. *Numbers 6:24–26*

COMMUNION OF THE SICK AND HOMEBOUND

1. This service is intended for those previously admitted to the Lord's Table.
2. If the entire service cannot be used, it may be shortened to the following: Confession and Absolution, Collect, Reading, Lord's Prayer, the Words of Our Lord, Distribution, and Benediction. Depending on the responsiveness of the communicant, the pastor may choose to omit certain parts of the service (e.g., the Preface).
3. Several forms of the confession of sins and other liturgical texts are provided, reflecting the several settings of the Divine Service in *Lutheran Service Book*. The pastor should lead the communicant in speaking or singing the form that is most familiar.
4. The seasonal Proper Preface may be substituted for the weekday preface provided in the rite.
5. This service may be reproduced according to local need and provided to the communicant and others present.
6. The table used for the celebration of the Sacrament is covered with a clean, white cloth. Two lighted candles (unless oxygen is being administered) and a crucifix or cross may be placed on the table.

INVOCATION
Matthew 28:19b

In the name of the Father and of the ✝ Son and of the Holy Spirit.
Amen.

CONFESSION AND ABSOLUTION

If the communicant desires to make a private confession, the pastor requests others present to leave the room. Otherwise, the pastor leads the sick person and others present in one of the following forms of Confession and Absolution, or one familiar to the communicant.

O almighty God, merciful Father, I, a poor, miserable sinner, confess unto You all my sins and iniquities with which I have ever offended You and justly deserved Your temporal and eternal punishment. But I am heartily sorry for them and sincerely repent of them, and I pray You of Your boundless mercy and for the sake of the holy, innocent, bitter sufferings and death of Your beloved Son, Jesus Christ, to be gracious and merciful to me, a poor, sinful being.

Most merciful God, we confess that we are by nature sinful and unclean. We have sinned against You in thought, word, and deed, by what we have done and by what we have left undone. We have not loved You with our whole heart; we have not loved our neighbors as ourselves. We justly deserve Your present and eternal punishment. For the sake of Your Son, Jesus Christ, have mercy on us. Forgive us, renew us, and lead us, so that we may delight in Your will and walk in Your ways to the glory of Your holy name. Amen.

If the communicant is unable to join in the confession, the pastor asks:

Is this your confession?
Yes.

The pastor lays his hand on the head of the communicant and says:

Almighty God in His mercy has given His Son to die for you and for His sake forgives you all your sins. As a called and ordained servant of Christ, and by His authority, I therefore forgive you all your sins in the name of the Father and of the ☩ Son and of the Holy Spirit. **Amen.**

[John 20:19–23]

COLLECT OF THE DAY

The Collect of the Day and/or one of the following collects is prayed.

Let us pray.

For the homebound

Gracious Father, You have assured us that we shall receive strength for every day of our lives. Grant Your servant ___name___, who is homebound, both the desire and the will to spend _his/her_ days as an obedient child, trusting in Your goodness and remembering with thankfulness Your mercies, which are new every morning; through Jesus Christ, Your Son, our Lord, who lives and reigns with You and the Holy Spirit, one God, now and forever. (520)

For the sick

O God, the strength of the weak and the consolation of all who put their trust in You, mercifully accept our prayers on behalf of Your servant ___name___ that by Your power ___his/her___ sickness may be turned to health according to Your good and gracious will; through Jesus Christ, Your Son, our Lord, who lives and reigns with You and the Holy Spirit, one God, now and forever. (521)

Amen.

READINGS

A reading for the week or one or more of the following are read.

Thus says the LORD,
    he who created you, O Jacob,
        he who formed you, O Israel:
"Fear not, for I have redeemed you;
    I have called you by name, you are mine.
When you pass through the waters, I will be with you;
    and through the rivers, they shall not overwhelm you;
when you walk through fire you shall not be burned,
    and the flame shall not consume you.
For I am the LORD your God,
    the Holy One of Israel, your Savior."

Isaiah 43:1–3a

Blessed be the God and Father of our Lord Jesus Christ, the Father of mercies and God of all comfort, who comforts us in all our affliction, so that we may be able to comfort those who are in any affliction, with the comfort with which we ourselves are comforted by God. For as we share abundantly in Christ's sufferings, so through Christ we share abundantly in comfort too.

2 Corinthians 1:3–5

Behold, some people brought to [Jesus] a paralytic, lying on a bed. And when Jesus saw their faith, he said to the paralytic, "Take heart, my son; your sins are forgiven." And behold, some of the scribes said to themselves, "This man is blaspheming." But Jesus, knowing their thoughts, said, "Why do you think evil in your hearts? For which is easier, to say, 'Your sins are forgiven,' or to say, 'Rise and walk'? But that you may know that the Son of Man has authority on earth to forgive sins"—he then said to the paralytic—"Rise, pick up your bed and go home." And he rose and went home. When the crowds saw it, they were afraid, and they glorified God, who had given such authority to men.

Matthew 9:2–8

Jesus answered him, "If anyone loves me, he will keep my word, and my Father will love him, and we will come to him and make our home with him."

John 14:23

BRIEF EXPOSITION OF THE WORD OF GOD

APOSTLES' CREED

I believe in God, the Father Almighty,
> **maker of heaven and earth.**
And in Jesus Christ, His only Son, our Lord,
> **who was conceived by the Holy Spirit,**
> **born of the virgin Mary,**
> **suffered under Pontius Pilate,**
> **was crucified, died and was buried.**
> **He descended into hell.**
> **The third day He rose again from the dead.**
> **He ascended into heaven**
> **and sits at the right hand of God the Father Almighty.**
> **From thence He will come to judge the living and the dead.**
I believe in the Holy Spirit,
> **the holy Christian Church,**
> > **the communion of saints,**
> **the forgiveness of sins,**
> **the resurrection of the body,**
> **and the life ⊹ everlasting. Amen.**

Christian: the ancient text reads "catholic," meaning the whole
Church as it confesses the wholeness of Christian doctrine.

PREFACE

The Lord be with you.   *2 Timothy 4:22*
And also with you.

Lift up your hearts.   *[Colossians 3:1]*
We lift them to the Lord.

Let us give thanks to the Lord our God.   *[Psalm 136]*
It is right to give Him thanks and praise.

The following or a seasonal PROPER PREFACE *(pages 49–55) is prayed:*

It is truly good, right, and salutary that we should at all times and
in all places give thanks to You, holy Lord, almighty Father, everlasting God, through Jesus Christ, our Lord. Therefore with angels
and archangels and with all the company of heaven we laud and
magnify Your glorious name, evermore praising You and saying:

SANCTUS

Isaiah 6:3; Matthew 21:9

Holy, holy, holy Lord God of
Sabaoth; heaven and
earth are full of Thy
glory. Hosanna, hosanna,
hosanna in the highest.
Blessed is He, blessed is He,
blessed is He that cometh
in the name of the Lord.
Hosanna, hosanna, hosan-
na in the highest.

Holy, holy, holy Lord, God of
power and might: heaven
and earth are full of Your
glory. Hosanna in the
highest.
Blessed is He who comes in
the name of the Lord.
Hosanna in the highest.

LORD'S PRAYER

Matthew 6:9–13

Our Father who art in heaven,
    hallowed be Thy name,
    Thy kingdom come,
    Thy will be done on earth as it is in heaven;
    give us this day our daily bread;
    and forgive us our trespasses
        as we forgive those who trespass against us;
    and lead us not into temptation,
    but deliver us from evil.
For Thine is the kingdom and the power and the glory
    forever and ever. Amen.

THE WORDS OF OUR LORD

Matthew 26:26–28; Mark 14:22–24
Luke 22:19–20; 1 Corinthians 11:23–25

Our Lord Jesus Christ, on the night when He was betrayed, took bread, and when He had given thanks, He broke it and gave it to the disciples and said: "Take, eat; this is My ✝ body, which is given for you. This do in remembrance of Me."

In the same way also He took the cup after supper, and when He had given thanks, He gave it to them, saying: "Drink of it, all of you; this cup is the new testament in My ✝ blood, which is shed for you for the forgiveness of sins. This do, as often as you drink it, in remembrance of Me."

PAX DOMINI

John 20:19

The peace of the Lord be with you always.
Amen.

AGNUS DEI

John 1:29

O Christ, Thou Lamb of God, that takest away the sin of the world, have mercy upon us.

O Christ, Thou Lamb of God, that takest away the sin of the world, have mercy upon us.

O Christ, Thou Lamb of God, that takest away the sin of the world, grant us Thy peace. Amen.

Lamb of God, You take away the sin of the world; have mercy on us.

Lamb of God, You take away the sin of the world; have mercy on us.

Lamb of God, You take away the sin of the world; grant us peace, grant us peace.

DISTRIBUTION

It is appropriate that the pastor receive the body and blood of the Lord with the sick or homebound person, together with those present who have previously been admitted to the Lord's Table. During the Distribution, *the pastor says:*

Take, eat; this is the true body of our Lord and Savior Jesus Christ, given into death for your sins.

Take, drink; this is the true blood of our Lord and Savior Jesus Christ, shed for the forgiveness of your sins.

After all have communed, the pastor says:

The body and blood of our Lord Jesus Christ strengthen and preserve you in body and soul to life everlasting.
Amen.

NUNC DIMITTIS

Luke 2:29–32

Lord, now lettest Thou Thy servant depart in peace according to Thy word,

for mine eyes have seen Thy salvation, which Thou hast prepared before the face of all people,

a light to lighten the Gentiles and the glory of Thy people Israel.

Glory be to the Father and to the Son and to the Holy Ghost; as it was in the beginning, is now, and ever shall be, world without end. Amen.

Lord, now You let Your servant go in peace; Your word has been fulfilled.

My own eyes have seen the salvation which You have prepared in the sight of every people:

a light to reveal You to the nations and the glory of Your people Israel.

Glory be to the Father and to the Son and to the Holy Spirit; as it was in the beginning, is now, and will be forever. Amen.

Nunc Dimittis

SONG OF SIMEON

POST-COMMUNION COLLECT

General

We give thanks to You, almighty God, that You have refreshed us through this salutary gift, and we implore You that of Your mercy You would strengthen us through the same in faith toward You and in fervent love toward one another; through Jesus Christ, Your Son, our Lord, who lives and reigns with You and the Holy Spirit, one God, now and forever. (402)

For the sick

Almighty God, heavenly Father, we give thanks that You have refreshed us with the body and blood of Your dear Son, Jesus Christ. Grant that this heavenly food which we have received will strengthen our faith that we may bear all crosses, sickness, and trials with patience and trust until You grant us deliverance, peace, and health; through Jesus Christ, our Lord, who lives and reigns with You and the Holy Spirit, one God, now and forever. (522)

Amen.

BENEDICTION

Numbers 6:24–26

The Lord bless you and keep you.
The Lord make His face shine upon you and be gracious unto you.
The Lord lift up His countenance upon you and ✝ give you peace.
Amen.

Seasonal Proper Prefaces

ADVENT

It is truly good, right, and salutary that we should at all times and in all places give thanks to You, holy Lord, almighty Father, everlasting God, through Jesus Christ, our Lord, whose way John the Baptist prepared, proclaiming Him the promised Messiah, the very Lamb of God who takes away the sin of the world, and calling sinners to repentance that they might escape from the wrath to be revealed when He comes again in glory. Therefore with angels and archangels and with all the company of heaven we laud and magnify Your glorious name, evermore praising You and saying:

CHRISTMAS

It is truly good, right, and salutary that we should at all times and in all places give thanks to You, holy Lord, almighty Father, everlasting God, through Jesus Christ, our Lord; for in the mystery of the Word made flesh You have given us a new revelation of Your glory that, seeing You in the person of Your Son, we may know and love those things which are not seen. Therefore with angels and archangels and with all the company of heaven we laud and magnify Your glorious name, evermore praising You and saying:

EPIPHANY

It is truly good, right, and salutary that we should at all times and in all places give thanks to You, holy Lord, almighty Father, everlasting God, through Jesus Christ, our Lord; for what had been hidden from before the foundation of the world You have made known to the nations in Your Son. In Him, being found in the substance of our mortal nature, You have manifested the fullness of Your glory. Therefore with angels and archangels and with all the company of heaven we laud and magnify Your glorious name, evermore praising You and saying:

THE BAPTISM OF OUR LORD

It is truly good, right, and salutary that we should at all times and in all places give thanks to You, holy Lord, almighty Father, everlasting God, through Jesus Christ, our Lord; for at His Baptism Your voice from heaven revealed Him as Your beloved Son, and the Holy Spirit descended on Him, confirming Him to be the Christ. Therefore with angels and archangels and with all the company of heaven we laud and magnify Your glorious name, evermore praising You and saying:

THE TRANSFIGURATION OF OUR LORD

It is truly good, right, and salutary that we should at all times and in all places give thanks to You, holy Lord, almighty Father, everlasting God, through Jesus Christ, our Lord, who at His transfiguration revealed His glory to His disciples that they might be strengthened to proclaim His cross and resurrection and with all the faithful look forward to the glory of life everlasting. Therefore with angels and archangels and with all the company of heaven we laud and magnify Your glorious name, evermore praising You and saying:

LENT

It is truly good, right, and salutary that we should at all times and in all places give thanks to You, holy Lord, almighty Father, everlasting God, through Jesus Christ, our Lord, who overcame the assaults of the devil and gave His life as a ransom for many that with cleansed hearts we might be prepared joyfully to celebrate the paschal feast in sincerity and truth. Therefore with angels and archangels and with all the company of heaven we laud and magnify Your glorious name, evermore praising You and saying:

HOLY WEEK

It is truly good, right, and salutary that we should at all times and in all places give thanks to You, holy Lord, almighty Father, everlasting God, through Jesus Christ, our Lord, who accomplished the salvation of mankind by the tree of the cross that, where death arose, there life also might rise again and that the serpent who overcame by the tree of the garden might likewise by the tree of the cross be overcome. Therefore with angels and archangels and with all the company of heaven we laud and magnify Your glorious name, evermore praising You and saying:

EASTER

It is truly good, right, and salutary that we should at all times and in all places give thanks to You, holy Lord, almighty Father, everlasting God. And most especially are we bound to praise You on this day for the glorious resurrection of Your Son, Jesus Christ, the very Paschal Lamb, who was sacrificed for us and bore the sins of the world. By His dying He has destroyed death, and by His rising again He has restored to us everlasting life. Therefore with Mary Magdalene, Peter and John, and with all the witnesses of the resurrection, with angels and archangels, and with all the company of heaven we laud and magnify Your glorious name, evermore praising You and saying:

ASCENSION

It is truly good, right, and salutary that we should at all times and in all places give thanks to You, holy Lord, almighty Father, everlasting God, through Jesus Christ, our Lord, who after His resurrection appeared openly to all His disciples and in their sight was taken up into heaven that He might make us partakers of His divine life. Therefore with angels and archangels and with all the company of heaven we laud and magnify Your glorious name, evermore praising You and saying:

PENTECOST

It is truly good, right, and salutary that we should at all times and in all places give thanks to You, holy Lord, almighty Father, everlasting God, through Jesus Christ, our Lord, who ascended above the heavens and, sitting at Your right hand, poured out on this day the promised Holy Spirit on His chosen disciples. For all this the whole earth rejoices with exceeding joy. Therefore with angels and archangels and with all the company of heaven we laud and magnify Your glorious name, evermore praising You and saying:

HOLY TRINITY

It is truly good, right, and salutary that we should at all times and in all places give thanks to You, holy Lord, almighty Father, everlasting God, who with Your only-begotten Son and the Holy Spirit are one God, one Lord. In the confession of the only true God, we worship the Trinity in person and the Unity in substance, of majesty coequal. Therefore with angels and archangels and with all the company of heaven we laud and magnify Your glorious name, evermore praising You and saying:

APOSTLES AND EVANGELISTS

It is truly good, right, and salutary that we should at all times and in all places give thanks to You, holy Lord, almighty Father, everlasting God; for You have mightily governed and protected Your holy Church, in which the blessed apostles and evangelists proclaimed Your divine and saving Gospel. Therefore with patriarchs and prophets, apostles and evangelists, [with Your servant *name of saint being commemorated*,] and with all the company of heaven we laud and magnify Your glorious name, evermore praising You and saying:

THE PRESENTATION OF OUR LORD

It is truly good, right, and salutary that we should at all times and in all places give thanks to You, holy Lord, almighty Father, everlasting God, through Jesus Christ, our Lord, who, sharing Your eternal splendor, was presented on this day in Your temple in the substance of our human flesh and revealed by the Spirit as the glory of Israel and the light of all peoples. Therefore with angels and archangels and with all the company of heaven we laud and magnify Your glorious name, evermore praising You and saying:

THE ANNUNCIATION OF OUR LORD
THE VISITATION
ST. MARY, MOTHER OF OUR LORD

It is truly good, right, and salutary that we should at all times and in all places give thanks to You, holy Lord, almighty Father, everlasting God, through Jesus Christ, our Lord; for by the Holy Spirit Your only-begotten Son was conceived in the womb of the blessed virgin Mary and brought forth in the substance of our human flesh that we might partake of His divine life. Therefore with angels and archangels and with all the company of heaven we laud and magnify Your glorious name, evermore praising You and saying:

ST. MICHAEL AND ALL ANGELS

It is truly good, right, and salutary that we should at all times and in all places give thanks to You, holy Lord, almighty Father, everlasting God, through Jesus Christ, our Lord. Through Him Your majesty is praised by all the holy angels and celebrated with one accord by the heavens and all the powers therein. The cherubim and seraphim sing Your praise, and with them we laud and magnify Your glorious name, evermore praising You and saying:

ALL SAINTS' DAY

It is truly good, right, and salutary that we should at all times and in all places give thanks to You, holy Lord, almighty Father, everlasting God. In the communion of all Your saints gathered into the one body of Your Son, You have surrounded us with so great a cloud of witnesses that we, encouraged by their faith and strengthened by their fellowship, may run with perseverance the race that is set before us and, together with them, receive the crown of glory that does not fade away. Therefore with angels and archangels and with all the company of heaven we laud and magnify Your glorious name, evermore praising You and saying:

COMMON I

It is truly good, right, and salutary that we should at all times and in all places give thanks to You, holy Lord, almighty Father, everlasting God, through Jesus Christ, our Lord, who on this day overcame death and the grave and by His glorious resurrection opened to us the way of everlasting life. Therefore with angels and archangels and with all the company of heaven we laud and magnify Your glorious name, evermore praising You and saying:

COMMON II

It is truly good, right, and salutary that we should at all times and in all places give thanks to You, holy Lord, almighty Father, everlasting God, through Jesus Christ, our Lord, who, having created all things, took on human flesh and was born of the virgin Mary. For our sake He died on the cross and rose from the dead to put an end to death, thus fulfilling Your will and gaining for You a holy people. Therefore with angels and archangels and with all the company of heaven we laud and magnify Your glorious name, evermore praising You and saying:

COMMON III

It is truly good, right, and salutary that we should at all times and in all places give thanks to You, holy Lord, almighty Father, everlasting God, through Jesus Christ, our Lord, who, out of love for His fallen creation, humbled Himself by taking on the form of a servant, becoming obedient unto death, even death upon a cross. Risen from the dead, He has freed us from eternal death and given us life everlasting. Therefore with angels and archangels and with all the company of heaven we laud and magnify Your glorious name, evermore praising You and saying:

BRIEF SERVICE OF THE WORD

This service is for use in nursing and convalescent homes, homes for the aged, or other care-giving institutions. It may be modified as circumstances dictate.

INVOCATION

P In the name of the Father and of the ☩ Son and of the Holy Spirit.

Matthew 28:19b

C **Amen.**

PSALMODY

One or more psalms are spoken or sung.

READING FROM HOLY SCRIPTURE

One or more readings from Holy Scripture are read. Each is introduced as follows:

P A reading from _____, chapter _____.

Each reading may conclude:

P This is the Word of the Lord.

C **Thanks be to God.**

SERMON OR MEDITATION

The Apostles' Creed may be confessed.

HYMN

PRAYERS

> Collect of the Day
>
> Intercessions and Thanksgivings

LORD'S PRAYER

Matthew 6:9–13

P Taught by our Lord and trusting His promises, we are bold to pray:

C Our Father who art in heaven,
>> hallowed be Thy name,
>> Thy kingdom come,
>> Thy will be done on earth as it is in heaven;
>> give us this day our daily bread;
>> and forgive us our trespasses
>>> as we forgive those who trespass against us;
>> and lead us not into temptation,
>> but deliver us from evil.
> For Thine is the kingdom and the power and the glory
>> forever and ever. Amen.

BLESSING

2 Corinthians 13:14

P The grace of our Lord ✠ Jesus Christ and the love of God and the communion of the Holy Spirit be with you all.

C Amen.

BLESSING OF A MOTHER AFTER CHILDBIRTH

1. Historically, this blessing was given when a mother returned to church after giving birth. It may be prayed with the mother prior to the service or in another setting.
2. The mother may be joined by her husband and other friends and relatives.
3. If the child has been baptized, then appropriate modification of the prayer before the blessing should be made.
4. In cases where the child did not survive childbirth, see pages 178–183 for appropriate resources.

In the name of the Father and of the ☩ Son and of the Holy Spirit.
Amen.

Matthew 28:19b

The psalm may be sung by whole verse or spoken by half verse.

This woman cried out and the Lord | heard her,*
    and saved her out of all her | troubles.

Liturgical text

I will bless the Lord at | all times;*
    his praise shall continually be | in my mouth.
My soul makes its boast | in the Lord;*
    let the humble hear | and be glad.
Oh, magnify the | Lord with me,*
    and let us exalt his name to- | gether!
I sought the Lord, and he | answered me*
    and delivered me from | all my fears.

▶

When the righteous cry for help, the | LORD hears*
    and delivers them out of all their | troubles.
Many are the afflictions of the | righteous,*
    but the LORD delivers him out | of them all.   *Psalm 34:1–4, 17, 19*

Glory be to the Father and | to the Son*
    and to the Holy | Spirit;
as it was in the be- | ginning,*
    is now, and will be forever. | Amen.
This woman cried out and the Lord | heard her,*
    and saved her out of all her | troubles.   *Liturgical text*

Taught by our Lord and trusting His promises, we are bold to pray:
Our Father who art in heaven,
    hallowed be Thy name,
    Thy kingdom come,
    Thy will be done on earth as it is in heaven;
    give us this day our daily bread;
    and forgive us our trespasses
        as we forgive those who trespass against us;
    and lead us not into temptation,
    but deliver us from evil.
For Thine is the kingdom and the power and the glory
    forever and ever. Amen.   *Matthew 6:9–13*

The Lord be with you.   *2 Timothy 4:22*
And also with you.

Let us pray.
Almighty and everlasting God, who turns the pains of the faithful
into joy at childbirth, we praise You for the great mercy which You
have shown to   *name of mother*   and her child(ren),   *name of
child(ren)* . Keep them always in Your fatherly care, and grant that
her   *child/children*   may be brought to the waters of Holy Baptism

and grow up in true fear, love, and trust of You; through Jesus Christ, Your Son, our Lord, who lives and reigns with You and the Holy Spirit, one God, now and forever. (523)
Amen.

The blessing of almighty God, the Father, the ✟ Son, and the Holy Spirit, be and remain with you always.
Amen.

HOLY MATRIMONY

General Notes

1. The rite of Holy Matrimony may be used at the beginning of the Divine Service or Daily Office. It may also stand by itself as an independent order of service.

2. If the rite is used at the beginning of the Divine Service, it comes before the Introit, Psalm, or Entrance Hymn. If it is used at the beginning of the Daily Office (Matins or Morning Prayer, Vespers or Evening Prayer), it precedes the opening versicles or psalmody.

3. Because of the solemn character of Holy Week, it is inappropriate to schedule a marriage during that time.

4. When used within the Divine Service, Holy Communion is offered to all eligible communicants and is not to be limited to the bride and bridegroom or the wedding party.

5. As in all worship in the house of God, the rite of Holy Matrimony invokes the presence and blessing of God. Therefore, it should avoid triteness and empty sentimentality.

6. Music selected for this rite should embody high standards of quality and be within the ability of the performers. The music should reflect the praise of God and His steadfast love in Christ as the foundation and model for marriage.

7. This rite is a more complete version of the corresponding rite in *Lutheran Service Book*, pages 275–277.

The Rite in Detail

1. According to the Church's usual order for processions, the wedding procession might be as follows:
   - The cross (and torches) may lead the procession.
   - The wedding attendants follow the cross (and torches), then followed by the bridegroom and the bride.
   - The bridegroom and bride may be escorted by their parents.
   - The pastor(s) conclude the procession.
2. A hymn may be sung during the procession of the wedding party. Other music may be based on hymn tunes used within the marriage service.
3. The wedding party may sit in the front pews or be provided with special seating.
4. The Propers for Holy Matrimony (*LSB Agenda*, pages 80–82) may be used in one of several ways:
   - If the rite of Holy Matrimony occurs in conjunction with a regularly scheduled service of the congregation, the Scripture readings for marriage are read within the marriage rite at the appointed place. The propers for the Divine Service or Daily Office that follows the rite are those of the Sunday or festival.
   - If the rite occurs in a specially scheduled Divine Service or Daily Office, the readings within the rite are omitted. The propers for the Divine Service or Daily Office that follows the rite are those appointed in the *LSB Agenda*, page 80.
   - If the rite stands by itself as an independent service, the Scripture readings for marriage are read within the rite at the appointed place.
5. Hymns appropriate for the rite of Holy Matrimony are listed in the *LSB Agenda*, page 82.
6. In the marriage vows, each person's first name is to be used.
7. Where legally required, the marriage license and marriage register are signed and witnessed after the service.

Stand

At the conclusion of the procession to the foot of the chancel, the pastor says:

P In the name of the Father and of the ☩ Son and of the Holy Spirit.

C **Amen.**   *Matthew 28:19b*

P Dearly beloved, we are gathered here in the sight of God and before His Church to witness the union of this man and this woman in holy matrimony. This is an honorable estate instituted and blessed by God in Paradise, before humanity's fall into sin.

In marriage we see a picture of the communion between Christ and His bride, the Church. Our Lord blessed and honored marriage with His presence and first miracle at Cana in Galilee. This estate is also commended to us by the apostle Paul as good and honorable. Therefore, marriage is not to be entered into inadvisedly or lightly, but reverently, deliberately, and in accordance with the purposes for which it was instituted by God.

The union of husband and wife in heart, body, and mind is intended by God for the mutual companionship, help, and support that each person ought to receive from the other, both in prosperity and adversity. Marriage was also ordained so that man and woman may find delight in one another. Therefore, all persons who marry shall take a spouse in holiness and honor, not in the passion of lust, for God has not called us to impurity but in holiness. God also established marriage for the procreation of children who are to be brought up in the fear and instruction of the Lord so that they may offer Him their praise.

For these reasons God has established the holy estate that ___*name*___ and ___*name*___ wish to enter. They desire our prayers as they begin their marriage in the Lord's name and with His blessing.

If this wedding rite is being used as an independent service (or when the rite precedes a regularly scheduled service of the congregation), the following or other appropriate passages from Holy Scripture are now read. Each reading may conclude with the response:

L This is the Word of the Lord.

C **Thanks be to God.**

When the rite stands alone, a sermon is also preached. A hymn may precede or follow. The wedding party may be seated throughout.

Genesis 2:7, 18–24

The Lord God formed the man of dust from the ground and breathed into his nostrils the breath of life, and the man became a living creature. . . .

Then the Lord God said, "It is not good that the man should be alone; I will make him a helper fit for him." So out of the ground the Lord God formed every beast of the field and every bird of the heavens and brought them to the man to see what he would call them. And whatever the man called every living creature, that was its name. The man gave names to all livestock and to the birds of the heavens and to every beast of the field. But for Adam there was not found a helper fit for him. So the Lord God caused a deep sleep to fall upon the man, and while he slept took one of his ribs and closed up its place with flesh. And the rib that the Lord God had taken from the man he made into a woman and brought her to the man. Then the man said,

"This at last is bone of my bones
    and flesh of my flesh;
she shall be called Woman,
    because she was taken out of Man."

Therefore a man shall leave his father and his mother and hold fast to his wife, and they shall become one flesh.

OR

Genesis 1:26–28

God said, "Let us make man in our image, after our likeness. And let them have dominion over the fish of the sea and over the birds of the heavens and over the livestock and over all the earth and over every creeping thing that creeps on the earth."

So God created man in his own image,
> in the image of God he created him;
> male and female he created them.

And God blessed them. And God said to them, "Be fruitful and multiply and fill the earth and subdue it and have dominion over the fish of the sea and over the birds of the heavens and over every living thing that moves on the earth."

Ephesians 5:1–2, 22–33

Be imitators of God, as beloved children. And walk in love, as Christ loved us and gave himself up for us, a fragrant offering and sacrifice to God. . . .

Wives, submit to your own husbands, as to the Lord. For the husband is the head of the wife even as Christ is the head of the church, his body, and is himself its Savior. Now as the church submits to Christ, so also wives should submit in everything to their husbands.

Husbands, love your wives, as Christ loved the church and gave himself up for her, that he might sanctify her, having cleansed her by the washing of water with the word, so that he might present the church to himself in splendor, without spot or wrinkle or any such thing, that she might be holy and without blemish. In the same way husbands should love their wives as their own bodies. He who loves his wife loves himself. For no one ever hated his own flesh, but nourishes and cherishes it, just as Christ does the church, because we are members of his body. "Therefore a man shall leave his father and mother and hold fast to his wife, and the two shall become one flesh." This mystery is profound, and I am saying that it refers to Christ and the church. However, let each one of you love his wife as himself, and let the wife see that she respects her husband.

Matthew 19:4–6

[Jesus answered the Pharisees:] "Have you not read that he who created them from the beginning made them male and female, and said, 'Therefore a man shall leave his father and his mother and hold fast to his wife, and they shall become one flesh'? So they are no longer two but one flesh. What therefore God has joined together, let not man separate."

OR

Mark 10:1–9

[Jesus] left there and went to the region of Judea and beyond the Jordan, and crowds gathered to him again. And again, as was his custom, he taught them. And Pharisees came up and in order to test him asked, "Is it lawful for a man to divorce his wife?" He answered them, "What did Moses command you?" They said, "Moses allowed a man to write a certificate of divorce and to send her away." And Jesus said to them, "Because of your hardness of heart he wrote you this commandment. But from the beginning of creation, 'God made them male and female.' 'Therefore a man shall leave his father and mother and hold fast to his wife, and they shall become one flesh.' So they are no longer two but one flesh. What therefore God has joined together, let not man separate."

If the wedding party has been seated, they now stand and take their places before the chancel steps.

The pastor asks the bridegroom:

P   ___Name of bridegroom___, will you have this woman to be your wedded wife, to live together in the holy estate of matrimony as God ordained it? Will you nourish and cherish her as Christ loved His body, the Church, giving Himself up for her? Will you love, honor, and keep her in sickness and in health and, forsaking all others, remain united to her alone, so long as you both shall live? Then say: I will.   *[Ephesians 5:29]*

R   *I will.*

The pastor asks the bride:

P   ___Name of bride___, will you have this man to be your wedded husband, to live together in the holy estate of matrimony as God ordained it? Will you submit to him as the Church submits to Christ? Will you love, honor, and keep him in sickness and in health and, forsaking all others, remain united to him alone, so long as you both shall live? Then say: I will.   *[Ephesians 5:24]*

R   *I will.*

If the bride is being given in marriage, the pastor may ask:

P   Who gives this woman to be married to this man?

R   ___We/I___ do.

The pastor may address the parents of the bridegroom and bride as follows:

P   Do you give your consent and blessing to this couple? Then say: We do.

R   *We do.*

P   Will you pray for and encourage ___name___ and ___name___ in their marriage, remembering at all times

that God wills them to live
within their vows until they
are parted by death? Then
say: We will.

R *We will.*

*The pastor leads the bridegroom and bride to the altar. The bride-
groom, taking the right hand of the bride and facing her, says after
the pastor:*

I, ___name of bridegroom___ ,
take you, ___name of bride___ ,
   to be my wedded wife,
to have and to hold from this day forward,
      for better, for worse,
      for richer, for poorer,
      in sickness and in health,
      to love and to cherish,
      till death us do part,
            according to God's holy will;
and I pledge to you my faithfulness.

The bride, in the same way, says after the pastor:

I, ___name of bride___ ,
take you, ___name of bridegroom___ ,
   to be my wedded husband,
to have and to hold from this day forward,
      for better, for worse,
      for richer, for poorer,
      in sickness and in health,
      to love and to cherish,
      till death us do part,
            according to God's holy will;
and I pledge to you my faithfulness.

The rings are presented to the pastor; then the following prayer is said:

P Almighty Father, You have generously created all things to serve
us for our good. Send Your blessing upon this couple who shall
wear these ✠ rings as a constant reminder of their marital fidelity. Grant that by Your mercy they may live gladly and faithfully in this holy estate; through Jesus Christ, Your Son, our Lord,
who lives and reigns with You and the Holy Spirit, one God, now
and forever. (525)

C **Amen.**

*The bridegroom and bride exchange rings beginning with the bridegroom.
While giving the ring, each says after the pastor one of the following:*

Receive this ring
    as a pledge and token
    of wedded love and
        faithfulness.
In the name of the Father
    and of the Son
    and of the Holy Spirit.
    Amen.
	With this ring I marry you,
	    my worldly goods
	        I give to you,
	    and with my body
	        I honor you.
	In the name of the Father
	    and of the Son
	    and of the Holy Spirit.
	    Amen.

The couple kneels.

P Now that ___*name*___ and ___*name*___ have committed themselves to
each other in holy matrimony, have given themselves to each other
by their solemn pledges, and have declared the same before God
and these witnesses, I pronounce them to be husband and wife, in
the name of the Father and of the ✠ Son and of the Holy Spirit.

C **Amen.**

P What God has joined together, let no one put asunder. *Matthew 19:6*

C **Amen.**

The pastor blesses the couple.

P The almighty and gracious God abundantly grant you His favor and sanctify and bless you with the blessing given to Adam and Eve in Paradise, that you may please Him in both body and soul and live together in holy love until your life's end.

C **Amen.**

If this rite precedes the Divine Service, the service continues with the INTROIT, PSALM, *or* ENTRANCE HYMN. *If this rite precedes the Daily Office, the service continues with the opening versicles or psalmody. If this rite stands by itself as an independent service, it concludes with the following. The bridegroom and bride remain kneeling.*

Stand

P Let us pray.
Almighty, everlasting God, our heavenly Father, grant that by Your blessing *name* and *name* may live together according to Your Word and promise. Strengthen them in faithfulness and love toward each other. Sustain and defend them in every trial and temptation. Help them to live in faith toward You, in the communion of Your holy Church, and in loving service to each other that they may ever enjoy Your heavenly blessing; through Jesus Christ, Your Son, our Lord, who lives and reigns with You and the Holy Spirit, one God, now and forever. (526)

C **Amen.**

P O God, our dwelling place in all generations, look with favor upon the homes of our land. Embrace husbands and wives, parents and children, in the arms of Your love, and grant that each, in reverence for Christ, fulfill the duties You have given. Bless our homes that they may ever be a shelter for the defenseless, a fortress for the tempted, a resting place for the weary, and a ►

71

foretaste of our eternal home with You; through Jesus Christ, Your Son, our Lord, who lives and reigns with You and the Holy Spirit, one God, now and forever. (527)

C **Amen.**

C **Our Father who art in heaven,**
>   **hallowed be Thy name,**
>   **Thy kingdom come,**
>   **Thy will be done on earth as it is in heaven;**
>   **give us this day our daily bread;**
>   **and forgive us our trespasses**
>   **as we forgive those who trespass against us;**
>   **and lead us not into temptation,**
>   **but deliver us from evil.**
> **For Thine is the kingdom and the power and the glory**
>   **forever and ever. Amen.**   *Matthew 6:9–13*

P The Lord bless you and keep you.
The Lord make His face shine upon you and be gracious unto you.
The Lord lift up His countenance upon you and ☩ give you peace.

C **Amen.**   *Numbers 6:24–26*

The wedding party departs in procession to the accompaniment of appropriate music.

Where legally required, the marriage license and marriage register are signed and witnessed after the service.

ANNIVERSARY OR AFFIRMATION OF HOLY MATRIMONY

General Notes

1. This rite is for use at the anniversary of a marriage, as an act of reconciliation, or in other appropriate circumstances. If a couple previously divorced is remarrying, the rite for Holy Matrimony is used.

2. The pastor should discuss the nature of this rite with the couple, making it clear that the rite is not a remarriage but rather an opportunity to hear God's Word, rejoice in His gift of marriage, and ask for His blessing.

3. If this rite is used as an act of public reconciliation, Individual Confession and Absolution may be used in pastoral care prior to this rite.

4. The rite of Anniversary or Affirmation of Holy Matrimony is designed for use at the beginning of the Divine Service or Daily Office. It may also stand by itself as an independent service.

5. If the rite is used at the beginning of the Divine Service, it comes before the Introit, Psalm, or Entrance Hymn. If this rite is used at the beginning of the Daily Office (Matins or Morning Prayer, Vespers or Evening Prayer), it precedes the opening versicles or psalmody.

6. Because of the solemn character of Holy Week, it is inappropriate to schedule this rite during that time.

7. When used within the Divine Service, Holy Communion is offered to all eligible communicants and is not to be limited to the husband and wife or the witnesses.

8. Additional resources for preparing couples for the use of this rite can be found on pages 377–382.

The Rite in Detail

1. The Propers for Holy Matrimony (*LSB Agenda,* page 80) may be used in one of several ways:
   - If the Anniversary or Affirmation of Holy Matrimony occurs in conjunction with a regularly scheduled service of the congregation, the Scripture readings are read at the appointed place. The propers for the Divine Service or Daily Office that follows the rite are those of the Sunday or festival.
   - If the rite occurs in a specially scheduled Divine Service or Daily Office, the readings within the rite are omitted. The propers for the Divine Service or Daily Office that follows the rite are those appointed in the *LSB Agenda,* page 80.
   - If the rite stands by itself as an independent service, the Scripture readings are read at the appointed place.
2. Hymns appropriate for the Anniversary or Affirmation of Holy Matrimony are listed in the *LSB Agenda,* page 82.
3. The restatement of marriage vows serves primarily as a sign of reconciliation between husband and wife. These words may be modified if the husband and wife wish to reaffirm their marriage pledge for other reasons.

The husband and wife (and witnesses) stand at the foot of the chancel. The pastor says:

P In the name of the Father and of the ☩ Son and of the Holy Spirit.

C **Amen.** *Matthew 28:19b*

P Beloved in the Lord, _ name _ and _ name _ have come before the Lord to commemorate [and renew] their solemn vows of holy matrimony which they first spoke to each other _____ years ago. Thankful for the mercy and kindness that our heavenly Father has showered upon them, they seek His continued gracious care. We also offer praise and thanksgiving to the Lord for holy matrimony and join with _ name _ and _ name _ in imploring His love and goodness.

Psalm 128 may be sung by whole verse or spoken by half verse.

Blessèd is everyone who | fears the LORD,*
   who walks | in his ways!
You shall eat the fruit of the labor | of your hands;*
   you shall be blessed, and it shall be | well with you.
Your wife will be like a fruitful vine with- | in your house;*
   your children will be like olive shoots around your | table.
Behold, thus shall the | man be blessed*
   who | fears the LORD.
The LORD bless you from | Zion!*
   May you see the prosperity of Jerusalem all the days | of your life!
May you see your children's | children!*
   Peace be upon | Israel!
Glory be to the Father and | to the Son*
   and to the Holy | Spirit;
as it was in the be- | ginning,*
   is now, and will be forever. | Amen.

One or both of the following Scripture readings are read.

The LORD God said, "It is not good that the man should be alone; I will make him a helper fit for him." So out of the ground the LORD God formed every beast of the field and every bird of the heavens and brought them to the man to see what he would call them. And whatever the man called every living creature, that was its name. The man gave names to all livestock and to the birds of the heavens and to every beast of the field. But for Adam there was not found a helper fit for him. So the LORD God caused a deep sleep to fall upon the man, and while he slept took one of his ribs and closed up its place with flesh. And the rib that the LORD God had taken from the man he made into a woman and brought her to the man. Then the man said,

   "This at last is bone of my bones
      and flesh of my flesh;

▶

she shall be called Woman,
because she was taken out of Man."
Therefore a man shall leave his father and his mother and hold fast to his wife, and they shall become one flesh.   *Genesis 2:18–24*

Put on then, as God's chosen ones, holy and beloved, compassion, kindness, humility, meekness, and patience, bearing with one another and, if one has a complaint against another, forgiving each other; as the Lord has forgiven you, so you also must forgive. And above all these put on love, which binds everything together in perfect harmony. And let the peace of Christ rule in your hearts, to which indeed you were called in one body. And be thankful. Let the word of Christ dwell in you richly, teaching and admonishing one another in all wisdom, singing psalms and hymns and spiritual songs, with thankfulness in your hearts to God. And whatever you do, in word or deed, do everything in the name of the Lord Jesus, giving thanks to God the Father through him. Wives, submit to your husbands, as is fitting in the Lord. Husbands, love your wives, and do not be harsh with them. *[Children, obey your parents in everything, for this pleases the Lord. Fathers, do not provoke your children, lest they become discouraged.]* Whatever you do, work heartily, as for the Lord and not for men, knowing that from the Lord you will receive the inheritance as your reward. You are serving the Lord Christ.
Colossians 3:12–19 [20–21] 23–24

If this rite stands by itself as an independent service, a sermon is preached. A hymn may precede or follow the sermon. The husband and wife (and witnesses) may be seated.

If the husband and wife (and witnesses) have been seated, they now stand and take their place before the altar, where the husband and wife face each other.

The pastor asks the following:

P   *Name of husband* , do you in the presence of God and of this congregation reaffirm the pledge you made when you took to yourself   *name of wife*   as your wife?

R   *I do.*

P   *Name of wife* , do you in the presence of God and of this congregation reaffirm the pledge you made when you took to yourself   *name of husband*   as your husband?

R   *I do.*

If vows are being renewed, each spouse says after the pastor:

   Name of wife , my beloved wife,
I reaffirm my sincere promise
      to be your husband,
and I implore the blessing
      of the Lord Jesus Christ
that, renewed by His loving-kindness
      and sustained by His grace,
I will be faithful until death parts us.

   Name of husband , my beloved husband,
I reaffirm my sincere promise
      to be your wife,
and I implore the blessing
      of the Lord Jesus Christ
that, renewed by His loving-kindness
      and sustained by His grace,
I will be faithful until death parts us.

The husband and wife may kneel for the blessing.

P   __*Name*__ and __*name*__, our merciful God and Father has sustained and blessed you throughout your wedded life. May He, who is ever faithful in love and compassion, continue to grant you His grace so that, with true fidelity and steadfast love, you may ever honor and keep your promises, grow in love toward Him and for each other, and come at last to the eternal joys that He has promised. In the name of the Father and of the ✝ Son and of the Holy Spirit.

C **Amen.**

P The almighty and gracious God continue to bless you that you may please Him in both body and soul and live together in holy love until your life's end.

C **Amen.**

If this rite precedes the Divine Service, the service continues with the Introit, Psalm, *or* Entrance Hymn. *If this rite precedes the Daily Office, the service continues with the opening versicles or psalmody. If this rite stands by itself as an independent service, it concludes as follows:*

Stand

One or both of the following may be prayed.

P Let us pray.
Lord God, heavenly Father, You instituted holy matrimony, blessed and honored it with the presence of Your Son at the marriage at Cana in Galilee, and continue to protect and preserve it. We thank You for the fatherly love and grace which You have bestowed upon __*name*__ and __*name*__ throughout their marriage. You have accompanied them with loving-kindness and tender mercy, visited them with Your comfort, strengthened them in sorrow and sickness, and crowned their life with every blessing. You have enabled them

to walk in marital love and fidelity, holding them to each other in sickness and in health, in adversity and prosperity, and granting them strength, patience, and faithfulness. Be with them, O Lord, until the end of their days, even as You have guided them in the past. Be their health, strength, refuge, and life. When the days of their earthly pilgrimage have ceased, graciously bring them to the marriage supper of Your Son, our Lord Jesus Christ, that they may dwell with You and all Your faithful and rejoice in Your joy forever; through the same Jesus Christ, Your Son, our Lord, who lives and reigns with You and the Holy Spirit, one God, now and forever. (528)

C Amen.

P O God, our dwelling place in all generations, look with favor upon the homes of our land. Embrace husbands and wives, parents and children, in the arms of Your love, and grant that each, in reverence for Christ, fulfill the duties You have given. Bless our homes that they may ever be a shelter for the defenseless, a fortress for the tempted, a resting place for the weary, and a foretaste of our eternal home with You; through Jesus Christ, Your Son, our Lord, who lives and reigns with You and the Holy Spirit, one God, now and forever. (527)

C Amen.

C **Our Father who art in heaven,**
    hallowed be Thy name,
    Thy kingdom come,
    Thy will be done on earth as it is in heaven;
    give us this day our daily bread;
    and forgive us our trespasses
        as we forgive those who trespass against us;
    and lead us not into temptation,
    but deliver us from evil.
For Thine is the kingdom and the power and the glory
    forever and ever. Amen.

Matthew 6:9–13

P _ Name _ and _ name _, may your hearts continue to be united in love and faithfulness and your home remain a dwelling place of the Lord. At the end of your pilgrimage here on earth, may you together see God face to face and enjoy that glory which He has promised to all who abide in His love to the end.

C **Amen.**

P The Lord bless you and keep you.
The Lord make His face shine upon you and be gracious unto you.
The Lord lift up His countenance upon you and ✠ give you peace.

C **Amen.** *Numbers 6:24–26*

COMMENDATION OF THE DYING

1. When a member of the Church is near death, the pastor should be called as soon as possible.
2. When death appears imminent, the rite may be abbreviated, using especially the Creed, Lord's Prayer, and commendation.
3. In some circumstances it may be appropriate that the pastor spend a prolonged period of time with the dying person and the family. The full rite may then be used, pacing the rite to the condition of the dying person.
4. In the event the pastor is not available to lead this rite, a member of the congregation or members of the family may use a revised version of this rite provided in the *LSB Agenda,* page 98.
5. When the body of the deceased has been willed for medical research, the Committal (pages 125–135), with appropriate modifications, may be used in the presence of the bereaved before the body is removed.
6. For additional resources when ministering to the dying, see pages 234–246.

P In the name of the Father and of the ✟ Son and of the Holy Spirit.

R *Amen.*   *Matthew 28:19b*

P The Lord be with you.

R *And also with you.*

P Let us pray.

Lord God, heavenly Father, look with favor upon Your child, ___name___ , forgive ___him/her___ all ___his/her___ sins, and comfort ___him/her___ with the promise of resurrection to life everlasting; through Your Son, Jesus Christ, our Lord, who lives and reigns with You and the Holy Spirit, one God, now and forever. (533)

R *Amen.*

If the dying person is conscious, the pastor may inquire whether he or she desires Individual Confession and Absolution (page 28). The pastor requests others present to leave the room to hear the confession. Otherwise, the pastor uses either form of confession provided here.

P Let us confess our sins.

P O almighty God, merciful Father,

R *I, a poor, miserable sinner, confess unto You all my sins and iniquities with which I have ever offended You and justly deserved Your temporal and eternal punishment. But I am heartily sorry for them and sincerely repent of them, and I pray You of Your boundless mercy and for the sake of the holy, innocent, bitter sufferings and death of Your beloved Son, Jesus Christ, to be gracious and merciful to me, a poor, sinful being.*

P Do you confess to almighty God that you are a poor, miserable sinner?

R *Yes.*

P Do you confess to our merciful Father that you have sinned against Him in thought, word, and deed?

R *Yes.*

P Do you confess that you justly deserve His temporal and eternal punishment?

R *Yes.*

P Do you believe that our Lord Jesus Christ died for you and shed His blood for you on the cross for the forgiveness of all your sins?

R *Yes.*

P Do you pray God, for the sake of the holy, innocent, bitter sufferings and death of His beloved Son, to be gracious and merciful to you?

R *Yes.*

P Upon this your confession, I, by virtue of my office, as a called and ordained servant of the Word, announce the grace of God to you, and in the stead and by the command of my Lord Jesus Christ I forgive you all your sins in the name of the Father and of the ✠ Son and of the Holy Spirit.

R *Amen.*

One of the following psalms is prayed. When copies of the rite are provided to those present, all may join in as the psalm is sung by whole verse or spoken by half verse. After the psalm and a time of silence, the psalm collect may be spoken. The use of one or more penitential psalms (6, 32, 38, 51, 102, 130, 143) is customary and appropriate when death is near. Other psalms and psalm collects are provided in the Resources for Christian Burial (LSB Agenda, page 140).

Sola Gratia

GRACE ALONE

Psalm 23

English Standard Version

The LORD is my | shepherd;*
  I | shall not want.
He makes me lie down in
green | pastures.*
    He leads me beside
    still | waters.
He re- | stores my soul.*
    He leads me in paths
    of righteousness for
    his | name's sake.
Even though I walk through
the valley of the shadow of
death, I will fear no evil, for
you are | with me;*
    your rod and your staff,
    they | comfort me.
You prepare a table before me in
the presence of my | enemies;*
    you anoint my head with
    oil; my cup | overflows.
Surely goodness and mercy
shall follow me all the
days | of my life,*
    and I shall dwell in the house
    of the LORD for- | ever.
**Glory be to the Father and | to
the Son***
    **and to the Holy | Spirit;
as it was in the be- | ginning,***
    **is now, and will be for-
    ever. | Amen.**

King James Version

The LORD is my | shepherd;*
  I | shall not want.
He maketh me to lie down in
green | pastures:*
    he leadeth me beside the
    still | waters.
He restoreth | my soul:*
    he leadeth me in the paths
    of righteousness for
    his | name's sake.
Yea, though I walk through
the valley of the shadow of
death, I will fear no evil: for
thou art | with me;*
    thy rod and thy staff
    they | comfort me.
Thou preparest a table before me
in the presence of mine | enemies:*
    thou anointest my head with
    oil; my cup runneth | over.
Surely goodness and mercy
shall follow me all the days | of
my life:*
    and I will dwell in the house
    of the LORD for- | ever.
**Glory be to the Father and | to
the Son***
    **and to the Holy | Spirit;
as it was in the be- | ginning,***
    **is now, and will be for-
    ever. | Amen.**

P O Lord, our shepherd, lead Your sheep in goodness and mercy as we pass with You through the valley of the shadow of death to Your eternal home, where You live and reign with the Father and the Holy Spirit, one God, now and forever. (534)

R *Amen.*

Psalm 130

Out | of the depths*
    I cry to you, | O LORD!
O Lord, | hear my voice!*
    Let your ears be attentive to the voice of my pleas for | mercy!
If you, O LORD, should mark in- | iquities,*
    O Lord, | who could stand?
But with you there is for- | giveness,*
    that you | may be feared.
I wait for the LORD, my | soul waits,*
    and in his | word I hope;
my soul waits for the Lord more than watchmen for the | morning,*
    more than watchmen for the | morning.
O Israel, hope in the LORD! For with the LORD there is | steadfast love,*
    and with him is plentiful re- | demption.
And he will redeem | Israel*
    from all his in- | iquities.
Glory be to the Father and | to the Son*
    and to the Holy | Spirit;
as it was in the be- | ginning,*
    is now, and will be forever. | Amen.

P O Lord, let Your ears be attentive to the voice of our cry, for there is forgiveness with You that You may be feared. By Your unfailing love deliver us from all our sin that our hope may be in You and in Your full redemption; through Jesus Christ, Your Son, our Lord, who lives and reigns with You and the Holy Spirit, one God, now and forever. (535)

R *Amen.*

The pastor reads from Holy Scripture and may give words of comfort based on the reading. Suggestions for additional readings are available in the Resources for Christian Burial (LSB Agenda, page 142).

My sheep hear My voice

[Jesus said:] "My sheep hear my voice, and I know them, and they follow me. I give them eternal life, and they will never perish, and no one will snatch them out of my hand. My Father, who has given them to me, is greater than all, and no one is able to snatch them out of the Father's hand."   *John 10:27–29*

Into Your hand I commit my spirit

Into your hand I commit my spirit;
you have redeemed me, O Lord, faithful God.   *Psalm 31:5*

I will give you rest

[Jesus said:] "Come to me, all who labor and are heavy laden, and I will give you rest. Take my yoke upon you, and learn from me, for I am gentle and lowly in heart, and you will find rest for your souls. For my yoke is easy, and my burden is light."   *Matthew 11:28–30*

God so loved the world

[Jesus said:] "For God so loved the world, that he gave his only Son, that whoever believes in him should not perish but have eternal life. For God did not send his Son into the world to condemn the world, but in order that the world might be saved through him. Whoever believes in him is not condemned, but whoever does not believe is condemned already, because he has not believed in the name of the only Son of God. And this is the judgment: the light has come into the world, and people loved the darkness rather than the light because their deeds were evil. For everyone who does wicked things hates the light and does not come to the light, lest his deeds should be exposed. But whoever does what is true comes to the light, so that it may be clearly seen that his deeds have been carried out in God."

John 3:16–21

The crucifixion of our Lord

Then the soldiers of the governor took Jesus into the governor's headquarters, and they gathered the whole battalion before him. And they stripped him and put a scarlet robe on him, and twisting together a crown of thorns, they put it on his head and put a reed in his right hand. And kneeling before him, they mocked him, saying, "Hail, King of the Jews!" And they spit on him and took the reed and struck him on the head. And when they had mocked him, they stripped him of the robe and put his own clothes on him and led him away to crucify him. As they went out, they found a man of Cyrene, Simon by name. They compelled this man to carry his cross.

And when they came to a place called Golgotha (which means Place of a Skull), they offered him wine to drink, mixed with gall, but when he tasted it, he would not drink it. And when they had crucified him, they divided his garments among them by casting lots. Then they sat down and kept watch over him there. And over his head they put the charge against him, which read, "This is Jesus, the King of the Jews." Then two robbers were crucified with him, one on the right and one on the left. And those who passed by derided him, wagging their heads and saying, "You who would destroy the temple and rebuild it in three days, save yourself! If you are the Son of God, come down from the cross." So also the chief priests, with the scribes and elders, mocked him, saying, "He saved others; he cannot save himself. He is the King of Israel; let him come down now from the cross, and we will believe in him. He trusts in God; let God deliver him now, if he desires him. For he said, 'I am the Son of God.'" And the robbers who were crucified with him also reviled him in the same way. ►

Now from the sixth hour there was darkness over all the land until the ninth hour. And about the ninth hour Jesus cried out with a loud voice, saying, "Eli, Eli, lema sabachthani?" that is, "My God, my God, why have you forsaken me?" And some of the bystanders, hearing it, said, "This man is calling Elijah." And one of them at once ran and took a sponge, filled it with sour wine, and put it on a reed and gave it to him to drink. But the others said, "Wait, let us see whether Elijah will come to save him." And Jesus cried out again with a loud voice and yielded up his spirit. And behold, the curtain of the temple was torn in two, from top to bottom. And the earth shook, and the rocks were split. The tombs also were opened. And many bodies of the saints who had fallen asleep were raised, and coming out of the tombs after his resurrection they went into the holy city and appeared to many. When the centurion and those who were with him, keeping watch over Jesus, saw the earthquake and what took place, they were filled with awe and said, "Truly this was the Son of God!"

Matthew 27:27–54

The resurrection of our Lord

Now on the first day of the week Mary Magdalene came to the tomb early, while it was still dark, and saw that the stone had been taken away from the tomb. So she ran and went to Simon Peter and the other disciple, the one whom Jesus loved, and said to them, "They have taken the Lord out of the tomb, and we do not know where they have laid him." So Peter went out with the other disciple, and they were going toward the tomb. Both of them were running together, but the other disciple outran Peter and reached the tomb first. And stooping to look in, he saw the linen cloths lying there, but he did not go in. Then Simon Peter came, following him, and went into the tomb. He saw the linen cloths lying there, and the face cloth, which had been on Jesus' head, not lying with the linen cloths but folded up in a place by itself. Then the other disciple, who had reached the tomb first, also went in, and he saw and believed; for as yet they did not understand the Scripture, that he must rise from the dead. Then the disciples went back to their homes.

But Mary stood weeping outside the tomb, and as she wept she stooped to look into the tomb. And she saw two angels in white, sitting where the body of Jesus had lain, one at the head and one at the feet. They said to her, "Woman, why are you weeping?" She said to them, "They have taken away my Lord, and I do not know where they have laid him." Having said this, she turned around and saw Jesus standing, but she did not know that it was Jesus. Jesus said to her, "Woman, why are you weeping? Whom are you seeking?" Supposing him to be the gardener, she said to him, "Sir, if you have carried him away, tell me where you have laid him, and I will take him away." Jesus said to her, "Mary." She turned and said to him in Aramaic, "Rabboni!" (which means Teacher). Jesus said to her, "Do not cling to me, for I have not yet ascended to the Father; but go to my brothers and say to them, 'I am ascending to my Father and your Father, to my God and your God.'" Mary Magdalene went and announced to the disciples, "I have seen the Lord"—and that he had said these things to her.

John 20:1–18

Standing before the throne and the Lamb

After this I looked, and behold, a great multitude that no one could number, from every nation, from all tribes and peoples and languages, standing before the throne and before the Lamb, clothed in white robes, with palm branches in their hands, and crying out with a loud voice, "Salvation belongs to our God who sits on the throne, and to the Lamb!" And all the angels were standing around the throne and around the elders and the four living creatures, and they fell on their faces before the throne and worshiped God, saying, "Amen! Blessing and glory and wisdom and thanksgiving and honor and power and might be to our God forever and ever! Amen."

▶

Then one of the elders addressed me, saying, "Who are these, clothed in white robes, and from where have they come?" I said to him, "Sir, you know." And he said to me, "These are the ones coming out of the great tribulation. They have washed their robes and made them white in the blood of the Lamb.

"Therefore they are before the throne of God,
    and serve him day and night in his temple;
    and he who sits on the throne will shelter them with his presence.
They shall hunger no more, neither thirst anymore;
    the sun shall not strike them,
    nor any scorching heat.
For the Lamb in the midst of the throne will be their shepherd,
    and he will guide them to springs of living water,
    and God will wipe away every tear from their eyes."

Revelation 7:9–17

The CREED *is confessed.*

I believe in God, the Father Almighty,
    maker of heaven and earth.
And in Jesus Christ, His only Son, our Lord,
    who was conceived by the Holy Spirit,
    born of the virgin Mary,
    suffered under Pontius Pilate,
    was crucified, died and was buried.
    He descended into hell.
    The third day He rose again from the dead.
    He ascended into heaven
    and sits at the right hand of God the Father Almighty.
    From thence He will come to judge the living and the dead.
I believe in the Holy Spirit,
    the holy Christian Church,
        the communion of saints,

the forgiveness of sins,
the resurrection of the body,
and the life ☩ everlasting. Amen.

> *Christian:* the ancient text reads "catholic," meaning the whole
> Church as it confesses the wholeness of Christian doctrine.

The Litany for the Dying may be prayed, either responsively or by the pastor.

O Lord,	**have mercy.**
O Christ,	**have mercy.**
O Lord,	**have mercy.**
God the Father in heaven,	**have mercy on us.**
God the Son, Redeemer of the world,	**have mercy on us.**
God the Holy Spirit,	**have mercy on us.**
Be gracious to us.	**Spare us, good Lord.**
Be gracious to us.	**Help us, good Lord.**
From all sin, from all evil, from all suffering,	**good Lord, deliver us.**
By Your incarnation, by Your cross and suffering, by Your death and burial,	**help us, good Lord.**
By Your resurrection and ascension, by the coming of Your Holy Spirit,	**help us, good Lord.**
We poor sinners implore You	**to hear us, good Lord.**
That You deliver Your servant *name* from all evil and from eternal death,	**we implore You to hear us, good Lord.**
That You forgive all *his/her* sins,	**we implore You to hear us, good Lord.**
That You give *him/her* refreshment and everlasting blessing,	**we implore You to hear us, good Lord.** ▶

That You give __*him/her*__ joy and glad-
ness in heaven with Your saints, **we implore You to hear us, good Lord.**

Christ, the Lamb of God,
who takes away the sin of the world, **have mercy on us.**
Christ, the Lamb of God,
who takes away the sin of the world, **have mercy on us.**
Christ, the Lamb of God,
who takes away the sin of the world, **grant us Your peace.**

O Lord, **have mercy.**
O Christ, **have mercy.**
O Lord, **have mercy.**

The pastor then prays:

P Almighty God, You breathed life into Adam and have given
earthly life also to __*name*__, Your dear child and servant. With
faith in Your power to heal and save, we commend __*him/her*__
to You; through Jesus Christ, Your Son, our Lord, who lives and
reigns with You and the Holy Spirit, one God, now and forever. (536)

R *Amen.*

The pastor lays his hands on the dying Christian as all pray:

Our Father who art in heaven,
hallowed be Thy name,
Thy kingdom come,
Thy will be done on earth as it is in heaven;
give us this day our daily bread;
and forgive us our trespasses
as we forgive those who trespass against us;
and lead us not into temptation,
but deliver us from evil.
For Thine is the kingdom and the power and the glory
forever and ever. Amen. *Matthew 6:9–13*

P   _Name_ , go in peace. May God the Father, who created you, may God the ✝ Son, who redeemed and saved you with His blood, may God the Holy Spirit, who sanctified you in the water of Holy Baptism, receive you into the company of saints and angels to await the resurrection and live in the light of His glory forevermore.

R   Amen.

The Nunc Dimittis is spoken or sung (LSB page 165, 182).

Lord, now You let Your servant go in peace;
    Your word has been fulfilled.
My own eyes have seen the salvation
    which You have prepared in the sight of every people:
a light to reveal You to the nations
    and the glory of Your people Israel.   *Luke 2:29–32*
Glory be to the Father and to the Son and to the Holy Spirit;
as it was in the beginning, is now, and will be forever. Amen.

The following hymn stanza may be sung or spoken:

Lord, let at last Thine angels come,
To Abr'ham's bosom bear me home,
    That I may die unfearing;
And in its narrow chamber keep
My body safe in peaceful sleep
    Until Thy reappearing.
And then from death awaken me,
That these mine eyes with joy may see,
    O Son of God, Thy glorious face,
    My Savior and my fount of grace.
Lord Jesus Christ,
    My prayer attend,
    My prayer attend,
    And I will praise Thee without end.   *Hymn 708:3*

Should death occur, the following prayer is said.

P O God the Father, fountain and source of all blessings, we give thanks that You have kept our ___brother/sister___ ___name___ in the faith and have now taken ___him/her___ to Yourself. Comfort us with Your holy Word, and give us strength that when our last hour comes we may peacefully fall asleep in You; through Jesus Christ, our Lord. (537)

R *Amen.*

The pastor concludes with the blessing.

P The Lord bless you and keep you.
The Lord make His face shine upon you and be gracious unto you.
The Lord lift up His countenance upon you and ✠ give you peace.

R *Amen.*   *Numbers 6:24–26*

COMFORTING THE BEREAVED

---

1. The first part of this rite (With the Family at the Viewing of the Body) is used with the immediate family when the body is viewed for the first time.
2. The second half of this rite (At the Visitation) may be used as a service with those gathered for the visitation or privately with the family before the public visitation.
3. A eulogy is not in the best Christian tradition. An obituary may be read which focuses on the Gospel promise of salvation by grace alone through faith alone in Christ our Lord, and not on the good deeds of the deceased. Examples of fitting obituaries are provided in the Resources for Christian Burial (*LSB Agenda,* page 148).
4. When used in the context of a large gathering, messages of Christian condolence and words giving thanks to God for the life of the deceased may be given. Family members may wish to acknowledge expressions of condolence that have been received.
5. For ongoing ministry to the bereaved, see the appropriate resources on pages 247–277.

With the Family at the Viewing of the Body

P In the name of the Father and of the ✠ Son and of the Holy Spirit.

R *Amen.*   *Matthew 28:19b*

P Hear the promise of Christ, our Lord: "I am the resurrection and the life. Whoever believes in me, though he die, yet shall he live, and everyone who lives and believes in me shall never die."

John 11:25–26

The pastor may speak words of consolation to the bereaved using the preceding or another passage of Holy Scripture.

P Let us pray.
Merciful Father, the generations rise and pass away before You. You are the strength of those who labor and the repose of the blessed dead. We give You thanks for all who have lived and died in the faith, especially for ___name___, our dear ___brother/sister___. In this body You gave ___him/her___ life and poured out Your Holy Spirit when You washed ___him/her___ in the renewing waters of Holy Baptism. By the same Spirit You led ___him/her___ to confess with ___his/her___ mouth that Jesus is Lord and to believe in ___his/her___ heart that You have raised Christ from the dead. Give us faith to commend our ___brother/sister___ to You and to await with confidence the resurrection of all Your saints, living and departed; through Jesus Christ, Your Son, our Lord, who lives and reigns with You and the Holy Spirit, one God, now and forever. (538)

R *Amen.*

At the Visitation

P In the name of the Father and of the ☩ Son and of the Holy Spirit.
R *Amen.*   *Matthew 28:19b*

One of the following psalms is prayed. When copies of the rite are provided to those present, all may join in as the psalm is sung by whole verse or spoken by half verse. After the psalm and a time of silence, the psalm collect may be spoken. Other psalms and psalm collects are provided in the Resources for Christian Burial (LSB Agenda, page 140).

Psalm 90

Lord, you have been our | dwelling place*
>> in all gener- | ations.
Before the mountains were brought forth, or ever you had formed the earth | and the world,*
>> from everlasting to everlasting | you are God.
You return | man to dust*
>> and say, "Return, O chil- | dren of man!"
For a thousand years in your sight are but as yesterday when | it is past,*
>> or as a watch | in the night.
You sweep them away as | with a flood;*
>> they are like a dream, like grass that is renewed in the | morning:
in the morning it flourishes and | is renewed;*
>> in the evening it fades and | withers.
For we are brought to an end by your | anger;*
>> by your wrath we | are dismayed.
You have set our iniquities be- | fore you,*
>> our secret sins in the light of your | presence.
For all our days pass away un- | der your wrath;*
>> we bring our years to an end | like a sigh.
The years of our life are seventy, or even by reason of strength | eighty;*
>> yet their span is but toil and trouble; they are soon gone, and we | fly away.
Who considers the power of your | anger,*
>> and your wrath according to the | fear of you?
So teach us to number | our days*
>> that we may get a heart of | wisdom.
Return, O Lord! | How long?*
>> Have pity on your | servants!
Satisfy us in the morning with your | steadfast love,*
>> that we may rejoice and be glad | all our days.
Make us glad for as many days as you have af- | flicted us,*
>> and for as many years as we have seen | evil.   ►

Let your work be shown to your | servants,*
 and your glorious power to their | children.
Let the favor of the Lord our God be up- | on us,*
 and establish the work of our hands upon us;
 yes, establish the work | of our hands!
Glory be to the Father and | to the Son*
 and to the Holy | Spirit;
as it was in the be- | ginning,*
 is now, and will be forever. | Amen.

P   O Lord, the refuge of every generation, we fade like withered
grass as You sweep us away in the sleep of death. Make us glad
for as many days as You have afflicted us, be gracious to us for
Jesus' sake, and awaken us in the joy of the resurrection to eternal life with Him who lives and reigns with You and the Holy
Spirit, one God, now and forever. (539)
R   *Amen.*

Psalm 27

The Lord is my light and my salvation; whom | shall I fear?*
 The Lord is the stronghold of my life; of whom shall I | be afraid?
When evildoers assail me to eat | up my flesh,*
 my adversaries and foes, it is they who stum- | ble and fall.
Though an army encamp against me, my heart | shall not fear;*
 though war arise against me, yet I will be | confident.
One thing have I asked of the Lord, that will I seek | after:*
 that I may dwell in the house of the Lord all the days of my life,
 to gaze upon the beauty of the Lord and to inquire in his | temple.
For he will hide me in his shelter in the day of | trouble;*
 he will conceal me under the cover of his tent; he will lift me
 high up- | on a rock.

And now my head shall be lifted up above my enemies all around me, and I will offer in his tent sacrifices with | shouts of joy;*
>I will sing and make melody | to the LORD.

Hear, O LORD, when I | cry aloud;*
>be gracious to me and | answer me!

You have said, | "Seek my face."*
>My heart says to you, "Your face, LORD, | do I seek."

Hide not your face from me. Turn not your servant away in | anger,*
>O you who have been my help. Cast me not off; forsake me not, O God of my sal- | vation!

For my father and my mother have for- | saken me,*
>but the LORD will | take me in.

Teach me your way, | O LORD,*
>and lead me on a level path because of my | enemies.

Give me not up to the will of my adver- | saries;*
>for false witnesses have risen against me, and they breathe out | violence.

I believe that I shall look upon the goodness | of the LORD*
>in the land of the | living!

Wait | for the LORD;*
>be strong, and let your heart take courage; wait | for the LORD!

Glory be to the Father and | to the Son*
>**and to the Holy | Spirit;**

as it was in the be- | ginning,*
>**is now, and will be forever. | Amen.**

P O Lord, our saving light and our shelter in the day of trouble, turn us not away in anger because of our sins. Calm our hearts, strengthen our faith, and lead us in Your straight paths until we see Your surpassing goodness in heaven with all those who live in Your Son, Jesus Christ, our Lord, who lives and reigns with You and the Holy Spirit, one God, now and forever. (540)

R *Amen.*

The reading of the obituary or words of thanksgiving for the life of the deceased may follow. See examples in the Resources for Christian Burial (LSB Agenda, page 148). Family members may wish to acknowledge expressions of condolence that have been received. The following is then prayed:

P Gracious Lord, we give You thanks for the days of earthly life You granted to ___name___, for the grace bestowed in Christ Jesus, for ___his/her___ adoption and rebirth in Holy Baptism, and for all the good ___he/she___ was permitted to give and to receive. We entrust ___him/her___ to Your mercy and pray for the sustaining comfort of Your Holy Spirit; through Jesus Christ, our Lord, who lives and reigns with You and the same Holy Spirit, one God, now and forever. (541)

R *Amen.*

One or more of the following may be read.

P Hear the Word of the Lord.

God our refuge

The eternal God is your refuge, and underneath are the everlasting arms.

Deuteronomy 33:27a NIV

Baptized into Christ's death and resurrection

Do you not know that all of us who have been baptized into Christ Jesus were baptized into his death? We were buried therefore with him by baptism into death, in order that, just as Christ was raised from the dead by the glory of the Father, we too might walk in newness of life. For if we have been united with him in a death like his, we shall certainly be united with him in a resurrection like his. We know that our old self was crucified with him in order that the body of sin might be brought to nothing, so that we would no longer be enslaved to sin. For one who has died has been set free from sin. Now if we have died with Christ, we believe that we will also live with him. We know that Christ being raised from the dead will never die again; death no longer has dominion over him. *Romans 6:3–9*

The life of Jesus manifested in our bodies

But we have this treasure in jars of clay, to show that the surpassing power belongs to God and not to us. We are afflicted in every way, but not crushed; perplexed, but not driven to despair; persecuted, but not forsaken; struck down, but not destroyed; always carrying in the body the death of Jesus, so that the life of Jesus may also be manifested in our bodies. For we who live are always being given over to death for Jesus' sake so that the life of Jesus also be manifested in our mortal flesh. So death is at work in us, but life in you. Since we have the same spirit of faith according to what has been written, "I believed, and so I spoke," we also believe, and so we also speak, knowing that he who raised the Lord Jesus will raise us also with Jesus and bring us with you into his presence. For it is all for your sake, so that as grace extends to more and more people it may increase thanksgiving, to the glory of God. So we do not lose heart. Though our outer nature is wasting away, our inner nature is being renewed day by day. For this slight momentary affliction is preparing for us an eternal weight of glory beyond all comparison, as we look not to the things that are seen but to the things that are unseen. For the things that are seen are transient, but the things that are unseen are eternal.

2 Corinthians 4:7–18

To live is Christ

It is my eager expectation and hope that I will not be at all ashamed, but that with full courage now as always Christ will be honored in my body, whether by life or by death. For to me to live is Christ, and to die is gain. *Philippians 1:20–21*

We grieve in hope

We do not want you to be uninformed, brothers, about those who are asleep, that you may not grieve as others do who have no hope. For since we believe that Jesus died and rose again, even so, through Jesus, God will bring with him those who have fallen asleep.

For this we declare to you by a word from the Lord, that we who are alive, who are left until the coming of the Lord, will not precede those who have fallen asleep. For the Lord himself will descend from heaven with a cry of command, with the voice of an archangel, and with the sound of the trumpet of God. And the dead in Christ will rise first. Then we who are alive, who are left, will be caught up together with them in the clouds to meet the Lord in the air, and so we will always be with the Lord. Therefore encourage one another with these words.

1 Thessalonians 4:13–18

Believers have eternal life

[Jesus said:] "Truly, truly, I say to you, whoever hears my word and believes him who sent me has eternal life. He does not come into judgment, but has passed from death to life." *John 5:24*

My sheep hear My voice

[Jesus said:] "My sheep hear my voice, and I know them, and they follow me. I give them eternal life, and they will never perish, and no one will snatch them out of my hand. My Father, who has given them to me, is greater than all, and no one is able to snatch them out of the Father's hand." *John 10:27–29*

Let not your hearts be troubled

[Jesus said:] "Let not your hearts be troubled. Believe in God; believe also in me. In my Father's house are many rooms. If it were not so, would I have told you that I go to prepare a place for you? And if I go and prepare a place for you, I will come again and will take you to myself, that where I am you may be also. And you know the way to where I am going." Thomas said to him, "Lord, we do not know where you are going. How can we know the way?" Jesus said to him, "I am the way, and the truth, and the life. No one comes to the Father except through me."

John 14:1–6

The pastor may speak words of consolation to the bereaved using these or other passages of Holy Scripture.

The following (Hymn 679) or another hymn may be sung or read. Other hymn suggestions are listed in the Resources for Christian Burial (LSB Agenda, page 146).

Oh, how blest are they whose toils are ended,
Who through death have unto God ascended!
They have arisen
From the cares which keep us still in prison.

We are still as in a dungeon living,
Still oppressed with sorrow and misgiving;
Our undertakings
Are but toils and troubles and heartbreakings.

They meanwhile are in their chambers sleeping,
Quiet and set free from all their weeping;
No cross or sadness
There can hinder their untroubled gladness.

Christ has wiped away their tears forever;
They have that for which we still endeavor.
By them are chanted
Songs that ne'er to mortal ears were granted.

▶

103

Come, O Christ, and loose the chains that bind us;
Lead us forth and cast this world behind us.
With You, th'Anointed,
Finds the soul its joy and rest appointed.

The CREED *is confessed.*

I believe in God, the Father Almighty,
    maker of heaven and earth.
And in Jesus Christ, His only Son, our Lord,
    who was conceived by the Holy Spirit,
    born of the virgin Mary,
    suffered under Pontius Pilate,
    was crucified, died and was buried.
    He descended into hell.
    The third day He rose again from the dead.
    He ascended into heaven
    and sits at the right hand of God the Father Almighty.
    From thence He will come to judge the living and the dead.
I believe in the Holy Spirit,
    the holy Christian Church,
        the communion of saints,
    the forgiveness of sins,
    the resurrection of the body,
    and the life ✠ everlasting. Amen.

Christian: the ancient text reads "catholic," meaning the whole
Church as it confesses the wholeness of Christian doctrine.

One or more of the following may be prayed.

P Let us pray.

Almighty and most merciful God, You bring us through suffering and death with our Lord Jesus Christ to enter with Him into glory. Grant us grace at all times to acknowledge and accept Your holy and gracious will, to remain in true faith, and to find peace and joy in the resurrection of the dead and the glory of everlasting life; through Jesus Christ, our Lord, who lives and reigns with You and the Holy Spirit, one God, now and forever. (542)

R *Amen.*

P Almighty God, heavenly Father, we thank and praise You that You called _____name_____ to the knowledge of Your dear Son, kept _____him/her_____ in the true faith, and granted _____him/her_____ a blessed end. We implore You, help us by Your Holy Spirit rightly to know and lament our sins and to be so strengthened in our faith in Christ that in all things we may grow up into Him who is our Head, evermore praising You in newness of life and cheerfully awaiting the glorious appearance of our Savior Jesus Christ, who lives and reigns with You and the Holy Spirit, one God, now and forever. (543)

R *Amen.*

At the death of a child:

P O Lord, heavenly Father, comfort _____name of parent(s)_____ and their family who grieve the loss of their dear child. Enable them in steadfast faith and confident hope to look for the blessed day of the completion of our salvation, when all who trust in You shall meet again in heavenly joy and glory; through Jesus Christ, our Lord. (544)

R *Amen.*

105

The prayers conclude with the LORD'S PRAYER.

P   Taught by our Lord and trusting His promises, we are bold to pray:
> **Our Father who art in heaven,**
> > **hallowed be Thy name,**
> > **Thy kingdom come,**
> > **Thy will be done on earth as it is in heaven;**
> > **give us this day our daily bread;**
> > **and forgive us our trespasses**
> > > **as we forgive those who trespass against us;**
> > **and lead us not into temptation,**
> > **but deliver us from evil.**
>
> **For Thine is the kingdom and the power and the glory**
> > **forever and ever. Amen.**

Matthew 6:9–13

The pastor blesses the bereaved.

P   The Lord bless you and keep you.
    The Lord make His face shine upon you and be gracious unto you.
    The Lord lift up His countenance upon you and ✠ give you peace.

R   *Amen.*

Numbers 6:24–26

ENTRANCE OF THE BODY INTO THE CHURCH

1. This rite may be used when the casket arrives at the church prior to the Funeral Service for viewing or visitation. It may also be used with the bereaved immediately prior to the Funeral Service.
2. If the casket is to be closed for visitation prior to the Funeral Service, the pall may be placed on the casket at the designated place in this rite.
3. If the casket is open for viewing prior to the Funeral Service, the pall is not placed on the casket until the Funeral Service.
4. The pastor, who may be vested, meets the casket, pallbearers, and the bereaved at the entrance to the church.

One of the following psalms is prayed.

I was glad when they | said to me,*
    "Let us go to the house | of the LORD!"
Our feet have been | standing*
    within your gates, O Je- | rusalem!
Pray for the peace of Je- | rusalem!*
    "May they be secure who | love you!
Peace be with- | in your walls*
    and security within your | towers!"
For my brothers and com- | panions' sake*
    I will say, "Peace be with- | in you!"
For the sake of the house of the | LORD our God,*
    I will | seek your good.

►

107

Glory be to the Father and | to the Son*
    and to the Holy | Spirit;
as it was in the be- | ginning,*
    is now, and will be forever. | Amen.
I was glad when they | said to me,*
    "Let us go to the house | of the LORD!"   *Psalm 122:1–2, 6–9*

OR

These things I remember, as I pour | out my soul:*
    how I would go with the throng and lead them in procession to
    the | house of God.
As a deer pants for | flowing streams,*
    so pants my soul for you, | O God.
My soul thirsts for God, for the | living God.*
    When shall I come and appear be- | fore God?
My tears have been my food | day and night,*
    while they say to me continually, "Where | is your God?"
These things I remember, as I pour | out my soul:*
    how I would go with the throng and lead them in procession to
    the | house of God
with glad shouts and | songs of praise,*
    a multitude keeping | festival.
Why are you cast down, O my soul, and why are you in turmoil
with- | in me?*
    Hope in God; for I shall again praise him, my salvation | and
    my God.
Glory be to the Father and | to the Son*
    and to the Holy | Spirit;
as it was in the be- | ginning,*
    is now, and will be forever. | Amen.
These things I remember, as I pour | out my soul:*
    how I would go with the throng and lead them in procession to
    the | house of God.   *Psalm 42:4a, 1–6a*

Remembrance of Baptism

P In Holy Baptism *name* was clothed with the robe of Christ's righteousness that covered all *his/her* sin. St. Paul says: "Do you not know that all of us who have been baptized into Christ Jesus were baptized into His death? We were buried therefore with Him by Baptism into death, in order that, just as Christ was raised from the dead by the glory of the Father, we too might walk in newness of life. For if we have been united with Him in a death like His, we shall certainly be united with Him in a resurrection like His."

Romans 6:3–5

The casket may be covered with a pall at this time.

P Let us pray.

Lord God, maker of heaven and earth and giver of life, we give thanks for all the mercies You granted *name* during *his/her* earthly life, especially for calling *him/her* to faith in Jesus Christ through Holy Baptism. Comfort all who mourn *his/her* death with the hope of the glorious resurrection of the body and a happy reunion in heaven. Remind us that we, too, are mortal, and prepare us to fall asleep in faith and on the Last Day receive the glory promised to all who trust in Your beloved Son, even Jesus Christ, our Lord, who lives and reigns with You and the Holy Spirit, one God, now and forever. (545)

R *Amen.*

P Peace be with you.

FUNERAL SERVICE

General Notes

1. The Funeral Service is intended for the burial of those who departed this life in the Christian faith.
2. The death of a member of the Church should be reported immediately to the pastor. No arrangements should be made without consultation with him.
3. Whenever possible, the Funeral Service of baptized members is conducted at the church.
4. Hymns and music in the Funeral Service should reflect Christian confidence, trust, and hope in the resurrection of the body and the life everlasting.
5. The liturgical color for the Funeral Service is the color of the season or day.
6. Floral arrangements express the Christian hope in the resurrection of the body. It is preferable that they not be placed on the casket or altar during the Funeral Service.
7. The Funeral Service may be used as a memorial service by omitting the placing of the pall and the rubric before the Nunc Dimittis.
8. A eulogy is not in the best Christian tradition. An obituary may be read which focuses on the Gospel promise of salvation by grace alone through faith alone in Christ our Lord, and not on the good deeds of the deceased.
9. Appropriate messages of Christian condolence may be given after the Lord's Prayer.
10. The ceremonies or tributes of social or other societies have no place within the service of the Church. Civic and military ceremonies or tributes should be held after the service of the Church,

normally following the committal.

11. This rite is a more complete version of the corresponding rite in *Lutheran Service Book*, pages 278–281.

The Service in Detail

1. A hymn or psalm may be sung or said, or appropriate organ or instrumental music may be played as the pastor leads the casket and the bereaved into the church. When there is no procession, the service begins when the pastor takes his customary place.

2. The procession into the church may be in this order: cross, torches, assisting ministers, pastor, casket and pallbearers, the bereaved, and other honored guests.

3. Prior to the service, the lighted paschal candle is placed near the center of the chancel, preferably near the head of the casket. When torches are included in the procession, they may be placed at the head and foot of the casket. The cross is placed in its customary place.

4. The casket is positioned before the altar at right angles to it. It is customary that the foot of the casket is positioned closest to the altar. For the funeral of a pastor, the head of the casket is positioned closest to the altar.

5. When the Invocation and Remembrance of Baptism are conducted at the entrance to the nave, the congregation stands and faces the entrance of the church. Following the Remembrance of Baptism, the pall is placed on the casket, and the procession proceeds into the nave during the Introit, Psalm, or Entrance Hymn.

6. The Kyrie may be spoken as provided in the rite, or a setting of the Kyrie familiar to the congregation may be sung.

7. Readings may include those previously used by the pastor in his ministry to the deceased. Readings of the Sunday or season in the Church Year may also be used. See additional suggestions provided in the Resources for Christian Burial (*LSB Agenda,* pages 143–145).

8. A choice of psalms is provided for the Introit and Gradual in the Resources for Christian Burial (*LSB Agenda,* page 143).

9. The Verse may be spoken or sung as provided in the rite, or a setting familiar to the congregation may be used.

10. When an obituary is read, it may be read in connection with the Sermon. Examples are provided in the Resources for Christian Burial (*LSB Agenda,* page 148).
11. Additional petitions that may be inserted in the Prayer of the Church are provided in this rite on pages 117–119.
12. When there is Holy Communion, the Prayer of the Church in the Funeral Service is followed by the Offertory and communion liturgy according to one of the settings of the Divine Service. Following the Distribution, the Funeral Service continues with the Nunc Dimittis in the Funeral Service.
13. Options for the Proper Preface include that of the season or day, the proper preface for All Saints' Day, or the one provided in the Resources for Christian Burial (*LSB Agenda,* page 147).
14. The Funeral Service concludes at the place of committal.
15. The procession out of the church forms in the same order as it entered. The cross may be taken to the place of committal.
16. The pall is removed at the church door and left in the church.

———————

A hymn or psalm may be sung or spoken.

Stand

INVOCATION

The sign of the cross ☩ may be made by all in remembrance of their Baptism.

P In the name of the Father and of the ☩ Son and of the Holy Spirit.
C **Amen.** *Matthew 28:19b*

REMEMBRANCE OF BAPTISM

The casket may be covered with a funeral pall.

P In Holy Baptism ___*name*___ was clothed with the robe of Christ's righteousness that covered all ___*his/her*___ sin. St. Paul says: "Do

112

you not know that all of us who have been baptized into Christ
Jesus were baptized into His death?"

C **We were buried therefore with Him by baptism into death, in
order that, just as Christ was raised from the dead by the
glory of the Father, we too might walk in newness of life. For
if we have been united with Him in a death like His, we shall
certainly be united with Him in a resurrection like His.**

Romans 6:3–5

INTROIT, PSALM, or ENTRANCE HYMN

KYRIE ~ *Lord, Have Mercy*   *Mark 10:47*

P Lord, have mercy upon us.
C **Christ, have mercy upon us.**
Lord, have mercy upon us.

SALUTATION and COLLECT OF THE DAY

P The Lord be with you.   *2 Timothy 4:22*
C **And also with you.**

P Let us pray.
O God of grace and mercy, we give thanks for Your loving-
kindness shown to *name* and to all Your servants who, having finished their course in faith, now rest from their labors.
Grant that we also may be faithful unto death and receive the
crown of eternal life; through Jesus Christ, Your Son, our Lord,
who lives and reigns with You and the Holy Spirit, one God,
now and forever. (546)
C **Amen.**

Sit

113

OLD TESTAMENT or FIRST READING

Ⓐ The _Old Testament/First_ Reading is from _____, chapter _____.

After the reading:

Ⓐ This is the Word of the Lord.
Ⓒ **Thanks be to God.**

PSALM or GRADUAL

EPISTLE or SECOND READING

Ⓐ The _Epistle/Second Reading_ is from _____, chapter _____.

After the reading:

Ⓐ This is the Word of the Lord.
Ⓒ **Thanks be to God.**

Stand

VERSE

General	Lent
Ⓐ Alleluia, alle- | luia.* 　Jesus Christ is the first- 　born | of the dead; Ⓒ **to Him be glory and power** **for- | ever.*** **Alle- | luia.** *[Revelation 1:5–6]*	Ⓐ If we have | died with Christ,* 　we shall also | live 　with Him; Ⓒ **if we are faithful | to the** **end,*** **we shall | reign with** **Him.** *2 Timothy 2:11b–12a*

HOLY GOSPEL

P The Holy Gospel according to St. _____, the _____ chapter.
C **Glory to You, O Lord.**

After the reading:

P This is the Gospel of the Lord.
C **Praise to You, O Christ.**

APOSTLES' CREED

P God has made us His people through our Baptism into Christ.
Living together in trust and hope, we confess our faith.
C **I believe in God, the Father Almighty,**
> **maker of heaven and earth.**
And in Jesus Christ, His only Son, our Lord,
> **who was conceived by the Holy Spirit,**
> **born of the virgin Mary,**
> **suffered under Pontius Pilate,**
> **was crucified, died and was buried.**
> **He descended into hell.**
> **The third day He rose again from the dead.**
> **He ascended into heaven**
> **and sits at the right hand of God the Father Almighty.**
> **From thence He will come to judge the living and the dead.**
I believe in the Holy Spirit,
> **the holy Christian Church,**
>> **the communion of saints,**
> **the forgiveness of sins,**
> **the resurrection of the body,**
> **and the life ✠ everlasting. Amen.**

> *Christian:* the ancient text reads "catholic," meaning the whole
> Church as it confesses the wholeness of Christian doctrine.

Sit

HYMN OF THE DAY

SERMON

Kneel/Stand

PRAYER OF THE CHURCH [1 Timothy 2:1–4]

P Let us pray to the Lord, our God and Father, who raised Jesus from the dead.

P Almighty God, You have knit Your chosen people together into one communion in the mystical body of Your Son, Jesus Christ, our Lord. Give to Your whole Church in heaven and on earth Your light and Your peace. Lord, in Your mercy,

C **hear our prayer.**

P Grant that all who have been baptized into Christ's death and resurrection may die to sin and rise to newness of life and so pass with Him through the gate of death and the grave to our joyful resurrection. Lord, in Your mercy,

C **hear our prayer.**

P Grant that all who have been nourished by the holy body and blood of Your Son may be raised to immortality and incorruption to be seated with Him at Your heavenly banquet. Lord, in Your mercy,

C **hear our prayer.**

P Give to the family of ___name___ and to all who mourn comfort in their grief and a sure confidence in Your loving care that, casting all their sorrow on You, they may know the consolation of Your love. Lord, in Your mercy,

C **hear our prayer.**

P Give courage and faith to the bereaved, that within the communion of Your Church they may have strength to meet the days ahead in the assurance of a holy and certain hope and in the joyful expectation of eternal life with those they love who have departed in the faith. Lord, in Your mercy,

C **hear our prayer.**

P Help us, we pray, in the midst of things we cannot understand, to believe and find comfort in the communion of saints, the forgiveness of sins, the resurrection of the body, and the life everlasting. Lord, in Your mercy,

C **hear our prayer.**

Additional petitions may be included here. If there are none, the prayers conclude on page 119.

Baptized Child

P Comfort   *name of deceased child's*   parents and family with the promise that through Holy Baptism   *he/she*   was delivered from sin and now lives in Your loving embrace. Lord, in Your mercy,

C **hear our prayer.** (568)

Young Person

P Hear our prayers at the death of   *name* , whose life has passed so quickly, that in our deep sadness we may remember how short our earthly pilgrimage is and seek those things that are above where Christ is seated. Lord, in Your mercy,

C **hear our prayer.** (569)

Husband and Father/Wife and Mother

P Look graciously upon those who mourn the death of a beloved   *husband and father / wife and mother*   and bring ▶

117

them to a joyous and blessed reunion in heaven. Lord, in
Your mercy,

C **hear our prayer.** (570)

Elderly Person

P We thank You that You have given _ name _ a long life of
grace and pray that You would grant that we, too, may die
in peace and receive the crown of everlasting glory. Lord,
in Your mercy,

C **hear our prayer.** (571)

Tragic Death

P Draw near to us in our deepest sorrow and comfort us in
the tragic death of _ name(s) _ with the protection of the
cross and resurrection. Lord, in Your mercy,

C **hear our prayer.** (572)

Sudden Death

P Comfort us at this sudden death of _ name _ and make us
always ready for Your final summons when we will depart
and be with Christ in glory. Lord, in Your mercy,

C **hear our prayer.** (573)

After a Long Illness

P Grant us grace to be conformed to the likeness of Christ
by sharing in His sufferings, even as _ name _ was in
_ his/her _ illness, that we may follow Christ in faith and
know the power of His resurrection. Lord, in Your mercy,

C **hear our prayer.** (574)

Pastor

P We thank You for ___name___ who faithfully shepherded Your flock here on earth. Grant that we, too, may be faithful until death and receive the crown of life. Lord, in Your mercy,

C **hear our prayer.** (575)

The prayers conclude:

P Receive our thanks for ___name___ and for all the blessings You bestowed on ___him/her___ in this earthly life. Bring us at last to our heavenly home that with ___him/her___ we may see You face to face in the joys of paradise. Lord, in Your mercy,

C **hear our prayer.** (547)

P O God of all grace, You sent Your Son, our Savior Jesus Christ, to bring life and immortality to light. We give You thanks that by His death He destroyed the power of death and by His resurrection He opened the kingdom of heaven to all believers. Strengthen us in the confidence that because He lives we shall live also, and that neither death nor life nor things present nor things to come will be able to separate us from Your love, which is in Christ Jesus, our Lord, who lives and reigns with You and the Holy Spirit, one God, now and forever. (548)

C **Amen.**

When there is Holy Communion, the service continues with the Of-FERTORY in the Divine Service; otherwise, the service continues with the LORD'S PRAYER.

LORD'S PRAYER

Matthew 6:9–13

P Taught by our Lord and trusting His promises, we are bold to pray:

C **Our Father who art in heaven,**
hallowed be Thy name,
Thy kingdom come,
Thy will be done on earth as it is in heaven;
give us this day our daily bread;
and forgive us our trespasses
as we forgive those who trespass against us;
and lead us not into temptation,
but deliver us from evil.
For Thine is the kingdom and the power and the glory
forever and ever. Amen.

Following the LORD'S PRAYER (or the DISTRIBUTION when there is Holy Communion), the pastor takes his place at the casket.

NUNC DIMITTIS ～ *Song of Simeon*

A "I am the resurrection and the life," says the Lord. "He who believes in Me will live, even though he dies; and whoever lives and believes in Me will never die." *John 11:25–26 NIV*

C **Lord, now You let Your servant go in peace;**
Your word has been fulfilled.
My own eyes have seen the salvation
which You have prepared in the sight of every people:
a light to reveal You to the nations
and the glory of Your people Israel. *Luke 2:29–32*
Glory be to the Father and to the Son and to the Holy Spirit;
as it was in the beginning, is now, and will be forever. Amen.

A "I am the resurrection and the life," says the Lord. "He who believes in Me will live, even though he dies; and whoever lives and believes in Me will never die."

CONCLUDING COLLECT

P The Lord be with you.   *2 Timothy 4:22*
C **And also with you.**

P Let us pray.
Lord God, our shepherd, You gather the lambs of Your flock into
the arms of Your mercy and bring them home. Comfort us with
the certain hope of the resurrection to everlasting life and a joyful reunion with those we love who have died in the faith;
through Jesus Christ, Your Son, our Lord, who lives and reigns
with You and the Holy Spirit, one God, now and forever. (549)
C **Amen.**

*When it is not possible for the Committal to be conducted at the
place of burial, it occurs here.*

*The pastor may place his hand on the head of the casket as he
says:*

P May God the Father, who created this body; may God the
✝ Son, who by His blood redeemed this body; may God
the Holy Spirit, who by Holy Baptism sanctified this body
to be His temple, keep these remains to the day of the resurrection of all flesh.
C **Amen.**

P Let us pray.
Almighty God, by the death of Your Son Jesus Christ You
destroyed death, by His rest in the tomb You sanctified the
graves of Your saints, and by His bodily resurrection You
brought life and immortality to light so that all who die in
Him abide in peace and hope. Receive our thanks for the
victory over death and the grave that He won for us. Keep
us in everlasting communion with all who wait for Him on ►

121

earth and with all in heaven who are with Him, for He is the resurrection and the life, even Jesus Christ, our Lord. (550)

C **Amen.**

BENEDICAMUS and BENEDICTION

A Let us bless the Lord. *[Psalm 103:1]*

C **Thanks be to God.**

P The Lord bless you and keep you.
The Lord make His face shine upon you and be gracious unto you.
The Lord lift up His countenance upon you and ☩ give you peace.

C **Amen.** *Numbers 6:24–26*

P Let us go forth in peace,

C **in the name of the Lord. Amen.**

A hymn may be sung as the casket is led in procession out of the church.

Suggested Psalms and Readings

The following are suggested psalms and readings for the Funeral Service. Page numbers refer to pages in this book where these readings occur. Readings in boldface have long-standing usage.

Psalm 16:1–2, 5, 8–9, 11	*Preserve me, O God*	p. 195
Psalm 23	*The Lord is my shepherd*	p. 84
Psalm 25:1–9, 16–21	*Make me to know Your ways*	p. 222
Psalm 27	*Wait for the Lord*	p. 98
Psalm 31:5	*Into Your hand I commit my spirit*	p. 86
Psalm 34:1–10	*Fear the Lord, you His saints*	p. 450

COMMITTAL

1. The Committal is used for interment in a place previously set apart for burial. When burial is in a public cemetery, the collect for the blessing of a grave is used. The Committal is also appropriate for the disposition of a body at sea.

2. In the case of cremation, the ashes are to be buried or interred at a cemetery plot, mausoleum, crypt, or columbarium. The practice of scattering the ashes of the deceased to the elements is discouraged among Christians.

3. When circumstances require that the burial occur at a later date, the Committal may include a sermon following the Scripture reading(s). The Apostles' Creed may also be confessed.

4. When feasible, the procession to the place of burial may form in the same order as at the Funeral Service, led by the processional cross. At the very least, the pastor leads the casket and bereaved to the place of burial.

5. The pastor may remain with the casket at the graveside until all the bereaved have left the cemetery as a sign of the eternal presence of Christ with the departed.

6. When the deceased was a member of the armed forces, military honors may follow the Committal.

7. If sand or earth is used during the Committal, it is never poured directly on the national flag. The head of the casket may be slightly uncovered for the application of the sand, after which the head of the casket may again be covered.

During the procession, one or more of the following may be sung or spoken, or other appropriate hymns or psalms may be sung.

Media vita in morte sumus *(14th-century hymn)*

In the midst of life we | are in death;*
 from whom can we | seek help?
From You alone, | O Lord,*
 who by our sins are justly | angered.
Holy God, holy and mighty, holy and merciful | Savior,*
 deliver us not into the bitterness of e- | ternal death.

Lord, You know the secrets | of our hearts;*
 shut not Your ears to our prayers, but spare us, | O Lord.
Holy God, holy and mighty, holy and merciful | Savior,*
 deliver us not into the bitterness of e- | ternal death.

O worthy and e- | ternal Judge,*
 do not let the pains of death turn us away from You at our | last hour.
Holy God, holy and mighty, holy and merciful | Savior,*
 deliver us not into the bitterness of e- | ternal death.

Psalm 118

Out of my distress I called | on the LORD;*
 the LORD answered me and | set me free.
It is better to take refuge | in the LORD*
 than to | trust in man.
It is better to take refuge | in the LORD*
 than to trust in | princes.
I was pushed hard, so that I was | falling,*
 but the LORD | helped me.
Glad songs of salvation are in the tents of the | righteous:*
 "The right hand of the LORD does | valiantly,

the right hand of the | Lord exalts,*
    the right hand of the Lord does | valiantly!"
I shall not die, but | I shall live,*
    and recount the deeds | of the Lord.
Open to me the gates of | righteousness,*
    that I may enter through them and give thanks | to the Lord.
This is the gate | of the Lord;*
    the righteous shall enter | through it.

Psalm 118:5, 8–9, 13, 15–17, 19–20

Glory be to the Father and | to the Son*
    and to the Holy | Spirit;
as it was in the be- | ginning,*
    is now, and will be forever. | Amen.

Psalm 130

Out | of the depths*
    I cry to you, | O Lord!
O Lord, | hear my voice!*
    Let your ears be attentive to the voice of my pleas for | mercy!
If you, O Lord, should mark in- | iquities,*
    O Lord, | who could stand?
But with you there is for- | giveness,*
    that you | may be feared.
I wait for the Lord, my | soul waits,*
    and in his | word I hope;
my soul waits for the Lord more than watchmen for the | morning,*
    more than watchmen for the | morning.
O Israel, hope in the Lord! For with the Lord there is | steadfast love,*
    and with him is plentiful re- | demption.
And he will redeem | Israel*
    from all his in- | iquities.

►

Glory be to the Father and | to the Son*
and to the Holy | Spirit;
as it was in the be- | ginning,*
is now, and will be forever. | Amen.

Nunc Dimittis

Lord, now You let Your servant go in peace;
Your word has been fulfilled.
My own eyes have seen the salvation
which You have prepared in the sight of every people:
a light to reveal You to the nations
and the glory of Your people Israel.   *Luke 2:29–32*
Glory be to the Father and to the Son and to the Holy Spirit;
as it was in the beginning, is now, and will be forever. Amen.

I know that my Redeemer lives

Oh, that my words were written! Oh, that they were inscribed in a
book! That they were engraved on a rock with an iron pen and lead,
forever! For I know that my Redeemer lives, and He shall stand at the
last on the earth. And after my skin is destroyed, this I know, that in
my flesh I shall see God, whom I shall see for myself, and my eyes
shall behold, and not another. How my heart yearns within me!

Job 19:23–27 NKJV

I am the resurrection and the life

Jesus said, "I am the resurrection and the life. Whoever believes in
me, though he die, yet shall he live, and everyone who lives and believes in me shall never die."   *John 11:25–26*

Psalm 16

Preserve me, | O God,*
>for in you I take | refuge.
I say to the LORD, "You | are my Lord;*
>I have no good a- | part from you."
As for the saints | in the land,*
>they are the excellent ones, in whom is all | my delight.
I have set the LORD always be- | fore me;*
>because he is at my right hand, I shall not be | shaken.
Therefore my heart is glad, and my whole being re- | joices;*
>my flesh also | dwells secure.
For you will not abandon my soul | to Sheol,*
>or let your holy one see cor- | ruption.
You make known to me the | path of life;*
>in your presence there is fullness of joy;
>at your right hand are pleasures for- | evermore.

Psalm 16:1–3, 8–11

Glory be to the Father and | to the Son*
>**and to the Holy | Spirit;**
as it was in the be- | ginning,*
>**is now, and will be forever. | Amen.**

Psalm 121

I lift up my eyes | to the hills.*
>From where does my | help come?
My help comes | from the LORD,*
>who made | heav'n and earth.
He will not let your | foot be moved;*
>he who keeps you will not | slumber.
Behold, he who keeps | Israel*
>will neither slum- | ber nor sleep.

▶

The LORD is your | keeper;*
    the LORD is your shade on your | right hand.
The sun shall not strike | you by day,*
    nor the | moon by night.
The LORD will keep you from all | evil;*
    he will | keep your life.
The LORD will keep your going out and your | coming in*
    from this time forth and for- | evermore.
Glory be to the Father and | to the Son*
    and to the Holy | Spirit;
as it was in the be- | ginning,*
    is now, and will be forever. | Amen.

The pastor stands at the head of the casket or next to the urn. When all have arrived at the place of interment, the prayer appropriate to the setting is spoken.

GLORY BE TO THE FATHER

If the grave is to be blessed:

P Let us pray.

O Lord Jesus Christ, by Your three-day rest in the tomb You hallowed the graves of all who believe in You, promising resurrection to our mortal bodies. Bless ✝ this grave that the body of our *brother/sister* may sleep here in peace until You awaken *him/her* to glory, when *he/she* will see You face to face and know the splendor of the eternal God, for You live and reign with the Father and the Holy Spirit, one God, now and forever. (551)

If the grave has already been blessed:

P Let us pray.

Merciful Father and Lord of life, with whom live the spirits of those who depart in the faith, we thank You for the blessings of body and soul that You granted this departed *brother/sister*, whose earthly remains we now lay to rest. Above all, we rejoice at Your gracious promise to all Your servants, both living and departed, that we shall be raised from death at the coming of our Lord Jesus Christ, who lives and reigns with You and the Holy Spirit, one God, now and forever. (552)

C Amen.

One or more of the following are read.

Grain of wheat

Jesus answered them, "The hour has come for the Son of Man to be glorified. Truly, truly, I say to you, unless a grain of wheat falls into the earth and dies, it remains alone; but if it dies, it bears much fruit. Whoever loves his life loses it, and whoever hates his life in this world will keep it for eternal life. If anyone serves me, he must follow me; and where I am, there will my servant be also. If anyone serves me, the Father will honor him." *John 12:23–26*

The perishable is raised imperishable

[The apostle Paul writes:] So is it with the resurrection of the dead. What is sown is perishable; what is raised is imperishable. It is sown in dishonor; it is raised in glory. It is sown in weakness; it is raised in power. It is sown a natural body; it is raised a spiritual body. If there is a natural body, there is also a spiritual body. Thus it is written, "The first man Adam became a living being"; the last Adam became a life-giving spirit. But it is not the spiritual that is first but the natural, and then the spiritual. The first man was from the earth, a man of dust; the second man is from heaven. As was the man of dust, so also are those who are of the dust, and as is the man of heaven, so also are those who are of heaven. Just as we have borne the image of the man of dust, we shall also bear the image of the man of heaven.

1 Corinthians 15:42–49

Changed in the twinkling of an eye

[The apostle Paul writes:] Behold! I tell you a mystery. We shall not all sleep, but we shall all be changed, in a moment, in the twinkling of an eye, at the last trumpet. For the trumpet will sound, and the dead will be raised imperishable, and we shall be changed. For this perishable body must put on the imperishable, and this mortal body must put on immortality. When the perishable puts on the imperishable, and the mortal puts on immortality, then shall come to pass the saying that is written: "Death is swallowed up in victory." "O death, where is your victory? O death, where is your sting?" The sting of death is sin, and the power of sin is the law. But thanks be to God, who gives us the victory through our Lord Jesus Christ.

1 Corinthians 15:51–57

We grieve in hope

[The apostle Paul writes:] But we do not want you to be uninformed, brothers, about those who are asleep, that you may not grieve as others do who have no hope. For since we believe that Jesus died and rose again, even so, through Jesus, God will bring with him those who have fallen asleep. For this we declare to you by a word from the Lord, that we who are alive, who are left until the coming of the Lord, will not precede those who have fallen asleep. For the Lord himself will descend from heaven with a cry of command, with the voice of an archangel, and with the sound of the trumpet of God. And the dead in Christ will rise first. Then we who are alive, who are left, will be caught up together with them in the clouds to meet the Lord in the air, and so we will always be with the Lord. *1 Thessalonians 4:13–17*

When the Committal does not immediately follow the Funeral Service, the CREED may be confessed.

P God has made us His people through our Baptism into Christ. Living together in trust and hope, we confess our faith.

C **I believe in God, the Father Almighty,**
maker of heaven and earth.

And in Jesus Christ, His only Son, our Lord,
who was conceived by the Holy Spirit,
born of the virgin Mary,
suffered under Pontius Pilate,
was crucified, died and was buried.
He descended into hell.
The third day He rose again from the dead.
He ascended into heaven
and sits at the right hand of God the Father Almighty.
From thence He will come to judge
the living and the dead. ▶

I believe in the Holy Spirit,
    the holy Christian Church,
        the communion of saints,
    the forgiveness of sins,
    the resurrection of the body,
    and the life ☩ everlasting. Amen.

> *Christian:* the ancient text reads "catholic," meaning the whole
> Church as it confesses the wholeness of Christian doctrine.

*Sand or earth may be poured on the casket in the sign of the cross
while the pastor says:*

P We now commit the body of our __brother/sister__ __name__ to
__the ground / its resting place / the deep__; earth to earth, ashes to
ashes, dust to dust, in the sure and certain hope of the resurrection
to eternal life through our Lord Jesus Christ, who will change our
lowly bodies so that they will be like His glorious body, by the
power that enables Him to subdue all things to Himself.

The pastor may place his hand on the head of the casket as he says:

P May God the Father, who created this body; may God the ☩ Son,
who by His blood redeemed this body; may God the Holy Spirit,
who by Holy Baptism sanctified this body to be His temple, keep
these remains to the day of the resurrection of all flesh.

C **Amen.**

P Taught by our Lord and trusting His promises, we are bold to pray:

C **Our Father who art in heaven,**
    hallowed be Thy name,
    Thy kingdom come,
    Thy will be done on earth as it is in heaven;
    give us this day our daily bread;
    and forgive us our trespasses
        as we forgive those who trespass against us;
    and lead us not into temptation,

but deliver us from evil.
For Thine is the kingdom and the power and the glory
forever and ever. Amen. *Matthew 6:9–13*

P Almighty God, by the death of Your Son Jesus Christ You destroyed death, by His rest in the tomb You sanctified the graves of Your saints, and by His bodily resurrection You brought life and immortality to light so that all who die in Him abide in peace and hope. Receive our thanks for the victory over death and the grave that He won for us. Keep us in everlasting communion with all who wait for Him on earth and with all in heaven who are with Him, for He is the resurrection and the life, even Jesus Christ, our Lord. (550)

C **Amen.**

The following or another appropriate hymn may be sung.

Abide with me, fast falls the eventide.
The darkness deepens; Lord, with me abide.
When other helpers fail and comforts flee,
Help of the helpless, O abide with me.

Hold Thou Thy cross before my closing eyes;
Shine through the gloom, and point me to the skies.
Heav'n's morning breaks, and earth's vain shadows flee;
In life, in death, O Lord, abide with me. *Hymn 878:1, 6*

P Alleluia! Christ is risen.
C **He is risen indeed. Alleluia!**
P Let us go forth in peace, in the name of the Lord.
C **Amen.**

P The Lord bless you and keep you.
    The Lord make His face shine upon you and be gracious unto you.
    The Lord lift up His countenance upon you and ✠ give you peace.
C **Amen.** *Numbers 6:24–26*

BURIAL FOR A STILLBORN CHILD OR UNBAPTIZED CHILD

1. This rite is intended for the burial of a stillborn child of Christian parents or a child of Christian parents who died before Baptism could be administered.
2. According to the circumstance, the rite may be conducted either publicly or privately at the church, funeral home, hospital, or the family home. With adaptation, the entire rite may also be held at the graveside.
3. When there is no body present, the Committal is omitted.

P In the name of the Father and of the ✢ Son and of the Holy Spirit.   *Matthew 28:19b*
C **Amen.**

P Beloved in the Lord, when God in His will for us allows our anticipation and joy to be changed into disappointment and grief, we turn to Him for comfort. In the midst of our sadness He calls us by the Gospel to a faith that will withstand such times of testing. Though we may not in this life have answers to the questions we ask, by the life, death, and resurrection of our Lord Jesus Christ we know that God is our loving Father, our Brother in suffering and death, and the Comforter who even now brings peace to our grief-stricken hearts.

While alive and in the womb, this child was brought and commended to Christ in our prayers. We should not doubt that these prayers have been heard, for we have God's own kind and comforting promises that such prayers in the name of Jesus Christ are heard by Him.

In love God has blessed His people with the washing of Holy Baptism, through which He gives rebirth in the Holy Spirit to us and to our children. When death comes before Baptism, we trust in His mercy that by His grace He has received this child to Himself for the sake of the death and resurrection of His Son, Jesus Christ, our Lord.

We take comfort in the confident hope that this child will be raised to life with Christ in the resurrection on the Last Day. The Lord grant that we remain steadfast in His Word and faith until we all come to the joys of life everlasting; for the sake of His dear Son, Jesus Christ, our Lord. Amen.

One or more of the following psalms is prayed.

Psalm 139

For you formed my | inward parts;*
    you knitted me together in my | mother's womb.
I praise you, for I am fearfully and wonder- | fully made.*
    Wonderful are your works; my soul knows it | very well.
My frame was not hid- | den from you,*
    when I was being made in secret, intricately woven in the depths | of the earth.
Your eyes saw my unformed substance; in your book were written, every | one of them,*
    the days that were formed for me, when as yet there were | none of them.   ►

How precious to me are your thoughts, | O God!*
    How vast is the | sum of them!
If I would count them, they are more | than the sand.*
    I awake, and I am still | with you.   *Psalm 139:13–18*
Glory be to the Father and | to the Son*
    and to the Holy | Spirit;
as it was in the be- | ginning,*
    is now, and will be forever. | Amen.

Psalm 23

English Standard Version

The LORD is my | shepherd;*
    I | shall not want.
He makes me lie down in
green | pastures.*
        He leads me beside
        still | waters.
He re- | stores my soul.*
        He leads me in paths
        of righteousness for
        his | name's sake.
Even though I walk through
the valley of the shadow of
death, I will fear no evil, for
you are | with me;*
        your rod and your staff,
        they | comfort me.
You prepare a table before me in
the presence of my | enemies;*
        you anoint my head with
        oil; my cup | overflows.

King James Version

The LORD is my | shepherd;*
    I | shall not want.
He maketh me to lie down in
green | pastures:*
        he leadeth me beside the
        still | waters.
He restoreth | my soul:*
        he leadeth me in the paths
        of righteousness for
        his | name's sake.
Yea, though I walk through
the valley of the shadow of
death, I will fear no evil: for
thou art | with me;*
        thy rod and thy staff
        they | comfort me.
Thou preparest a table before me
in the presence of mine | enemies:*
        thou anointest my head with
        oil; my cup runneth | over.

Surely goodness and mercy
shall follow me all the
days | of my life,*
    and I shall dwell in the house
    of the LORD for- | ever.
**Glory be to the Father and | to
the Son***
    and to the Holy | Spirit;
as it was in the be- | ginning,*
    **is now, and will be for-
    ever. | Amen.**

Surely goodness and mercy
shall follow me all the days | of
my life:*
    and I will dwell in the house
    of the LORD for- | ever.
**Glory be to the Father and | to
the Son***
    and to the Holy | Spirit;
as it was in the be- | ginning,*
    **is now, and will be for-
    ever. | Amen.**

Psalm 130

Out | of the depths*
    I cry to you, | O LORD!
O Lord, | hear my voice!*
    Let your ears be attentive to the voice of my pleas for | mercy!
If you, O LORD, should mark in- | iquities,*
    O Lord, | who could stand?
But with you there is for- | giveness,*
    that you | may be feared.
I wait for the LORD, my | soul waits,*
    and in his | word I hope;
my soul waits for the Lord more than watchmen for the | morning,*
    more than watchmen for the | morning.
O Israel, hope in the LORD! For with the LORD there is | steadfast love,*
    and with him is plentiful re- | demption.
And he will redeem | Israel*
    from all his in- | iquities.
Glory be to the Father and | to the Son*
    and to the Holy | Spirit;
as it was in the be- | ginning,*
    is now, and will be forever. | Amen.

One or more of the following passages from Holy Scripture are read. The first reading is introduced by the following:

P Hear the Word of God from _____, chapter _____.

Additional readings may be introduced by citing the biblical reference. After each reading, the following is said:

P This is the Word of the Lord.
C **Thanks be to God.**

Rachel weeps for her children

Thus says the LORD: "A voice is heard in Ramah,
    lamentation and bitter weeping.
Rachel is weeping for her children;
    she refuses to be comforted for her children,
    because they are no more."
Thus says the LORD: "Keep your voice from weeping,
    and your eyes from tears, for there is a reward for your work,
    declares the LORD,
and they shall come back from the land of the enemy.
There is hope for your future, declares the LORD,
    and your children shall come back to their own country."

Jeremiah 31:15–17

The Lord gives, the Lord takes away

[Job] said, "Naked I came from my mother's womb, and naked shall I return. The LORD gave, and the LORD has taken away; blessed be the name of the LORD."

Job 1:21

Nothing shall separate us from the love of God

What then shall we say to these things? If God is for us, who can be against us? He who did not spare his own Son but gave him up for us all, how will he not also with him graciously give us all things? Who shall bring any charge against God's elect? It is God who justifies. Who is to condemn? Christ Jesus is the one who died—more than that, who was raised—who is at the right hand of God, who indeed is interceding for us. Who shall separate us from the love of Christ? Shall tribulation, or distress, or persecution, or famine, or nakedness, or danger, or sword? As it is written,

"For your sake we are being killed all the day long;
we are regarded as sheep to be slaughtered."

No, in all these things we are more than conquerors through him who loved us. For I am sure that neither death nor life, nor angels nor rulers, nor things present nor things to come, nor powers, nor height nor depth, nor anything else in all creation, will be able to separate us from the love of God in Christ Jesus our Lord. *Romans 8:31–39*

We live to the Lord

None of us lives to himself, and none of us dies to himself. If we live, we live to the Lord, and if we die, we die to the Lord. So then, whether we live or whether we die, we are the Lord's. For to this end Christ died and lived again, that he might be Lord both of the dead and of the living. *Romans 14:7–9*

He will wipe away all tears

Then I saw a new heaven and a new earth, for the first heaven and the first earth had passed away, and the sea was no more. And I saw the holy city, the new Jerusalem, coming down out of heaven from God, prepared as a bride adorned for her husband. And I heard a loud voice from the throne saying, "Behold, the dwelling place of God is with man. He will dwell with them, and they will be his people, and God himself will be with them as their God. He will wipe away every tear from their eyes, and death shall be no more, neither shall there be mourning nor crying nor pain anymore, for the former things ▶

have passed away." And he who was seated on the throne said, "Behold, I am making all things new." Also he said, "Write this down, for these words are trustworthy and true." And he said to me, "It is done! I am the Alpha and the Omega, the beginning and the end. To the thirsty I will give from the spring of the water of life without payment. The one who conquers will have this heritage, and I will be his God and he will be my son."

Revelation 21:1–7

Their angels always see the Father's face

The disciples came to Jesus, saying, "Who is the greatest in the kingdom of heaven?" And calling to him a child, he put him in the midst of them and said, "Truly, I say to you, unless you turn and become like children, you will never enter the kingdom of heaven. Whoever humbles himself like this child is the greatest in the kingdom of heaven. Whoever receives one such child in my name receives me. See that you do not despise one of these little ones. For I tell you that in heaven their angels always see the face of my Father who is in heaven."

Matthew 18:1–5, 10–11

Let the children come to Me

They were bringing children to him that he might touch them, and the disciples rebuked them. But when Jesus saw it, he was indignant and said to them, "Let the children come to me; do not hinder them, for to such belongs the kingdom of God. Truly, I say to you, whoever does not receive the kingdom of God like a child shall not enter it." And He took them in his arms and blessed them, laying his hands on them.

Mark 10:13–16

I will give you rest

Jesus declared, "I thank you, Father, Lord of heaven and earth, that you have hidden these things from the wise and understanding and revealed them to little children; yes, Father, for such was your gracious will. All things have been handed over to me by my Father, and no one knows the Son except the Father, and no one knows the Father except the Son and anyone to whom the Son chooses to reveal him. Come to me, all who labor and are heavy laden, and I will give you rest. Take my yoke upon you, and learn from me, for I am gentle and lowly in heart, and you will find rest for your souls. For my yoke is easy, and my burden is light." *Matthew 11:25–30*

The pastor may speak words of consolation to the bereaved.

A hymn may be sung.

P Let us pray.
Heavenly Father, Your Son bore all our griefs and carried all our sorrows. Strengthen the faith of these grieving parents and all who bear this heavy burden. Help them to rely on Your boundless mercy and to trust that their little one, who has been gathered into Your loving arms, will rise on the Last Day; through Jesus Christ, Your Son, our Lord, who lives and reigns with You and the Holy Spirit, one God, now and forever. (553)

C **Amen.**

> *If the body of the deceased has been present during this service but will not be buried, the following is spoken:*
>
> P May God the Father, the ☩ Son, and the Holy Spirit keep these remains to the day of the resurrection of all flesh.
>
> C **Amen.**

If the service is taking place at the place of burial, the LORD'S PRAYER and BENEDICTION are omitted here.

P Taught by our Lord and trusting His promises, we are bold to pray:

C **Our Father who art in heaven,**
   hallowed be Thy name,
   Thy kingdom come,
   Thy will be done on earth as it is in heaven;
   give us this day our daily bread;
   and forgive us our trespasses
      as we forgive those who trespass against us;
   and lead us not into temptation,
   but deliver us from evil.
   For Thine is the kingdom and the power and the glory
      forever and ever. Amen.   *Matthew 6:9–13*

P The Lord bless you and keep you.
   The Lord make His face shine upon you and be gracious unto you.
   The Lord lift up His countenance upon you and ☩ give you peace.

C **Amen.**   *Numbers 6:24–26*

Committal

The pastor leads the casket and the family to the place of interment.
The following may be sung or said:

Media vita in morte sumus *(14th-century hymn)*

In the midst of life we | are in death;*
   from whom can we | seek help?
From You alone, | O Lord,*
   who by our sins are justly | angered.
Holy God, holy and mighty, holy and merciful | Savior,*
   deliver us not into the bitterness of e- | ternal death.

Lord, You know the secrets | of our hearts;*
   shut not Your ears to our prayers, but spare us, | O Lord.

144

Holy God, holy and mighty, holy and merciful | Savior,*
 deliver us not into the bitterness of e- | ternal death.

O worthy and e- | ternal Judge,*
 do not let the pains of death turn us away from You at our | last hour.
Holy God, holy and mighty, holy and merciful | Savior,*
 deliver us not into the bitterness of e- | ternal death.

P Let us pray.
  O Lord Jesus Christ, by Your three-day rest in the tomb You hallowed the graves of all Your children, promising resurrection to our mortal bodies. (Bless ✝ this grave and) grant that the body of this child may sleep here in peace until You awaken _him/her_ to glory, when _he/she_ will see You face to face and know the splendor of the eternal God, for You live and reign with the Father and the Holy Spirit, one God, now and forever. (551)

C **Amen.**

The following passage from Holy Scripture is read.

P The apostle Paul comforts us concerning the resurrection of the dead:

 So is it with the resurrection of the dead. What is sown is perishable; what is raised is imperishable. It is sown in dishonor; it is raised in glory. It is sown in weakness; it is raised in power. It is sown a natural body; it is raised a spiritual body. If there is a natural body, there is also a spiritual body. . . . When the perishable puts on the imperishable, and the mortal puts on immortality, then shall come to pass the saying that is written: "Death is swallowed up in victory." "O death, where is your victory? O death, where is your sting?" The sting of death is sin, and the power of sin is the law. But thanks be to God, who gives us the victory through our Lord Jesus Christ.   *1 Corinthians 15:42–44, 54–57*

145

Sand or earth may be poured on the casket in the sign of the cross while the pastor says:

P It has pleased our heavenly Father in His wise providence to call this child to Himself. We now commit ___his/her___ body to ___the ground / its resting place___ ; earth to earth, ashes to ashes, dust to dust, in the sure and certain hope of the resurrection to eternal life through our Lord Jesus Christ, who will change our lowly bodies so that they will be like His glorious body, by the power that enables Him to subdue all things to Himself.

C **Amen.**

The pastor may place his hand on the head of the casket as he says:

P May God the Father, the ✠ Son, and the Holy Spirit keep these remains to the day of the resurrection of all flesh.

C **Amen.**

P Taught by our Lord and trusting His promises, we are bold to pray:

C **Our Father who art in heaven,**
    hallowed be Thy name,
    Thy kingdom come,
    Thy will be done on earth as it is in heaven;
    give us this day our daily bread;
    and forgive us our trespasses
      as we forgive those who trespass against us;
    and lead us not into temptation,
    but deliver us from evil.
  For Thine is the kingdom and the power and the glory
    forever and ever. Amen. *Matthew 6:9–13*

P Almighty God, by the death of Your Son Jesus Christ You destroyed death and redeemed and saved Your little ones. By His bodily resurrection You brought life and immortality to light so that all who die in Him abide in peace and hope. Receive our thanks for the victory over death and the grave that He won for us. Keep us in everlasting communion with all who wait for Him on earth and with all in heaven who are with Him, for He is the resurrection and the life, even Jesus Christ, our Lord. (550)

C **Amen.**

An appropriate hymn may be sung.

P Alleluia! Christ is risen.

C **He is risen indeed. Alleluia!**

P Let us go forth in peace, in the name of the Lord.

C **Amen.**

P The Lord bless you and keep you.
The Lord make His face shine upon you and be gracious unto you.
The Lord lift up His countenance upon you and ✠ give you peace.

C **Amen.** *Numbers 6:24–26*

BLESSING OF A HOME

1. It is appropriate that homes of Christians be blessed by the Word of God and prayer. This rite may be used when a new home is occupied, when a family moves to another home, or at other appropriate times (e.g., following a robbery or vandalizing of a home, following an assault or murder in the home, following fire or other destruction, following renovation of a home).

2. Homes may be blessed annually. Usually this is done during the season of the Epiphany due to the connection of the visitation of the Magi to the home of the infant Christ (Matt. 2:1–11; John 1:14). On such annual observances of this rite, the Magnificat with antiphon (see page 150) may be chanted in place of the Psalmody.

3. Those present at the Blessing of a Home may include all family members, as well as friends and relatives. Because of the responsive nature of this rite, copies should be made available to all participants.

4. As desired, one or more individual rooms may be blessed. The sequence may be adjusted according to the layout of the house.

5. The pastor of the congregation presides. He may vest in his customary vestments, using the color of the day or season.

6. If family members and guests serve as assistants **A**, the pastor may assign readings to them in advance.

7. Because of the solemn character of Holy Week, it is inappropriate to schedule this rite during that time.

8. The head of the household should be encouraged to pray regularly with the family, read the Scriptures, and sing hymns throughout the year, especially in times of distress.

The pastor, family, and guests gather in the living room of the home or in another convenient place.

GREETING

P Peace be to this home ✛ and to all who dwell here.　　*Luke 10:5b alt.*
C **Amen.**

The following psalm may be sung by whole verse or spoken by half verse. During Epiphany, the Magnificat may be used in place of the Psalmody, sung or spoken in the same fashion.

PSALMODY

Our help is in the name | of the LORD,*
　　who made | heaven and earth.　　　　　　　*Psalm 124:8*
I lift up my eyes | to the hills.*
　　From where does my | help come?
My help comes | from the LORD,*
　　who made | heaven and earth.
He will not let your | foot be moved;*
　　he who keeps you will not | slumber.
Behold, he who keeps | Israel*
　　will neither slum- | ber nor sleep.
The LORD is your | keeper;*
　　the LORD is your shade on your | right hand.
The sun shall not strike | you by day,*
　　nor the | moon by night.
The LORD will keep you from all | evil;*
　　he will | keep your life.
The LORD will keep your going out and your | coming in*
　　from this time forth and for- | evermore.　　　*Psalm 121*
Glory be to the Father and | to the Son*
　　and to the Holy | Spirit;　　　　　　　　　►

as it was in the be- | ginning,*
    is now, and will be forever. | Amen.
Our help is in the name | of the Lord,*
    who made | heaven and earth.   *Psalm 124:8*

OR

MAGNIFICAT

Magi from the East came in- | to the house*
    and wor- | shiped the Lord,
and when they had opened their treasures,
they presented | gifts to Him:*
    gold, frankin- | cense, and myrrh.   *Matthew 2:11 alt.*
My soul magni- | fies the Lord,*
    and my spirit rejoices in God, my | Savior;
for He has re- | garded*
    the lowliness of His | handmaiden.
For, behold, | from this day*
    all generations will call me | blessèd.
For the Mighty One has done great | things to me,*
    and Holy | is His name;
and His mercy is on those who | fear Him*
    from generation to gener- | ation.
He has shown strength | with His arm;*
    He has scattered the proud in the imagination | of their hearts.
He has cast down the mighty | from their thrones,*
    and has exalted the | lowly.
He has filled the hungry | with good things,*
    and the rich He has sent emp- | ty away.
He has helped His servant | Israel*
    in remembrance of His | mercy,
as He spoke to our | fathers,*
    to Abraham, and to his seed for- | ever.   *Luke 1:46–55 alt.*

150

Glory be to the Father and | to the Son*
    and to the Holy | Spirit;
as it was in the be- | ginning,*
    is now, and will be forever. | Amen.
Magi from the East came in- | to the house*
    and wor- | shiped the Lord,
and when they had opened their treasures,
they presented | gifts to Him:*
    gold, frankin- | cense, and myrrh.   *Matthew 2:11 alt.*

READING FROM HOLY SCRIPTURE

One or more of the following passages of Holy Scripture are read, preferably from the family Bible. Each reading is introduced with the following:

P   A reading from _____, chapter _____.

After each reading:

P   This is the Word of the Lord.
C   **Thanks be to God.**

"Everyone then who hears these words of mine and does them will be like a wise man who built his house on the rock. And the rain fell, and the floods came, and the winds blew and beat on that house, but it did not fall, because it had been founded on the rock. And everyone who hears these words of mine and does not do them will be like a foolish man who built his house on the sand. And the rain fell, and the floods came, and the winds blew and beat against that house, and it fell, and great was the fall of it." And when Jesus finished these sayings, the crowds were astonished at his teaching, for he was teaching them as one who had authority, and not as their scribes.   *Matthew 7:24–29*

As they went on their way, Jesus entered a village. And a woman named Martha welcomed him into her house. And she had a sister called Mary, who sat at the Lord's feet and listened to his teaching. But Martha was distracted with much serving. And she went up to him and said, "Lord, do you not care that my sister has left me to serve alone? Tell her then to help me." But the Lord answered her, "Martha, Martha, you are anxious and troubled about many things, but one thing is necessary. Mary has chosen the good portion, which will not be taken away from her."

Luke 10:38–42

The true light, which enlightens everyone, was coming into the world. He was in the world, and the world was made through him, yet the world did not know him. He came to his own, and his own people did not receive him. But to all who did receive him, who believed in his name, he gave the right to become children of God, who were born, not of blood nor of the will of the flesh nor of the will of man, but of God. And the Word became flesh and dwelt among us, and we have seen his glory, glory as of the only Son from the Father, full of grace and truth.

John 1:9–14

The following may be read during the season of Epiphany.

Now after Jesus was born in Bethlehem of Judea in the days of Herod the king, behold, wise men from the east came to Jerusalem, saying, "Where is he who has been born king of the Jews? For we saw his star when it rose and have come to worship him." When Herod the king heard this, he was troubled, and all Jerusalem with him; and assembling all the chief priests and scribes of the people, he inquired of them where the Christ was to be born. They told him, "In Bethlehem of Judea, for so it is written by the prophet:

"'And you, O Bethlehem, in the land of Judah,
    are by no means least among the rulers of Judah;
for from you shall come a ruler
    who will shepherd my people Israel.'"

Then Herod summoned the wise men secretly and ascertained from them what time the star had appeared. And he sent them to Bethlehem, saying, "Go and search diligently for the child, and when you have found him, bring me word, that I too may come and worship him." After listening to the king, they went on their way. And behold, the star that they had seen when it rose went before them until it came to rest over the place where the child was. When they saw the star, they rejoiced exceedingly with great joy. And going into the house they saw the child with Mary his mother, and they fell down and worshiped him. Then, opening their treasures, they offered him gifts, gold and frankincense and myrrh. And being warned in a dream not to return to Herod, they departed to their own country by another way.   *Matthew 2:1–12*

Following the reading from Holy Scripture, the pastor may deliver a brief homily.

HYMN

C   Oh, blest the house, whate'er befall,
    Where Jesus Christ is all in all!
    A home that is not wholly His—
    How sad and poor and dark it is!

    Oh, blest that house where faith is found
    And all in hope and love abound;
    They trust their God and serve Him still
    And do in all His holy will!

    ▶

Oh, blest the parents who give heed
Unto their children's foremost need
And weary not of care or cost.
May none to them and heav'n be lost!

Oh, blest that house; it prospers well.
In peace and joy the parents dwell,
And in their children's lives is shown
How richly God can bless His own.

Then here will I and mine today
A solemn promise make and say:
Though all the world forsake His Word,
I and my house will serve the Lord!

Hymn 862

BLESSING OF ROOMS

One or more of the following rooms may be blessed. All those assembled move in procession throughout the house, stopping in each room for the following readings and prayers. Family members and guests may serve as assistant readers Ⓐ. *If individual rooms are not to be blessed, the rite continues with the* LORD'S PRAYER *on page 156.*

LIVING ROOM

Ⓐ Hear the Word of the Lord.

Be renewed in the spirit of your minds. . . . Therefore, having put away falsehood, let each one of you speak the truth with his neighbor, for we are members one of another. . . . Let no corrupting talk come out of your mouths, but only such as is good for building up, as fits the occasion, that it may give grace to those who hear. And do not grieve the Holy Spirit of God, by whom you were sealed for the day of redemption. Let all bitterness and wrath and anger and clamor and slander be put away from you, along with all malice. Be kind to one another, tenderhearted, forgiving one another, as God in Christ forgave you.

Ephesians 4:23, 25, 29–32

P Let us pray.

Blessed be the God and Father of our Lord Jesus Christ, the Father of all mercies and the God of all comfort. What manner of love You have bestowed on us, that we should be called the children of God. As You have in Christ forgiven us, grant us also to live in that forgiveness toward one another, free from fear and misgivings and held together confidently in Your love, which covers the multitude of our sins for Jesus' sake. (656)

C Amen.

ENTRANCE TO THE HOME

A God settles the solitary in a home. Therefore welcome one another as Christ has welcomed you, for the glory of God.

Psalm 68:6a; Romans 15:7

P Lord God, protect and guide those who live here as they come and go. Let them show hospitality to all who visit this home, so that those who enter here may find peace; through Jesus Christ, our Lord. (657)

C Amen.

BEDROOM

A In peace I will both lie down and sleep; for you alone, O Lord, make me dwell in safety.

Psalm 4:8

P For each new morning and its light
For rest and shelter of the night,
For health and food, for love and friends,
For every gift Your goodness sends,
We thank You, gracious Lord. (658)

C Amen.

STUDY

A Give instruction to a wise man, and he will be still wiser; teach a righteous man, and he will increase in learning. *Proverbs 9:9*

P O Lord, You desire truth in the inward being; therefore teach us to know wisdom; through Jesus Christ, our Lord. (659)
C **Amen.**

FAMILY ROOM

A Finally, brothers, whatever is true, whatever is honorable, whatever is just, whatever is pure, whatever is lovely, whatever is commendable, if there is any excellence, if there is anything worthy of praise, think about these things. *Philippians 4:8*

P Lord of all creation, give us a right judgment in all things, that we may rejoice in all that is good and be defended against all that is evil; through Jesus Christ, our Lord. (660)
C **Amen.**

KITCHEN/DINING ROOM

A You shall eat in plenty and be satisfied, and praise the name of the LORD your God, who has dealt wondrously with you. *Joel 2:26a*

P Give us ever grateful hearts for daily bread, O Lord, and keep us ever mindful of the needs of others; through Jesus Christ, our Lord. (661)
C **Amen.**

P Taught by our Lord and trusting His promises, we are bold to pray:
C **Our Father who art in heaven,**
hallowed be Thy name,
Thy kingdom come,

Thy will be done on earth as it is in heaven;
give us this day our daily bread;
and forgive us our trespasses
    as we forgive those who trespass against us;
and lead us not into temptation,
but deliver us from evil.
For Thine is the kingdom and the power and the glory
forever and ever. Amen.

Matthew 6:9–13

P The Lord be with you.
C **And also with you.**

P Let us pray.
Lord God Almighty, we implore You to bless and sanctify this home, its occupants, and its possessions, enriching them in every way. Drive from here the snares of the evil one and send Your holy angel to guard, protect, visit, and defend all who dwell in this home. Mercifully hear their prayers and, when their last hour comes, grant them safe haven in Your heavenly mansions; through Jesus Christ, our Lord. (662)
C **Amen.**

During the season of Epiphany, the following collect may be prayed:

P O God, by the leading of a star You led the Magi to the home in which Christ our Lord dwelt, thereby making known Your only-be-gotten Son to the Gentiles. Mercifully grant that we who know You now by faith may after this life know the fullness of Your glorious Godhead; through Jesus Christ, our Lord, who lives and reigns with You and the Holy Spirit, one God, now and forever. (663)
C **Amen.**

BLESSING

P Let us bless the Lord.

C **Thanks be to God.**

P The Lord Almighty, the Father, the ☩ Son, and the Holy Spirit, be and remain on this home and on all who live here.

C **Amen.**

HYMN

C Now thank we all our God
    With hearts and hands and voices,
Who wondrous things has done,
    In whom His world rejoices;
Who from our mothers' arms
    Has blest us on our way
With countless gifts of love
    And still is ours today.

Hymn 895:1

RESOURCES
FOR
PASTORAL CARE

AT THE TIME OF BIRTH

Before Childbirth
Preparing the Parents

Childbirth is normally a time of happy excitement and anticipation. The child to be born is the Creator's gift, formed by Him in the womb. The joy of the prospective parents may be mingled with anxiety over the changes that a new life will bring. There may be concerns during the pregnancy for the health of the child and/or the mother. The child may not have been planned, and one or both of the parents may not be looking forward to the work and cost of a new baby. Because the months leading to the birth are usually busy, it is easy to neglect seeking the Lord's benediction during these important days. The pastor will want to use this special time as an opportunity to direct the focus of the expectant parents on God as the giver of all good gifts.

PSALMODY
Psalm 139:1–18, 23–24   *You knitted me together*

¹ O LORD, you have searched me and | known me!*
> ²You know when I sit down and when I rise up; you discern
> my thoughts | from afar.

³ You search out my path and my | lying down*
> and are acquainted with | all my ways.

⁴ Even before a word is | on my tongue,*
> behold, O LORD, you know it alto- | gether.

►

161

⁵ You hem me in, behind | and before, *
    and lay your hand up- | on me.
⁶ Such knowledge is too wonder- | ful for me; *
    it is high; I cannot | attain it.
⁷ Where shall I go from your | Spirit? *
    Or where shall I flee from your | presence?
⁸ If I ascend to heaven, | you are there! *
    If I make my bed in Sheol, | you are there!
⁹ If I take the wings of the | morning *
    and dwell in the uttermost parts | of the sea,
¹⁰ even there your hand shall | lead me, *
    and your right hand shall | hold me.
¹¹ If I say, "Surely the darkness shall | cover me, *
    and the light about me | be night,"
¹² even the darkness is not | dark to you; *
    the night is bright as the day, for darkness is as | light with you.
¹³ For you formed my | inward parts; *
    you knitted me together in my | mother's womb.
¹⁴ I praise you, for I am fearfully and wonder- | fully made. *
    Wonderful are your works; my soul knows it | very well.
¹⁵ My frame was not hid- | den from you, *
    when I was being made in secret, intricately woven in the
    depths | of the earth.
¹⁶ Your eyes saw my unformed substance; in your book were
  written, every | one of them, *
    the days that were formed for me, when as yet there
    were | none of them.
¹⁷ How precious to me are your thoughts, | O God! *
    How vast is the | sum of them!
¹⁸ If I would count them, they are more | than the sand. *
    I awake, and I am still | with you.
²³ Search me, O God, and | know my heart! *
    Try me and | know my thoughts!

²⁴ And see if there be any grievous | way in me,*
    and lead me in the way ever- | lasting!

Psalm 91:1–2, 9–12   *His angels will guard you*

¹ He who dwells in the shelter of the | Most High*
    will abide in the shadow of the Al- | mighty.
² I will say to the LORD, "My refuge and my | fortress,*
    my God, in | whom I trust."
⁹ Because you have made the LORD your | dwelling place—*
    the Most High, who is my | refuge—
¹⁰ no evil shall be allowed to be- | fall you,*
    no plague come | near your tent.
¹¹ For he will command his angels con- | cerning you*
    to guard you in | all your ways.
¹² On their hands they will | bear you up,*
    lest you strike your foot a- | gainst a stone.

ADDITIONAL PSALMODY

Psalm 8   *How majestic is Your name*
Psalm 148   *Praise the Lord!*

READINGS
Mark 10:13–16   *Jesus blesses the children*

¹³They were bringing children to [Jesus] that he might touch them, and the disciples rebuked them. ¹⁴But when Jesus saw it, he was indignant and said to them, "Let the children come to me; do not hinder them, for to such belongs the kingdom of God. ¹⁵Truly, I say to you, whoever does not receive the kingdom of God like a child shall not enter it." ¹⁶And he took them in his arms and blessed them, laying his hands on them.

Matthew 18:1–6   *Whoever humbles himself*

¹The disciples came to Jesus, saying, "Who is the greatest in the kingdom of heaven?" ²And calling to him a child, he put him in the midst of them ³and said, "Truly, I say to you, unless you turn and become like children, you will never enter the kingdom of heaven. ⁴Whoever humbles himself like this child is the greatest in the kingdom of heaven.

    ⁵"Whoever receives one such child in my name receives me, ⁶but whoever causes one of these little ones who believe in me to sin, it would be better for him to have a great millstone fastened around his neck and to be drowned in the depth of the sea."

ADDITIONAL READINGS

Is. 41:8–10	*Do not fear, for God is with you*
Is. 43:1–7	*He who created you says, "Fear not"*
Luke 1:39–55	*Mary visits Elizabeth and praises the Lord*

PRAYERS

Lord of life, receive our prayer for   *name of mother*   and for the child she carries, that they may safely come to the time of birth. Grant that by water and the Word this child may be brought to new birth in Christ; who lives and reigns with You and the Holy Spirit, one God, now and forever. (728)

Heavenly Father, we thank You for blessing the union of   *names of parents* . Look favorably upon   *name of mother*   and the child she carries, and grant that throughout this time of pregnancy these expectant parents may be drawn nearer to You and to each other in the certainty of Your love; through Jesus Christ, our Lord, who lives and reigns with You and the Holy Spirit, one God, now and forever. (729)

HYMN
The Lord, My God, Be Praised

LSB 794

The Lord, my God, be praised,
　　My light, my life from heaven;
My maker, who to me
　　Has soul and body given;
My Father, who will shield
　　And keep me day by day
And make each moment yield
　　New blessings on my way. (st. 1)

Before Childbirth
In Event of Potential Problems

When there are indications that the baby, the mother, or both could be facing problems that threaten a safe delivery or physical health, there is at least worry if not fear as well. Such testing of faith is simultaneously the opportunity for the deepening of faith. Pastoral ministrations will work toward being at peace with the knowledge that everything is in the hands of Him who will not fail no matter what the baby or the parents must face.

PSALMODY
Psalm 37:3–7a

Wait patiently for the Lord

³ Trust in the Lord, | and do good;*
　　dwell in the land and befriend | faithfulness.
⁴ Delight yourself | in the Lord,*
　　and he will give you the desires | of your heart.
⁵ Commit your way | to the Lord;*
　　trust in him, and | he will act.

　►

⁶ He will bring forth your righteousness | as the light,*
    and your justice as the | noonday.
⁷ Be still be- | fore the LORD*
    and wait patiently | for him.

Psalm 55:22   *Cast your anxieties on the Lord*

²² Cast your burden on the LORD, and he will sus- | tain you;*
    he will never permit the righteous to | be moved.

Psalm 57:1, 7–10   *Take refuge in the Lord's mercy*

¹ Be merciful to me, O God, be merciful to me, for in you my soul
takes | refuge;*
    in the shadow of your wings I will take refuge, till the storms
    of destruction | pass by.
⁷ My heart is steadfast, O God, my heart is | steadfast!*
    I will sing and make | melody!
⁸ Awake, my glory! Awake, O | harp and lyre!*
    I will a- | wake the dawn!
⁹ I will give thanks to you, O Lord, among the | peoples;*
    I will sing praises to you among the | nations.
¹⁰ For your steadfast love is great to the | heavens,*
    your faithfulness | to the clouds.

ADDITIONAL PSALMODY

Psalm 130   *Hope in the Lord*
Psalm 139:1–18, 23–24   *The Lord knows even my heart*

READINGS

Romans 8:15–28   *Creation groans in childbirth*

¹⁵You did not receive the spirit of slavery to fall back into fear, but
you have received the Spirit of adoption as sons, by whom we cry,
"Abba! Father!" ¹⁶The Spirit himself bears witness with our spirit

that we are children of God, [17]and if children, then heirs—heirs of God and fellow heirs with Christ, provided we suffer with him in order that we may also be glorified with him.

[18]For I consider that the sufferings of this present time are not worth comparing with the glory that is to be revealed to us. [19]For the creation waits with eager longing for the revealing of the sons of God. [20]For the creation was subjected to futility, not willingly, but because of him who subjected it, in hope [21]that the creation itself will be set free from its bondage to decay and obtain the freedom of the glory of the children of God. [22]For we know that the whole creation has been groaning together in the pains of childbirth until now. [23]And not only the creation, but we ourselves, who have the firstfruits of the Spirit, groan inwardly as we wait eagerly for adoption as sons, the redemption of our bodies. [24]For in this hope we were saved. Now hope that is seen is not hope. For who hopes for what he sees? [25]But if we hope for what we do not see, we wait for it with patience.

[26]Likewise the Spirit helps us in our weakness. For we do not know what to pray for as we ought, but the Spirit himself intercedes for us with groanings too deep for words. [27]And he who searches hearts knows what is the mind of the Spirit, because the Spirit intercedes for the saints according to the will of God. [28]And we know that for those who love God all things work together for good, for those who are called according to his purpose.

1 Corinthians 10:13 *Able to endure temptation*

[13]No temptation has overtaken you that is not common to man. God is faithful, and he will not let you be tempted beyond your ability, but with the temptation he will also provide the way of escape, that you may be able to endure it.

1 Peter 5:6–7 *Cast your anxieties on the Lord*

[6]Humble yourselves, therefore, under the mighty hand of God so that at the proper time he may exalt you, [7]casting all your anxieties on him, because he cares for you.

ADDITIONAL READINGS

Rom. 8:28, 31–35, 37–39   *We are more than conquerors*
Phil. 4:4–7   *The peace of God will guard you*
Heb. 13:5b–6   *Confidence in view of God's presence*

PRAYER

Father and creator of us all, our lives are in Your hands. Our hearts are weighed down with the knowledge that   *name of mother*   and her unborn child are in danger. According to Your will preserve and protect both mother and child. Grant an increase of faith to   *names of parents*   to trust that You work all things together for our ultimate good. Into Your hands we commend them and their loved ones, trusting in Your mercy; through Jesus Christ, Your Son, our Lord, who lives and reigns with You and the Holy Spirit, one God, now and forever. (730)

HYMN

O Jesus Christ, Thy Manger Is   *LSB 372*

> He whom the sea
> And wind obey
Doth come to serve the sinner in great meekness.
> Thou, God's own Son,
> With us art one,
Dost join us and our children in our weakness. (st. 2)

> Thou Christian heart,
> Whoe'er thou art,
Be of good cheer and let no sorrow move thee!
> For God's own Child,
> In mercy mild,
Joins thee to Him; how greatly God must love thee! (st. 4)

© 1941 Concordia Publishing House

ADDITIONAL HYMNS

Be Still, My Soul, before the Lord   *LSB 771*
Entrust Your Days and Burdens   *LSB 754:3–4*

At the Time of Labor and Delivery

As the hopes and expectations of new parents are realized in the birth of their child, wonder and joy fill their hearts. Praise to God is on their lips, thanking Him for the miracle of His creation. Should difficulties with labor and/or delivery develop, the truth and comfort of God's Word along with prayer will be needed to calm the fears and address the doubts and concerns of all the members of the family.

PSALMODY

Psalm 103:13–18   *The Father's compassion*

¹³ As a father shows compassion to his | children,*
    so the LORD shows compassion to those who | fear him.
¹⁴ For he | knows our frame;*
    he remembers that | we are dust.
¹⁵ As for man, his days | are like grass;*
    he flourishes like a flower | of the field;
¹⁶ for the wind passes over it, and | it is gone,*
    and its place knows | it no more.
¹⁷ But the steadfast love of the LORD is from everlasting to
everlasting on those who | fear him,*
    and his righteousness to children's | children,
¹⁸ to those who keep his | covenant*
    and remember to do his com- | mandments.

Psalm 138   *Give thanks, the Lord preserves life*

¹ I give you thanks, O LORD, with | my whole heart;*
    before the gods I | sing your praise;
² I bow down toward your holy temple and give thanks to your
name for your steadfast love and your | faithfulness,*
    for you have exalted above all things your name | and your word.
³ On the day I called, you | answered me;*
    my strength of soul | you increased.   ▶

169

⁴ All the kings of the earth shall give you thanks, | O LORD,*
    for they have heard the words | of your mouth,
⁵ and they shall sing of the ways | of the LORD,*
    for great is the glory | of the LORD.
⁶ For though the LORD is high, he regards the | lowly,*
    but the haughty he knows | from afar.
⁷ Though I walk in the midst of trouble, you pre- | serve my life;*
    you stretch out your hand against the wrath of my enemies,
    and your right hand de- | livers me.
⁸ The LORD will fulfill his pur- | pose for me;*
    your steadfast love, O LORD, endures forever. Do not forsake
    the work | of your hands.

ADDITIONAL PSALMODY

Psalm 71:1–8   *Deliver and rescue me*
Psalm 113   *Who is like the Lord?*

READINGS

Genesis 1:26–28, 31   *Man in God's image is fruitful*

²⁶God said, "Let us make man in our image, after our likeness. And let them have dominion over the fish of the sea and over the birds of the heavens and over the livestock and over all the earth and over every creeping thing that creeps on the earth."

    ²⁷So God created man in his own image,
        in the image of God he created him;
        male and female he created them.

²⁸And God blessed them. And God said to them, "Be fruitful and multiply and fill the earth and subdue it and have dominion over the fish of the sea and over the birds of the heavens and over every living thing that moves on the earth."

²⁸¹And God saw everything that he had made, and behold, it was very good. And there was evening and there was morning, the sixth day.

Luke 18:15–17

Jesus blesses infants

[15]They were bringing even infants to [Jesus] that he might touch them. And when the disciples saw it, they rebuked them. [16]But Jesus called him to him, saying, "Let the children come to me, and do not hinder them, for to such belongs the kingdom of God. [17]Truly, I say to you, whoever does not receive the kingdom of God like a child shall not enter it."

John 16:21

The pain of childbirth gives way to joy

[21]When a woman is giving birth, she has sorrow because her hour has come, but when she has delivered the baby, she no longer remembers the anguish, for joy that a human being has been born into the world.

ADDITIONAL READINGS

Rom. 8:28–39   *God graciously gives us all things*
1 Cor. 10:13   *God sustains us in all temptations*

PRAYER

Almighty God, You are an ever-present help in trouble. We humbly ask You to assist *name of mother* in her labor and bring forth in safety the *child/children* she is delivering. Sustain and comfort her and her husband with Your all-sufficient grace in Christ, that they may trust in You and Your love and not be afraid; through the same Jesus Christ, our Lord, who lives and reigns with You and the Holy Spirit, one God, now and forever. (731)

HYMNS
Lord Jesus, Think on Me
LSB 610

Lord Jesus, think on me,
    By anxious thoughts oppressed;
Let me Your loving servant be
    And taste Your promised rest.

Lord Jesus, think on me
    Amid the battle's strife;
In all my pain and misery,
    O be my health and life! (sts. 2–3)

We All Believe in One True God
LSB 954

We all believe in one true God,
    Who created earth and heaven,
The Father, who to us in love
    Has the right of children given.
He in soul and body feeds us;
    All we need His hand provides us;
Through all snares and perils leads us,
    Watching that no harm betide us.
He cares for us by day and night;
All things are governed by His might. (st. 1)

ADDITIONAL HYMN

Be Still, My Soul, before the Lord
LSB 771

172

Following Childbirth

Following many months of waiting and planning, parents are given the gift of children in a vivid demonstration of the Father's work as the creator and giver of life. Along with physical birth comes the anticipation of the second birth in Holy Baptism. Children are not ours to keep, but are given in trust from the Lord to be entrusted to His care. Among the many responsibilities given to new parents is the need to teach the Christian faith to the next generation.

PSALMODY

Psalm 127   *Children are a heritage from the Lord*

¹ Unless the LORD builds the house, those who build it la- | bor in vain.*

    Unless the LORD watches over the city, the watchman stays a- | wake in vain.

² It is in vain that you rise up early and go late to rest, eating the bread of | anxious toil;*

    for he gives to his be- | lovèd sleep.

³ Behold, children are a heritage | from the LORD,*

    the fruit of the womb | a reward.

⁴ Like arrows in the hand of a | warrior*

    are the children | of one's youth.

⁵ Blessèd is the man who fills his quiver | with them!*

    He shall not be put to shame when he speaks with his enemies | in the gate.

Psalm 128   *Your wife, a fruitful vine*

¹ Blessèd is everyone who | fears the LORD,*

    who walks | in his ways!

² You shall eat the fruit of the labor | of your hands;*

    you shall be blessed, and it shall be | well with you.

▶

³ Your wife will be like a fruitful vine with- | in your house;*
  your children will be like olive shoots around your | table.
⁴ Behold, thus shall the | man be blessed*
  who | fears the LORD.
⁵ The LORD bless you from | Zion!*
  May you see the prosperity of Jerusalem all the days | of
  your life!
⁶ May you see your children's | children!*
  Peace be upon | Israel!

ADDITIONAL PSALMODY

Psalm 78:1–7   *Tell the next generation*
Psalm 100   *Praise the Lord who made us*

READINGS

Genesis 21:1–8   *Sarah gives birth to Isaac*

¹The LORD visited Sarah as he had said, and the LORD did to Sarah as he had promised. ²And Sarah conceived and bore Abraham a son in his old age at the time of which God had spoken to him. ³Abraham called the name of his son who was born to him, whom Sarah bore him, Isaac. ⁴And Abraham circumcised his son Isaac when he was eight days old, as God had commanded him. ⁵Abraham was a hundred years old when his son Isaac was born to him. ⁶And Sarah said, "God has made laughter for me; everyone who hears will laugh over me." ⁷And she said, "Who would have said to Abraham that Sarah would nurse children? Yet I have borne him a son in his old age."

⁸And the child grew and was weaned. And Abraham made a great feast on the day that Isaac was weaned.

1 Samuel 1:19–20   *Hannah conceived and bore Samuel*

¹⁹They rose early in the morning and worshiped before the LORD; then they went back to their house at Ramah. And Elkanah knew Hannah his wife, and the LORD remembered her. ²⁰And in due time

Hannah conceived and bore a son, and she called his name Samuel, for she said, "I have asked for him from the LORD."

Mark 10:13–16 *Receive the kingdom like a little child*

[13]They were bringing children to [Jesus] that he might touch them, and the disciples rebuked them. [14]But when Jesus saw it, he was indignant and said to them, "Let the children come to me; do not hinder them, for to such belongs the kingdom of God. [15]Truly, I say to you, whoever does not receive the kingdom of God like a child shall not enter it." [16]And he took them in his arms and blessed them, laying his hands on them.

ADDITIONAL READINGS

1 Sam. 2:1–10	*Hannah's prayer of praise and thanksgiving*
Is. 66:7–14	*Jerusalem like a child at its mother's breast*
Luke 11:11–13	*The goodness of earthly fathers*
Acts 2:38–39	*The promise is for you and your children*

PRAYERS

For the child

Heavenly Father, receive our heartfelt thanks for this child, a gift of Your grace and love for us in Your beloved Son, Jesus Christ. Send Your holy angels to shield _him/her_ from all dangers of body and soul. Preserve _him/her_ according to Your good pleasure until that day when _he/she_ is brought to the waters of Holy Baptism to receive the washing of rebirth and renewal by the Holy Spirit; through Jesus Christ, our Lord, who lives and reigns with You and the same Holy Spirit, one God, now and forever. (732)

Heavenly Father, You sent Your own Son into this world as the child of Mary. We thank You for the life of this child, _name_, entrusted to our care. Bring _him/her_ to the saving waters of Holy Baptism, and grant _him/her_ that precious inheritance awaiting _him/her_ in Your eternal kingdom; for the sake of Jesus Christ, our Lord. (300)

For father and mother

Gracious God, we thank You for hearing and answering the prayers of _ name of parents _ by granting them the gift of a child. At all times, let them see in this child an undeserved gift from Your hand. Strengthen them and all who bear the sign of the cross to be teachers and examples of the Christian faith to this child, and by the gracious leading of Your Holy Spirit fulfill what we are unable to do; through Jesus Christ, our Lord, who lives and reigns with You and the Holy Spirit, one God, now and forever. (733)

For the father

Merciful Father, from whom every good and perfect gift comes, receive our thanks and praise for the child You have brought into this world. Grant Your blessing to _ name of father _, _ his/her _ father, and by Your Holy Spirit strengthen him in his faith that he may fulfill his sacred responsibilities toward this child and lead his family in the way of Your righteousness and peace; through Jesus Christ, our Lord, who lives and reigns with You and the Holy Spirit, one God, now and forever. (734)

For the mother

O almighty God, You have delivered Your servant _ name _ from the pain and peril of childbirth and granted her a safe delivery. Keep mother and child always in Your tender care; and grant that this child may be brought to the waters of Holy Baptism and grow up in true fear, love, and trust of You; through Jesus Christ, our Lord. (303)

For young siblings

The following prayer may be prayed by young children repeating each phrase after the pastor.

Dear heavenly Father, thank You for the gift of the baby _ brother/sister _ You have given. Keep _ him/her _ safe, and help us all to love _ him/her _; through Jesus Christ, our Lord. (735)

For grandparents

Our Father in heaven, by Your blessing You grant us the joy of beholding our children's children. Grant Your wisdom to _name of grandparents_ that they may love and guide their grandchild(ren) and help _him/her/them_ reach full stature in Your gracious kingdom; through Jesus Christ, our Lord, who lives and reigns with You and the Holy Spirit, one God, now and forever. (736)

At the home

O Lord our God, creator of all that exists, we thank You for the joy of new life begun and for the privilege bestowed upon us of being participants with You in the ongoing stream of life. Grant that these blessings may be continued to our children and our children's children, that all generations may praise Your holy name; through Jesus Christ, our Lord. (737)

HYMN

Now Thank We All Our God
LSB 895

Now thank we all our God
   With hearts and hands and voices,
Who wondrous things has done,
   In whom His world rejoices;
Who from our mothers' arms
   Has blest us on our way
With countless gifts of love
   And still is ours today. (st. 1)

ADDITIONAL HYMNS

My Soul Now Magnifies the Lord   *LSB 934*
Oh, Blest the House   *LSB 862*

Special Situations

Because ours is a fallen world, the joy of expectant parents or of new parents is sometimes tempered or shattered by any of a number of challenging circumstances: miscarriage, stillbirth, death shortly after birth, premature birth, medical complications, a decision to give up a child for adoption, or permanent disabilities. Pastoral care at such times concerns not only the child but also the parents and the wide range of agonizing questions, unsettling doubts and discouragement, and rollercoaster emotions with which they may be struggling. As in all evangelical ministry, the comforting Gospel of God's grace and mercy in Christ for us sinners must be the predominating Word.

PSALMODY

Psalm 23   *The Lord is my shepherd*

¹ The LORD is my | shepherd;*
    I | shall not want.
² He makes me lie down in green | pastures.*
    He leads me beside still | waters.
³ He re- | stores my soul.*
    He leads me in paths of righteousness for his | name's sake.
⁴ Even though I walk through the valley of the shadow of death,
    I will fear no evil, for you are | with me;*
    your rod and your staff, they | comfort me.
⁵ You prepare a table before me in the presence of my | enemies;*
    you anoint my head with oil; my cup | overflows.
⁶ Surely goodness and mercy shall follow me all the days | of my life,*
    and I shall dwell in the house of the LORD for- | ever.

Psalm 77:1–15   *In the day of trouble, seek the Lord*

¹ I cry a- | loud to God,*
    aloud to God, and he will | hear me.

2 In the day of my trouble I | seek the Lord;*
>> in the night my hand is stretched out without wearying;
>> my soul refuses to be | comforted.

3 When I remember | God, I moan;*
>> when I meditate, my | spirit faints.

4 You hold my eyelids | open;*
>> I am so troubled that I | cannot speak.

5 I consider the | days of old,*
>> the years | long ago.

6 I said, "Let me remember my song in the night;
> let me meditate | in my heart."*
>> Then my spirit made a dil- | igent search:

7 "Will the Lord spurn for- | ever,*
>> and never again be | favorable?

8 Has his steadfast love for- | ever ceased?*
>> Are his promises at an end | for all time?

9 Has God forgotten to be | gracious?*
>> Has he in anger shut up his com- | passion?"

10 Then I said, "I will ap- | peal to this,*
>> to the years of the right hand of the | Most High."

11 I will remember the deeds | of the LORD;*
>> yes, I will remember your won- | ders of old.

12 I will ponder | all your work,*
>> and meditate on your | mighty deeds.

13 Your way, O God, is | holy.*
>> What god is great | like our God?

14 You are the God who works | wonders;*
>> you have made known your might among the | peoples.

15 You with your arm redeemed your | people,*
>> the children of Jacob and | Joseph.

ADDITIONAL PSALMODY

Psalm 46:1–5, 11   *God is our fortress in time of trouble*
Psalm 88   *My soul is full of troubles, hear my cry*
Psalm 90:1–6, 12–17   *Your power overshadows our concerns*
Psalm 91:1–4, 14–16   *My refuge and my fortress*
Psalm 130   *I wait for the Lord*
Psalm 139:13–18   *Fearfully and wonderfully made*

READINGS

Exodus 34:5–7a   *The Lord is compassionate and gracious*

⁵The Lord descended in the cloud and stood with him there, and proclaimed the name of the Lord. ⁶The Lord passed before him and proclaimed, "The Lord, the Lord, a God merciful and gracious, slow to anger, and abounding in steadfast love and faithfulness, ⁷keeping steadfast love for thousands, forgiving iniquity and transgression and sin."

Mark 10:13–16   *Let the children come to Me*

¹³They were bringing children to [Jesus] that he might touch them, and the disciples rebuked them. ¹⁴But when Jesus saw it, he was indignant and said to them, "Let the children come to me; do not hinder them, for to such belongs the kingdom of God. ¹⁵ Truly, I say to you, whoever does not receive the kingdom of God like a child shall not enter it." ¹⁶And he took them in his arms and blessed them, laying his hands on them.

Lamentations 3:22–26   *His mercies are new every morning*

²² The steadfast love of the Lord never ceases;
    his mercies never come to an end;
²³ they are new every morning;
    great is your faithfulness.
²⁴ "The Lord is my portion," says my soul,
    "therefore I will hope in him."
²⁵ The Lord is good to those who wait for him,
    to the soul who seeks him.

²⁶ It is good that one should wait quietly
  for the salvation of the LORD.

Romans 11:33–36
God's wisdom is unsearchable

³³Oh, the depth of the riches and wisdom and knowledge of God! How unsearchable are his judgments and how inscrutable his ways!
    ³⁴ "For who has known the mind of the Lord,
      or who has been his counselor?"
    ³⁵ "Or who has given a gift to him
      that he might be repaid?"
³⁶For from him and through him and to him are all things. To him be glory forever. Amen.

ADDITIONAL READINGS

1 Sam. 3:18	*The Lord does what seems best to Him*
Job 1:21–22	*The Lord gave, and the Lord has taken away*
Is. 43:1–7	*Fear not, for I am with you*
Rom. 14:7–9	*Whether we live or die, we are the Lord's*
2 Cor. 1:2–7	*God comforts us in all our affliction*

PRAYERS
Miscarriage

Almighty God, gracious Father, Your ways are often beyond our understanding. In Your hidden wisdom the hopes of *names of parents* have been turned from joy to sadness. In Your mercy help them to accept Your good and gracious will. Comfort them in their hour of sorrow with Your life-giving Word for the sake of Jesus Christ, Your Son, our Lord, who lives and reigns with You and the Holy Spirit, one God, now and forever. (738)

Lord God, Father of mercies and God of all comfort, we thank You for Your care in this time of trial and sadness. Console and comfort *name of parents* with the assurance of Your tender compassion ▶

and unfailing love; through Jesus Christ, our Lord, who lives and reigns with You and the Holy Spirit, one God, now and forever. (739)

Stillbirth/Death shortly after birth

Almighty and eternal God, You have given, and You have taken away. Comfort _name of parents_, whose hopes have been turned to sorrow. Strengthen their faith in this time of sadness that they may trust in You. Teach them to depend on Your boundless mercy, confident that their little one has been invited into the arms of Your Son, Jesus Christ, our Lord, who lives and reigns with You and the Holy Spirit, one God, now and forever. (740)

Heavenly Father, Your Son bore all our griefs and carried all our sorrows. Strengthen the faith of _name of parents_ and all who bear this heavy burden of sorrow and loss. Help them to rely on Your boundless mercy and to trust that their child, who has been gathered into Your loving arms, remains in Your abiding care; through Jesus Christ, our Lord. (273)

Premature birth

Heavenly Father, our lives are in Your care and keeping. Look in mercy upon the fragile life of _name of child / this child_. Preserve _his/her_ life, and nurture _him/her_ that _he/she_ may grow and develop in both body and soul. Grant patience to _name of parents_, and dispel their fears that with confidence they may rely on Your promises; through Jesus Christ, our Lord, who lives and reigns with You and the Holy Spirit, one God, now and forever. (741)

Medical complications/permanent disabilities

Heavenly Father, we thank You for _name of child_, whom You have entrusted to _name of parents_. Be with this child and those who wait and watch over _him/her_ in _his/her_ affliction. Grant that Your loving will for ___*him/her*___ be done. Encourage the parents with the certainty of Your providential care that they may know Your peace and strength and, relying on You, may bring up ___*name of child*___ as one of Your dear children; through Jesus Christ, our Lord, who lives and reigns with You and the Holy Spirit, one God, now and forever. (742)

HYMNS

Entrust Your Days and Burdens
LSB 754

Take heart, have hope, my spirit,
    And do not be dismayed;
God helps in ev'ry trial
    And makes you unafraid.
Await His time with patience
    Through darkest hours of night
Until the sun you hoped for
    Delights your eager sight. (st. 3)

O God, Forsake Me Not
LSB 731

O God, forsake me not!
    Lord, I am Yours forever.
O keep me strong in faith
    That I may leave You never.
Grant me a blessèd end
    When my good fight is fought;
Help me in life and death—
    O God, forsake me not! (st. 4)

ADDITIONAL HYMNS

Great Is Thy Faithfulness	*LSB 809*
In the Very Midst of Life	*LSB 755:2*
What God Ordains Is Always Good	*LSB 760*

Infertility

Advancements in medical technology can easily lead to the false notion that life can be manufactured rather than received as a gift of God. The Lord gives children through, and sometimes in spite of, such technology. The pastor will want to assist the couple in discerning God-pleasing uses of these technologies. Adoption may also be a godly option for the couple to consider. In any case, when the Lord chooses not to bless a couple with children, in no way does this mean that He has withdrawn His favor from them. There are many ways in which a couple not granted physical children of their own can participate in the blessings of family life.

CANTICLE

1 Samuel 2:1b–9 *The Song of Hannah*

1b "My heart exults in the LORD; my strength is exalted | in the LORD.*
    My mouth derides my enemies, because I rejoice in your sal- | vation.

2 "There is none holy like the LORD; there is none be- | sides you;*
    there is no rock | like our God.

3 Talk no more so very | proudly,*
    let not arrogance come | from your mouth;
 for the LORD is a God of | knowledge,*
    and by him actions | are weighed.

4 The bows of the mighty are | broken,*
    but the feeble | bind on strength.

5 Those who were full have hired themselves | out for bread,*
    but those who were hungry have ceased to | hunger.
 The barren has borne | seven,*
    but she who has many children | is forlorn.

6 The LORD kills and | brings to life;*
    he brings down to Sheol and | raises up.

⁷ The LORD makes poor and | makes rich;*
  he brings low and | he exalts.
⁸ He raises up the poor | from the dust;*
  he lifts the needy from the ash heap to make them sit with
  princes and inherit a seat of | honor.
For the pillars of the earth | are the LORD's,*
  and on them he has | set the world.
⁹ "He will guard the feet of his faithful ones, but the wicked shall
be cut off in | darkness,*
  for not by might shall a | man prevail."

ADDITIONAL PSALMODY

Psalm 113   *Who is like the Lord?*
Psalm 130:5–8   *I wait for the Lord*

READINGS

Matthew 6:33   *Seek first the kingdom of God*

³³Seek first the kingdom of God and his righteousness, and all these
things will be added to you.

2 Corinthians 12:9   *The Lord's grace is sufficient*

⁹[The Lord] said to me, "My grace is sufficient for you, for my power
is made perfect in weakness." Therefore I will boast all the more gladly
of my weaknesses, so that the power of Christ may rest upon me.

1 Thessalonians 5:9–11   *God has destined us for salvation*

⁹God has not destined us for wrath, but to obtain salvation through
our Lord Jesus Christ, ¹⁰who died for us so that whether we are awake
or asleep we might live with him. ¹¹Therefore encourage one another
and build one another up, just as you are doing.

ADDITIONAL READINGS

Gen. 30:1–2	*The gift of children comes only from God*
1 Sam. 1:1–11	*Hannah prays for a child*
Is. 55:8–9	*God's thoughts and ways are not ours*

PRAYERS

For those desiring a child

Heavenly Father, You create and sustain all living things. _Names of husband and wife_ sincerely desire the gift of children. Look on them with Your mercy, give them patience and understanding, and, according to Your will, grant them the gift of a child; through Jesus Christ, Your Son, our Lord, who lives and reigns with You and the Holy Spirit, one God, now and forever. (743)

For those who cannot conceive

Heavenly Father, You never forsake those who call on You. Hear the prayers of _names of husband and wife_, who are unable to have children. Grant them grace to accept Your holy will, and bestow on them an increase of faith to cast this and every care on You; through Jesus Christ, our Lord, who lives and reigns with You and the Holy Spirit, one God, now and forever. (744)

HYMNS

From God Can Nothing Move Me *LSB 713*

The Lord my life arranges;
  Who can His work destroy?
In His good time He changes
  All sorrow into joy.
  So let me then be still:
My body, soul, and spirit
His tender care inherit
  According to His will.

186

Each day at His good pleasure
   God's gracious will is done.
He sent His greatest treasure
   In Jesus Christ, His Son.
   He ev'ry gift imparts.
The bread of earth and heaven
Are by His kindness given.
   Praise Him with thankful hearts! (sts. 3–4)

© 2006 Concordia Publishing House

If Thou But Trust in God to Guide Thee   *LSB 750*

Be patient and await His leisure
   In cheerful hope, with heart content
To take whate'er thy Father's pleasure
   And His discerning love hath sent,
Nor doubt our inmost wants are known
To Him who chose us for His own. (st. 3)

ADDITIONAL HYMNS

Entrust Your Days and Burdens   *LSB 754:2–3*
Jesus, Lead Thou On   *LSB 718:3–4*

Adoption

Those contemplating adoption will engage in much discussion, thought, and prayer. The pastor will lead husband and wife to see that the love that moves them to adopt a child born to another is like the love of God for us in Christ, who has adopted us into the family of faith. Holy Baptism is the visible means by which God accomplishes this also for the adopted child.

PSALMODY

Psalm 68:4–6a
Father of the fatherless

⁴ Sing to God, sing praises | to his name;*
    lift up a song to him who rides through the deserts;
    his name is the LORD; exult be- | fore him!
⁵ Father of the fatherless and protector of | widows*
    is God in his holy habi- | tation.
⁶ God settles the solitary | in a home;*
    he leads out the prisoners to pros- | perity.

ADDITIONAL PSALMODY

Psalm 72:1–4, 18–19
The Lord delivers the needy children

READINGS

John 19:25–27
Jesus provides for His mother

²⁵Standing by the cross of Jesus were his mother and his mother's sister, Mary the wife of Clopas, and Mary Magdalene. ²⁶When Jesus saw his mother and the disciple whom he loved standing nearby, he said to his mother, "Woman, behold, your son!" ²⁷Then he said to the disciple, "Behold, your mother!" And from that hour the disciple took her to his own home.

Romans 8:14–17 *We have received the Spirit of adoption*

¹⁴All who are led by the Spirit of God are sons of God. ¹⁵For you did not receive the spirit of slavery to fall back into fear, but you have received the Spirit of adoption as sons, by whom we cry, "Abba! Father!" ¹⁶The Spirit himself bears witness with our spirit that we are children of God, ¹⁷and if children, then heirs—heirs of God and fellow heirs with Christ, provided we suffer with him in order that we may also be glorified with him.

ADDITIONAL READINGS

| Gal. 4:4–7 | *That we might receive adoption as sons* |
| Eph. 1:3–6 | *In love God predestined us for adoption* |

PRAYERS

Those seeking to adopt

Heavenly Father, before the foundation of the world You chose us in Christ to be Your sons and daughters. Look with favor upon *names of parents* as they *seek to adopt / prepare to receive* a child into their family. Give them patience during their time of waiting, and encourage them with Your love; through Jesus Christ, Your Son, our Lord, who lives and reigns with You and the Holy Spirit, one God, now and forever. (745)

Thanksgiving upon adoption

Heavenly Father, You have adopted us as Your sons and daughters by grace. We give You thanks that *names of parents* have been granted the gift of a *son/daughter* . Fill this family with wisdom and patience that they may live together in faith and love; through Jesus Christ, Your Son, our Lord, who lives and reigns with You and the Holy Spirit, one God, now and forever. (746)

HYMNS

Now Thank We All Our God
LSB 895

Now thank we all our God
  With hearts and hands and voices,
Who wondrous things has done,
  In whom His world rejoices;
Who from our mothers' arms
  Has blest us on our way
With countless gifts of love
  And still is ours today. (st. 1)

See This Wonder in the Making
LSB 593

See this wonder in the making:
God Himself this child is taking
As a lamb safe in His keeping,
His to be, awake or sleeping. (st. 1)

Far more tender than a mother,
Far more caring than a father,
God, into Your arms we place _him/her/them_ ,
With Your love and peace embrace _him/her/them_ . (st. 3)

ADDITIONAL HYMNS

Baptized into Your Name Most Holy   *LSB 590*
Father Welcomes   *LSB 605*
O Gracious Lord, with Love Draw Near   *LSB 599:1, 5*
Our Father, by Whose Name   *LSB 863*

Abortion

Whether a pregnant woman is contemplating an abortion or has already aborted her unborn child, the situation is emotionally and spiritually challenging. As the pastor has opportunity to apply the Word of God, he must proceed with patience, love, and wisdom, choosing his words carefully and with discretion, being sensitive to the vulnerable position and/or the guilt and shame of the woman and others involved. At all times, the sanctity of human life must be upheld. If abortion is being contemplated, options other than abortion should be encouraged.

The pastor may direct the mother and others involved to Individual Confession and Absolution, *LSB* page 292.

PSALMODY

Psalm 6:1–9   *Save me for Your love's sake*

¹ O LORD, rebuke me not in your | anger,*
   nor discipline me | in your wrath.
² Be gracious to me, O LORD, for I am | languishing;*
   heal me, O LORD, for my bones are | troubled.
³ My soul also is greatly | troubled.*
   But you, O LORD— | how long?
⁴ Turn, O LORD, deliv- | er my life;*
   save me for the sake of your | steadfast love.
⁵ For in death there is no remem- | brance of you;*
   in Sheol who will | give you praise?
⁶ I am weary with my moaning; every night I flood my | bed with tears;*
   I drench my couch with my | weeping.
⁷ My eye wastes away be- | cause of grief;*
   it grows weak because of | all my foes.

▶

⁸ Depart from me, all you workers of | evil,*
　　for the LORD has heard the sound of my | weeping.
⁹ The LORD has | heard my plea;*
　　the LORD ac- | cepts my prayer.

Psalm 139:13–17　　　　　　　　*You formed me in the womb*

¹³ For you formed my | inward parts;*
　　you knitted me together in my | mother's womb.
¹⁴ I praise you, for I am fearfully and wonder- | fully made.*
　　Wonderful are your works; my soul knows it | very well.
¹⁵ My frame was not hid- | den from you,*
　　when I was being made in secret, intricately woven in the
　　depths | of the earth.
¹⁶ Your eyes saw my unformed substance; in your book were
　　written, every | one of them,*
　　the days that were formed for me, when as yet there
　　were | none of them.
¹⁷ How precious to me are your thoughts, | O God!*
　　How vast is the | sum of them!

ADDITIONAL PSALMODY

Psalm 36:5–10　　　　　　　　*How precious is Your steadfast love*
Psalm 103:8–18　　　　　　　　*The Lord is merciful and gracious*

READINGS

Jeremiah 1:4–5　　　　　　　*He knows us in the womb*

⁴ The word of the LORD came to me, saying,
⁵ "Before I formed you in the womb I knew you,
　　and before you were born I consecrated you;
　　I appointed you a prophet to the nations."

Mark 10:14b *Let the children come to Me*

14b[Jesus] said to them, "Let the children come to me; do not hinder them, for to such belongs the kingdom of God."

John 10:10 *Jesus came to give life*

10[Jesus said:] "The thief comes only to steal and kill and destroy. I came that they may have life and have it abundantly."

1 Corinthians 6:19–20 *Our bodies are the Lord's*

19Do you not know that your body is a temple of the Holy Spirit within you, whom you have from God? You are not your own, 20for you were bought with a price. So glorify God in your body.

ADDITIONAL READINGS

2 Sam. 12:15–23	*After his child's death, David carries on*
Job 10:8–12	*Job proclaims that he was formed by God*
Prov. 24:11–12; 31:8	*Rescue those being taken to death*

PRAYERS

When a mother is considering an abortion

God of all grace, out of fatherly, divine goodness and mercy You have given us life and commanded us not to hurt or harm our neighbor in his body. Teach us to care for this unborn child whom You have created in Your image. Grant Your grace to _ name of mother _ that, by Your Word and Spirit, she may live according to Your will and have the courage to nurture and cherish her child. Surround her with those who will rejoice in this child, and provide for her needs of body and soul; through Jesus Christ, Your Son, our Lord, who lives and reigns with You and the Holy Spirit, one God, now and forever. (747)

For the comfort of one who has undergone an abortion

Gracious Father in heaven, look with mercy on Your daughter ___name___, who suffers the shame of abortion. For the sake of Christ Jesus, our Savior, forgive her all her sins, and remove all feelings of guilt and despair. Protect her from the accusing voices of others and the accusations from within. By Your Spirit increase her faith that she may entrust herself and her child into Your fatherly hands; through Jesus Christ, Your Son, our Lord, who lives and reigns with You and the Holy Spirit, one God, now and forever. (748)

HYMN
If Your Beloved Son, O God
LSB 568

My guilt, O Father, You have laid
    On Christ, Your Son, my Savior.
Lord Jesus, You my debt have paid
    And gained for me God's favor.
O Holy Spirit, Fount of grace,
The good in me to You I trace;
    In faith and hope preserve me. (st. 5)

ADDITIONAL HYMN
From Depths of Woe I Cry to Thee
LSB 607

MINISTERING TO THE SICK

Times of Illness

Pastoral visitation during an illness may be a once-in-a-lifetime opportunity for ministry to a particular individual. The pastor will want to remind the person that Christ has carried all of our sicknesses and infirmities. In this light, the afflicted are rightly invited to cling to Christ and His cross and receive His salvation delivered in the Gospel and the blessed Sacraments.

PSALMODY

Psalm 16:1–2, 5, 8–9, 11
Preserve me, O God

¹ Preserve me, | O God,*
> for in you I take | refuge.

² I say to the LORD, "You | are my Lord;*
> I have no good a- | part from you."

⁵ The LORD is my chosen portion | and my cup;*
> you | hold my lot.

⁸ I have set the LORD always be- | fore me;*
> because he is at my right hand, I shall not be | shaken.

⁹ Therefore my heart is glad, and my whole being re- | joices;*
> my flesh also | dwells secure.

¹¹ You make known to me the | path of life;*
> in your presence there is fullness of joy; at your right hand
> are pleasures for- | evermore.

Psalm 27:1, 4–5, 7–8, 13–14   *The Lord is my light*

¹ The LORD is my light and my salvation; whom | shall I fear?*
    The LORD is the stronghold of my life; of whom shall I | be afraid?

⁴ One thing have I asked of the LORD, that will I seek | after:*
    that I may dwell in the house of the LORD all the days of my life, to gaze upon the beauty of the LORD and to inquire in his | temple.

⁵ For he will hide me in his shelter in the day of | trouble;*
    he will conceal me under the cover of his tent; he will lift me high up- | on a rock.

⁷ Hear, O LORD, when I | cry aloud;*
    be gracious to me and | answer me!

⁸ You have said, | "Seek my face."*
    My heart says to you, "Your face, LORD, | do I seek."

¹³ I believe that I shall look upon the goodness | of the LORD*
    in the land of the | living!

¹⁴ Wait | for the LORD;*
    be strong, and let your heart take courage; wait | for the LORD!

ADDITIONAL PSALMODY

Psalm 25:1–2a, 6, 16–18, 20	*In You I trust*
Psalm 28:1–2, 6–9	*The Lord is my strength and shield*
Psalm 32:1–7	*Don't keep silent, but pray to Him for help*
Psalm 34:1–9, 17–19, 22	*Taste and see that the Lord is good*
Psalm 91:1–2, 9–12, 14–16	*He will command His angels*
Psalm 100	*The Lord made us; we are His*
Psalm 103:1–5	*Bless the Lord, O my soul*
Psalm 116:1–2, 7, 12–14, 17–18	*I will call on Him*

READINGS

Matthew 4:23–24 *Jesus healed every disease*

[23][Jesus] went throughout all Galilee, teaching in their synagogues and proclaiming the gospel of the kingdom and healing every disease and every affliction among the people. [24]So his fame spread throughout all Syria, and they brought him all the sick, those afflicted with various diseases and pains, those oppressed by demons, epileptics, and paralytics, and he healed them.

Romans 8:26–32, 35–39 *He who did not spare His own Son*

[26]The Spirit helps us in our weakness. For we do not know what to pray for as we ought, but the Spirit himself intercedes for us with groanings too deep for words. [27]And he who searches hearts knows what is the mind of the Spirit, because the Spirit intercedes for the saints according to the will of God. [28]And we know that for those who love God all things work together for good, for those who are called according to his purpose. [29]For those whom he foreknew he also predestined to be conformed to the image of his Son, in order that he might be the firstborn among many brothers. [30]And those whom he predestined he also called, and those whom he called he also justified, and those whom he justified he also glorified.

[31]What then shall we say to these things? If God is for us, who can be against us? [32]He who did not spare his own Son but gave him up for us all, how will he not also with him graciously give us all things?

[35]Who shall separate us from the love of Christ? Shall tribulation, or distress, or persecution, or famine, or nakedness, or danger, or sword? [36]As it is written,

> "For your sake we are being killed all the day long;
>   we are regarded as sheep to be slaughtered."

[37]No, in all these things we are more than conquerors through him who loved us. [38]For I am sure that neither death nor life, nor angels nor rulers, nor things present nor things to come, nor powers, [39]nor ►

height nor depth, nor anything else in all creation, will be able to separate us from the love of God in Christ Jesus our Lord.

Isaiah 41:9b–10   *Fear not, I am with you*

9b "You are my servant,
    I have chosen you and not cast you off";
10 fear not, for I am with you;
    be not dismayed, for I am your God;
I will strengthen you, I will help you,
    I will uphold you with my righteous right hand.

Lamentations 3:22–26   *The love of the Lord never ceases*

22 The steadfast love of the LORD never ceases;
    his mercies never come to an end;
23 they are new every morning;
    great is your faithfulness.
24 "The LORD is my portion," says my soul,
    "therefore I will hope in him."
25 The LORD is good to those who wait for him,
    to the soul who seeks him.
26 It is good that one should wait quietly
    for the salvation of the LORD.

ADDITIONAL READINGS

Is. 45:5–7	*The Lord makes well-being and creates calamity*
Rom. 5:1–5	*We rejoice in our sufferings*
1 Cor. 10:9–13	*The Lord provides escape from temptation*
2 Cor. 1:3–5	*God comforts us in all our afflictions*
2 Cor. 4:16–18	*Inner nature being renewed*
Col. 3:1–4	*Seek the things that are above*
1 Peter 5:6–11	*Cast all your anxieties on Him*

PRAYERS

O Lord, look down from heaven; behold, visit, and relieve Your servant _name_ for whom we pray. Look upon _him/her_ with the eyes of Your mercy, and give _him/her_ comfort and sure confidence in You. Defend _him/her_ from every danger to body and soul, and keep _him/her_ in peace and safety; through Jesus Christ, our Lord, who lives and reigns with You and the Holy Spirit, one God, now and forever. (749)

Father of mercies and God of all comfort, our only help in time of need, look with favor upon Your servant(s) _name(s)_ . Assure _him/her/them_ of Your mercy, comfort _him/her/them_ with the awareness of Your goodness, preserve _him/her/them_ from the temptations of the evil one, and give _him/her/them_ patience in _his/her/their_ tribulation. If it please You, restore _him/her/them_ to health, or give _him/her/them_ grace to accept this affliction; through Jesus Christ, our Lord, who lives and reigns with You and the Holy Spirit, one God, now and forever. (254 alt.)

Lord God, the strength of the weak and the consolation of those who suffer, mercifully hear our prayers, and grant to _name_ the help of Your power, that _his/her_ sickness may be turned to health and our sorrow into joy; through Jesus Christ, our Lord, who lives and reigns with You and the Holy Spirit, one God, now and forever. (750)

Father of all mercy, You never fail to help those who call on You for help. Give strength and confidence to Your _son/daughter_ in _his/her_ time of great need that _he/she_ may know that You are near and that You uphold _him/her_ with Your everlasting arms. Grant that, resting on Your protection, _he/she_ may fear no evil, for You are with _him/her_ to comfort and deliver _him/her_ ; through Jesus Christ, our Lord, who lives and reigns with You and the Holy Spirit, one God, now and forever. (751)

Heavenly Father, You forgive all our iniquities and heal all our diseases. You sent Your only-begotten Son to bear our griefs and carry our sorrows. Be merciful to _name_ , pardon all _his/her_ sins, and restore _his/her_ health according to Your will. Preserve _his/her_ faith, and keep _him/her_ and _his/her_ family in Your peace and safety; through Jesus Christ, our Lord, who lives and reigns with You and the Holy Spirit, one God, now and forever. (752)

Critical illness

O Lord, You are the great Physician of soul and body; You chasten and You heal. Show mercy to Your servant(s) _name(s)_ . Spare _his/her/their_ life (lives) and restore _his/her/their_ strength. Even as You gave Your Son to bear our infirmities and sicknesses, deal compassionately with _name(s)_ and bless _him/her/them_ with Your healing power. We commit _him/her/them_ to Your gracious mercy and protection; through Jesus Christ, our Lord, who lives and reigns with You and the Holy Spirit, one God, now and forever. (255)

Emergency

Almighty God, our refuge and strength, a very present help in trouble, look in mercy upon _name_ in _his/her_ time of great need. Sustain _his/her_ faith and defend _him/her_ from every danger to body and soul. Grant _him/her_ the certainty that, upholding _his/her_ with Your everlasting arms, You are at work for _his/her_ good and for the honor and glory of Your name; through Jesus Christ, our Lord, who lives and reigns with You and the Holy Spirit, one God, now and forever. (753)

For a critically ill child

Almighty God, Father in heaven, watch over Your child _name_ now afflicted with sickness. Mercifully spare the life You have given. Relieve _his/her_ pain, guard _him/her_ from all danger, and restore _his/her_ health according to Your gracious will, that _he/she_ may be raised to a life of faithful service to You; through Jesus Christ, our Lord, who lives and reigns with You and the Holy Spirit, one God, now and forever. (258)

Praying with a young child

When praying with a young child, the pastor may also pray in simple language such as the following:

Dear Jesus, _name_ is _hurting/sick_. We know that You love _him/her_. Watch over _him/her_ and help _him/her_ to get better; in Your name we pray. (754)

Before medical testing

Almighty God, graciously comfort _name_ in _his/her_ suffering, and be with _him/her_ as _he/she_ undergoes medical testing. Take away _his/her_ fear, and strengthen _his/her_ faith that _he/she_ may trust in Your merciful will and cling to Your salvation; through Jesus Christ, our Lord, who lives and reigns with You and the Holy Spirit, one God, now and forever. (755)

After medical testing

Lord God, heavenly Father, receive our humble thanks for protecting _name_ during _his/her_ medical _test/procedure_. Graciously keep _him/her_ in Your love and care, granting _him/her_ patience and trust, for we know that whoever believes in Christ will not be forsaken; through the same Jesus Christ, our Lord, who lives and reigns with You and the Holy Spirit, one God, now and forever. (756)

Before surgery

Lord Jesus Christ, in Your ministry You healed many with frail and diseased bodies. Be present with _name_ as _he/she_ undergoes surgery. Bless _him/her_ with faith in Your loving-kindness and ▶

protection. Endow the surgeon(s) and the medical team with skill and alertness so that this surgery may help Your servant to a speedy restoration of health and strength according to Your gracious will. Hear us for Your name's sake as you live and reign with the Father and the Holy Spirit, one God, now and forever. (757)

After surgery

Lord Jesus Christ, receive our thanks for hearing our prayers on behalf of _name_, who has successfully undergone surgery, and for giving to the surgeon(s) and the medical team the skills that have been effectually administered. Restore _him/her_ fully to health and strength, in Your time and according to Your good and gracious will; for You live and reign with the Father and the Holy Spirit, one God, now and forever. (758)

At the time of diagnosis

Almighty God, merciful Lord, our times are in Your hand. Look in favor on _name_, whose illness has been diagnosed and for whose healing we humbly pray. Sustain _him/her_ by Your grace that _his/her_ patience and hope may not fail. Calm all fear and anxiety in _him/her_ and in _his/her_ loved ones, and grant them faith to accept Your will and firmly believe that what You ordain is always good; through Jesus Christ, our Lord, who lives and reigns with You and the Holy Spirit, one God, now and forever. (759)

For doctors, surgeons, nurses, and other medical personnel

Lord God, be with the doctors and nurses and all others who will be ministering to the bodily needs of Your servant _name_ that, blessed by You, their tender care may serve to the healing of _his/her_ sickness and lead to a speedy return to health; through Jesus Christ, our Lord, who lives and reigns with You and the Holy Spirit, one God, now and forever. (760)

HYMNS

I Lay My Sins on Jesus

LSB 606

I lay my wants on Jesus;
    All fullness dwells in Him;
He heals all my diseases;
    My soul He does redeem.
I lay my griefs on Jesus,
    My burdens and my cares;
He from them all releases;
    He all my sorrows shares. (st. 2)

Your Hand, O Lord, in Days of Old

LSB 846

Your touch then, Lord, brought life and health,
    Gave speech and strength and sight;
And youth renewed and frenzy calmed
    Revealed You, Lord of light.
And now, O Lord, be near to bless,
    Almighty as before,
In crowded street, by beds of pain,
    As by Gennes'ret's shore.

O be our great deliv'rer still,
    The Lord of life and death;
Restore and quicken, soothe and bless,
    With Your life-giving breath.
To hands that work and eyes that see
    Give wisdom's healing pow'r
That whole and sick and weak and strong
    May praise You evermore. (sts. 2–3)

Salvation unto Us Has Come

LSB 555

Since Christ has full atonement made
    And brought to us salvation,
Each Christian therefore may be glad
    And build on this foundation.
Your grace alone, dear Lord, I plead,
Your death is now my life indeed,
    For You have paid my ransom.

Let me not doubt, but truly see
    Your Word cannot be broken;
Your call rings out, "Come unto Me!"
    No falsehood have You spoken.
Baptized into Your precious name,
My faith cannot be put to shame,
    And I shall never perish. (sts. 6–7)

ADDITIONAL HYMNS

How Firm a Foundation	LSB 728:2–4
O Son of God, in Galilee	LSB 841
When to Our World the Savior Came	LSB 551

Chronic Illness

The caring pastor will certainly be sensitive to the expression of guilt or fear, cynicism or hopelessness or denial often made by the chronically or terminally ill. A wise pastor will also be open to family members who struggle with conflicted feelings about caring for their loved ones. Only through the Word of the Gospel are forgiveness and strength imparted to God's people, with the promise of the resurrection of the body and life eternal with Christ in the world to come.

PSALMODY

Psalm 23 *The Lord is my shepherd*

¹ The LORD is my | shepherd;*
  I | shall not want.
² He makes me lie down in green | pastures.*
  He leads me beside still | waters.
³ He re- | stores my soul.*
  He leads me in paths of righteousness for his | name's sake.
⁴ Even though I walk through the valley of the shadow of death, I will fear no evil, for you are | with me;*
  your rod and your staff, they | comfort me.
⁵ You prepare a table before me in the presence of my | enemies;*
  you anoint my head with oil; my cup | overflows.
⁶ Surely goodness and mercy shall follow me all the days | of my life,*
  and I shall dwell in the house of the LORD for- | ever.

Psalm 31:1–5, 7, 16 *I take refuge in Your love*

¹ In you, O LORD, do I take refuge; let me never be | put to shame;*
  in your righteousness de- | liver me!
² Incline your ear to me; rescue me | speedily!*
  Be a rock of refuge for me, a strong fortress to | save me!
³ For you are my rock and my | fortress;*
  and for your name's sake you lead me and | guide me; ►

⁴ you take me out of the net they have hidden | for me,*
>> for you are my | refuge.

⁵ Into your hand I commit my | spirit;*
>> you have redeemed me, O LORD, | faithful God.

⁷ I will rejoice and be glad in your | steadfast love,*
>> because you have seen my affliction; you have known the
>> distress | of my soul.

¹⁶ Make your face shine on your | servant;*
>> save me in your | steadfast love!

Psalm 51:1–12
Have mercy; restore the joy of salvation

¹ Have mercy on me, O God, according to your | steadfast love;*
>> according to your abundant mercy blot out my
>> trans- | gressions.

² Wash me thoroughly from my in- | iquity,*
>> and cleanse me | from my sin!

³ For I know my trans- | gressions,*
>> and my sin is ever be- | fore me.

⁴ Against you, you only, have I sinned and done what is evil | in
your sight,*
>> so that you may be justified in your words and blameless in
>> your | judgment.

⁵ Behold, I was brought forth in in- | iquity,*
>> and in sin did my mother con- | ceive me.

⁶ Behold, you delight in truth in the inward | being,*
>> and you teach me wisdom in the | secret heart.

⁷ Purge me with hyssop, and I | shall be clean;*
>> wash me, and I shall be whit- | er than snow.

⁸ Let me hear joy and | gladness;*
>> let the bones that you have bro- | ken rejoice.

⁹ Hide your face | from my sins,*
>> and blot out all my in- | iquities.

¹⁰ Create in me a clean heart, | O God,*

and renew a right spirit with- | in me.
¹¹ Cast me not away from your | presence,*
  and take not your Holy Spirit | from me.
¹² Restore to me the joy of your sal- | vation,*
  and uphold me with a willing | spirit.

Psalm 139:1–3, 7–10, 17–18, 23–24 *Lord, You have known me*

¹ O LORD, you have searched me and | known me!*
  ² You know when I sit down and when I rise up;
  you discern my thoughts | from afar.
³ You search out my path and my | lying down*
  and are acquainted with | all my ways.
⁷ Where shall I go from your | Spirit?*
  Or where shall I flee from your | presence?
⁸ If I ascend to heaven, | you are there!*
  If I make my bed in Sheol, | you are there!
⁹ If I take the wings of the | morning*
  and dwell in the uttermost parts | of the sea,
¹⁰ even there your hand shall | lead me,*
  and your right hand shall | hold me.
¹⁷ How precious to me are your thoughts, | O God!*
  How vast is the | sum of them!
¹⁸ If I would count them, they are more | than the sand.*
  I awake, and I am still | with you.
²³ Search me, O God, and | know my heart!*
  Try me and | know my thoughts!
²⁴ And see if there be any grievous | way in me,*
  and lead me in the way ever- | lasting!

ADDITIONAL PSALMODY

Psalm 25:1–2a, 4–7   *I wait for the Lord all the day*
Psalm 34:1–4, 8–15, 17–19   *O taste and see that the Lord is good*
Psalm 39:4, 7, 12a   *Hear my prayer, O Lord*

Psalm 42:1–2, 5–6a, 7–8, 11   *Hope in God*
Psalm 44:1–4, 8, 26   *As You helped Israel, help us*
Psalm 46:1–5, 7, 10–11   *God is our refuge and strength*
Psalm 90:1–4, 12, 14–15, 17a   *Teach us to number our days*
Psalm 145:1–2, 13–18   *The Lord is near to all who call on Him*

READINGS

2 Corinthians 4:16—5:9   *Groaning in our bodies for Christ*

[16]We do not lose heart. Though our outer nature is wasting away, our inner nature is being renewed day by day. [17]For this slight momentary affliction is preparing for us an eternal weight of glory beyond all comparison, [18]as we look not to the things that are seen but to the things that are unseen. For the things that are seen are transient, but the things that are unseen are eternal.

[5:1]For we know that if the tent, which is our earthly home, is destroyed, we have a building from God, a house not made with hands, eternal in the heavens. [2]For in this tent we groan, longing to put on our heavenly dwelling, [3]if indeed by putting it on we may not be found naked. [4]For while we are still in this tent, we groan, being burdened—not that we would be unclothed, but that we would be further clothed, so that what is mortal may be swallowed up by life. [5]He who has prepared us for this very thing is God, who has given us the Spirit as a guarantee.

[6]So we are always of good courage. We know that while we are at home in the body we are away from the Lord, [7]for we walk by faith, not by sight. [8]Yes, we are of good courage, and we would rather be away from the body and at home with the Lord. [9]So whether we are at home or away, we make it our aim to please him.

2 Corinthians 12:7–10   *My grace is sufficient for you*

[7]To keep me from being too elated by the surpassing greatness of the revelations, a thorn was given me in the flesh, a messenger of Satan to harass me, to keep me from being too elated. [8]Three times I

pleaded with the Lord about this, that it should leave me. ⁹But he said to me, "My grace is sufficient for you, for my power is made perfect in weakness." Therefore I will boast all the more gladly of my weaknesses, so that the power of Christ may rest upon me. ¹⁰For the sake of Christ, then, I am content with weaknesses, insults, hardships, persecutions, and calamities. For when I am weak, then I am strong.

2 Corinthians 1:3–7   *He comforts us in all our afflictions*

³Blessed be the God and Father of our Lord Jesus Christ, the Father of mercies and God of all comfort, ⁴who comforts us in all our affliction, so that we may be able to comfort those who are in any affliction, with the comfort with which we ourselves are comforted by God. ⁵For as we share abundantly in Christ's sufferings, so through Christ we share abundantly in comfort too. ⁶If we are afflicted, it is for your comfort and salvation; and if we are comforted, it is for your comfort, which you experience when you patiently endure the same sufferings that we suffer. ⁷Our hope for you is unshaken, for we know that as you share in our sufferings, you will also share in our comfort.

ADDITIONAL READINGS

Matt. 25:31–40	*The least of Christ's brothers*
Luke 23:38–43	*You will be with me in paradise*
John 14:1–3	*I go to prepare a place for you*
Acts 20:32–35	*More blessed to give than to receive*
Rom. 5:1–5	*We rejoice in our sufferings*
Rom. 8:18, 28, 31–35, 37–39	*Present sufferings and future glory*
1 Cor. 13:1–7, 13	*Love bears all things*
2 Cor. 6:4–10	*Paul commends himself to the Lord*
Gal. 6:2, 9–10	*Let us not grow weary of doing good*
James 5:7–8, 10–11	*Be patient*

PRAYERS

Father of mercies and God of all comfort, our only help in time of need, look with favor upon Your servant(s) __name(s)__. Assure __him/her/them__ of Your mercy, comfort __him/her/them__ with the awareness of Your goodness, preserve __him/her/them__ from the temptations of the evil one, and give __him/her/them__ patience in __his/her/their__ tribulation. If it please You, restore __him/her/them__ to health, or give __him/her/them__ grace to accept this affliction; through Jesus Christ, our Lord, who lives and reigns with You and the Holy Spirit, one God, now and forever. (254 alt.)

Terminally ill

Eternal Father, You alone make the decisions concerning life and death. Have mercy on __name__, whose illness seems irreversible. If it be Your will, restore __him/her__ and lengthen __his/her__ earthly life; if not, O Father, keep __him/her__ in __his/her__ baptismal grace, and prepare __him/her__ to commit __himself/herself__ to Your eternal care. Give __him/her__ a repentant heart, firm faith, and a lively hope that the pain or fear of death may not cause __him/her__ to waver in confidence and trust. When __his/her__ days on earth are ended, grant __him/her__ a joyous entrance into everlasting life with the glorious company of all Your saints; through Jesus Christ, our Lord, who lives and reigns with You and the Holy Spirit, one God, now and forever. (761)

Lord of all grace, You sent Your Son, our Savior Jesus Christ, to bring life and immortality to light. We give You thanks that by His death He destroyed the power of death and by His resurrection He opened the kingdom of heaven to all believers. Strengthen __name__ in the confidence that because Christ lives __he/she__ shall live also, and that neither death nor life nor things present nor things to come will be able to separate __him/her__ from Your love, which is in Christ Jesus, our Lord, who lives and reigns with You and the Holy Spirit, one God, now and forever. (548 alt.)

For the physically disabled

Lord God, heavenly Father, receive our thanks for the gift of life and for everything in Your creation that enriches our physical lives. By Your merciful guidance, aid and strengthen _name_ , and enable _him/her_ to find fulfillment in _his/her_ life and encouragement and support for all _his/her_ endeavors; through Jesus Christ, our Lord, who lives and reigns with You and the Holy Spirit, one God, now and forever. (285 alt.)

Lord Jesus Christ, give _name_ at all times a patient spirit, willing and ready to wait and pray, that _he/she_ may not weary of You, but cast every care upon You with all cheerfulness and confidence and always hope for the best from You, who live and reign with the Father and the Holy Spirit, one God, now and forever. (762)

Patience to bear afflictions

Heavenly Father, You teach us in Your holy Word that You do not willingly afflict or grieve Your children. Look with compassion on _name_ , for whom we pray. Remember _him/her_ in mercy, strengthen _him/her_ in patience, comfort _him/her_ with the memory of Your goodness, and let Your face shine on _him/her_ that _he/she_ may be guarded by Your peace in Christ Jesus, who lives and reigns with You and the Holy Spirit, one God, now and forever. (763)

For the caretakers (family)

Almighty God, gracious Lord, look in mercy on the family (and friends) of _name_ as they care for _him/her_ . Grant them Your Holy Spirit that they may have faith equal to the task before them. Sustain them that by Your grace they may reflect Your love through their patient service to _name_ and each other; through Jesus Christ, our Lord, who lives and reigns with You and the Holy Spirit, one God, now and forever. (764)

HYMNS

Fight the Good Fight

LSB 664

Cast care aside, lean on your guide;
His boundless mercy will provide.
Trust, and enduring faith shall prove
Christ is your life and Christ your love.

Faint not nor fear, His arms are near;
He changes not who holds you dear;
Only believe, and you will see
That Christ is all eternally. (sts. 3–4)

I Trust, O Lord, Your Holy Name

LSB 734

Bow down Your gracious ear to me
And hear my cry, my prayer, my plea;
> Make haste for my protection,
>> For woes and fear
>> Surround me here.
> Help me in my affliction.

You are my strength, my shield, my rock,
My fortress that withstands each shock,
> My help, my life, my tower,
>> My battle sword,
>> Almighty Lord—
> Who can resist Your power? (sts. 2–3)

ADDITIONAL HYMNS

Entrust Your Days and Burdens   LSB 754:2–3
Lord, Thee I Love with All My Heart   LSB 708:1–2
When to Our World the Savior Came   LSB 551

Returning Home from the Hospital

A patient's discharge from the hospital is usually accompanied by a sense of relief and an eager desire to return home. Healing undoubtedly will need to continue, the body as well as the mind and soul requiring further therapy and strengthening. Those therapeutic days before returning to normalcy are blessed times for prayer, praise, and thanksgiving.

PSALMODY

Psalm 28:6–9 *The Lord is my strength and shield*

6 Blessèd | be the LORD!*
  For he has heard the voice of my pleas for | mercy.
7 The LORD is my strength and my shield; in him my heart trusts,
  and | I am helped;*
    my heart exults, and with my song I give | thanks to him.
8 The LORD is the strength of his | people;*
    he is the saving refuge of his a- | nointed.
9 Oh, save your people and bless your | heritage!*
    Be their shepherd and carry them for- | ever.

Psalm 103:1–12 *The Lord forgives iniquity and heals diseases*

1 Bless the LORD, | O my soul,*
    and all that is within me, bless his | holy name!
2 Bless the LORD, | O my soul,*
    and forget not all his | benefits,
3 who forgives all your in- | iquity,*
    who heals all your dis- | eases,
4 who redeems your life | from the pit,*
    who crowns you with steadfast love and | mercy,
5 who satisfies | you with good*
    so that your youth is renewed like the | eagle's.   ►

⁶ The LORD works | righteousness*
    and justice for all who | are oppressed.
⁷ He made known his ways to | Moses,*
    his acts to the people of | Israel.
⁸ The LORD is merciful and | gracious,*
    slow to anger and abounding in | steadfast love.
⁹ He will not | always chide,*
    nor will he keep his anger for- | ever.
¹⁰ He does not deal with us according | to our sins,*
    nor repay us according to our in- | iquities.
¹¹ For as high as the heavens are a- | bove the earth,*
    so great is his steadfast love toward those who | fear him;
¹² as far as the east is | from the west,*
    so far does he remove our transgres- | sions from us.

ADDITIONAL PSALMODY

Psalm 34:1–6, 22	*I sought the Lord, and He answered me*
Psalm 41:1–3, 13	*The Lord is our strength in weakness*
Psalm 92:1–5	*It is good to give thanks to the Lord*
Psalm 145:1–5, 9–10	*Great is the Lord*

READINGS

Ephesians 1:3–10   *Blessed be the God and Father*

³Blessed be the God and Father of our Lord Jesus Christ, who has blessed us in Christ with every spiritual blessing in the heavenly places, ⁴even as he chose us in him before the foundation of the world, that we should be holy and blameless before him. In love ⁵he predestined us for adoption as sons through Jesus Christ, according to the purpose of his will, ⁶to the praise of his glorious grace, with which he has blessed us in the Beloved. ⁷In him we have redemption through his blood, the forgiveness of our trespasses, according to the riches of his grace, ⁸which he lavished upon us, in all wisdom and in-

sight ⁹making known to us the mystery of his will, according to his purpose, which he set forth in Christ ¹⁰as a plan for the fullness of time, to unite all things in him, things in heaven and things on earth.

Romans 5:1–5   *Justified by faith, we have peace with God*

¹Since we have been justified by faith, we have peace with God through our Lord Jesus Christ. ²Through him we have also obtained access by faith into this grace in which we stand, and we rejoice in hope of the glory of God. ³More than that, we rejoice in our sufferings, knowing that suffering produces endurance, ⁴and endurance produces character, and character produces hope, ⁵and hope does not put us to shame, because God's love has been poured into our hearts through the Holy Spirit who has been given to us.

ADDITIONAL READINGS

Is. 40:28–31	*They shall renew their strength*
Acts 3:1–10	*The lame beggar healed*
Rom. 8:28–30	*All things work together for good*
2 Cor. 4:16–18	*We look to the things that are unseen*
Eph. 3:14–20	*To Him be glory in the Church*

PRAYERS

Lord God, heavenly Father, we praise Your wonderful goodness for blessing _ name _ during _ his/her _ stay at the hospital and for bringing _ him/her _ safely home. Be with _ him/her _, and grant that _ he/she _ may be restored to wholeness and strength for service in Your kingdom; through Jesus Christ, our Lord, who lives and reigns with You and the Holy Spirit, one God, now and forever. (765)

Lord God, You care for Your children in all their needs. Restore _ name _, and look upon _ him/her _ in Your mercy. Give _ him/her _ comfort and sure confidence in You. Defend _ him/her _ from danger and harm, and keep _ him/her _ in perpetual peace and safety; ▶

through Jesus Christ, our Lord, who lives and reigns with You and the Holy Spirit, one God, now and forever. (766)

HYMN
Sing Praise to God, the Highest Good
LSB 819

Sing praise to God, the highest good,
    The author of creation,
The God of love who understood
    Our need for His salvation.
With healing balm our souls He fills
And ev'ry faithless murmur stills:
    To God all praise and glory!

What God's almighty pow'r has made,
    In mercy He is keeping.
By morning glow or evening shade
    His eye is never sleeping.
Within the kingdom of His might
All things are just and good and right:
    To God all praise and glory!

We sought the Lord in our distress;
    O God, in mercy hear us.
Our Savior saw our helplessness
    And came with peace to cheer us.
For this we thank and praise the Lord,
Who is by one and all adored:
    To God all praise and glory! (sts. 1–3)

ADDITIONAL HYMNS

Give Thanks with a Grateful Heart LSB 806
Praise to You and Adoration LSB 692

Thanksgiving for Healing

Once the pain has eased and the stress of potential danger and the irritation of disease are behind, the heart of the child of God can leap for joy as God's healing hand is personally experienced in body, mind, and soul. Because of the sinful flesh, it is all too easy to forget one's previous condition before the healing. A faithful heart overflowing with thanks pleases the Lord and keeps the baptized Christian attuned to God's mercy and grace.

PSALMODY

Psalm 30:1–2, 4–5, 10–12   *I cried to You, and You answered me*

¹ I will extol you, O LORD, for you have | drawn me up*
    and have not let my foes rejoice | over me.
² O LORD my God, I cried to | you for help,*
    and you have | healed me.
⁴ Sing praises to the LORD, O | you his saints,*
    and give thanks to his | holy name.
⁵ For his anger is but for a moment, and his favor is for a | lifetime.*
    Weeping may tarry for the night, but joy comes with
    the | morning.
¹⁰ Hear, O LORD, and be merci- | ful to me!*
    O LORD, be my | helper!
¹¹ You have turned for me my mourning into | dancing;*
    you have loosed my sackcloth and clothed me with | gladness,
¹² that my glory may sing your praise and not be | silent.*
    O LORD my God, I will give thanks to you for- | ever!

Psalm 145:1–3, 13–20a, 21   *The Lord is faithful in all His words*

¹ I will extol you, my | God and King,*
    and bless your name forever and | ever.
² Every day I will | bless you*
    and praise your name forever and | ever.

▶

3 Great is the LORD, and greatly | to be praised,*
    and his greatness is un- | searchable.

13 Your kingdom is an everlasting | kingdom,*
    and your dominion endures throughout all gener- | ations.
  The LORD is faithful in | all his words*
    and kind in | all his works.

14 The LORD upholds all who are | falling*
    and raises up all who are | bowed down.

15 The eyes of all | look to you,*
    and you give them their food in due | season.

16 You open | your hand;*
    you satisfy the desire of every | living thing.

17 The LORD is righteous in | all his ways*
    and kind in | all his works.

18 The LORD is near to all who | call on him,*
    to all who call on | him in truth.

19 He fulfills the desire of those who fear him;
  he also hears their cry and | saves them.*
    20 The LORD preserves all who | love him.

21 My mouth will speak the praise | of the LORD,*
    and let all flesh bless his holy name forever and | ever.

ADDITIONAL PSALMODY

Psalm 103:1–5, 8, 20–22   *Bless the Lord, O my soul*
Psalm 116:1–7, 12–14   *The Lord heard my voice*
Psalm 119:65–72   *It is good for me that I was afflicted*
Psalm 138:1–3, 8a   *On the day I called, You answered me*
Psalm 150   *Praise the Lord!*

READINGS

Luke 17:11–17   *Cleansing of the ten lepers*

11On the way to Jerusalem he was passing along between Samaria and Galilee. 12And as he entered a village, he was met by ten lepers, who stood at a distance [13]and lifted up their voices, saying, "Jesus, Master, have mercy on us." [14]When he saw them he said to them, "Go and show yourselves to the priests." And as they went they were cleansed. [15]Then one of them, when he saw that he was healed, turned back, praising God with a loud voice; [16]and he fell on his face at Jesus' feet, giving him thanks. Now he was a Samaritan. [17]Then Jesus answered, "Were not ten cleansed? Where are the nine?"

1 Chronicles 16:8–11, 24–25, 34   *David's song of thanksgiving*

[8] Oh give thanks to the LORD; call upon his name;
   make known his deeds among the peoples!

[9] Sing to him; sing praises to him;
   tell of all his wondrous works!

[10] Glory in his holy name;
   let the hearts of those who seek the LORD rejoice!

[11] Seek the LORD and his strength;
   seek his presence continually!

[24] Declare his glory among the nations,
   his marvelous works among all the peoples!

[25] For great is the LORD, and greatly to be praised,
   and he is to be held in awe above all gods.

[34] Oh give thanks to the LORD, for he is good;
   for his steadfast love endures forever!

ADDITIONAL READINGS

1 Chron. 29:10–13   *We thank You, our God*
Phil. 1:3–6   *I thank my God in all my remembrance of you*
1 Peter 1:3–9   *Blessed be the God and Father*

PRAYERS

Gracious God, giver of life, health, safety, and strength: receive our thanks and praise for blessing *name* with recovery from sickness and pain. Fill *his/her* heart with daily remembrance of Your ▶

goodness that _he/she_ may serve You with a holy and obedient life; through Jesus Christ, Your Son, our Lord, who lives and reigns with You and the Holy Spirit, one God, now and forever. (298 alt.)

Almighty God, we give thanks that You have restored the health of _name_, on whose behalf we bless and praise Your name. Grant that _he/she_ may continue the work You have given _him/her_ in this life and finally receive eternal glory at the appearing of Your Son, Jesus Christ, our Lord, who lives and reigns with You and the Holy Spirit, one God, now and forever. (297 alt.)

HYMNS

Now Thank We All Our God
LSB 895

Now thank we all our God
    With hearts and hands and voices,
Who wondrous things has done,
    In whom His world rejoices;
Who from our mothers' arms
    Has blest us on our way
With countless gifts of love
    And still is ours today. (st. 1)

Praise, My Soul, the King of Heaven
LSB 793

Praise Him for His grace and favor
    To His people in distress;
Praise Him still the same as ever,
    Slow to chide and swift to bless:
        Alleluia, alleluia!
    Glorious in His faithfulness.

Fatherlike He tends and spares us;
    Well our feeble frame He knows;
In His hand He gently bears us,
    Rescues us from all our foes.
        Alleluia, alleluia!
    Widely yet His mercy flows. (sts. 2–3)

ADDITIONAL HYMNS

We Praise You, O God	*LSB 785*
When in the Hour of Deepest Need	*LSB 615:6*

End of Life Decisions

Care of the irretrievably dying always includes provision of those ordinary items needed to sustain life (nutrition and hydration). Once the dying person's vital processes have ceased their spontaneous functions, the decision may be made to discontinue the use of artificial means to prolong life or extraordinary forms of treatment. While never aiming for death, the Christian will not hold on to physical life as the only or the highest good. The same Lord who gives life also takes it away. Therefore when the time of death comes, Christians do not cling to life in defiance or fear. The pastor will be prepared to guide his people in thinking through decisions regarding the end of life within the scope of God's will revealed through the Scriptures. Trusting in the sure promises of our Lord's resurrection, the pastor will use God's Word to comfort and strengthen family members as they commend their dying loved one to the hands of a merciful Savior.

When death is near, the Commendation of the Dying (pages 81–94) is used.

PSALMODY
Psalm 25:1–9, 16–21   *Make me to know Your ways*

1 To you, | O Lord,*
     I lift | up my soul.
2 O my God, in you I trust; let me not be | put to shame;*
     let not my enemies exult | over me.
3 Indeed, none who wait for you shall be | put to shame;*
     they shall be ashamed who are wantonly | treacherous.
4 Make me to know your ways, | O Lord;*
     teach me | your paths.
5 Lead me in your truth and teach me, for you are the God of my
sal- | vation;*
     for you I wait all the | day long.
6 Remember your mercy, O Lord, and your | steadfast love,*
     for they have been | from of old.
7 Remember not the sins of my youth or my trans- | gressions;*
     according to your steadfast love remember me, for the sake
of your goodness, | O Lord!
8 Good and upright | is the Lord;*
     therefore he instructs sinners | in the way.
9 He leads the humble in | what is right,*
     and teaches the humble | his way.
16 Turn to me and be gra- | cious to me,*
     for I am lonely and af- | flicted.
17 The troubles of my heart | are enlarged;*
     bring me out of my dis- | tresses.
18 Consider my affliction and my | trouble,*
     and forgive | all my sins.
19 Consider how many | are my foes,*
     and with what violent hatred they | hate me.
20 Oh, guard my soul, and de- | liver me!*
     Let me not be put to shame, for I take ref- | uge in you.

²¹ May integrity and uprightness pre- | serve me,*
    for I | wait for you.

Psalm 143:1–2, 5–8   *I stretch out my hands to You*

¹ Hear my prayer, O LORD; give ear to my pleas for | mercy!*
    In your faithfulness answer me, in your | righteousness!
² Enter not into judgment with your | servant,*
    for no one living is righteous be- | fore you.
⁵ I remember the days of old; I meditate on all that | you have done;*
    I ponder the work | of your hands.
⁶ I stretch out my | hands to you;*
    my soul thirsts for you like a | parched land.
⁷ Answer me quickly, O LORD! My | spirit fails!*
    Hide not your face from me, lest I be like those who go
    down | to the pit.
⁸ Let me hear in the morning of your steadfast love, for in | you I
    trust.*
    Make me know the way I should go, for to you I lift | up my
    soul.

ADDITIONAL PSALMODY

Psalm 18:1–6, 16–18, 20–21   *I call upon the Lord and am saved*
Psalm 31:5–10, 16–17, 21–24   *The Lord preserves the faithful*
Psalm 34:4–9, 15, 17–18, 22   *The Lord hears His servants*
Psalm 90   *Teach us to number our days*
Psalm 116:1–9, 15–17   *The Lord has loosed my bonds*
Psalm 139:1–4, 13–18   *You have searched me and known me*

READINGS

Luke 22:39–43   *Jesus prays in Gethsemane*

³⁹ [Jesus] came out and went, as was his custom, to the Mount of Olives,
and the disciples followed him. ⁴⁰And when he came to the place,
he said to them, "Pray that you may not enter into temptation." ▶

[41]And he withdrew from them about a stone's throw, and knelt down and prayed, [42]saying, "Father, if you are willing, remove this cup from me. Nevertheless, not my will, but yours, be done." [43]And there appeared to him an angel from heaven, strengthening him.

Ecclesiastes 3:1–8 *For everything there is a season*

[1]For everything there is a season, and a time for every matter under heaven:

> [2] a time to be born, and a time to die;
> a time to plant, and a time to pluck up what is planted;
> [3] a time to kill, and a time to heal;
> a time to break down, and a time to build up;
> [4] a time to weep, and a time to laugh;
> a time to mourn, and a time to dance;
> [5] a time to cast away stones, and a time to gather stones together;
> a time to embrace, and a time to refrain from embracing;
> [6] a time to seek, and a time to lose;
> a time to keep, and a time to cast away;
> [7] a time to tear, and a time to sew;
> a time to keep silence, and a time to speak;
> [8] a time to love, and a time to hate;
> a time for war, and a time for peace.

John 11:1–4 *Lazarus' illness is for the glory of God*

[1]Now a certain man was ill, Lazarus of Bethany, the village of Mary and her sister Martha. [2]It was Mary who anointed the Lord with ointment and wiped his feet with her hair, whose brother Lazarus was ill. [3]So the sisters sent to him, saying, "Lord, he whom you love is ill." [4]But when Jesus heard it he said, "This illness does not lead to death. It is for the glory of God, so that the Son of God may be glorified through it."

Philippians 1:19–26   *To live is Christ, to die is gain*

¹⁹I know that through your prayers and the help of the Spirit of Jesus Christ this will turn out for my deliverance, ²⁰as it is my eager expectation and hope that I will not be at all ashamed, but that with full courage now as always Christ will be honored in my body, whether by life or by death. ²¹For to me to live is Christ, and to die is gain. ²²If I am to live in the flesh, that means fruitful labor for me. Yet which I shall choose I cannot tell. ²³I am hard pressed between the two. My desire is to depart and be with Christ, for that is far better. ²⁴But to remain in the flesh is more necessary on your account. ²⁵Convinced of this, I know that I will remain and continue with you all, for your progress and joy in the faith, ²⁶so that in me you may have ample cause to glory in Christ Jesus, because of my coming to you again.

Romans 14:7–9   *Whether we live or die, we are the Lord's*

⁷None of us lives to himself, and none of us dies to himself. ⁸If we live, we live to the Lord, and if we die, we die to the Lord. So then, whether we live or whether we die, we are the Lord's. ⁹For to this end Christ died and lived again, that he might be Lord both of the dead and of the living.

ADDITIONAL READINGS

Job 1:21–22   *The Lord gives; the Lord takes away*
Job 19:25–27   *I know that my Redeemer lives*
Matt. 7:7–8   *Ask, and it will be given to you*
Luke 23:46   *Into Your hands I commit My spirit*
John 10:27–30   *No one will snatch them out of My hand*
Rom. 8:22–30   *We eagerly await the redemption of our bodies*
1 Cor. 15:22–26   *In Christ shall all be made alive*

PRAYERS

Almighty God, You breathed life into Adam and have given earthly life also to _name_ , Your dear child and servant. Trusting in Your ▶

225

compassion, we commend __him/her__ to You; through Jesus Christ, Your Son, our Lord, who lives and reigns with You and the Holy Spirit, one God, now and forever. (767)

Merciful Father, God of all truth, we commend __name__ into Your gracious keeping, for You have redeemed __him/her__. Guard and shield __him/her__ from all the powers of darkness as __he/she__ walks through the valley of the shadow of death. Grant that __he/she__ may fall asleep in peace and awaken to the bright joy of Your eternal presence; through Jesus Christ, Your Son, our Lord, who lives and reigns with You and the Holy Spirit, one God, now and forever. (768)

For the family in deliberation

Heavenly Father, we thank You for the truth of Your Word that nothing in death or life will separate us from Your love in Christ Jesus and that whether we live or die we belong to You. By Your gracious Spirit strengthen the family of __name__ in this confidence, and guide them as they face difficult decisions concerning __his/her__ medical care so that their actions may be in agreement with Your holy will. Do not forsake them, but uphold and keep them in Your love and peace; through Jesus Christ, Your Son, our Lord, who lives and reigns with You and the Holy Spirit, one God, now and forever. (769)

HYMN
O Sacred Head, Now Wounded   _LSB 450_

My Shepherd, now receive me;
    My Guardian, own me Thine.
Great blessings Thou didst give me,
    O Source of gifts divine.
Thy lips have often fed me
    With words of truth and love;
Thy Spirit oft hath led me
    To heav'nly joys above. (st. 4)

My Savior, be Thou near me
    When death is at my door;
Then let Thy presence cheer me,
    Forsake me nevermore!
When soul and body languish,
    O leave me not alone,
But take away mine anguish
    By virtue of Thine own! (st. 6)

Be Thou my consolation,
    My shield, when I must die;
Remind me of Thy passion
    When my last hour draws nigh.
Mine eyes shall then behold Thee,
    Upon Thy cross shall dwell,
My heart by faith enfold Thee.
    Who dieth thus dies well. (st. 7)

ADDITIONAL HYMNS

If Thou But Trust in God to Guide Thee   *LSB 750:7*
No Saint on Earth Lives Life to Self Alone   *LSB 747*

Ministering to Caregivers

The task of caring for those in need provides opportunity for Christ-like self-sacrifice. This can be a taxing labor of love. The pastor may need to minister as much to the caregivers as to those for whom they care. He will remind them of their own need for God's Word and prayer, and he will encourage them to find refreshment in the company of others.

PSALMODY
Psalm 28:6–9 *The Lord is my strength*

6 Blessèd | be the LORD!*
   For he has heard the voice of my pleas for | mercy.
7 The LORD is my strength and my shield; in him my heart trusts, and | I am helped:*
   my heart exults, and with my song I give | thanks to him.
8 The LORD is the strength of his | people;*
   he is the saving refuge of his a- | nointed.
9 Oh, save your people and bless your | heritage!*
   Be their shepherd and carry them for- | ever.

Psalm 42:1–2, 5–6a, 8–9, 11 *Hope in God*

1 As a deer pants for | flowing streams,*
   so pants my soul for you, | O God.
2 My soul thirsts for God, for the | living God.*
   When shall I come and appear be- | fore God?
5 Why are you cast down, O my soul, and why are you in turmoil with- | in me?*
   Hope in God; for I shall again praise him,
   my salvation | 6 and my God.
8 By day the LORD commands his steadfast love, and at night his song is | with me,*
   a prayer to the God | of my life.

⁹ I say to God, my rock: "Why have you for- | gotten me?*
    Why do I go mourning because of the oppression of
    the | enemy?"
¹¹ Why are you cast down, O my soul, and why are you in turmoil
    with- | in me?*
    Hope in God; for I shall again praise him,
    my salvation | and my God.

Psalm 116:5–9   *The Lord has dealt bountifully*

⁵ Gracious is the LORD, and | righteous;*
    our God is | merciful.
⁶ The LORD preserves the | simple;*
    when I was brought low, he | saved me.
⁷ Return, O my soul, | to your rest;*
    for the LORD has dealt bountifully | with you.
⁸ For you have delivered my | soul from death,*
    my eyes from tears, my feet from | stumbling;
⁹ I will walk be- | fore the LORD*
    in the land of the | living.

ADDITIONAL PSALMODY

Psalm 27:1, 3, 5, 7, 11, 13–14   *The Lord is my light and salvation*
Psalm 36:5–10   *His steadfast love is precious*

READINGS

1 Peter 4:8–10   *Love and show hospitality*

⁸Above all, keep loving one another earnestly, since love covers a
multitude of sins. ⁹Show hospitality to one another without grum-
bling. ¹⁰As each has received a gift, use it to serve one another, as
good stewards of God's varied grace.

Proverbs 6:20; 23:22   *The father and mother who gave you life*

²⁰ My son, keep your father's commandment,
    and forsake not your mother's teaching.
²² Listen to your father who gave you life,
    and do not despise your mother when she is old.

Romans 12:6–13   *Doing all with the grace that God gives*

⁶Having gifts that differ according to the grace given to us, let us use them: if prophecy, in proportion to our faith; ⁷if service, in our serving; the one who teaches, in his teaching; ⁸the one who exhorts, in his exhortation; the one who contributes, in generosity; the one who leads, with zeal; the one who does acts of mercy, with cheerfulness.

⁹Let love be genuine. Abhor what is evil; hold fast to what is good. ¹⁰Love one another with brotherly affection. Outdo one another in showing honor. ¹¹Do not be slothful in zeal, be fervent in spirit, serve the Lord. ¹²Rejoice in hope, be patient in tribulation, be constant in prayer. ¹³Contribute to the needs of the saints and seek to show hospitality.

ADDITIONAL READINGS

Matt. 6:25–34   *Do not be anxious*
James 5:13–16   *James instructs on ministering to the sick*

PRAYERS

For related caregivers

God of all compassion, give to Your servant(s) *name of caregiver(s)* a special measure of compassion and patience as *he/she/they* care(s) for *name of parent / child / relative* . Comfort *him/her/them* in times of frustration and distress and give *him/her/them* (an) understanding heart(s) as *he/she/they* extend(s) *his/her/their* hands in acts of mercy. Enable *him/her/them* to rejoice in the opportunity You have given *him/her/them* to serve *his/her/their*   *mother /*

father / daughter / son / other relationship in this way. Cause *name of caregiver(s)* to find time to care for *himself/herself/themselves* so that *he/she/they* may continue to serve with a joyful heart; through Jesus Christ, our Lord. (770)

For related caregivers of the elderly

God of all compassion, give to Your servant(s) *name of caregiver(s)* a special measure of compassion and patience as *she/he/they* care(s) for *name of parent / relative* in *his/her* twilight years. Comfort *her/him/them* in times of frustration and distress and give *her/him/them* (an) understanding heart(s) as *she/he/they* extend(s) *her/his/their* hands in acts of mercy. Enable *her/him/them* to rejoice in the opportunity You have given to honor *her/his/their mother / father / parents / grandparent(s)* in this way and bless what remaining time they have together. Cause *name of caregiver(s)* to find time to care for *herself/himself/themselves* so that *she/he/they* may continue to serve with a joyful heart; through Jesus Christ, our Lord. (771)

For non-related caregivers

Most merciful God, give to *name of caregiver(s)* a special measure of compassion and patience as *she/he/they* care(s) for _____. Comfort *her/him/them* in times of distress and anxiety, and give *her/him/them* (an) understanding heart(s) as *she/he/they* extend(s) *her/his/their* hands in acts of mercy to _____, who can no longer care adequately for *himself/herself/themselves*. Enable *name of caregiver(s)* to find time to care for *herself/himself/themselves* so that *she/he/they* may continue to serve with a joyful heart; through Jesus Christ, our Lord. (772)

HYMNS

Lord of Glory, You Have Bought Us
LSB 851

Grant us hearts, dear Lord, to give You
    Gladly, freely of Your own.
With the sunshine of Your goodness
    Melt our thankless hearts of stone
Till our cold and selfish natures,
    Warmed by You, at length believe
That more happy and more blessèd
    'Tis to give than to receive.

Wondrous honor You have given
    To our humblest charity
In Your own mysterious sentence,
    "You have done it all to Me."
Can it be, O gracious Master,
    That You deign for alms to sue,
Saying by Your poor and needy,
    "Give as I have giv'n to you"?

Lord of glory, You have bought us
    With Your lifeblood as the price,
Never grudging for the lost ones
    That tremendous sacrifice.
Give us faith to trust You boldly,
    Hope, to stay our souls on You;
But, oh, best of all Your graces,
    With Your love our love renew. (sts. 2–4)

O God of Mercy, God of Might

LSB 852

Teach us the lesson Thou hast taught:
To feel for those Thy blood hath bought,
That ev'ry word and deed and thought
    May work a work for Thee. (st. 3)

In sickness, sorrow, want, or care,
May we each other's burdens share;
May we, where help is needed, there
    Give help as unto Thee! (st. 5)

ADDITIONAL HYMNS

Christ, Our Human Likeness Sharing	*LSB 847*
For All the Faithful Women	*LSB 855:1, 12, 3–4*
Gracious God, You Send Great Blessings	*LSB 782*
Lord, Help Us Walk Your Servant Way	*LSB 857*
Lord, Whose Love through Humble Service	*LSB 848:1, 4*
O Son of God, in Galilee	*LSB 841*
Where Charity and Love Prevail	*LSB 845*
With the Lord Begin Your Task	*LSB 869:1–2, 5*

AT THE TIME OF DEATH

Ministering to the Dying

Death is the inevitable consequence of sin and, for the unbeliever, the ultimate enemy. For the believer death is the defeated enemy and the doorway to eternal life. Nevertheless, the process of dying can be a frightening one. In ministering to the dying, the pastor brings the consolation of the forgiveness of sins won for us by the death of Christ. He will comfort the dying with the sure and certain hope of the resurrection of the body, guaranteed by our Lord's own resurrection.

When death appears imminent, the Commendation of the Dying (pages 81–94) is used.

PSALMODY

Psalm 4:8   *Sleep in peace*

⁸ In peace I will both lie | down and sleep;*
    for you alone, O LORD, make me dwell in | safety.

Psalm 27:1   *The Lord is my light*

¹ The LORD is my light and my salvation; whom | shall I fear?*
    The LORD is the stronghold of my life; of whom shall I | be afraid?

Psalm 31:5

I commit my spirit

5 Into your hand I commit my | spirit;*
  you have redeemed me, O LORD, | faithful God.

Psalm 73:26

God is my strength

26 My flesh and my | heart may fail,*
  but God is the strength of my heart and my portion for- | ever.

Psalm 23

The Lord is my shepherd

English Standard Version

1 The LORD is my | shepherd;*
  I | shall not want.
2 He makes me lie down in green | pastures.*
  He leads me beside still | waters.
3 He re- | stores my soul.*
  He leads me in paths of righteousness for his | name's sake.
4 Even though I walk through the valley of the shadow of death,
  I will fear no evil, for you are | with me;*
  your rod and your staff, they | comfort me.
5 You prepare a table before me in the presence of my | enemies;*
  you anoint my head with oil; my cup | overflows.
6 Surely goodness and mercy shall follow me all the days | of my
  life,*
  and I shall dwell in the house of the LORD for- | ever.

King James Version

1 The LORD is my | shepherd;*
  I | shall not want.
2 He maketh me to lie down in green | pastures:*
  he leadeth me beside the still | waters.
3 He restoreth | my soul:*
  he leadeth me in the paths of righteousness for his | name's
  sake. ►

235

4 Yea, though I walk through the valley of the shadow of death,
   I will fear no evil: for thou art | with me;*
      thy rod and thy staff they | comfort me.
5 Thou preparest a table before me in the presence of
   mine | enemies:*
      thou anointest my head with oil; my cup runneth | over.
6 Surely goodness and mercy shall follow me all the days | of my
   life:*
      and I will dwell in the house of the LORD for- | ever.

Psalm 90   *The years of our life are soon gone*

1 Lord, you have been our | dwelling place*
      in all gener- | ations.
2 Before the mountains were brought forth, or ever you had formed
   the earth | and the world,*
      from everlasting to everlasting | you are God.
3 You return | man to dust*
      and say, "Return, O chil- | dren of man!"
4 For a thousand years in your sight are but as yesterday when | it
   is past,*
      or as a watch | in the night.
5 You sweep them away as | with a flood;*
      they are like a dream, like grass that is renewed in the | morning:
6 in the morning it flourishes and | is renewed;*
      in the evening it fades and | withers.
7 For we are brought to an end by your | anger;*
      by your wrath we | are dismayed.
8 You have set our iniquities be- | fore you,*
      our secret sins in the light of your | presence.
9 For all our days pass away un- | der your wrath;*
      we bring our years to an end | like a sigh.
10 The years of our life are seventy, or even by reason of
   strength | eighty;*

    yet their span is but toil and trouble; they are soon gone, and
    we | fly away.

11 Who considers the power of your | anger,*
    and your wrath according to the | fear of you?

12 So teach us to number | our days*
    that we may get a heart of | wisdom.

13 Return, O LORD! | How long?*
    Have pity on your | servants!

14 Satisfy us in the morning with your | steadfast love,*
    that we may rejoice and be glad | all our days.

15 Make us glad for as many days as you have af- | flicted us,*
    and for as many years as we have seen | evil.

16 Let your work be shown to your | servants,*
    and your glorious power to their | children.

17 Let the favor of the Lord our God be upon us, and establish the
    work of our hands up- | on us;*
       yes, establish the work | of our hands!

Psalm 116:1–9, 15–19   *You deliver my soul from death*

1 I love the LORD, because | he has heard*
    my voice and my pleas for | mercy.

2 Because he inclined his | ear to me,*
    therefore I will call on him as long | as I live.

3 The snares of death encompassed me; the pangs of Sheol
    laid | hold on me;*
    I suffered distress and | anguish.

4 Then I called on the name | of the LORD:*
    "O LORD, I pray, deliv- | er my soul!"

5 Gracious is the LORD, and | righteous;*
    our God is | merciful.

6 The LORD preserves the | simple;*
    when I was brought low, he | saved me.   ▶

⁷ Return, O my soul, | to your rest;*
    for the Lord has dealt bountifully | with you.
⁸ For you have delivered my | soul from death,*
    my eyes from tears, my feet from | stumbling;
⁹ I will walk be- | fore the Lord*
    in the land of the | living.
¹⁵ Precious in the sight | of the Lord*
    is the death | of his saints.
¹⁶ O Lord, I am your | servant;*
    I am your servant, the son of your maidservant.
    You have | loosed my bonds.
¹⁷ I will offer to you the sacrifice of thanks- | giving*
    and call on the name | of the Lord.
¹⁸ I will pay my vows | to the Lord*
    in the presence of all his | people,
¹⁹ in the courts of the house | of the Lord,*
    in your midst, O Jerusalem. | Praise the Lord!

Psalm 130:1–5   *With You there is forgiveness*

¹ Out | of the depths*
    I cry to you, | O Lord!
² O Lord, | hear my voice!*
    Let your ears be attentive to the voice of my pleas for | mercy!
³ If you, O Lord, should mark in- | iquities,*
    O Lord, | who could stand?
⁴ But with you there is for- | giveness,*
    that you | may be feared.
⁵ I wait for the Lord, my | soul waits,*
    and in his | word I hope.

Psalm 118:17, 19–20 *I shall not die but live*

¹⁷ I shall not die, but | I shall live,*
    and recount the deeds | of the LORD.
¹⁹ Open to me the gates of | righteousness,*
    that I may enter through them and give thanks | to the LORD.
²⁰ This is the gate | of the LORD;*
    the righteous shall enter | through it.

Psalm 121:7–8 *Your going out and coming in*

⁷ The LORD will keep you from all | evil;*
    he will | keep your life.
⁸ The LORD will keep your going out and your | coming in*
    from this time forth and for- | evermore.

ADDITIONAL PSALMODY

Psalm 16:1–2, 5, 9–11	*The Lord will not abandon my soul*
Psalm 25:6–7	*Remember Your mercy, O Lord*
Psalm 91	*The Lord, my refuge and fortress*

READINGS
Luke 2:25–32 *Lord, let Your servant depart in peace*

²⁵There was a man in Jerusalem, whose name was Simeon, and this man was righteous and devout, waiting for the consolation of Israel, and the Holy Spirit was upon him. ²⁶And it had been revealed to him by the Holy Spirit that he would not see death before he had seen the Lord's Christ. ²⁷And he came in the Spirit into the temple, and when the parents brought in the child Jesus, to do for him according to the custom of the Law, ²⁸he took him up in his arms and blessed God and said,

²⁹ "Lord, now you are letting your servant depart in peace,
    according to your word;
³⁰ for my eyes have seen your salvation
    ³¹ that you have prepared in the presence of all peoples, ►

³² a light for revelation to the Gentiles,
    and for glory to your people Israel."

John 3:16 *God so loved the world*

¹⁶For God so loved the world, that he gave his only Son, that whoever believes in him should not perish but have eternal life.

John 10:14–15 *I am the Good Shepherd*

¹⁴I am the good shepherd. I know my own and my own know me, ¹⁵just as the Father knows me and I know the Father; and I lay down my life for the sheep.

John 10:27–28 *My sheep hear My voice*

²⁷My sheep hear my voice, and I know them, and they follow me. ²⁸I give them eternal life, and they will never perish, and no one will snatch them out of my hand.

Mark 16:1–7 *The resurrection of our Lord*

¹When the Sabbath was past, Mary Magdalene and Mary the mother of James and Salome bought spices, so that they might go and anoint him. ²And very early on the first day of the week, when the sun had risen, they went to the tomb. ³And they were saying to one another, "Who will roll away the stone for us from the entrance of the tomb?" ⁴And looking up, they saw that the stone had been rolled back—it was very large. ⁵And entering the tomb, they saw a young man sitting on the right side, dressed in a white robe, and they were alarmed. ⁶And he said to them, "Do not be alarmed. You seek Jesus of Nazareth, who was crucified. He has risen; he is not here. See the place where they laid him. ⁷But go, tell his disciples and Peter that he is going before you to Galilee. There you will see him, just as he told you."

John 11:25–26a   *I am the resurrection and the life*

²⁵Jesus said to her, "I am the resurrection and the life. Whoever believes in me, though he die, yet shall he live, ²⁶and everyone who lives and believes in me shall never die."

John 20:19–31   *The risen Lord forgives sin*

¹⁹On the evening of that day, the first day of the week, the doors being locked where the disciples were for fear of the Jews, Jesus came and stood among them and said to them, "Peace be with you." ²⁰When he had said this, he showed them his hands and his side. Then the disciples were glad when they saw the Lord. ²¹Jesus said to them again, "Peace be with you. As the Father has sent me, even so I am sending you." ²²And when he had said this, he breathed on them and said to them, "Receive the Holy Spirit. ²³If you forgive the sins of anyone, they are forgiven; if you withhold forgiveness from anyone, it is withheld."

²⁴Now Thomas, one of the Twelve, called the Twin, was not with them when Jesus came. ²⁵So the other disciples told him, "We have seen the Lord." But he said to them, "Unless I see in his hands the mark of the nails, and place my finger into the mark of the nails, and place my hand into his side, I will never believe."

²⁶Eight days later, his disciples were inside again, and Thomas was with them. Although the doors were locked, Jesus came and stood among them and said, "Peace be with you." ²⁷Then he said to Thomas, "Put your finger here, and see my hands; and put out your hand, and place it in my side. Do not disbelieve, but believe." ²⁸Thomas answered him, "My Lord and my God!" ²⁹Jesus said to him, "Have you believed because you have seen me? Blessed are those who have not seen and yet have believed."

³⁰Now Jesus did many other signs in the presence of the disciples, which are not written in this book; ³¹but these are written so that you may believe that Jesus is the Christ, the Son of God, and that by believing you may have life in his name.

Philippians 1:21–23 *To live is Christ, to die is gain*

²¹For to me to live is Christ, and to die is gain. ²²If I am to live in the flesh, that means fruitful labor for me. Yet which I shall choose I cannot tell. ²³I am hard pressed between the two. My desire is to depart and be with Christ, for that is far better.

ADDITIONAL READINGS

Is. 53:4–5	*He was wounded for our transgressions*
Luke 23:39–43	*Today you will be with me in paradise*
John 11:21–27	*Jesus comforts Martha*
Rom. 14:7–9	*Whether we live or die, we are the Lord's*
2 Cor. 5:1–10	*We have a building from God*
2 Tim. 4:6–8	*The time of my departure has come*
Rev. 7:9–17	*The redeemed standing before the Lamb*

PRAYERS

Eternal Father, You alone make the decisions concerning life and death. Be gracious and merciful to _ name _, whose death seems imminent. Keep _ him/her _ in _ his/her _ baptismal grace, and prepare _ him/her _ to commit _ himself/herself _ to Your eternal care and keeping. Give _ him/her _ a repentant heart, firm faith, and a lively hope. Let not the fear of death cause _ him/her _ to waver in confidence and trust. At Your chosen time, grant _ him/her _ a peaceful departure and a joyous entrance into everlasting life with the glorious company of all Your saints; through Jesus Christ, Your Son, our Lord, who lives and reigns with You and the Holy Spirit, one God, now and forever. (262 alt.)

Almighty and eternal God, faithful heavenly Father, comfort and strengthen _ name _ in Your great mercy. Help _ him/her _ in all discomfort and distress. In Your good time, take _ him/her _ to Yourself in Your kingdom, for You have redeemed _ him/her _ through the blood of Jesus Christ, Your Son, our Lord, who lives and reigns with You and the Holy Spirit, one God, now and forever. (773)

For those in a hospice

Almighty God, gracious Father, look in mercy on _name_ , [lying in great weakness]. Forgive all _his/her_ sins and strengthen _his/her_ faith in Christ Jesus and in His salvation. By Your Holy Spirit grant _him/her_ a living hope and a sure confidence in Christ until that time when You shall receive _him/her_ into Your eternal kingdom; through Jesus Christ, Your Son, our Lord, who lives and reigns with You and the Holy Spirit, one God, now and forever. (774)

Prayer for forgiveness

Almighty God, gracious Lord, You forgive the sins of all who truly repent and believe in Christ. Hear _name_ , who calls upon You, and absolve _him/her_ of all _his/her_ iniquity. In mercy grant _him/her_ Your peace, and by Your Holy Spirit preserve _him/her_ in the true faith to life everlasting; through Jesus Christ, Your Son, our Lord, who lives and reigns with You and the Holy Spirit, one God, now and forever. (775)

For the caregivers (family)

Almighty God, gracious Lord, look in mercy on the family (and friends) of _name_ as they care for _him/her_ . Grant them Your Holy Spirit that they may have faith equal to the task before them. Sustain them that by Your grace they may reflect Your love through their patient service to _name_ and each other; through Jesus Christ, our Lord, who lives and reigns with You and the Holy Spirit, one God, now and forever. (776)

HYMNS

Lord, Thee I Love with All My Heart
LSB 708

Lord, let at last Thine angels come,
To Abr'ham's bosom bear me home,
    That I may die unfearing;
And in its narrow chamber keep
My body safe in peaceful sleep
    Until Thy reappearing.
And then from death awaken me,
That these mine eyes with joy may see,
    O Son of God, Thy glorious face,
    My Savior and my fount of grace.
Lord Jesus Christ, my prayer attend, my prayer attend,
And I will praise Thee without end. (st. 3)

I Walk in Danger All the Way
LSB 716

My walk is heav'nward all the way;
    Await, my soul, the morrow,
When God's good healing shall allay
    All suff'ring, sin, and sorrow.
Then, worldly pomp, begone!
To heav'n I now press on.
    For all the world I would not stay;
    My walk is heav'nward all the way. (st. 6)

Let Us Ever Walk with Jesus
LSB 685

Let us gladly die with Jesus.
    Since by death He conquered death,
He will free us from destruction,
    Give to us immortal breath.
Let us mortify all passion
    That would lead us into sin;

And the grave that shuts us in
Shall but prove the gate to heaven.
Jesus, here with You I die,
There to live with You on high. (st. 3)

ADDITIONAL HYMNS

Abide with Me	*LSB 878:1, 5–6*
For Me to Live Is Jesus	*LSB 742*
In Peace and Joy I Now Depart	*LSB 938*
Lord, Take My Hand and Lead Me	*LSB 722:3*
No Saint on Earth Lives Life to Self Alone	*LSB 747*
Precious Lord, Take My Hand	*LSB 739*

The use of Confession and Absolution is always appropriate for one who is near death. The pastor is encouraged to speak the Confession and Absolution even if the dying person is not able to speak or respond.

Confession of Sins

O almighty God, merciful Father, I, a poor, miserable sinner, confess unto You all my sins and iniquities with which I have ever offended You and justly deserved Your temporal and eternal punishment. But I am heartily sorry for them and sincerely repent of them, and I pray You of Your boundless mercy and for the sake of the holy, innocent, bitter sufferings and death of Your beloved Son, Jesus Christ, to be gracious and merciful to me, a poor, sinful being.

OR

Do you confess to almighty God that you are a poor, miserable sinner?
Yes.

Do you confess to our merciful Father that you have sinned against Him in thought, word, and deed?
Yes.

▶

245

Do you confess that you justly deserve His temporal and eternal punishment?
Yes.

Do you believe that our Lord Jesus Christ died for you and shed His blood for you on the cross for the forgiveness of all your sins?
Yes.

Do you pray God, for the sake of the holy, innocent, bitter sufferings and death of His beloved Son, to be gracious and merciful to you?
Yes.

Finally, do you believe that my forgiveness is God's forgiveness?
Yes.

Absolution

  Name , I, by virtue of my office, as a called and ordained servant of the Word, announce the grace of God to you, and in the stead and by the command of my Lord Jesus Christ I forgive you all your sins in the name of the Father and of the ✙ Son and of the Holy Spirit. Amen.

Create in Me
LSB 192/956

Create in me a clean heart, O God,
    and renew a right spirit within me.
Cast me not away from Thy presence,
    and take not Thy Holy Spirit from me.
Restore unto me the joy of Thy salvation,
    and uphold me with Thy free spirit. Amen.   *Psalm 51:10–12*

Ministering to the Bereaved

Pastors can be called to minister to the bereaved at any time and in a wide variety of informal settings. These resources are intended to supplement the rites and resources for Christian burial provided in the *Lutheran Service Book: Agenda* and elsewhere in this volume. This ministry to the bereaved does not end with the funeral; anniversaries, birthdays, and holidays may also be especially difficult or painful. The pastor uses these and other occasions to provide ongoing consolation to the bereaved. The pastor will proclaim the hope of the resurrection and eternal life in Christ and encourage the bereaved to draw strength from Christ's Word and Sacraments in the fellowship of the congregation.

For resources in the days immediately following death, see the rite for Comforting the Bereaved (pages 95–106).

See also Burial for a Stillborn Child or Unbaptized Child (pages 136–147).

PSALMODY

Psalm 23

The Lord is my shepherd

¹ The LORD is my | shepherd;*
　　I | shall not want.
² He makes me lie down in green | pastures.*
　　He leads me beside still | waters.
³ He re- | stores my soul.*
　　He leads me in paths of righteousness for his | name's sake.
⁴ Even though I walk through the valley of the shadow of death,
　I will fear no evil, for you are | with me;*
　　your rod and your staff, they | comfort me.
⁵ You prepare a table before me in the presence of my | enemies;*
　　you anoint my head with oil; my cup | overflows. ►

⁶ Surely goodness and mercy shall follow me all the days | of my
life,*
> and I shall dwell in the house of the Lord for- | ever.

Psalm 90   *Lord, You have been our dwelling place*

¹ Lord, you have been our | dwelling place*
> in all gener- | ations.

² Before the mountains were brought forth, or ever you had
formed the earth | and the world,*
> from everlasting to everlasting | you are God.

³ You return | man to dust*
> and say, "Return, O chil- | dren of man!"

⁴ For a thousand years in your sight are but as yesterday when | it
is past,*
> or as a watch | in the night.

⁵ You sweep them away as | with a flood;*
> they are like a dream, like grass that is renewed in the | morning:

⁶ in the morning it flourishes and | is renewed;*
> in the evening it fades and | withers.

⁷ For we are brought to an end by your | anger;*
> by your wrath we | are dismayed.

⁸ You have set our iniquities be- | fore you,*
> our secret sins in the light of your | presence.

⁹ For all our days pass away un- | der your wrath;*
> we bring our years to an end | like a sigh.

¹⁰ The years of our life are seventy, or even by reason of
strength | eighty;*
> yet their span is but toil and trouble; they are soon gone, and
> we | fly away.

¹¹ Who considers the power of your | anger,*
> and your wrath according to the | fear of you?

¹² So teach us to number | our days*
>   that we may get a heart of | wisdom.

¹³ Return, O Lᴏʀᴅ! | How long?*
>   Have pity on your | servants!

¹⁴ Satisfy us in the morning with your | steadfast love,*
>   that we may rejoice and be glad | all our days.

¹⁵ Make us glad for as many days as you have af- | flicted us,*
>   and for as many years as we have seen | evil.

¹⁶ Let your work be shown to your | servants,*
>   and your glorious power to their | children.

¹⁷ Let the favor of the Lord our God be upon us, and establish the work of our hands up- | on us;*
>   yes, establish the work | of our hands!

ADDITIONAL PSALMODY

Psalm 46	*God is our refuge and strength*
Psalm 103	*The Lord shows compassion*
Psalm 116	*When I was brought low, He saved me*
Psalm 121	*My help comes from the Lord*

READINGS

Isaiah 25:6–9   *The Lord will swallow up death forever*

⁶ On this mountain the Lᴏʀᴅ of hosts will make for all peoples
>   a feast of rich food, a feast of well-aged wine,
>   of rich food full of marrow, of aged wine well refined.

⁷ And he will swallow up on this mountain
>   the covering that is cast over all peoples,
>   the veil that is spread over all nations.

⁸ He will swallow up death forever;
and the Lord Gᴏᴅ will wipe away tears from all faces,
>   and the reproach of his people he will take away from all the
>   earth, for the Lᴏʀᴅ has spoken.   ▶

9 It will be said on that day,
>"Behold, this is our God; we have waited for him,
>that he might save us.
>This is the LORD; we have waited for him;
>let us be glad and rejoice in his salvation."

Romans 6:3–9 *Baptized into Christ's death and resurrection*

3Do you not know that all of us who have been baptized into Christ Jesus were baptized into his death? 4We were buried therefore with him by baptism into death, in order that, just as Christ was raised from the dead by the glory of the Father, we too might walk in newness of life.

5For if we have been united with him in a death like his, we shall certainly be united with him in a resurrection like his. 6We know that our old self was crucified with him in order that the body of sin might be brought to nothing, so that we would no longer be enslaved to sin. 7For one who has died has been set free from sin. 8Now if we have died with Christ, we believe that we will also live with him. 9We know that Christ being raised from the dead will never die again; death no longer has dominion over him.

Job 19:23–27a *I know that my Redeemer lives*

23 Oh that my words were written!
>Oh that they were inscribed in a book!
24 Oh that with an iron pen and lead
>they were engraved in the rock forever!
25 For I know that my Redeemer lives,
>and at the last he will stand upon the earth.
26 And after my skin has been thus destroyed,
>yet in my flesh I shall see God,
27 whom I shall see for myself,
>and my eyes shall behold, and not another.

John 11:20–27   *Jesus is the resurrection and the life*

²⁰When Martha heard that Jesus was coming, she went and met him, but Mary remained seated in the house. ²¹Martha said to Jesus, "Lord, if you had been here, my brother would not have died. ²²But even now I know that whatever you ask from God, God will give you." ²³Jesus said to her, "Your brother will rise again." ²⁴Martha said to him, "I know that he will rise again in the resurrection on the last day." ²⁵Jesus said to her, "I am the resurrection and the life. Whoever believes in me, though he die, yet shall he live, ²⁶and everyone who lives and believes in me shall never die. Do you believe this?" ²⁷She said to him, "Yes, Lord; I believe that you are the Christ, the Son of God, who is coming into the world."

Romans 8:31–35, 37–39   *Nothing shall separate us*

³¹What then shall we say to these things? If God is for us, who can be against us? ³²He who did not spare his own Son but gave him up for us all, how will he not also with him graciously give us all things? ³³Who shall bring any charge against God's elect? It is God who justifies. ³⁴Who is to condemn? Christ Jesus is the one who died—more than that, who was raised—who is at the right hand of God, who indeed is interceding for us. ³⁵Who shall separate us from the love of Christ? Shall tribulation, or distress, or persecution, or famine, or nakedness, or danger, or sword?

³⁷No, in all these things we are more than conquerors through him who loved us. ³⁸For I am sure that neither death nor life, nor angels nor rulers, nor things present nor things to come, nor powers, ³⁹nor height nor depth, nor anything else in all creation, will be able to separate us from the love of God in Christ Jesus our Lord.

ADDITIONAL READINGS

Lam. 3:22–26	*Great is Your faithfulness*
Mark 10:13–16	*Jesus blesses the children*
Mark 16:1–7	*He has risen*

Luke 9:28–36	*Jesus is transfigured*
John 3:14–21	*Whoever believes has eternal life*
John 10:14–15, 27–30	*The Shepherd's sheep will never perish*
1 Cor. 15:12–26	*In Christ shall all be made alive*
1 Cor. 15:51–58	*God gives us the victory over death*
1 Thess. 4:13–18	*The Lord will raise the dead*
Heb. 12:18–24	*You have come to the city of the living God*
Rev. 14:13	*Blessed are the dead who die in the Lord*
Rev. 21:1–7	*The new Jerusalem*

PRAYERS

Lord God, heavenly Father, receive our humble thanks for all Your mercies granted to our _brother/sister_ _name_ during _his/her_ earthly life, especially for calling _him/her_ by the Gospel and sustaining _him/her_ in the true faith until _his/her_ departure. Comfort those who mourn _his/her_ death with the hope of the glorious resurrection and a happy reunion in heaven. Help us to remember that we are mortal, that we may ever prepare ourselves to fall asleep in faith and finally receive the glory promised to all who trust in Your beloved Son, Jesus Christ, our Lord, who lives and reigns with You and the Holy Spirit, one God, now and forever. (545)

Almighty and most merciful God, You bring us through suffering and death with our Lord Jesus Christ to enter with Him into glory. Grant us grace at all times to acknowledge and accept Your holy and gracious will, to remain in true faith, and to find peace and joy in the resurrection of the dead and the glory of everlasting life; through Jesus Christ, Your Son, our Lord, who lives and reigns with You and the Holy Spirit, one God, now and forever. (279 alt.)

At the death of a spouse

Merciful God and Father, look graciously upon _name_, who grieves at the death of _his wife / her husband_, _name_. Teach us ever to remember that all things work together for the good of those who love You. Receive our thanks for blessing _name_ and _name_ in holy matrimony and for the love and support they gave each other. Comfort _name_ with Your everlasting Gospel, and lead _him/her_ by Your Holy Spirit until You take _him/her_ with all Your saints to the marriage feast of the Lamb in His kingdom, which has no end; through the same Jesus Christ, Your Son, our Lord, who lives and reigns with You and the Holy Spirit, one God, now and forever. (777)

At the death of a parent/grandparent

Eternal God and Father, look graciously upon _name(s)_, who grieve(s) at the death of _his/her/their_ _father / mother / grandfather / grandmother_. Teach us to remember that all things work together for the good of those who love You. Help us to recall with thanksgiving the many mercies You gave _his/her/their_ _father / mother / grandfather / grandmother_, especially that You adopted _him/her_ as Your child in Holy Baptism and kept _him/her_ in the true faith unto the glories of heaven. Comfort us with Your everlasting Gospel, and lead us by Your Holy Spirit until You take us with all Your saints to a joyous and blessed reunion in heaven; through Jesus Christ, Your Son, our Lord, who lives and reigns with You and the Holy Spirit, one God, now and forever. (778)

At the death of a baptized young child

Blessed Lord, according to Your wisdom and grace You give and You take away. Receive our humble thanks for all the mercies You granted to this child, _name_, during _his/her_ short time on earth and for taking _him/her_ to Yourself in heaven. Strengthen _his/her_ parents to accept Your holy will. Comfort and console them with the truth that in Holy Baptism their dear child was delivered from sin and is now among the saints in glory. Keep us all in Your grace that when our last hour comes we may depart in peace; through Jesus Christ, Your Son, our Lord, who lives and reigns with You and the Holy Spirit, one God, now and forever. (271 alt.)

For parents of an unbaptized young child

Heavenly Father, Your Son bore all our griefs and carried all our sorrows. Strengthen the faith of _name(s) of parent(s)_, who bear this heavy burden. Help them to rely on Your boundless mercy and to trust that their little one, who has been gathered into Your loving arms, will rise on the Last Day; through Jesus Christ, Your Son, our Lord, who lives and reigns with You and the Holy Spirit, one God, now and forever. (273 alt.)

For parents of adult children

Blessed Lord, according to Your wisdom and grace You give and You take away. Receive our humble thanks for all the mercies You granted to _name_ during _his/her_ life and for taking _him/her_ to Yourself in heaven. Strengthen _name(s) of parent(s)_ to accept Your holy will. Comfort and console _him/her/them_ with the truth that in Holy Baptism _his/her/their_ _son/daughter_ was delivered from sin and is now among the saints in glory. Keep us all in Your grace that when our last hour comes we may depart in peace; through Jesus Christ, Your Son, our Lord, who lives and reigns with You and the Holy Spirit, one God, now and forever. (271 alt.)

At the death of a Christian friend

O God of grace and glory, we remember our _brother/sister_ _name_, who is now in Your eternal presence. We thank You for giving _him/her_ to us to know and to love as a friend on our earthly pilgrimage. In Your boundless compassion console us in this time of sorrow. Give us faith to see that death is the gate of eternal life so that in quiet confidence we may continue our course on earth until by Your call we are reunited with those who in saving faith have gone before us; through Jesus Christ, Your Son, our Lord, who lives and reigns with You and the Holy Spirit, one God, now and forever. (268)

For those who mourn the death of one whose faith is in question

Almighty God, Father of mercies and God of all comfort, deal graciously with ___name(s)___ and all who mourn that, casting every care on You, they may know the consolation of Your love; through Jesus Christ, Your Son, our Lord, who lives and reigns with You and the Holy Spirit, one God, now and forever. (264 alt.)

Collects for other specific circumstances may be found in the Lutheran Service Book: Altar Book.

HYMNS

Be Still, My Soul

LSB 752

Be still, my soul; the Lord is on your side;
    Bear patiently the cross of grief or pain;
Leave to your God to order and provide;
    In ev'ry change He faithful will remain.
Be still, my soul; your best, your heav'nly Friend
Through thorny ways leads to a joyful end. (st. 1)

Be still, my soul; though dearest friends depart
    And all is darkened in this vale of tears;
Then you will better know His love, His heart,
    Who comes to soothe your sorrows and your fears.
Be still, my soul; your Jesus can repay
From His own fullness all He takes away. (st. 3)

Be still, my soul; the hour is hast'ning on
    When we shall be forever with the Lord,
When disappointment, grief, and fear are gone,
    Sorrow forgot, love's purest joys restored.
Be still, my soul; when change and tears are past,
All safe and blessèd we shall meet at last. (st. 4)

Jesus Christ, My Sure Defense

LSB 741

Jesus Christ, my sure defense
 And my Savior, now is living!
Knowing this, my confidence
 Rests upon the hope here given,
Though the night of death be fraught
Still with many an anxious thought. (st. 1)

Then take comfort and rejoice,
 For His members Christ will cherish.
Fear not, they will hear His voice;
 Dying, they will never perish;
For the very grave is stirred
When the trumpet's blast is heard. (st. 6)

Laugh to scorn the gloomy grave
 And at death no longer tremble;
He, the Lord, who came to save
 Will at last His own assemble.
They will go their Lord to meet,
Treading death beneath their feet. (st. 7)

ADDITIONAL HYMNS

Awake, My Heart, with Gladness	*LSB 467:6*
He's Risen, He's Risen	*LSB 480:4*
I Know That My Redeemer Lives	*LSB 461:1, 5, 8*
Jesus Lives! The Victory's Won	*LSB 490:1, 5*
This Body in the Grave We Lay	*LSB 759*

For Those Whose Grief Is Persistent

While grief and sorrow are expected reactions to death, persistent and consuming grief obscures the hope of the Gospel. While the cemetery is a place for recalling memories of loved ones, Christ gives us another place to go—His Word and Supper, which offer more than memories. Through the Good News of Jesus' victory over death, the Spirit draws us to the Lord's sanctuary where there is communion with Him and one another in Christ, and also with those who have gone before us in the faith.

PSALMODY
Psalm 118:5, 8–9, 13–17   *I shall not die, but I shall live*

⁵ Out of my distress I called | on the LORD;*
    the LORD answered me and | set me free.
⁸ It is better to take refuge | in the LORD*
    than to | trust in man.
⁹ It is better to take refuge | in the LORD*
    than to trust in | princes.
¹³ I was pushed hard, so that I was | falling,*
    but the LORD | helped me.
¹⁴ The LORD is my strength | and my song;*
    he has become my sal- | vation.
¹⁵ Glad songs of salvation are in the tents of the | righteous:*
    "The right hand of the LORD does | valiantly,
¹⁶ the right hand of the | LORD exalts,*
    the right hand of the LORD does | valiantly!"
¹⁷ I shall not die, but | I shall live,*
    and recount the deeds | of the LORD.

Psalm 13 *I have trusted in Your steadfast love*

¹ How long, O LORD? Will you forget me for- | ever?*
How long will you hide your | face from me?

² How long must I take counsel in my soul and have sorrow in my
heart | all the day?*
How long shall my enemy be exalted | over me?

³ Consider and answer me, O | LORD my God;*
light up my eyes, lest I sleep the | sleep of death,

⁴ lest my enemy say, "I have prevailed | over him,"*
lest my foes rejoice because I am | shaken.

⁵ But I have trusted in your | steadfast love;*
my heart shall rejoice in your sal- | vation.

⁶ I will sing | to the LORD,*
because he has dealt bountifully | with me.

ADDITIONAL PSALMODY

Psalm 34:1–9, 15, 17–20, 22	*When the righteous cry, the Lord hears*
Psalm 77	*I cry aloud to God, and He will hear me*
Psalm 90	*The Lord has saved us. Save us again.*
Psalm 102:1–7, 11–13, 16–17	*He regards the prayer of the destitute*
Psalm 116	*When I was brought low, He saved me*
Psalm 130	*Lord, hear my cry for mercy*
Psalm 143:1–2, 6–8, 11	*Answer me quickly, O Lord*
Psalm 145:1–14	*Great is the Lord*

READINGS

John 5:24–29 *The dead will hear and live*

²⁴Truly, truly, I say to you, whoever hears my word and believes him
who sent me has eternal life. He does not come into judgment, but
has passed from death to life.

²⁵Truly, truly, I say to you, an hour is coming, and is now here,
when the dead will hear the voice of the Son of God, and those who
hear will live. ²⁶For as the Father has life in himself, so he has granted

the Son also to have life in himself. ^{27}And he has given him authority to execute judgment, because he is the Son of Man. ^{28}Do not marvel at this, for an hour is coming when all who are in the tombs will hear his voice ^{29}and come out, those who have done good to the resurrection of life, and those who have done evil to the resurrection of judgment.

1 Thessalonians 4:13–18   *We grieve in hope*

^{13}We do not want you to be uninformed, brothers, about those who are asleep, that you may not grieve as others do who have no hope. ^{14}For since we believe that Jesus died and rose again, even so, through Jesus, God will bring with him those who have fallen asleep. ^{15}For this we declare to you by a word from the Lord, that we who are alive, who are left until the coming of the Lord, will not precede those who have fallen asleep. ^{16}For the Lord himself will descend from heaven with a cry of command, with the voice of an archangel, and with the sound of the trumpet of God. And the dead in Christ will rise first. ^{17}Then we who are alive, who are left, will be caught up together with them in the clouds to meet the Lord in the air, and so we will always be with the Lord. ^{18}Therefore encourage one another with these words.

1 Peter 5:6–11   *Cast all your anxieties on Him*

^{6}Humble yourselves, therefore, under the mighty hand of God so that at the proper time he may exalt you, ^{7}casting all your anxieties on him, because he cares for you. ^{8}Be sober-minded; be watchful. Your adversary the devil prowls around like a roaring lion, seeking someone to devour. ^{9}Resist him, firm in your faith, knowing that the same kinds of suffering are being experienced by your brotherhood throughout the world. ^{10}And after you have suffered a little while, the God of all grace, who has called you to his eternal glory in Christ, will himself restore, confirm, strengthen, and establish you. ^{11}To him be the dominion forever and ever. Amen.

ADDITIONAL READINGS

Job 42:1–6	*God's purposes are supreme*
Eccl. 3:1–8	*A time for everything*
Is. 35:3–10	*God saves those with an anxious heart*
Matt. 11:25–30	*Jesus promises rest to the heavy-laden*
1 Cor. 15:20–26	*In Christ shall all be made alive*
1 Cor. 15:51–58	*We shall all be changed*
1 Peter 1:3–9	*For a little while you have been grieved*
Rev. 7:9–17	*Standing before the Lamb*
Rev. 21:9–10, 22—22:7	*The new Jerusalem*

PRAYERS

For the survivors of a deceased Christian

Heavenly Father, You would not have us grieve as those who have no hope but, rather, You call us to live in the confidence that all who die in faith are with You in everlasting life and eternal peace. By Your Word and Spirit, strengthen _ name _ in the knowledge that _ his/her _ loved one is at home in Your heavenly kingdom. Give _ him/her _ the courage to walk by faith until that day when all who belong to You will be reunited around the throne of the Lamb, who lives and reigns with You and the Holy Spirit, one God, now and forever. (780)

For comfort in sorrow

Almighty God, heavenly Father, Your judgments are mysterious and Your ways beyond our understanding. By the grace of Your Holy Spirit, show us Your loving purpose in all things. Have mercy on _ name of mourner _, who continues to mourn the death of _ name of deceased _. Strengthen _ name of mourner's _ faith, and ease _ his/her _ distress that _ he/she _ may abide in Your peace; through Jesus Christ, Your Son, our Lord, who lives and reigns with You and the Holy Spirit, one God, now and forever. (781)

Anniversary of a death

Almighty and everlasting God, in Your glorious presence live all who depart in the Lord. Receive our thanks for Your loving-kindness shown to _name of deceased_ , who has finished _his/her_ course in the faith and who rests from _his/her_ labors. Mercifully grant that _name of mourner(s)_ and all who mourn may persevere in running the race set before us, until we are finally gathered with all Your faithful people in eternal glory; through Jesus Christ, Your Son, our Lord, who lives and reigns with You and the Holy Spirit, one God, now and forever. (782)

HYMNS

The Will of God Is Always Best

LSB 758

The will of God is always best
    And shall be done forever;
And they who trust in Him are blest;
    He will forsake them never.
        He helps indeed
        In time of need;
He chastens with forbearing.
        They who depend
        On God, their friend,
Shall not be left despairing. (st. 1)

When life's brief course on earth is run
    And I this world am leaving,
Grant me to say, "Your will be done,"
    Your faithful Word believing.
        My dearest Friend,
        I now commend
My soul into Your keeping;
        From sin and hell,
        And death as well,
By You the vict'ry reaping. (st. 4)

Across the Sky the Shades of Night

LSB 899

We now remember, as we pray,
  Our dear ones in Your caring
Who brightly shine in endless day,
  Past death and all despairing.
At our life's end, Lord, as Your own,
Bring us with them around Your throne,
  The joys of heaven sharing. (st. 4)

ADDITIONAL HYMNS

Be Still, My Soul	LSB 752:3–4
There Is a Time for Everything	LSB 762
What God Ordains Is Always Good	LSB 760:1, 4–5
When Aimless Violence Takes Those We Love	LSB 764
Who Are You Who Walk in Sorrow	LSB 476

Sudden or Accidental Death

When ministering to those shocked by the sudden death of a loved one, the pastor's very presence and readiness to listen may bring a measure of comfort. He will avoid offering explanations for unanswerable questions. Ultimately, it is the Word of God that brings Christ to them, bestowing on them the peace that passes all understanding.

PSALMODY
Psalm 18:1–6

The Lord is my rock and my fortress

¹ I | love you,*
   O | Lord, my strength.
² The Lord is my rock and my fortress and my de- | liverer,*
   my God, my rock, in whom I take refuge, my shield, and the horn of my salvation, my | stronghold.
³ I call upon the Lord, who is worthy | to be praised,*
   and I am saved from my | enemies.
⁴ The cords of death en- | compassed me;*
   the torrents of destruction as- | sailed me;
⁵ the cords of Sheol en- | tangled me;*
   the snares of death con- | fronted me.
⁶ In my distress I called upon the Lord; to my God I | cried for help.*
   From his temple he heard my voice, and my cry to him | reached his ears.

Psalm 130

Out of the depths I cry to You

¹ Out | of the depths*
   I cry to you, | O Lord!
² O Lord, | hear my voice!*
   Let your ears be attentive to the voice of my pleas for | mercy!
³ If you, O Lord, should mark in- | iquities,*
   O Lord, | who could stand?

▶

4 But with you there is for- | giveness,*
    that you | may be feared.
5 I wait for the LORD, my | soul waits,*
    and in his | word I hope;
6 my soul waits for the Lord more than watchmen for the | morning,*
    more than watchmen for the | morning.
7 O Israel, hope in the LORD! For with the LORD there is | steadfast love,*
    and with him is plentiful re- | demption.
8 And he will redeem | Israel*
    from all his in- | iquities.

ADDITIONAL PSALMODY

Psalm 23   *The Lord is my shepherd*
Psalm 46:1–5, 10–11   *God is our refuge and strength*
Psalm 57:1–3   *I take refuge in God, for He will save me*
Psalm 116:1–6, 10, 15   *When I was brought low, He saved me*

READINGS

Lamentations 3:22–26, 31–33   *The love of the Lord never ceases*

22 The steadfast love of the LORD never ceases;
    his mercies never come to an end;
23 they are new every morning;
    great is your faithfulness.
24 "The LORD is my portion," says my soul,
    "therefore I will hope in him."
25 The LORD is good to those who wait for him,
    to the soul who seeks him.
26 It is good that one should wait quietly
    for the salvation of the LORD.
31 For the LORD will not
    cast off forever,

³² but, though he cause grief, he will have compassion
according to the abundance of his steadfast love;
³³ for he does not willingly afflict
or grieve the children of men.

John 11:20–27 *Lord, if You had been here*

²⁰When Martha heard that Jesus was coming, she went and met him, but Mary remained seated in the house. ²¹Martha said to Jesus, "Lord, if you had been here, my brother would not have died. ²²But even now I know that whatever you ask from God, God will give you." ²³Jesus said to her, "Your brother will rise again." ²⁴Martha said to him, "I know that he will rise again in the resurrection on the last day." ²⁵Jesus said to her, "I am the resurrection and the life. Whoever believes in me, though he die, yet shall he live, ²⁶and everyone who lives and believes in me shall never die. Do you believe this?" ²⁷She said to him, "Yes, Lord; I believe that you are the Christ, the Son of God, who is coming into the world."

Philippians 4:6–7 *Let your requests be known to God*

⁶Do not be anxious about anything, but in everything by prayer and supplication with thanksgiving let your requests be made known to God. ⁷And the peace of God, which surpasses all understanding, will guard your hearts and your minds in Christ Jesus.

ADDITIONAL READINGS

Mark 16:1–7 *Christ is risen*
John 10:14–15, 27–30 *His sheep will never perish*
Rom. 8:28–35, 37–39 *Nothing can separate us*
2 Cor. 1:3–4 *Blessed be the God of all comfort*
2 Cor. 4:7–12 *We carry in our bodies the death of Jesus*

PRAYERS

Lord God, heavenly Father, You promise that nothing shall separate us from Your love, which is in Christ Jesus, our Lord. Comfort the members of this family and all who mourn the sudden death of __name__. Grant that we may ever be prepared for Your final summons when we will depart and be with Christ in blessedness and glory; through Jesus Christ, Your Son, our Lord, who lives and reigns with You and the Holy Spirit, one God, now and forever. (783)

Merciful God and Father, graciously look upon the family of our departed __brother/sister__ __name__. Remember us in all our sorrow and grief. Support us when we are unable to understand the things that happen to us and those we love. Comfort and console us, and grant that through Your merciful help we may have courage to face the days ahead; through Jesus Christ, Your Son, our Lord, who lives and reigns with You and the Holy Spirit, one God, now and forever. (784)

HYMNS

What God Ordains Is Always Good
LSB 760

What God ordains is always good:
    His will is just and holy.
As He directs my life for me,
    I follow meek and lowly.
        My God indeed
        In ev'ry need
Knows well how He will shield me;
To Him, then, I will yield me. (st. 1)

What God ordains is always good:
    This truth remains unshaken.
Though sorrow, need, or death be mine,
    I shall not be forsaken.

I fear no harm,
    For with His arm
He shall embrace and shield me;
So to my God I yield me. (st. 6)

Awake, My Heart, with Gladness   *LSB 467*

Now I will cling forever
    To Christ, my Savior true;
My Lord will leave me never,
    Whate'er He passes through.
He rends death's iron chain;
He breaks through sin and pain;
    He shatters hell's grim thrall;
    I follow Him through all. (st. 6)

ADDITIONAL HYMNS

Be Still, My Soul   *LSB 752:1–3*
Entrust Your Days and Burdens   *LSB 754:3–4*
The Will of God Is Always Best   *LSB 758:1, 3–4*
When Aimless Violence Takes Those We Love   *LSB 764*

Suicide

Suicide challenges the pastor to speak evangelically without offering false hope. Suicide is a sin for which Christ died. In the face of things that cannot be understood, the pastor will direct survivors to the sure promises of God in Christ Jesus, encouraging them to walk by faith, not sight.

PSALMODY

Psalm 34:17–20, 22   *The Lord is near to the brokenhearted*

¹⁷ When the righteous cry for help, the | Lord hears*
     and delivers them out of all their | troubles.
¹⁸ The Lord is near to the broken- | hearted*
     and saves the crushed in | spirit.
¹⁹ Many are the afflictions of the | righteous,*
     but the Lord delivers him out | of them all.
²⁰ He keeps | all his bones;*
     not one of them is | broken.
²² The Lord redeems the life of his | servants;*
     none of those who take refuge in him will | be condemned.

Psalm 23   *I will fear no evil, for You are with me*

¹ The Lord is my | shepherd;*
     I | shall not want.
² He makes me lie down in green | pastures.*
     He leads me beside still | waters.
³ He re- | stores my soul.*
     He leads me in paths of righteousness for his | name's sake.
⁴ Even though I walk through the valley of the shadow of death,
     I will fear no evil, for you are | with me;*
     your rod and your staff, they | comfort me.
⁵ You prepare a table before me in the presence of my | enemies;*
     you anoint my head with oil; my cup | overflows.

⁶ Surely goodness and mercy shall follow me all the days | of my life,*
and I shall dwell in the house of the LORD for- | ever.

ADDITIONAL PSALMODY

Psalm 46:1–5, 10–11 — *God is our refuge and strength*
Psalm 90:12–17 — *Teach us to number our days*
Psalm 103:8, 10–14 — *The Lord is merciful and gracious*

READINGS

John 6:37–40 — *The will of God is to save*

³⁷All that the Father gives me will come to me, and whoever comes
to me I will never cast out. ³⁸For I have come down from heaven, not
to do my own will but the will of him who sent me. ³⁹And this is the
will of him who sent me, that I should lose nothing of all that he has
given me, but raise it up on the last day. ⁴⁰For this is the will of my
Father, that everyone who looks on the Son and believes in him
should have eternal life, and I will raise him up on the last day.

2 Corinthians 1:3–4 — *God comforts us in all our afflictions*

³Blessed be the God and Father of our Lord Jesus Christ, the Father
of mercies and God of all comfort, ⁴who comforts us in all our affliction, so that we may be able to comfort those who are in any affliction, with the comfort with which we ourselves are comforted by God.

ADDITIONAL READINGS

Is. 41:8–11, 13 — *Fear not, I am the one who helps you*
John 10:27–29 — *No one can snatch them out of My hand*
Rom. 8:26–28, 38–39 — *Nothing can separate us from God's love*
Rom. 14:7–9 — *Whether we live or die, we are the Lord's*
2 Cor. 4:6–11 — *We are afflicted, but not crushed*

PRAYERS

Merciful Father, our life and salvation rest in Your grace alone. Your strength is made perfect in our weakness. Apart from Your love in Christ we cannot stand against the attacks of the evil one. We are troubled, but not crushed; sometimes in doubt, but never in despair; dejected, but not destroyed. In these dark hours strengthen us by Your Word and Sacrament. Grant us Your abiding presence in the midst of what we cannot understand. Take into Your care _names of survivors_ , whose hearts are heavy with sorrow and grief. Lead them to look to You for confidence and strength as they face the future. Sustain them with Your comforting love, and finally receive us all into Your eternal glory, where You will wipe all tears from our eyes; through Jesus Christ, our only mediator and redeemer, who lives and reigns with You and the Holy Spirit, one God, now and forever. (277 alt.)

Father of mercies and God of all comfort, be with the family of _name_ who has died by _his/her_ own hand. Graciously comfort them in their grief and surround them with Your unfailing love that by Your Word and Spirit they may be strengthened and preserved in the true faith; through Jesus Christ, Your Son, our Lord, who lives and reigns with You and the Holy Spirit, one God, now and forever. (278 alt.)

HYMNS

I Walk in Danger All the Way
LSB 716

I walk with Jesus all the way,
    His guidance never fails me;
Within His wounds I find a stay
    When Satan's pow'r assails me;
And by His footsteps led,
My path I safely tread.
    No evil leads my soul astray;
    I walk with Jesus all the way. (st. 5)

270

O God, Forsake Me Not
LSB 731

O God, forsake me not!
    Your gracious presence lend me;
Lord, lead Your helpless child;
    Your Holy Spirit send me
That I my course may run.
    O be my light, my lot,
My staff, my rock, my shield—
    O God, forsake me not! (st. 1)

O God, forsake me not!
    Lord, hear my supplication!
In ev'ry evil hour
    Help me resist temptation;
And when the prince of hell
    My conscience seeks to blot,
Be then not far from me—
    O God, forsake me not! (st. 3)

Lamb of God, Pure and Holy
LSB 434

Lamb of God, pure and holy,
    Who on the cross didst suffer,
Ever patient and lowly,
    Thyself to scorn didst offer.
All sins Thou borest for us,
Else had despair reigned o'er us:
    Thy peace be with us, O Jesus! O Jesus! (st. 3)

ADDITIONAL HYMNS

In the Cross of Christ I Glory   *LSB 427:1–2*
Jesus, Refuge of the Weary   *LSB 423:1*
My Hope Is Built on Nothing Less   *LSB 575/576:1–2*

Murder

Survivors of a murder victim are confronted with the profound grief that accompanies a tragic death as well as the temptation to harbor vengefulness and hatred toward the murderer. Recognizing that retribution belongs to the authorities that God has put in place to punish evildoers, the pastor will direct the mourners to Christ, who came to destroy the works of the devil by His innocent suffering and death. In His cross and resurrection alone is there comfort, peace, and security for those whose lives have been scarred by the murder of a loved one.

When a murder has occurred in a home, the rite for the Blessing of a Home (pages 148–158) may be used.

PSALMODY

Psalm 37:7–15, 39–40   *Refrain from anger; wait for the Lord*

⁷ Be still before the LORD and wait patiently | for him;*
   fret not yourself over the one who prospers in his way, over the man who carries out evil de- | vices!

⁸ Refrain from anger, and for- | sake wrath!*
   Fret not yourself; it tends only to | evil.

⁹ For the evildoers shall be | cut off,*
   but those who wait for the LORD shall inher- | it the land.

¹⁰ In just a little while, the wicked will | be no more;*
   though you look carefully at his place, he will | not be there.

¹¹ But the meek shall inher- | it the land*
   and delight themselves in a- | bundant peace.

¹² The wicked plots against the | righteous*
   and gnashes his | teeth at him,

¹³ but the Lord laughs at the | wicked,*
   for he sees that his day is | coming.

¹⁴ The wicked draw the sword and | bend their bows*
   to bring down the poor and needy, to slay those whose way is | upright;

¹⁵ their sword shall enter | their own heart,*
    and their bows shall be | broken.
³⁹ The salvation of the righteous is | from the LORD;*
    he is their stronghold in the time of | trouble.
⁴⁰ The LORD helps them and de- | livers them;*
    he delivers them from the wicked and saves them, because
    they take ref- | uge in him.

Psalm 140   *The Lord delivers us from the evil man*

¹ Deliver me, O LORD, from | evil men;*
    preserve me from | violent men,
² who plan evil things | in their heart*
    and stir up wars con- | tinually.
³ They make their tongue sharp as a | serpent's,*
    and under their lips is the ven- | om of asps.
⁴ Guard me, O LORD, from the hands of the wicked; preserve me
  from | violent men,*
    who have planned to trip | up my feet.
⁵ The arrogant have hidden a trap for me, and with cords they
  have | spread a net;*
    beside the way they have set | snares for me.
⁶ I say to the LORD, You | are my God;*
    give ear to the voice of my pleas for mercy, | O LORD!
⁷ O LORD, my Lord, the strength of my sal- | vation,*
    you have covered my head in the day of | battle.
⁸ Grant not, O LORD, the desires of the | wicked;*
    do not further their evil plot or they will be ex- | alted!
⁹ As for the head of those who sur- | round me,*
    let the mischief of their lips over- | whelm them!
¹⁰ Let burning coals fall up- | on them!*
    Let them be cast into fire, into miry pits, no | more to rise!
¹¹ Let not the slanderer be established | in the land;*
    let evil hunt down the violent man | speedily!   ►

¹² I know that the LORD will maintain the cause of the af- | flicted,*
   and will execute justice for the | needy.
¹³ Surely the righteous shall give thanks | to your name;*
   the upright shall dwell in your | presence.

ADDITIONAL PSALMODY

Psalm 23   *The Lord is my shepherd*
Psalm 143:7–11   *Answer me quickly, O Lord*
Psalm 145:18–20   *The Lord preserves all who love Him*

READINGS
John 10:14–15, 27–30   *My sheep will never perish*

¹⁴[Jesus said:] "I am the good shepherd. I know my own and my own
know me, ¹⁵just as the Father knows me and I know the Father; and
I lay down my life for the sheep.

²⁷"My sheep hear my voice, and I know them, and they follow
me. ²⁸I give them eternal life, and they will never perish, and no one
will snatch them out of my hand. ²⁹My Father, who has given them
to me, is greater than all, and no one is able to snatch them out of the
Father's hand. ³⁰I and the Father are one."

Luke 23:33–46   *Jesus' crucifixion: Father, forgive them*

³³When they came to the place that is called The Skull, there they crucified [Jesus], and the criminals, one on his right and one on his left.
³⁴And Jesus said, "Father, forgive them, for they know not what they
do." And they cast lots to divide his garments. ³⁵And the people stood
by, watching, but the rulers scoffed at him, saying, "He saved others;
let him save himself, if he is the Christ of God, his Chosen One!" ³⁶The
soldiers also mocked him, coming up and offering him sour wine ³⁷and
saying, "If you are the King of the Jews, save yourself!" ³⁸There was
also an inscription over him, "This is the King of the Jews."

³⁹One of the criminals who were hanged railed at him, saying,

"Are you not the Christ? Save yourself and us!" ⁴⁰But the other rebuked him, saying, "Do you not fear God, since you are under the same sentence of condemnation? ⁴¹And we indeed justly, for we are receiving the due reward of our deeds; but this man has done nothing wrong." ⁴²And he said, "Jesus, remember me when you come into your kingdom." ⁴³And he said to him, "Truly, I say to you, today you will be with me in Paradise."

⁴⁴It was now about the sixth hour, and there was darkness over the whole land until the ninth hour, ⁴⁵while the sun's light failed. And the curtain of the temple was torn in two. ⁴⁶Then Jesus, calling out with a loud voice, said, "Father, into your hands I commit my spirit!" And having said this he breathed his last.

ADDITIONAL READINGS

Rom. 5:1–5	*By faith we have access into God's grace*
Rom. 8:31–39	*Nothing can separate us from God's love*
Rom. 12:17–19	*Do not avenge yourselves, but leave it to God*
Rom. 13:1–4	*God has established the authorities*
2 Cor. 5:1–10	*We have a building from God*

PRAYERS

Almighty God, merciful Lord, be gracious to the family of _ name _, whose life has been tragically ended and who is now at rest with You. Comfort them in their grief, deliver them from anger, and sustain them with the knowledge that they are upheld by Your everlasting arms. Grant them Your Holy Spirit that they may meet the days to come with steadfastness and patience, and with the hope of the glorious resurrection and a blessed reunion in heaven with those they love who have departed in the faith; through Jesus Christ, Your Son, our Lord, who lives and reigns with You and the Holy Spirit, one God, now and forever. (785)

Almighty God, grant comfort to the family of __name__ as they mourn
__his/her__ death. Since You are judge over all, guide the civil authorities charged with the investigation of this crime that the evidence
may be carefully considered and those responsible be brought to justice. Give the family patience in their waiting, and lead them to forgive, even as You have so graciously forgiven us; through Jesus
Christ, Your Son, our Lord, who lives and reigns with You and the
Holy Spirit, one God, now and forever. (786)

HYMNS

When Aimless Violence Takes Those We Love   LSB 764

When aimless violence takes those we love,
    When random death strikes childhood's promise down,
When wrenching loss becomes our daily bread,
    We know, O God, You leave us not alone. (st. 1)

Because Your Son knew agony and loss,
    Felt desolation, grief and scorn and shame,
We know You will be with us, come what may,
    Your loving presence near, always the same. (st. 4)

Through long grief-darkened days help us, dear Lord,
    To trust Your grace for courage to endure,
To rest our souls in Your supporting love,
    And find our hope within Your mercy sure. (st. 5)

Joy F. Patterson
© *1994, 1997 Hope Publishing Co.*

In the Very Midst of Life   LSB 755

In the midst of death's dark vale
    Pow'rs of hell o'ertake us.
Who will help when they assail,
    Who secure will make us?
        Thou only, Lord, Thou only!

Thy heart is moved with tenderness,
Pities us in our distress.
> Holy and righteous God!
> Holy and mighty God!
> Holy and all-merciful Savior!
> Eternal Lord God!
Save us from the terror
Of the fiery pit of hell.
> Have mercy, O Lord! (st. 2)

ADDITIONAL HYMNS

Christ Jesus Lay in Death's Strong Bands	*LSB 458:2–4*
Jesus, in Your Dying Woes	*LSB 447:1–3*
O Dearest Jesus, What Law Hast Thou Broken	*LSB 439:1–2, 4*

TIMES OF SPIRITUAL DISTRESS

Anxiety, Apprehension, Fear

God's people are often confronted by a variety of issues and circumstances that lead to feelings of fear and anxiety. The cause of these fears is ultimately rooted in a lack of trust in God's gracious ordering of the universe for the well-being of His people. The pastor will be careful to proclaim the trust-worthy promises of God that nothing will separate us from His love in Christ Jesus.

PSALMODY

Psalm 4   *The Lord alone makes me dwell in safety*

¹ Answer me when I call, O God of my righteousness! You have given me relief when I was | in distress.*
    Be gracious to me and | hear my prayer!
² O men, how long shall my honor be turned | into shame?*
    How long will you love vain words and seek | after lies?
³ But know that the LORD has set apart the godly | for himself;*
    the LORD hears when I | call to him.
⁴ Be angry, and | do not sin;*
    ponder in your own hearts on your beds, and be | silent.
⁵ Offer right sacri- | fices,*
    and put your trust | in the LORD.
⁶ There are many who say, "Who will show | us some good?*
    Lift up the light of your face upon us, | O LORD!"

7 You have put more joy | in my heart*
    than they have when their grain and | wine abound.
8 In peace I will both lie | down and sleep;*
    for you alone, O LORD, make me dwell in | safety.

Psalm 34:4–9, 19, 22   *The Lord delivers from all afflictions*

4 I sought the LORD, and he | answered me*
    and delivered me from | all my fears.
5 Those who look to him are | radiant,*
    and their faces shall never | be ashamed.
6 This poor man cried, and the LORD | heard him*
    and saved him out of all his | troubles.
7 The angel of the LORD encamps around those who | fear him,*
    and de- | livers them.
8 Oh, taste and see that the | LORD is good!*
    Blessèd is the man who takes ref- | uge in him!
9 Oh, fear the LORD, | you his saints,*
    for those who fear him | have no lack!
19 Many are the afflictions of the | righteous,*
    but the LORD delivers him out | of them all.
22 The LORD redeems the life of his | servants;*
    none of those who take refuge in him will | be condemned.

Psalm 118:5–9, 13–14   *It is better to take refuge in the Lord*

5 Out of my distress I called | on the LORD;*
    the LORD answered me and | set me free.
6 The LORD is on my side; I | will not fear.*
    What can man | do to me?
7 The LORD is on my side as my | helper;*
    I shall look in triumph on those who | hate me.
8 It is better to take refuge | in the LORD*
    than to | trust in man.

▶

279

⁹ It is better to take refuge | in the LORD*
　　than to trust in | princes.
¹³ I was pushed hard, so that I was | falling,*
　　but the LORD | helped me.
¹⁴ The LORD is my strength | and my song;*
　　he has become my sal- | vation.

Psalm 27:1 *The Lord is my light and my salvation*

¹ The LORD is my light and my salvation; whom | shall I fear?*
　　The LORD is the stronghold of my life; of whom shall I | be
　　afraid?

ADDITIONAL PSALMODY

Psalm 23	*I will fear no evil, for You are with me*
Psalm 27:1–5, 14	*The Lord is my light and my salvation*
Psalm 46:1–3, 10–11	*God is our refuge and strength*
Psalm 56:3–4, 10–13	*In God I trust; I shall not be afraid*
Psalm 91	*The Lord, my refuge and my fortress*
Psalm 94:14, 17–19, 22	*The Lord cheers my soul*

READINGS
Matthew 6:25–34 *Seek first the kingdom of God*

²⁵[Jesus said:] "Do not be anxious about your life, what you will eat or what you will drink, nor about your body, what you will put on. Is not life more than food, and the body more than clothing? ²⁶Look at the birds of the air: they neither sow nor reap nor gather into barns, and yet your heavenly Father feeds them. Are you not of more value than they? ²⁷And which of you by being anxious can add a single hour to his span of life? ²⁸And why are you anxious about clothing? Consider the lilies of the field, how they grow: they neither toil nor spin, ²⁹yet I tell you, even Solomon in all his glory was not arrayed like one of these. ³⁰But if God so clothes the grass of the field, which today is alive and to-morrow is thrown into the oven, will he not much more clothe you, O

ANXIETY, APPREHENSION, FEAR

you of little faith? ³¹Therefore do not be anxious, saying, 'What shall we eat?' or 'What shall we drink?' or 'What shall we wear?' ³²For the Gentiles seek after all these things, and your heavenly Father knows that you need them all. ³³But seek first the kingdom of God and his righteousness, and all these things will be added to you.

³⁴"Therefore do not be anxious about tomorrow, for tomorrow will be anxious for itself. Sufficient for the day is its own trouble."

Romans 8:28–39   *If God is for us, who can be against us?*

²⁸We know that for those who love God all things work together for good, for those who are called according to his purpose. ²⁹For those whom he foreknew he also predestined to be conformed to the image of his Son, in order that he might be the firstborn among many brothers. ³⁰And those whom he predestined he also called, and those whom he called he also justified, and those whom he justified he also glorified.

³¹What then shall we say to these things? If God is for us, who can be against us? ³²He who did not spare his own Son but gave him up for us all, how will he not also with him graciously give us all things? ³³Who shall bring any charge against God's elect? It is God who justifies. ³⁴Who is to condemn? Christ Jesus is the one who died—more than that, who was raised—who is at the right hand of God, who indeed is interceding for us. ³⁵Who shall separate us from the love of Christ? Shall tribulation, or distress, or persecution, or famine, or nakedness, or danger, or sword? ³⁶As it is written,

> "For your sake we are being killed all the day long;
>   we are regarded as sheep to be slaughtered."

³⁷No, in all these things we are more than conquerors through him who loved us. ³⁸For I am sure that neither death nor life, nor angels nor rulers, nor things present nor things to come, nor powers, ³⁹nor height nor depth, nor anything else in all creation, will be able to separate us from the love of God in Christ Jesus our Lord.

Mark 4:35–41 *The wind and the waves obey Him*

[35]On that day, when evening had come, [Jesus] said to them, "Let us go across to the other side." [36]And leaving the crowd, they took him with them in the boat, just as he was. And other boats were with him. [37]And a great windstorm arose, and the waves were breaking into the boat, so that the boat was already filling. [38]But he was in the stern, asleep on the cushion. And they woke him and said to him, "Teacher, do you not care that we are perishing?" [39]And he awoke and rebuked the wind and said to the sea, "Peace! Be still!" And the wind ceased, and there was a great calm. [40]He said to them, "Why are you so afraid? Have you still no faith?" [41]And they were filled with great fear and said to one another, "Who then is this, that even wind and sea obey him?"

Philippians 4:4–7 *Let your requests be made known to God*

[4]Rejoice in the Lord always; again I will say, Rejoice. [5]Let your reasonableness be known to everyone. The Lord is at hand; [6]do not be anxious about anything, but in everything by prayer and supplication with thanksgiving let your requests be made known to God. [7]And the peace of God, which surpasses all understanding, will guard your hearts and your minds in Christ Jesus.

ADDITIONAL READINGS

Ex. 14:10–14	*Israel at the Red Sea*
2 Kings 6:8–19	*The Lord sends armies to protect His people*
Prov. 29:25	*Whoever trusts in the Lord is safe*
Is. 35:3–4	*Be strong; fear not*
Is. 41:8–14	*Fear not; I am the one who helps you*
Lam. 3:55–58	*Do not fear*
Dan. 6:16–23	*Daniel in the lions' den*
Matt. 10:26–31	*Do not fear those who kill the body*
Luke 10:38–42	*Jesus at the home of Mary and Martha*
John 14:1–6	*Let not your hearts be troubled*
1 Cor. 7:29–32a	*I want you to be free from anxieties*

Heb. 2:14–18
1 Peter 5:6–7
1 John 4:18

Our brother Christ delivers us
Cast all your anxieties on Him
Perfect love casts out fear

PRAYERS

O most loving Father, You want us to give thanks for all things, to fear nothing except losing You, and to lay all our cares on You, knowing that You care for us. Strengthen _ name _ in _ his/her _ faith in You. Grant that the fears and anxieties of this mortal life may not separate _ him/her _ from Your love shown to us in Jesus Christ, Your Son, our Lord, who lives and reigns with You and the Holy Spirit, one God, now and forever. (787)

Lord Jesus Christ, You commanded the wind and the waves, and they obeyed You. Speak peace to _ name _, who is troubled by fear. By the power of Your Word, calm _ his/her _ anxious heart and the raging storms of _ his/her _ spirit; for You live and reign with the Father and the Holy Spirit, one God, now and forever. (788)

HYMNS

Lord, Take My Hand and Lead Me   *LSB 722*

Lord, when the tempest rages,
 I need not fear,
For You, the Rock of Ages,
 Are always near.
Close by Your side abiding,
 I fear no foe,
For when Your hand is guiding,
 In peace I go. (st. 2)

© 1978 Lutheran Book of Worship

A Mighty Fortress Is Our God
LSB 656

Though devils all the world should fill,
    All eager to devour us,
We tremble not, we fear no ill;
    They shall not overpow'r us.
This world's prince may still
Scowl fierce as he will,
    He can harm us none.
    He's judged; the deed is done;
One little word can fell him. (st. 3)

How Firm a Foundation
LSB 728

"Fear not! I am with you, O be not dismayed,
For I am your God and will still give you aid;
I'll strengthen you, help you, and cause you to stand,
Upheld by My righteous, omnipotent hand." (st. 2)

ADDITIONAL HYMNS

Have No Fear, Little Flock	*LSB 735*
I Know My Faith Is Founded	*LSB 587:2*
Jesus, Savior, Pilot Me	*LSB 715*
On Eagles' Wings	*LSB 727*
Who Trusts in God a Strong Abode	*LSB 714*

Spiritual Doubt and Affliction

A person experiencing doubt and affliction may be asking questions such as:

- Does God love me?
- Why is this happening to me?
- Has God abandoned me?
- Am I saved?

The pastor will recognize that the devil always targets the First Commandment, tempting Christians to forsake the sure promises of God. In his care of such afflicted Christians the pastor will point to Holy Baptism as a sure sign of God's unfailing grace in Christ. He will encourage the continued hearing of God's Word and reception of the Lord's Supper as the means by which God strengthens the struggling Christian to trust His certain promises.

PSALMODY

Psalm 13 *I trust in Your steadfast love*

¹ How long, O Lord? Will you forget me for- | ever?*
　　How long will you hide your | face from me?
² How long must I take counsel in my soul and have sorrow in my heart | all the day?*
　　How long shall my enemy be exalted | over me?
³ Consider and answer me, O | Lord my God;*
　　light up my eyes, lest I sleep the | sleep of death,
⁴ lest my enemy say, "I have prevailed | over him,"*
　　lest my foes rejoice because I am | shaken.
⁵ But I have trusted in your | steadfast love;*
　　my heart shall rejoice in your sal- | vation.
⁶ I will sing | to the Lord,*
　　because he has dealt bountifully | with me.

Psalm 143:1, 7–12   *Make me know the way I should go*

1 Hear my prayer, O LORD; give ear to my pleas for | mercy!*
   In your faithfulness answer me, in your | righteousness!

7 Answer me quickly, O LORD! My | spirit fails!*
   Hide not your face from me, lest I be like those who go
   down | to the pit.

8 Let me hear in the morning of your steadfast love, for in | you
   I trust.*
   Make me know the way I should go, for to you I lift | up my soul.

9 Deliver me from my enemies, | O LORD!*
   I have fled to you for | refuge!

10 Teach me to do your will, for you | are my God!*
   Let your good Spirit lead me on | level ground!

11 For your name's sake, O LORD, pre- | serve my life!*
   In your righteousness bring my soul out of | trouble!

12 And in your steadfast love you will cut off my | enemies,*
   and you will destroy all the adversaries of my soul, for I am
   your | servant.

ADDITIONAL PSALMODY

Psalm 10:12–18	*Why, O Lord, do You stand far off?*
Psalm 38:9–18, 21–22	*Do not forsake me; be not far from me*
Psalm 88	*I cry to You, O Lord*
Psalm 89:49–52	*Lord, where is Your steadfast love?*
Psalm 94:12–19	*The Lord will not forsake His people*
Psalm 119:65–72	*I was afflicted that I may learn*
Psalm 130	*Out of the depths I cry to You, O Lord*

READINGS

John 20:24–31   *The resurrected Lord appears to Thomas*

24Now Thomas, one of the Twelve, called the Twin, was not with
them when Jesus came. 25So the other disciples told him, "We have
seen the Lord." But he said to them, "Unless I see in his hands the

mark of the nails, and place my finger into the mark of the nails, and place my hand into his side, I will never believe."

[26]Eight days later, his disciples were inside again, and Thomas was with them. Although the doors were locked, Jesus came and stood among them and said, "Peace be with you." [27]Then he said to Thomas, "Put your finger here, and see my hands; and put out your hand, and place it in my side. Do not disbelieve, but believe." [28]Thomas answered him, "My Lord and my God!" [29]Jesus said to him, "Have you believed because you have seen me? Blessed are those who have not seen and yet have believed."

[30]Now Jesus did many other signs in the presence of the disciples, which are not written in this book; [31]but these are written so that you may believe that Jesus is the Christ, the Son of God, and that by believing you may have life in his name.

Romans 5:1–5   *Justified by faith, we have peace with God*

[1]Since we have been justified by faith, we have peace with God through our Lord Jesus Christ. [2]Through him we have also obtained access by faith into this grace in which we stand, and we rejoice in hope of the glory of God. [3]More than that, we rejoice in our sufferings, knowing that suffering produces endurance, [4]and endurance produces character, and character produces hope, [5]and hope does not put us to shame, because God's love has been poured into our hearts through the Holy Spirit who has been given to us.

Hebrews 12:1–13   *The Lord fixes our faith on Jesus*

[1]Since we are surrounded by so great a cloud of witnesses, let us also lay aside every weight, and sin which clings so closely, and let us run with endurance the race that is set before us, [2]looking to Jesus, the founder and perfecter of our faith, who for the joy that was set before him endured the cross, despising the shame, and is seated at the right hand of the throne of God.

[3]Consider him who endured from sinners such hostility against ▶

himself, so that you may not grow weary or fainthearted. [4]In your struggle against sin you have not yet resisted to the point of shedding your blood. [5]And have you forgotten the exhortation that addresses you as sons?

> "My son, do not regard lightly the discipline of the Lord,
>   nor be weary when reproved by him.
> [6]For the Lord disciplines the one he loves,
>   and chastises every son whom he receives."

[7]It is for discipline that you have to endure. God is treating you as sons. For what son is there whom his father does not discipline? [8]If you are left without discipline, in which all have participated, then you are illegitimate children and not sons. [9]Besides this, we have had earthly fathers who disciplined us and we respected them. Shall we not much more be subject to the Father of spirits and live? [10]For they disciplined us for a short time as it seemed best to them, but he disciplines us for our good, that we may share his holiness. [11]For the moment all discipline seems painful rather than pleasant, but later it yields the peaceful fruit of righteousness to those who have been trained by it.

[12]Therefore lift your drooping hands and strengthen your weak knees, [13]and make straight paths for your feet, so that what is lame may not be put out of joint but rather be healed.

ADDITIONAL READINGS

Job 5:17–18	*Blessed is the one whom God reproves*
Hos. 6:1–3, 5–6	*He has torn us, that He may heal us*
Matt. 5:10–12	*Blessed are the persecuted*
Matt. 15:21–28	*The Canaanite woman*
2 Cor. 1:3–7	*God comforts us in all our affliction*
2 Cor. 4:7–12	*Afflicted in every way, but not crushed*
2 Cor. 12:7–10	*My grace is sufficient for you*
Heb. 4:14–16	*Our High Priest sympathizes with our weaknesses*
James 1:2–5	*Count it all joy when you meet trials*
1 Peter 1:3–9	*Grieved for a little while*

PRAYERS

Almighty God, heavenly Father, of Your tender love toward us sinners You have given us Your Son that, believing in Him, we may have everlasting life. By Your Spirit comfort _name_ in all _his/her_ troubles, and protect _him/her_ from all doubt so that _he/she_ may remain steadfast in the faith and come at last to life eternal; through Jesus Christ, our Lord, who lives and reigns with You and the Holy Spirit, one God, now and forever. (789)

Almighty God, our heavenly Father, You have given to all who believe exceedingly great and precious promises. Grant Your Holy Spirit to _name_ that _he/she_ may without all doubt trust in Your Son, Jesus Christ, so that _his/her_ faith in Your sight may never be found wanting; through the same Jesus Christ, our Lord, who lives and reigns with You and the Holy Spirit, one God, now and forever. (790)

Almighty and everlasting God, You are the consolation of the sorrowful and the strength of the weak. Hear the prayers of _name_, who is in tribulation and distress, so that in all _his/her_ necessities _he/she_ may mark and receive Your abundant help and comfort; through Jesus Christ, Your Son, our Lord, who lives and reigns with You and the Holy Spirit, one God, now and forever. (791)

HYMNS

Salvation unto Us Has Come

LSB 555

Since Christ has full atonement made
    And brought to us salvation,
Each Christian therefore may be glad
    And build on this foundation.
Your grace alone, dear Lord, I plead,
Your death is now my life indeed,
    For You have paid my ransom.

Let me not doubt, but truly see
　　Your Word cannot be broken;
Your call rings out, "Come unto Me!"
　　No falsehood have You spoken.
Baptized into Your precious name,
My faith cannot be put to shame,
　　And I shall never perish. (sts. 6–7)

I Trust, O Lord, Your Holy Name　　　　*LSB 734*

You are my strength, my shield, my rock,
My fortress that withstands each shock,
　　My help, my life, my tower,
　　　　My battle sword,
　　　　Almighty Lord—
　　Who can resist Your power?

With You, O Lord, I cast my lot;
O faithful God, forsake me not,
　　To You my soul commending.
　　　　Lord, be my stay,
　　　　And lead the way
　　Now and when life is ending. (sts. 3–4)

ADDITIONAL HYMNS

God's Own Child, I Gladly Say It	*LSB 594*
How Firm a Foundation	*LSB 728*
In God, My Faithful God	*LSB 745*
Jesus, Priceless Treasure	*LSB 743*

Loneliness

God created mankind to be in communion with Him and with each other. Though loneliness can take many forms (e.g., being shut-in, moving to a new place, loss of a loved one, self-inflicted loneliness), the pastor will proclaim the good news that Christ is our Immanuel and that in Him we are given life together in the Christian congregation. The pastor will encourage those who are able to seek companionship in that fellowship and will likewise encourage the congregation to provide comfort for the lonely.

PSALMODY

Psalm 68:4–6 *Father of the fatherless and protector of widows*

⁴ Sing to God, sing praises | to his name;*
 lift up a song to him who rides through the deserts; his name
 is the LORD; exult be- | fore him!
⁵ Father of the fatherless and protector of | widows*
 is God in his holy habi- | tation.
⁶ God settles the solitary in a home; he leads out the prisoners to
 pros- | perity,*
 but the rebellious dwell in a | parched land.

Psalm 142 *When my spirit faints, You know my way*

¹ With my voice I cry out | to the LORD;*
 with my voice I plead for mercy | to the LORD.
² I pour out my complaint be- | fore him;*
 I tell my trouble be- | fore him.
³ When my spirit faints within me, you | know my way!*
 In the path where I walk they have hidden a | trap for me.
⁴ Look to the right and see: there is none who takes notice | of me;*
 no refuge remains to me; no one cares | for my soul.
⁵ I cry to you, | O LORD;*
 I say, "You are my refuge, my portion in the land of the | living." ▶

⁶ Attend to my cry, for I am brought | very low!*
   Deliver me from my persecutors, for they are too | strong for me!
⁷ Bring me out of prison, that I may give thanks | to your name!*
   The righteous will surround me, for you will deal
   bountifully | with me.

Psalm 38:1–11, 15, 21–22   *The loneliness of being a sinner*

¹ O LORD, rebuke me not in your | anger,*
   nor discipline me | in your wrath!
² For your arrows have sunk | into me,*
   and your hand has come | down on me.
³ There is no soundness in my flesh because of your indig- | nation;*
   there is no health in my bones because | of my sin.
⁴ For my iniquities have gone o- | ver my head;*
   like a heavy burden, they are too heav- | y for me.
⁵ My wounds stink and | fester*
   because of my | foolishness,
⁶ I am utterly bowed down and | prostrate;*
   all the day I go about | mourning.
⁷ For my sides are filled with | burning,*
   and there is no soundness | in my flesh.
⁸ I am feeble | and crushed;*
   I groan because of the tumult | of my heart.
⁹ O Lord, all my longing is be- | fore you;*
   my sighing is not hid- | den from you.
¹⁰ My heart throbs; my strength | fails me,*
   and the light of my eyes—it also has | gone from me.
¹¹ My friends and companions stand aloof | from my plague,*
   and my nearest kin stand | far off.
¹⁵ But for you, O LORD, | do I wait;*
   it is you, O Lord my God, who will | answer.
²¹ Do not forsake me, | O LORD!*
   O my God, be not | far from me!

²² Make haste to | help me,*
  O Lord, my sal- | vation!

ADDITIONAL PSALMODY

Psalm 16:7–11	*The Lord will not abandon my soul*
Psalm 22:1–5, 19	*Our fathers trusted in You*
Psalm 31:1–3, 9–10, 14–16, 24	*Lord, be my rock and rescue me*
Psalm 73:25–28	*My flesh fails, but God is my strength*
Psalm 88:1–9	*My soul is full of troubles; hear my cry*
Psalm 109:21–31	*Let them curse, but the Lord will bless*
Psalm 139:1–17	*The Lord knows my very heart*

READINGS

Isaiah 49:13–16a   *The Lord will not forget you*

¹³ Sing for joy, O heavens, and exult, O earth;
    break forth, O mountains, into singing!
For the LORD has comforted his people
    and will have compassion on his afflicted.
¹⁴ But Zion said, "The LORD has forsaken me;
    my Lord has forgotten me."
¹⁵ "Can a woman forget her nursing child,
    that she should have no compassion on the son of her womb?
Even these may forget,
    yet I will not forget you.
¹⁶ Behold, I have engraved you on the palms of my hands."

John 14:16–21   *The Lord will not leave you as orphans*

¹⁶[Jesus said:] "I will ask the Father, and he will give you another Helper, to be with you forever, ¹⁷even the Spirit of truth, whom the world cannot receive, because it neither sees him nor knows him. You know him, for he dwells with you and will be in you.

¹⁸"I will not leave you as orphans; I will come to you. ¹⁹Yet a little while and the world will see me no more, but you will see me. ▶

Because I live, you also will live. [20]In that day you will know that I am in my Father, and you in me, and I in you. [21]Whoever has my commandments and keeps them, he it is who loves me. And he who loves me will be loved by my Father, and I will love him and manifest myself to him."

Hebrews 13:5   *Be content; I will never leave you*

[5]Keep your life free from love of money, and be content with what you have, for he has said, "I will never leave you nor forsake you."

ADDITIONAL READINGS

Joshua 1:9	*The Lord is with you wherever you go*
1 Kings 19:9b–18	*The Lord speaks to Elijah*
2 Kings 6:8–17	*God's angels watch over His people*
Is. 46:3–4	*God carries His people throughout their lives*
Mark 15:33–34	*Jesus forsaken by God for us*
Eph. 2:11–13, 19–20	*Members of God's household*
2 Tim. 4:16–18	*Paul deserted by all except the Lord*
Heb. 12:1–2	*Surrounded by a cloud of witnesses*
1 Peter 1:3–9	*God has given us a new birth*

PRAYERS

Almighty God, You set the solitary in families. Look upon _name_ in _his/her_ loneliness. Embrace _him/her_ with Your love that in the midst of _his/her_ pain _he/she_ may know Your abiding presence. Help _him/her_ to see Your love and care in the communion of saints and the company of angels; through Jesus Christ, Your Son, our Lord, who lives and reigns with You and the Holy Spirit, one God, now and forever. (792)

Almighty God, merciful Father, by Word and Sacrament You have created Your Church in this world to be a godly communion and a caring family. Grant Your blessing to those who dwell in loneliness that they may find a place of healthful solace and pleasant fellowship among people faithful to You; through Jesus Christ, Your Son, our Lord, who lives and reigns with You and the Holy Spirit, one God, now and forever. (282)

Lord Jesus, You promise never to leave us or forsake us. Grant that in the midst of *his/her* loneliness *name* may find fulfillment through faith in You and through loving service to *his/her* neighbor; for You live and reign with the Father and the Holy Spirit, one God, now and forever. (880)

HYMNS

Why Should Cross and Trial Grieve Me   *LSB 756*

Why should cross and trial grieve me?
    Christ is near
    With His cheer;
Never will He leave me.
Who can rob me of the heaven
    That God's Son
    For me won
When His life was given? (st. 1)

From God's joy can nothing sever,
    For I am
    His dear lamb,
He, my Shepherd ever.
I am His because He gave me
    His own blood
    For my good,
By His death to save me. (st. 4)

© 2004 Stephen P. Starke
Admin. Concordia Publishing House

The Lord's My Shepherd, I'll Not Want   *LSB 710*

Yea, though I walk in death's dark vale,
    Yet will I fear no ill;
For Thou art with me, and Thy rod
    And staff me comfort still. (st. 3)

ADDITIONAL HYMNS

Hear Us, Father, When We Pray	*LSB 773*
I Am Jesus' Little Lamb	*LSB 740*
If God Himself Be for Me	*LSB 724*
Through Jesus' Blood and Merit	*LSB 746*

Thoughts of Suicide

For many, thoughts of suicide are the result of a profound sense of hopelessness and desperation. While one in such desperation may require the assistance of other professionals, the pastor's work is to proclaim the life and hope that are ours in Jesus Christ. Using the Word of God, the pastor will draw the suicidal person away from a desperate focus on self to fix his or her eyes on Jesus and His righteousness. In Him alone we have the hope that does not disappoint.

PSALMODY
Psalm 22:1–11, 19–26   *My God, why have You forsaken me*

¹ My God, my God, why have you for- | saken me?*
> Why are you so far from saving me, from the words of my | groaning?

² O my God, I cry by day, but you do not | answer,*
> and by night, but I | find no rest.

³ Yet you are | holy,*
> enthroned on the praises of | Israel.

⁴ In you our fathers | trusted;*
> they trusted, and you de- | livered them.

⁵ To you they cried and were | rescued;*
> in you they trusted and were not | put to shame.

⁶ But I am a worm and | not a man,*
        scorned by mankind and despised by the | people.
⁷ All who see me | mock me;*
        they make mouths at me; they | wag their heads;
⁸ "He trusts in the LORD; let him de- | liver him;*
        let him rescue him, for he de- | lights in him!"
⁹ Yet you are he who took me | from the womb;*
        you made me trust you at my | mother's breasts.
¹⁰ On you was I cast | from my birth,*
        and from my mother's womb you have | been my God.
¹¹ Be not far from me, for trouble | is near,*
        and there is | none to help.
¹⁹ But you, O LORD, do not be | far off!*
        O you my help, come quickly | to my aid!
²⁰ Deliver my soul | from the sword,*
        my precious life from the power | of the dog!
²¹ Save me from the mouth of the | lion!*
        You have rescued me from the horns of the wild | oxen!
²² I will tell of your name to my | brothers;*
        in the midst of the congregation I will | praise you:
²³ You who fear the LORD, praise him! All you offspring of Jacob,
        glo- | rify him,*
        and stand in awe of him, all you offspring of | Israel!
²⁴ For he has not despised or abhorred the affliction of the afflicted,
        and he has not hidden his | face from him,*
        but has heard, when he | cried to him.
²⁵ From you comes my praise in the great congre- | gation;*
        my vows I will perform before those who | fear him.
²⁶ The afflicted shall eat and be satisfied; those who seek him
        shall | praise the LORD!*
        May your hearts live for- | ever!

Psalm 54

Lord, save me by Your name

¹ O God, save me, | by your name,*
    and vindicate me | by your might.
² O God, | hear my prayer;*
    give ear to the words | of my mouth.
³ For strangers have risen against me; ruthless men | seek my life;*
    they do not set God be- | fore themselves.
⁴ Behold, God is my | helper;*
    the Lord is the upholder | of my life.
⁵ He will return the evil to my | enemies;*
    in your faithfulness put an | end to them.
⁶ With a freewill offering I will sacri- | fice to you;*
    I will give thanks to your name, O Lord, for | it is good.
⁷ For he has delivered me from every | trouble,*
    and my eye has looked in triumph on my | enemies.

ADDITIONAL PSALMODY

Psalm 18:1–6, 46–50	*I called to God in my distress, and He heard me*
Psalm 23	*I will not fear darkness, for He is with me*
Psalm 31:1–4, 10, 14, 24	*Hear me, O Lord, for my strength fails*
Psalm 32:1–7	*Acknowledge your sin, and the Lord forgives*
Psalm 43	*Why are you cast down, O my soul?*
Psalm 55:1–8, 16–18	*I call to God, and He will save me*
Psalm 71:1–6, 14, 19–20	*You will revive me again from the depths*
Psalm 121	*The Lord will keep you forever*
Psalm 124	*Our help is in the name of the Lord*
Psalm 130	*Out of the depths I cry to the Lord*
Psalm 139:1–18	*The Lord has made me and knows me*

READINGS

Hebrews 13:5b–6

I will never leave you

⁵ᵇ"I will never leave you nor forsake you." ⁶So we can confidently
say,

298

"The Lord is my helper;
    I will not fear;
what can man do to me?"

John 10:10b–15, 27–30 *The good shepherd protects His sheep*

10b[Jesus said:] "I came that they may have life and have it abundantly. 11I am the good shepherd. The good shepherd lays down his life for the sheep. 12He who is a hired hand and not a shepherd, who does not own the sheep, sees the wolf coming and leaves the sheep and flees, and the wolf snatches them and scatters them. 13He flees because he is a hired hand and cares nothing for the sheep. 14I am the good shepherd. I know my own and my own know me, 15just as the Father knows me and I know the Father; and I lay down my life for the sheep.

27"My sheep hear my voice, and I know them, and they follow me. 28I give them eternal life, and they will never perish, and no one will snatch them out of my hand. 29My Father, who has given them to me, is greater than all, and no one is able to snatch them out of the Father's hand. 30I and the Father are one."

1 Corinthians 10:13 *God provides the way of escape*

13No temptation has overtaken you that is not common to man. God is faithful, and he will not let you be tempted beyond your ability, but with the temptation he will also provide the way of escape, that you may be able to endure it.

ADDITIONAL READINGS

Job 19:20–27	*I know that my Redeemer lives*
Prov. 3:5–8	*Trust in the Lord, not your own understanding*
Is. 43:1–3a	*Fear not, you are Mine*
Lam. 3:19, 31–33	*The Lord will have compassion*
John 3:16–17	*God so loved the world*
John 8:10–12	*Whoever follows Jesus has the light of life*
Rom. 8:1, 26–39	*The Spirit helps us in our weakness*

Rom. 12:1–2	*Be transformed by the renewal of your mind*
Phil. 4:6–7	*God's peace will guard us*
Phil. 4:8–9	*Think about whatever is true, honorable, just*
Col. 3:1–10	*You have put off the old self and put on the new*
Heb. 4:14–16	*A High Priest who sympathizes with our weakness*
Heb. 12:1–2	*Let us fix our eyes on Jesus*
1 Peter 1:2b–5	*God has given us new birth with a living hope*

PRAYERS

Heavenly Father, be with *name* in *his/her* deep distress and sorrow, and sustain *him/her* by Your Word. Because of what Jesus has done for us upon the cross, forgive *him/her* all *his/her* sins, strengthen *his/her* faith, and grant *him/her* Your deliverance and peace. Renew *him/her* in the knowledge that You are a compassionate God who knows and loves *him/her* . Let Your holy angel be with *him/her* that the evil foe may have no power over *him/her* ; through Jesus Christ, Your Son, our Lord, who lives and reigns with You and the Holy Spirit, one God, now and forever. (793)

Almighty, everlasting God, look down from heaven and behold Your servant *name* , for whom we pray. Look upon *him/her* with the eyes of Your mercy and forgiveness. Give *him/her* comfort and sure confidence in You, defend *him/her* from the danger of the enemy, and keep *him/her* in Your peace and safety; through Jesus Christ, Your Son, our Lord, who lives and reigns with You and the Holy Spirit, one God, now and forever. (794)

Almighty and everlasting God, the consolation of the sorrowful and the strength of the weak, may the prayers of those who in any tribulation or distress cry to You graciously come before You, so that in every situation they may recognize and receive Your gracious help, comfort, and peace; through Jesus Christ, Your Son, our Lord, who lives and reigns with You and the Holy Spirit, one God, now and forever. (280)

HYMNS

Jesus, Priceless Treasure
LSB 743

In Thine arms I rest me;
Foes who would molest me
    Cannot reach me here.
Though the earth be shaking,
Ev'ry heart be quaking,
    Jesus calms my fear.
        Lightnings flash
        And thunders crash;
Yet, though sin and hell assail me,
Jesus will not fail me. (st. 2)

Dear Christians, One and All, Rejoice
LSB 556

Fast bound in Satan's chains I lay;
    Death brooded darkly o'er me.
Sin was my torment night and day;
    In sin my mother bore me.
But daily deeper still I fell;
My life became a living hell,
    So firmly sin possessed me. (st. 2)

But God had seen my wretched state
    Before the world's foundation,
And mindful of His mercies great,
    He planned for my salvation.
He turned to me a father's heart;
He did not choose the easy part
    But gave His dearest treasure. (st. 4)

►

To me He said: "Stay close to Me,
    I am your rock and castle.
Your ransom I Myself will be;
    For you I strive and wrestle.
For I am yours, and you are Mine,
And where I am you may remain;
    The foe shall not divide us." (st. 7)

ADDITIONAL HYMNS

Before the Throne of God Above	*LSB 574*
Lord, It Belongs Not to My Care	*LSB 757:3*
Not unto Us	*LSB 558:2–4*
O God, Forsake Me Not	*LSB 731*
Salvation unto Us Has Come	*LSB 555:6–7*

Mental Disorders

The extent to which sin ravages the human mind includes a wide range of mental disorders. In addition to encouraging and supporting other appropriate professional assistance for the one who is troubled, the pastor will specifically provide a ministry of consolation that brings peace to the troubled mind. He will speak familiar passages from the Word of God that calm troubled hearts and give rest to the weary.

PSALMODY
Psalm 18:1–6, 28, 30–31   *I love You, O Lord, my strength*

¹ I | love you,*
    O | LORD, my strength.

2 The LORD is my rock and my fortress and my de- | liverer,*
    my God, my rock, in whom I take refuge, my shield, and the
    horn of my salvation, my | stronghold.

3 I call upon the LORD, who is worthy | to be praised,*
    and I am saved from my | enemies.

4 The cords of death en- | compassed me;*
    the torrents of destruction as- | sailed me;

5 the cords of Sheol en- | tangled me;*
    the snares of death con- | fronted me.

6 In my distress I called upon the LORD; to my God I | cried for help.*
    From his temple he heard my voice, and my cry to
    him | reached his ears.

28 For it is you who | light my lamp;*
    the LORD my God lightens my | darkness.

30 This God—his way is | perfect;*
    the word of the LORD proves true; he is a shield for all those
    who take ref- | uge in him.

31 For who is God, | but the LORD?*
    And who is a rock, ex- | cept our God?

Psalm 22:9–11, 23–24   *He has not hidden His face*

9 Yet you are he who took me | from the womb;*
    you made me trust you at my | mother's breasts.

10 On you was I cast | from my birth,*
    and from my mother's womb you have | been my God.

11 Be not far from me, for trouble | is near,*
    and there is | none to help.

23 You who fear the LORD, praise him! All you offspring of Jacob,
glo- | rify him,*
    and stand in awe of him, all you offspring of | Israel!

24 For he has not despised or abhorred the affliction of the afflicted,
and he has not hidden his | face from him,*
    but has heard, when he | cried to him.

ADDITIONAL PSALMODY

Psalm 23	*The Lord is my shepherd*
Psalm 46	*Be still, and know that I am God*
Psalm 69:1–3, 13–21, 29–30	*Deliver me from the deep waters*
Psalm 121	*The Lord will keep your life*
Psalm 124	*Our help is in the name of the Lord*

READINGS

Matthew 11:28–30 *Come to Me; I will give you rest*

28[Jesus said:] "Come to me, all who labor and are heavy laden, and I will give you rest. 29Take my yoke upon you, and learn from me, for I am gentle and lowly in heart, and you will find rest for your souls. 30For my yoke is easy, and my burden is light."

John 14:26–27 *Peace I leave with you*

26[Jesus said:] "The Helper, the Holy Spirit, whom the Father will send in my name, he will teach you all things and bring to your remembrance all that I have said to you. 27Peace I leave with you; my peace I give to you. Not as the world gives do I give to you. Let not your hearts be troubled, neither let them be afraid."

Romans 8:35–39 *Who shall separate us from the love of Christ?*

35Who shall separate us from the love of Christ? Shall tribulation, or distress, or persecution, or famine, or nakedness, or danger, or sword? 36As it is written,

> "For your sake we are being killed all the day long;
>   we are regarded as sheep to be slaughtered."

37No, in all these things we are more than conquerors through him who loved us. 38For I am sure that neither death nor life, nor angels nor rulers, nor things present nor things to come, nor powers, 39nor height nor depth, nor anything else in all creation, will be able to separate us from the love of God in Christ Jesus our Lord.

ADDITIONAL READINGS

1 Sam. 16:14–23	*The case of Saul*
Lam. 3:17–33	*Hope for the anguished soul*
Dan. 4:28–37	*The case of Nebuchadnezzar*
Matt. 8:23–27	*Jesus calms the storm*
Matt. 14:22–33	*Jesus rescues Peter from the waves*
John 3:14–17	*God sent His Son to save us*
Phil. 4:4–9	*God's peace guards your hearts and minds*
1 Thess. 5:23–24	*May the God of peace sanctify you completely*

PRAYERS

Gracious Lord, have mercy on __*name*__. Sustain and strengthen __*him/her*__ by Your Word and Spirit that no distress may separate __*him/her*__ from You. According to Your will, grant __*him/her*__ healing and deliverance from this affliction; through Jesus Christ, Your Son, our Lord, who lives and reigns with You and the Holy Spirit, one God, now and forever. (795)

Lord God, merciful Father, sustain and comfort Your servant __*name*__, who is mentally ill. Do not allow the evil one to trouble __*him/her*__, but provide __*him/her*__ with people who, in wisdom and sympathy, will help __*him/her*__. Strengthen __*him/her*__ and those who surround __*him/her*__ in the knowledge of Your redeeming love so that they may ever look to You for healing and peace; through Jesus Christ, Your Son, our Lord, who lives and reigns with You and the Holy Spirit, one God, now and forever. (283 alt.)

HYMNS

Lord, Take My Hand and Lead Me
LSB 722

Lord, when the tempest rages,
    I need not fear,
For You, the Rock of Ages,
    Are always near.
Close by Your side abiding,
    I fear no foe,
For when Your hand is guiding,
    In peace I go. (st. 2)
                    © *1978 Lutheran Book of Worship*

How Firm a Foundation
LSB 728

"The soul that on Jesus has leaned for repose
I will not, I will not, desert to his foes;
That soul, though all hell should endeavor to shake,
I'll never, no never, no never, forsake!" (st. 3)

Be Still, My Soul
LSB 752

Be still, my soul; the Lord is on your side;
    Bear patiently the cross of grief or pain;
Leave to your God to order and provide;
    In ev'ry change He faithful will remain.
Be still, my soul; your best, your heav'nly Friend
Through thorny ways leads to a joyful end. (st. 1)

ADDITIONAL HYMNS

God Loved the World So That He Gave	*LSB 571*
Grant Peace, We Pray, in Mercy, Lord	*LSB 777/778*
I Am Jesus' Little Lamb	*LSB 740*
I Am Trusting Thee, Lord Jesus	*LSB 729*

Guilt and Shame

The conscience terrified by the memories of sin finds itself living under the condemnation of the Law, which offers no peace or rest. For the Christian who is driven by the Law to despair of the mercies of Christ Jesus, the pastor must "set the whole Decalogue aside" (Luther) and make the most of the Gospel. The pastor will guide the besieged Christian to find consolation in the word of absolution, a word that provides forgiveness for the guilty and covering for those who stand in shame on account of their sin.

The rite of Individual Confession and Absolution is found on pages 28–30.

PSALMODY

Psalm 51:1–12 *Create in me a clean heart*

¹ Have mercy on me, O God, according to your | steadfast love;*
  according to your abundant mercy blot out my trans- | gressions.

² Wash me thoroughly from my in- | iquity,*
  and cleanse me | from my sin!

³ For I know my trans- | gressions,*
  and my sin is ever be- | fore me.

⁴ Against you, you only, have I sinned and done what is evil | in your sight,*
    so that you may be justified in your words and blameless in your | judgment.

⁵ Behold, I was brought forth in in- | iquity,*
  and in sin did my mother con- | ceive me.

⁶ Behold, you delight in truth in the inward | being,*
  and you teach me wisdom in the | secret heart.

⁷ Purge me with hyssop, and I | shall be clean;*
  wash me, and I shall be whit- | er than snow.

⁸ Let me hear joy and | gladness;*
  let the bones that you have bro- | ken rejoice.

▶

⁹ Hide your face | from my sins,*
    and blot out all my in- | iquities.
¹⁰ Create in me a clean heart, | O God,*
    and renew a right spirit with- | in me.
¹¹ Cast me not away from your | presence,*
    and take not your Holy Spirit | from me.
¹² Restore to me the joy of your sal- | vation,*
    and uphold me with a willing | spirit.

Psalm 32:1–5   *I confessed my sin, and You forgave*

¹ Blessèd is the one whose transgression is for- | given,*
    whose sin is | covered.
² Blessèd is the man against whom the Lord counts no in- | iquity,*
    and in whose spirit there is | no deceit.
³ For when I kept silent, my bones wast- | ed away*
    through my groaning | all day long.
⁴ For day and night your hand was heavy up- | on me;*
    my strength was dried up as by the heat of | summer.
⁵ I acknowledged my sin to you, and I did not cover my in- | iquity;*
    I said, "I will confess my transgressions to the Lord," and
    you forgave the iniquity | of my sin.

Psalm 25:1–11, 16–20   *Let me not be put to shame*

¹ To you, | O Lord,*
    I lift | up my soul.
² O my God, in you I trust; let me not be | put to shame;*
    let not my enemies exult | over me.
³ Indeed, none who wait for you shall be | put to shame;*
    they shall be ashamed who are wantonly | treacherous.
⁴ Make me to know your ways, | O Lord;*
    teach me | your paths.
⁵ Lead me in your truth and teach me, for you are the God of my
    sal- | vation;*

for you I wait all the | day long.

6 Remember your mercy, O Lord, and your | steadfast love,*
  for they have been | from of old.

7 Remember not the sins of my youth or my trans- | gressions;*
  according to your steadfast love remember me, for the sake
  of your goodness, | O Lord!

8 Good and upright | is the Lord;*
  therefore he instructs sinners | in the way.

9 He leads the humble in | what is right,*
  and teaches the humble | his way.

10 All the paths of the Lord are steadfast love and | faithfulness,*
  for those who keep his covenant and his testi- | monies.

11 For your name's sake, | O Lord,*
  pardon my guilt, for | it is great.

16 Turn to me and be gra- | cious to me,*
  for I am lonely and af- | flicted.

17 The troubles of my heart | are enlarged;*
  bring me out of my dis- | tresses.

18 Consider my affliction and my | trouble,*
  and forgive | all my sins.

19 Consider how many | are my foes,*
  and with what violent hatred they | hate me.

20 Oh, guard my soul, and de- | liver me!*
  Let me not be put to shame, for I take ref- | uge in you.

ADDITIONAL PSALMODY

Psalm 6	*The Lord has heard my plea*
Psalm 31	*He heard my cry for mercy*
Psalm 38	*I am feeble and crushed*
Psalm 102	*The Lord regards the prayer of the destitute*
Psalm 103:8–18	*He removes our sin as far as east from west*
Psalm 130	*With You there is forgiveness*
Psalm 143	*Hear my pleas for mercy*

READINGS

Hebrews 12:1–2 *Looking to Jesus, the founder of our faith*

¹Since we are surrounded by so great a cloud of witnesses, let us also lay aside every weight, and sin which clings so closely, and let us run with endurance the race that is set before us, ²looking to Jesus, the founder and perfecter of our faith, who for the joy that was set before him endured the cross, despising the shame, and is seated at the right hand of the throne of God.

John 1:29 *Behold, the Lamb of God*

²⁹The next day [John] saw Jesus coming toward him, and said, "Behold, the Lamb of God, who takes away the sin of the world!"

Genesis 3:1–15, 21 *Adam's shame and God's first promise*

¹Now the serpent was more crafty than any other beast of the field that the LORD God had made. He said to the woman, "Did God actually say, 'You shall not eat of any tree in the garden'?" ²And the woman said to the serpent, "We may eat of the fruit of the trees in the garden, ³but God said, 'You shall not eat of the fruit of the tree that is in the midst of the garden, neither shall you touch it, lest you die.'" ⁴But the serpent said to the woman, "You will not surely die. ⁵For God knows that when you eat of it your eyes will be opened, and you will be like God, knowing good and evil." ⁶So when the woman saw that the tree was good for food, and that it was a delight to the eyes, and that the tree was to be desired to make one wise, she took of its fruit and ate, and she also gave some to her husband who was with her, and he ate. ⁷Then the eyes of both were opened, and they knew that they were naked. And they sewed fig leaves together and made themselves loincloths.

⁸And they heard the sound of the LORD God walking in the garden in the cool of the day, and the man and his wife hid themselves from the presence of the LORD God among the trees of the garden.

⁹But the LORD God called to the man and said to him, "Where are you?" ¹⁰And he said, "I heard the sound of you in the garden, and I was afraid, because I was naked, and I hid myself." ¹¹He said, "Who told you that you were naked? Have you eaten of the tree of which I commanded you not to eat?" ¹²The man said, "The woman whom you gave to be with me, she gave me fruit of the tree, and I ate." ¹³Then the LORD God said to the woman, "What is this that you have done?" The woman said, "The serpent deceived me, and I ate." ¹⁴The LORD God said to the serpent,

> "Because you have done this,
>> cursed are you above all livestock
>> and above all beasts of the field;
> on your belly you shall go,
>> and dust you shall eat
>> all the days of your life.
> ¹⁵I will put enmity between you and the woman,
>> and between your offspring and her offspring;
> he shall bruise your head,
>> and you shall bruise his heel."

²¹And the LORD God made for Adam and for his wife garments of skins and clothed them.

John 8:1b–11   *The woman caught in adultery is not condemned*

¹ᵇJesus went to the Mount of Olives. ²Early in the morning he came again to the temple. All the people came to him, and he sat down and taught them. ³The scribes and the Pharisees brought a woman who had been caught in adultery, and placing her in the midst ⁴they said to him, "Teacher, this woman has been caught in the act of adultery. ⁵Now in the Law Moses commanded us to stone such women. So what do you say?" ⁶This they said to test him, that they might have some charge to bring against him. Jesus bent down and wrote with his finger on the ground. ⁷And as they continued to ask him, he stood ▶

up and said to them, "Let him who is without sin among you be the first to throw a stone at her." ⁸And once more he bent down and wrote on the ground. ⁹But when they heard it, they went away one by one, beginning with the older ones, and Jesus was left alone with the woman standing before him.¹⁰Jesus stood up and said to her, "Woman, where are they? Has no one condemned you?" ¹¹She said, "No one, Lord." And Jesus said, "Neither do I condemn you; go, and from now on sin no more."

ADDITIONAL READINGS

2 Sam. 12:1–14	*David's sin is taken away by the Lord*
Ezra 9:5–9	*Ezra admits his shame*
Dan. 9:4–19	*Daniel confesses and prays for forgiveness*
Luke 18:9–14	*The Pharisee and the tax collector*
John 3:14–21	*God sent His Son to save the world*
Rom. 8:1, 33–34	*It is God who justifies*
2 Cor. 5:18—6:2	*Be reconciled to God*
Col. 1:19–23	*Through Christ God reconciled to Himself all things*
1 Peter 3:13–22	*Baptism saves you*
1 John 1:5–9	*If we confess our sins, He will forgive us*
1 John 2:28	*Believers will not shrink from Christ in shame*

PRAYERS

Lord Jesus Christ, through Your shameful death on the cross You embraced the guilt of our sin and atoned for our iniquities. Forgive Your servant __name__ . Assure __him/her__ that You have cleansed __him/her__ of __his/her__ guilt and taken away __his/her__ shame that __he/she__ may rejoice in the freedom of sins forgiven and in Your everlasting peace; even as You live and reign with the Father and the Holy Spirit, one God, now and forever. (796)

Gracious Lord, for the sake of Your holy name forgive __name__ all __his/her__ sins and rescue __him/her__ whom You have redeemed through the precious blood of Your dear Son. Deal with Your servant

312

not according to _his/her_ weakness and guilt but according to Your love and goodness, and grant _him/her_ Your peace; through Jesus Christ, Your Son, our Lord, who lives and reigns with You and the Holy Spirit, one God, now and forever. (797)

Heavenly Father, You do not wish sinners to die but to repent and live. According to Your great compassion be merciful to _name_. Take away _his/her_ sin, deliver _him/her_ from _his/her_ guilt, and restore to _him/her_ the joy of Your salvation; through Jesus Christ, Your Son, our Lord, who lives and reigns with You and the Holy Spirit, one God, now and forever. (798)

Almighty and everlasting God, You despise nothing You have made and forgive the sins of all who are penitent. Create in _name_ a new and contrite heart that, lamenting _his/her_ sins and acknowledging _his/her_ wretchedness, _he/she_ may receive from You full pardon and forgiveness; through Jesus Christ, Your Son, our Lord, who lives and reigns with You and the Holy Spirit, one God, now and forever. (L22)

HYMNS

Jesus Sinners Doth Receive

LSB 609

We deserve but grief and shame,
 Yet His words, rich grace revealing,
Pardon, peace, and life proclaim;
 Here our ills have perfect healing.
Firmly in these words believe:
Jesus sinners doth receive. (st. 2)

I, a sinner, come to Thee
 With a penitent confession.
Savior, mercy show to me;
 Grant for all my sins remission.
Let these words my soul relieve:
Jesus sinners doth receive. (st. 4)

▶

Now my conscience is at peace;
    From the Law I stand acquitted.
Christ hath purchased my release
    And my ev'ry sin remitted.
Naught remains my soul to grieve:
Jesus sinners doth receive. (st. 6)

All Christians Who Have Been Baptized   *LSB 596*

In Baptism we now put on Christ—
    Our shame is fully covered
With all that He once sacrificed
    And freely for us suffered.
For here the flood of His own blood
Now makes us holy, right, and good
      Before our heav'nly Father. (st. 4)

© 2004 Concordia Publishing House

ADDITIONAL HYMNS

Baptismal Waters Cover Me	*LSB 616*
From Depths of Woe I Cry to Thee	*LSB 607*
Jesus, Thy Blood and Righteousness	*LSB 563*
To Thee, Omniscient Lord of All	*LSB 613*

Anger and Bitterness

Sinful anger and bitterness are destructive emotional responses expressed by an unwillingness to forgive others. When not dealt with, they devastate a person's relationship with God and the neighbor. The pastor will use the Law to reveal such anger and bitterness as a fruit of unbelief. Proclaiming the unconditional forgiveness won by Christ, the pastor will point to the love of Christ, which constrains us to relinquish anger and to forgive those who have sinned against us even as God in Christ has forgiven us.

PSALMODY
Psalm 73:1–5, 8–9, 12–14, 16–19, 21–28

The embittered soul turns to the Lord

¹ Truly God is good to | Israel,*
> to those who are | pure in heart.

² But as for me, my feet had almost | stumbled,*
> my steps had | nearly slipped.

³ For I was envious of the | arrogant*
> when I saw the prosperity of the | wicked.

⁴ For they have no pangs | until death;*
> their bodies are | fat and sleek.

⁵ They are not in trouble as | others are;*
> they are not stricken like the rest of | mankind.

⁸ They scoff and speak with | malice;*
> loftily they threaten op- | pression.

⁹ They set their mouths against the | heavens,*
> and their tongue struts | through the earth.

¹² Behold, these are the | wicked;*
> always at ease, they increase in | riches.

¹³ All in vain have I kept my | heart clean*
> and washed my hands in | innocence.

►

¹⁴ For all the day long I have been | stricken*
    and rebuked every | morning.

¹⁶ But when I thought how to under- | stand this,*
    it seemed to me a | wearisome task,

¹⁷ until I went into the sanctuary | of God;*
    then I dis- | cerned their end.

¹⁸ Truly you set them in slippery | places;*
    you make them fall to | ruin.

¹⁹ How they are destroyed in a | moment,*
    swept away utterly by | terrors!

²¹ When my soul was em- | bittered,*
    when I was | pricked in heart,

²² I was brutish and | ignorant;*
    I was like a | beast toward you.

²³ Nevertheless, I am continually | with you;*
    you hold my | right hand.

²⁴ You guide me with your | counsel,*
    and afterward you will receive me to | glory.

²⁵ Whom have I in | heaven but you?*
    And there is nothing on earth that I desire be- | sides you.

²⁶ My flesh and my | heart may fail,*
    but God is the strength of my heart and my portion for- | ever.

²⁷ For behold, those who are far from you shall | perish;*
    you put an end to everyone who is unfaithful | to you.

²⁸ But for me it is good to be | near God;*
    I have made the Lord GOD my refuge, that I may tell of | all
    your works.

Psalm 133
Brothers dwell together in unity

¹ Behold, how good and pleas- | ant it is*
    when brothers dwell in | unity!

² It is like the precious oil on the head, running down on the
    beard, on the beard of | Aaron,*

running down on the collar | of his robes!

³ It is like the dew of Hermon, which falls on the mountains of | Zion!*

For there the LORD has commanded the blessing, life for- | evermore.

Psalm 34:11–22   *Turn away from evil*

¹¹ Come, O children, lis- | ten to me;*
    I will teach you the fear | of the LORD.

¹² What man is there who de- | sires life*
    and loves many days, that he may | see good?

¹³ Keep your tongue from | evil*
    and your lips from speak- | ing deceit.

¹⁴ Turn away from evil | and do good;*
    seek peace and pur- | sue it.

¹⁵ The eyes of the LORD are toward the | righteous*
    and his ears | toward their cry.

¹⁶ The face of the LORD is against those who do | evil,*
    to cut off the memory of them | from the earth.

¹⁷ When the righteous cry for help, the | LORD hears*
    and delivers them out of all their | troubles.

¹⁸ The LORD is near to the broken- | hearted*
    and saves the crushed in | spirit.

¹⁹ Many are the afflictions of the | righteous,*
    but the LORD delivers him out | of them all.

²⁰ He keeps | all his bones;*
    not one of them is | broken.

²¹ Affliction will slay the | wicked,*
    and those who hate the righteous will | be condemned.

²² The LORD redeems the life of his | servants;*
    none of those who take refuge in him will | be condemned.

ADDITIONAL PSALMODY

Psalm 19:12–14	*Let my words and heart be acceptable*
Psalm 25	*Lead me in Your truth and teach me*
Psalm 122:6–9	*Pray for the peace of others*
Psalm 143	*Make me to know the way I should go*

READINGS

Genesis 50:15–21
Joseph forgives his brothers

¹⁵When Joseph's brothers saw that their father was dead, they said, "It may be that Joseph will hate us and pay us back for all the evil that we did to him." ¹⁶So they sent a message to Joseph, saying, "Your father gave this command before he died, ¹⁷'Say to Joseph, Please forgive the transgression of your brothers and their sin, because they did evil to you.' And now, please forgive the transgression of the servants of the God of your father." Joseph wept when they spoke to him. ¹⁸His brothers also came and fell down before him and said, "Behold, we are your servants." ¹⁹But Joseph said to them, "Do not fear, for am I in the place of God? ²⁰As for you, you meant evil against me, but God meant it for good, to bring it about that many people should be kept alive, as they are today. ²¹So do not fear; I will provide for you and your little ones." Thus he comforted them and spoke kindly to them.

Matthew 5:21–24
Whoever is angry is liable to judgment

²¹[Jesus said:] "You have heard that it was said to those of old, 'You shall not murder; and whoever murders will be liable to judgment.' ²²But I say to you that everyone who is angry with his brother will be liable to judgment; whoever insults his brother will be liable to the council; and whoever says, 'You fool!' will be liable to the hell of fire. ²³So if you are offering your gift at the altar and there remember that your brother has something against you, ²⁴leave your gift there before the altar and go. First be reconciled to your brother, and then come and offer your gift."

318

Ephesians 4:26–27, 31–32   *Put away all bitterness and anger*

²⁶Be angry and do not sin; do not let the sun go down on your anger, ²⁷and give no opportunity to the devil.

³¹Let all bitterness and wrath and anger and clamor and slander be put away from you, along with all malice. ³²Be kind to one another, tenderhearted, forgiving one another, as God in Christ forgave you.

Romans 12:14–21   *Repay no one evil for evil*

¹⁴Bless those who persecute you; bless and do not curse them. ¹⁵Rejoice with those who rejoice, weep with those who weep. ¹⁶Live in harmony with one another. Do not be haughty, but associate with the lowly. Never be conceited. ¹⁷Repay no one evil for evil, but give thought to do what is honorable in the sight of all. ¹⁸If possible, so far as it depends on you, live peaceably with all. ¹⁹Beloved, never avenge yourselves, but leave it to the wrath of God, for it is written, "Vengeance is mine, I will repay, says the Lord." ²⁰To the contrary, "if your enemy is hungry, feed him; if he is thirsty, give him something to drink; for by so doing you will heap burning coals on his head." ²¹Do not be overcome by evil, but overcome evil with good.

ADDITIONAL READINGS

Gen. 4:1–7	*Cain was angry with God and his brother*
Job 19:13–15, 23–27a	*Job clings to his redeemer*
Prov. 14:29	*Be slow to anger*
Prov. 19:11	*The wise are slow to anger*
Matt. 18:15–17	*Reconcile with your brother*
1 Cor. 13:4–7	*Love is patient and keeps no record of wrongs*
Phil. 2:1–11	*Having the mind of Christ*
1 Tim. 2:8	*Pray without anger or quarreling*
Heb. 12:12–15	*See to it that no root of bitterness springs up*
James 1:19–21	*Be slow to become angry*
1 Peter 2:19–25	*Do not revile when you are reviled*

PRAYERS

Lord Jesus Christ, in Your love for us and for our salvation You suffered the Father's wrath upon the cross. Deliver __name__ from anger and resentment, hatred and revenge. Grant that __he/she__ may forgive as __he/she__ has been forgiven and stand reconciled before You in Your righteousness and purity; for You live and reign with the Father and the Holy Spirit, one God, now and forever. (799)

O God, from whom come all holy desires, all good counsels, and all just works, give to us, Your servants, that peace which the world cannot give, that our hearts may be set to obey Your commandments and also that we, being defended from the fear of our enemies, may live in peace and quietness; through Jesus Christ, Your Son, our Lord, who lives and reigns with You and the Holy Spirit, one God, now and forever. (410)

HYMNS

These Are the Holy Ten Commands

LSB 581

"You shall not murder, hurt, nor hate;
Your anger dare not dominate.
Be kind and patient; help, defend,
And treat your foe as your friend."
    Have mercy, Lord! (st. 6)

Our works cannot salvation gain;
They merit only endless pain.
Forgive us, Lord! To Christ we flee,
Who pleads for us endlessly.
    Have mercy, Lord! (st. 12)

Our Father, Who from Heaven Above   *LSB 766*

Forgive our sins, Lord, we implore,
That they may trouble us no more;
> We, too, will gladly those forgive
> Who hurt us by the way they live.
Help us in our community
To serve each other willingly. (st. 6)

ADDITIONAL HYMNS

"Forgive Our Sins as We Forgive"   *LSB 843*
Where Charity and Love Prevail   *LSB 845*

Depression and Discouragement

Depression is a complex malady that may require the assistance of other professional help. The pastor's ministry to one who is depressed or discouraged is to focus chiefly on the spiritual battles of the afflicted person. Proclaiming that Jesus is our brother and defender, even in the depths of life, the pastor will comfort the depressed person with the promise that God rescues and restores those who call upon Him.

PSALMODY

Psalm 42:3–8   *My soul is cast down; I remember the Lord*

3 My tears have been my food | day and night,*
> while they say to me continually, "Where | is your God?"
4 These things I remember, as I pour | out my soul:*
> how I would go with the throng and lead them in procession
> to the | house of God
with glad shouts and | songs of praise,*
> a multitude keeping | festival.   ►

5 Why are you cast down, O my soul, and why are you in turmoil with- | in me?*

    Hope in God; for I shall again praise him, my salvation | 6and my God.

My soul is cast down with- | in me;*

    therefore I remember you from the land of Jordan and of Hermon, from Mount | Mizar.

7 Deep calls to deep at the roar of your | waterfalls;*

    all your breakers and your waves have gone | over me.

8 By day the LORD commands his steadfast love, and at night his song is | with me,*

    a prayer to the God | of my life.

Psalm 142   *When my spirit faints, You know my way*

1 With my voice I cry out | to the LORD;*

    with my voice I plead for mercy | to the LORD.

2 I pour out my complaint be- | fore him;*

    I tell my trouble be- | fore him.

3 When my spirit faints within me, you | know my way!*

    In the path where I walk they have hidden a | trap for me.

4 Look to the right and see: there is none who takes notice | of me;*

    no refuge remains to me; no one cares | for my soul.

5 I cry to you, | O LORD;*

    I say, "You are my refuge, my portion in the land of the | living."

6 Attend to my cry, for I am brought | very low!*

    Deliver me from my persecutors, for they are too | strong for me!

7 Bring me out of prison, that I may give thanks | to your name!*

    The righteous will surround me, for you will deal bountifully | with me.

Psalm 130   *The Lord's word of forgiveness is my hope*

1 Out | of the depths*

    I cry to you, | O LORD!

² O Lord, | hear my voice!*

    Let your ears be attentive to the voice of my pleas for | mercy!

³ If you, O LORD, should mark in- | iquities,*

    O Lord, | who could stand?

⁴ But with you there is for- | giveness,*

    that you | may be feared.

⁵ I wait for the LORD, my | soul waits,*

    and in his | word I hope;

⁶ my soul waits for the Lord more than watchmen for the | morning,*

    more than watchmen for the | morning.

⁷ O Israel, hope in the LORD! For with the LORD there is | steadfast love,*

    and with him is plentiful re- | demption.

⁸ And he will redeem | Israel*

    from all his in- | iquities.

ADDITIONAL PSALMODY

Psalm 6	*My soul is greatly troubled*
Psalm 9:1–18	*The Lord is a stronghold in times of trouble*
Psalm 25:15–22	*Bring me out of my distress*
Psalm 27:7–14	*Hear when I cry aloud*
Psalm 30:8–12	*You have turned my mourning into dancing*
Psalm 34:1–10	*Those who seek the Lord lack no good thing*
Psalm 40:1–3	*He drew me up out of the miry bog*
Psalm 68:19–20	*The Lord daily bears us up*
Psalm 84:8–12	*Blessed is the one who trusts in You*
Psalm 88	*I cry out day and night before You*
Psalm 107:1–2, 20–22, 31–32, 43	*The Lord has redeemed His people*
Psalm 139	*The Lord knows all, even my heart*

READINGS

2 Corinthians 12:7–10   *My grace is sufficient for you*

⁷To keep me from being too elated by the surpassing greatness of the revelations, a thorn was given me in the flesh, a messenger of ▶

Satan to harass me, to keep me from being too elated. [8]Three times I pleaded with the Lord about this, that it should leave me. [9]But he said to me, "My grace is sufficient for you, for my power is made perfect in weakness." Therefore I will boast all the more gladly of my weaknesses, so that the power of Christ may rest upon me. [10]For the sake of Christ, then, I am content with weaknesses, insults, hardships, persecutions, and calamities. For when I am weak, then I am strong.

Romans 8:35–39 *Nothing shall separate us from the love of Christ*

[35]Who shall separate us from the love of Christ? Shall tribulation, or distress, or persecution, or famine, or nakedness, or danger, or sword? [36]As it is written,

> "For your sake we are being killed all the day long;
> we are regarded as sheep to be slaughtered."

[37]No, in all these things we are more than conquerors through him who loved us. [38]For I am sure that neither death nor life, nor angels nor rulers, nor things present nor things to come, nor powers, [39]nor height nor depth, nor anything else in all creation, will be able to separate us from the love of God in Christ Jesus our Lord.

Isaiah 40:28–31 *You shall run and not be weary*

[28] Have you not known? Have you not heard?
   The LORD is the everlasting God,
      the Creator of the ends of the earth.
   He does not faint or grow weary;
      his understanding is unsearchable.
[29] He gives power to the faint,
      and to him who has no might he increases strength.
[30] Even youths shall faint and be weary,
      and young men shall fall exhausted;
[31] but they who wait for the LORD shall renew their strength;
      they shall mount up with wings like eagles;

they shall run and not be weary;
they shall walk and not faint.

ADDITIONAL READINGS

1 Kings 19:1–18	*The Lord speaks to discouraged Elijah*
Eccl. 2:17–25	*Without God, everything is meaningless*
Is. 38:10–20	*Hezekiah's song of recovery*
Is. 41:9b–10	*God exhorts His people not to be dismayed*
Lam. 3:19–26, 31–33	*Remembering the Lord's compassion*
Luke 4:14–21	*Jesus the Christ gives liberty to the captives*
Luke 24:13–35	*Christ transforms the Emmaus disciples*
Rom. 8:26–28	*The Holy Spirit intercedes for us*
Eph. 1:2–8	*God chose us in Christ*
1 Peter 1:3–9	*We are born again to a living hope*

PRAYERS

Lord Jesus Christ, Your precious blood washes away our sins and revives our spirits. Look with compassion on _ name _, and restore hope and well-being to _ him/her _. Banish the spirit of depression, strengthen _ his/her _ faith, disperse the cloud of despair that covers _ him/her _, and grant _ him/her _ the comfort of Your Holy Spirit and the joy of Your salvation; for You live and reign with the Father and the same Holy Spirit, one God, now and forever. (800)

Keep in remembrance, O Lord, the tempted and the distressed. Gently guide _ name _ and by Your great goodness bring _ him/her _ into the way of peace. Let the light of Your truth shine on all who are in trouble, danger, temptation, and bondage of sin. In Your mercy draw them to Yourself for the sake of Jesus Christ, Your Son, our Lord, who lives and reigns with You and the Holy Spirit, one God, now and forever. (801)

Almighty God, do not cast away Your people who cry to You in their distress and tribulation, but for the glory of Your name be pleased to help and deliver them; through Jesus Christ, Your Son, our Lord, who lives and reigns with You and the Holy Spirit, one God, now and forever. (802)

HYMN

When in the Hour of Deepest Need

LSB 615

Then is our comfort this alone
That we may meet before Your throne;
To You, O faithful God, we cry
For rescue in our misery.

For You have promised, Lord, to heed
Your children's cries in time of need
Through Him whose name alone is great,
Our Savior and our advocate.

And so we come, O God, today
And all our woes before You lay;
For sorely tried, cast down, we stand,
Perplexed by fears on ev'ry hand.

O from our sins, Lord, turn Your face;
Absolve us through Your boundless grace.
Be with us in our anguish still;
Free us at last from ev'ry ill. (sts. 2–5)

ADDITIONAL HYMNS

Eternal Spirit of the Living Christ	LSB 769
Hear Us, Father, When We Pray	LSB 773:1–2
If Your Beloved Son, O God	LSB 568:1–3
Lead Me, Guide Me	LSB 721

Reconciliation with Other Christians

Sin is the cause of all conflict and estrangement among Christians. Reconciliation can take place only in conjunction with the forgiveness of sins. The Law is used to lead Christians who are estranged from one another to acknowledge their sins and to confess them to God and each other. Then the pastor can speak the Gospel of forgiveness, which frees those who are estranged to forgive one another. Part of the reconciliation process might include the use of either the rite of Individual Confession and Absolution (pages 28–30) or the Service of Corporate Confession and Absolution (*LSB,* pages 290–291).

PSALMODY

Psalm 124
If the Lord had not been on our side

¹ If it had not been the Lord who was | on our side—*
  let Israel | now say—
² if it had not been the Lord who was | on our side*
  when people rose up a- | gainst us,
³ then they would have swallowed us | up alive,*
  when their anger was kindled a- | gainst us;
⁴ then the flood would have swept | us away,*
  the torrent would have gone | over us;
⁵ then over us | would have gone*
  the raging | waters.
⁶ Blessèd | be the Lord,*
  who has not given us as prey | to their teeth!
⁷ We have escaped like a bird from the snare of the | fowlers;*
  the snare is broken, and we | have escaped!
⁸ Our help is in the name | of the Lord,*
  who made | heaven and earth.

Psalm 38   *O Lord, rebuke me not in Your anger*

¹ O LORD, rebuke me not in your | anger,*
　　nor discipline me | in your wrath!

² For your arrows have sunk | into me,*
　　and your hand has come | down on me.

³ There is no soundness in my flesh because of your indig- | nation;*
　　there is no health in my bones because | of my sin.

⁴ For my iniquities have gone o- | ver my head;*
　　like a heavy burden, they are too heav- | y for me.

⁵ My wounds stink and | fester*
　　because of my | foolishness,

⁶ I am utterly bowed down and | prostrate;*
　　all the day I go about | mourning.

⁷ For my sides are filled with | burning,*
　　and there is no soundness | in my flesh.

⁸ I am feeble | and crushed;*
　　I groan because of the tumult | of my heart.

⁹ O Lord, all my longing is be- | fore you;*
　　my sighing is not hid- | den from you.

¹⁰ My heart throbs; my strength | fails me,*
　　and the light of my eyes—it also has | gone from me.

¹¹ My friends and companions stand aloof | from my plague,*
　　and my nearest kin stand | far off.

¹² Those who seek my life lay their snares; those who seek my hurt speak of | ruin*
　　and meditate treachery | all day long.

¹³ But I am like a deaf man; I | do not hear,*
　　like a mute man who does not o- | pen his mouth.

¹⁴ I have become like a man who | does not hear,*
　　and in whose mouth are | no rebukes.

¹⁵ But for you, O LORD, | do I wait;*
　　it is you, O Lord my God, who will | answer.

¹⁶ For I said, "Only let them not rejoice | over me,*

who boast against me when my | foot slips!"

¹⁷ For I am read- | y to fall,*
    and my pain is ever be- | fore me.

¹⁸ I confess my in- | iquity;*
    I am sorry | for my sin.

¹⁹ But my foes are vigorous, they are | mighty,*
    and many are those who hate me | wrongfully.

²⁰ Those who render me e- | vil for good*
    accuse me because I follow | after good.

²¹ Do not forsake me, | O LORD!*
    O my God, be not | far from me!

²² Make haste to | help me,*
    O Lord, my sal- | vation!

ADDITIONAL PSALMODY

Psalm 51:1–12, 18	*Forgive my sin and renew me*
Psalm 55	*Cast your burden on the Lord*
Psalm 130	*With You there is forgiveness*
Psalm 133	*When brothers dwell in unity*

READINGS

Genesis 50:15–21   *Joseph forgives his brothers*

¹⁵When Joseph's brothers saw that their father was dead, they said, "It may be that Joseph will hate us and pay us back for all the evil that we did to him." ¹⁶So they sent a message to Joseph, saying, "Your father gave this command before he died, ¹⁷'Say to Joseph, Please forgive the transgression of your brothers and their sin, because they did evil to you.' And now, please forgive the transgression of the servants of the God of your father." Joseph wept when they spoke to him. ¹⁸His brothers also came and fell down before him and said, "Behold, we are your servants." ¹⁹But Joseph said to them, "Do not fear, for am I in the place of God? ²⁰As for you, you meant evil against me, but God meant it for good, to bring it about that many ►

people should be kept alive, as they are today. ²¹So do not fear; I will provide for you and your little ones." Thus he comforted them and spoke kindly to them.

Matthew 5:21–26   *Be reconciled to your brother*

²¹[Jesus said:] "You have heard that it was said to those of old, 'You shall not murder; and whoever murders will be liable to judgment.' ²²But I say to you that everyone who is angry with his brother will be liable to judgment; whoever insults his brother will be liable to the council; and whoever says, 'You fool!' will be liable to the hell of fire. ²³So if you are offering your gift at the altar and there remember that your brother has something against you, ²⁴leave your gift there before the altar and go. First be reconciled to your brother, and then come and offer your gift. ²⁵Come to terms quickly with your accuser while you are going with him to court, lest your accuser hand you over to the judge, and the judge to the guard, and you be put in prison. ²⁶Truly, I say to you, you will never get out until you have paid the last penny."

Matthew 5:43–48   *Love your enemies*

⁴³[Jesus said:] "You have heard that it was said, 'You shall love your neighbor and hate your enemy.' ⁴⁴But I say to you, Love your enemies and pray for those who persecute you, ⁴⁵so that you may be sons of your Father who is in heaven. For he makes his sun rise on the evil and on the good, and sends rain on the just and on the unjust. ⁴⁶For if you love those who love you, what reward do you have? Do not even the tax collectors do the same? ⁴⁷And if you greet only your brothers, what more are you doing than others? Do not even the Gentiles do the same? ⁴⁸You therefore must be perfect, as your heavenly Father is perfect."

ADDITIONAL READINGS

Gen. 13:1–12	*Abram and Lot settle their strife*
Matt. 18:15–20	*Reconcile with your brother*
Luke 22:24–27	*I am among you as one who serves*
Rom. 15:4–7	*God grant you to live in harmony*
1 Cor. 1:10–13	*Let there be no divisions among you*
1 Cor. 6:1–8	*Settling disputes between brothers*
Gal. 5:16–26	*Enmity and strife versus love and peace*
Eph. 2:11–22	*Jews and Gentiles are made one in Christ*
1 Tim. 2:8	*Pray without anger or quarreling*
James 3:13–18	*The wisdom from above is full of mercy*
1 Peter 3:8–17	*Have unity of mind, sympathy, brotherly love*
1 John 4:7–11	*Beloved, let us love one another*

PRAYERS

God of love, through Your Son You have commanded us to love one another. By the guidance of Your Word and Spirit, deliver us from impenitence and teach us the truth that we might confess our sins, receive Your forgiveness, and be reconciled to one another; through Jesus Christ, Your Son, our Lord, who lives and reigns with You and the Holy Spirit, one God, now and forever. (206)

Father of mercies and God of all consolation, come to the aid of ___names___, turning them from their sin to live for You alone. Give them the power of Your Holy Spirit that they may attend to Your Word, confess their sins, receive Your forgiveness, and grow into the fullness of Your Son, Jesus Christ, our Lord and our Redeemer, who lives and reigns with You and the Holy Spirit, one God, now and forever. (803)

For an impenitent who is absent

Almighty, everlasting God, through Your only Son, our blessed Lord, You commanded us to love our enemies, to do good to those who hate us, and to pray for those who persecute us. Therefore, we earnestly implore You that by Your gracious working ___name of absent impenitent___ may be led to true repentance and receive Your ►

forgiveness, that ___he/she/they___ may have the same love toward us as we have toward ___him/her/them___, and that ___he/she/they___ may be of one accord and of one mind and heart with us and with Your whole Church; through Jesus Christ, Your Son, our Lord, who lives and reigns with You and the Holy Spirit, one God, now and forever. (110 alt.)

Thanksgiving for reconciliation achieved

O God, through Your Son, Jesus Christ, You reconciled the world to Yourself and have given to Your Church the ministry of reconciliation. We give You thanks that by Your grace ___name___ and ___name___ have forgiven one another and are at peace. Strengthened by Your forgiveness, grant that they may continue to live in the unity of the Spirit and the bond of peace; through Jesus Christ, Your Son, our Lord, who lives and reigns with You and the Holy Spirit, one God, now and forever. (804)

When reconciliation does not occur

O God, You desire all to live in the unity of the Spirit and the bond of peace. With sorrow we lament that ___name___ and ___name___ have not been reconciled to each other. We commend them to Your mercy, imploring You by Your Word and Spirit to work repentance that they might yet rejoice in the reconciliation that You have won for us in Your Son, Jesus Christ, our Lord, who lives and reigns with You and the Holy Spirit, one God, now and forever. (805)

HYMN
Our Father, Who from Heaven Above
LSB 766

Our Father, who from heav'n above
Bids all of us to live in love
    As members of one family
    And pray to You in unity,
Teach us no thoughtless words to say
But from our inmost hearts to pray. (st. 1)

Give us this day our daily bread,
And let us all be clothed and fed.
    Save us from hardship, war, and strife;
    In plague and famine, spare our life,
That we in honest peace may live,
To care and greed no entrance give. (st. 5)

Forgive our sins, Lord, we implore,
That they may trouble us no more;
    We, too, will gladly those forgive
    Who hurt us by the way they live.
Help us in our community
To serve each other willingly. (st. 6)

Stanza 5 © 1980 Concordia Publishing House

ADDITIONAL HYMNS

"Forgive Our Sins as We Forgive"	*LSB 843*
These Are the Holy Ten Commands	*LSB 581:6, 12*
Where Charity and Love Prevail	*LSB 845*

Coping with Change

Changes in life—especially changes that cause grief and heartache—may lead the faithful to forget the Lord's unchanging promises and His holy and gracious will. To those who are troubled by uncertainties concerning the future or the inability to control the circumstances and events of their lives, the pastor will proclaim the steadfastness of the Lord in keeping His word of promise. He will remind God's people that even in the midst of change "Jesus Christ is the same yesterday, today, and forever" (Heb. 13:8) and that in Him they will stand secure.

PSALMODY

Psalm 90   *Lord, You have been our dwelling place*

¹ Lord, you have been our | dwelling place*
   in all gener- | ations.
² Before the mountains were brought forth, or ever you had
   formed the earth | and the world,*
      from everlasting to everlasting | you are God.
³ You return | man to dust*
      and say, "Return, O chil- | dren of man!"
⁴ For a thousand years in your sight are but as yesterday when | it
   is past,*
      or as a watch | in the night.
⁵ You sweep them away as | with a flood;*
      they are like a dream, like grass that is renewed in the | morning:
⁶ in the morning it flourishes and | is renewed;*
      in the evening it fades and | withers.
⁷ For we are brought to an end by your | anger;*
      by your wrath we | are dismayed.
⁸ You have set our iniquities be- | fore you,*
      our secret sins in the light of your | presence.

⁹ For all our days pass away un- | der your wrath;*
    we bring our years to an end | like a sigh.

¹⁰ The years of our life are seventy, or even by reason of
strength | eighty;*
        yet their span is but toil and trouble; they are soon gone, and
        we | fly away.

¹¹ Who considers the power of your | anger,*
    and your wrath according to the | fear of you?

¹² So teach us to number | our days*
    that we may get a heart of | wisdom.

¹³ Return, O LORD! | How long?*
    Have pity on your | servants!

¹⁴ Satisfy us in the morning with your | steadfast love,*
    that we may rejoice and be glad | all our days.

¹⁵ Make us glad for as many days as you have af- | flicted us,*
    and for as many years as we have seen | evil.

¹⁶ Let your work be shown to your | servants,*
    and your glorious power to their | children.

¹⁷ Let the favor of the Lord our God be upon us, and establish the
work of our hands up- | on us;*
    yes, establish the work | of our hands!

Psalm 111   *The works of the Lord are established forever*

¹ Praise the LORD! I will give thanks to the LORD with my | whole
heart,*
    in the company of the upright, in the congre- | gation.

² Great are the works | of the LORD,*
    studied by all who de- | light in them.

³ Full of splendor and majesty | is his work,*
    and his righteousness endures for- | ever.

⁴ He has caused his wondrous works to be re- | membered;*
    the LORD is gracious and | merciful.

                                     ▶

⁵ He provides food for those who | fear him;*
  he remembers his covenant for- | ever.
⁶ He has shown his people the power | of his works,*
  in giving them the inheritance of the | nations.
⁷ The works of his hands are faith- | ful and just;*
  all his precepts are | trustworthy;
⁸ they are established forever and | ever,*
  to be performed with faithfulness and up- | rightness.
⁹ He sent redemption to his people; he has commanded his
  covenant for- | ever.*
  Holy and awesome | is his name!
¹⁰ The fear of the LORD is the beginning of wisdom; all those who
  practice it have a good under- | standing.*
  His praise endures for- | ever!

ADDITIONAL PSALMODY

Psalm 33:10–12	*The counsel of the Lord stands forever*
Psalm 62:1–2, 5–8, 11–12a	*God is my fortress*
Psalm 102:1–5, 11–13, 27–28	*The Lord is forever*
Psalm 103:15–18	*The love of the Lord is everlasting*
Psalm 145:1–9	*One generation will tell the next*

READINGS

Luke 9:23–26   *Take up your cross and follow Me*

²³[Jesus] said to all, "If anyone would come after me, let him deny himself and take up his cross daily and follow me. ²⁴For whoever would save his life will lose it, but whoever loses his life for my sake will save it. ²⁵For what does it profit a man if he gains the whole world and loses or forfeits himself? ²⁶For whoever is ashamed of me and of my words, of him will the Son of Man be ashamed when he comes in his glory and the glory of the Father and of the holy angels."

Isaiah 40:6–8   *The Word of our God stands forever*

⁶ A voice says, "Cry!"
>   And I said, "What shall I cry?"
> All flesh is grass,
>   and all its beauty is like the flower of the field.
⁷ The grass withers, the flower fades
>   when the breath of the LORD blows on it;
>   surely the people are grass.
⁸ The grass withers, the flower fades,
>   but the word of our God will stand forever.

Hebrews 13:8   *Jesus Christ is the same forever*

⁸Jesus Christ is the same yesterday and today and forever.

Ecclesiastes 1:9–11   *There is nothing new under the sun*

⁹ What has been is what will be,
>   and what has been done is what will be done,
>   and there is nothing new under the sun.
¹⁰ Is there a thing of which it is said,
>   "See, this is new"?
> It has been already
>   in the ages before us.
¹¹ There is no remembrance of former things,
>   nor will there be any remembrance
> of later things yet to be
>   among those who come after.

ADDITIONAL READINGS

Eccl. 12:13–14   *The conclusion of the matter*
Rom. 8:31–39   *Nothing will be able to separate us from God's love*
2 Cor. 4:16–18   *Our inner nature is being renewed*
Eph. 1:3–14   *Your election in God is sure*
Heb. 11:8–10   *Abraham's trust in God in the midst of change*

James 1:16–18   *The Father of lights*
Rev. 21:1–5a   *A new heaven and a new earth*

PRAYERS

Heavenly Father, You make the minds of Your faithful to be of one will. Grant that Your servant __name__ may love what You command and desire what You promise, that among the many changes of this world __his/her__ heart may ever be fixed where true joys are to be found; through Jesus Christ, Your Son, our Lord, who lives and reigns with You and the Holy Spirit, one God, now and forever. (L45 alt.)

Lord God, You have called Your servants to ventures of which we cannot see the ending, by paths as yet untrodden, through perils unknown. Give us faith to go out with good courage, not knowing where we go but only that Your hand is leading us and Your love supporting us; through Jesus Christ, Your Son, our Lord, who lives and reigns with You and the Holy Spirit, one God, now and forever. (193)

Heavenly Father, in whom we live and move and have our being, we humbly pray You so to guide and govern us by Your Word and Spirit that in all the cares and occupations of our life we may not forget You but remember that we are ever walking in Your sight; through Jesus Christ, Your Son, our Lord, who lives and reigns with You and the Holy Spirit, one God, now and forever. (806)

HYMNS

Abide with Me   LSB 878

Swift to its close ebbs out life's little day;
Earth's joys grow dim, its glories pass away;
Change and decay in all around I see;
O Thou who changest not, abide with me. (st. 4)

O God, Our Help in Ages Past

LSB 733

O God, our help in ages past,
    Our hope for years to come,
Our shelter from the stormy blast,
    And our eternal home:

Under the shadow of Thy throne
    Thy saints have dwelt secure;
Sufficient is Thine arm alone,
    And our defense is sure.

Before the hills in order stood
    Or earth received her frame,
From everlasting Thou art God,
    To endless years the same. (sts. 1–3)

ADDITIONAL HYMNS

Entrust Your Days and Burdens	*LSB 754*
Great Is Thy Faithfulness	*LSB 809*
Seek Ye First	*LSB 712*

Impatience

When the problems and challenges of life are not resolved quickly and to our personal satisfaction, the devil, the world, and our sinful nature can lead us to impatience. Impatience is a sign of not trusting God. Patience, on the other hand, is a fruit of the Spirit that is born of the Gospel. Christians battling impatience will find hope and direction in the faithfulness of Christ, who, in the face of sin and death, commended Himself to the Father and by His patient suffering and death won their forgiveness.

PSALMODY

Psalm 27

Wait for the Lord

¹ The LORD is my light and my salvation; whom | shall I fear?*
  The LORD is the stronghold of my life; of whom shall I | be afraid?

² When evildoers assail me to eat | up my flesh,*
  my adversaries and foes, it is they who stum- | ble and fall.

³ Though an army encamp against me, my heart | shall not fear;*
  though war arise against me, yet I will be | confident.

⁴ One thing have I asked of the LORD, that will I seek | after:*
  that I may dwell in the house of the LORD all the days of my life, to gaze upon the beauty of the LORD and to inquire in his | temple.

⁵ For he will hide me in his shelter in the day of | trouble;*
  he will conceal me under the cover of his tent; he will lift me high up- | on a rock.

⁶ And now my head shall be lifted up above my enemies all around me, and I will offer in his tent sacrifices with | shouts of joy;*
  I will sing and make melody | to the LORD.

⁷ Hear, O LORD, when I | cry aloud;*
  be gracious to me and | answer me!

⁸ You have said, | "Seek my face."*

My heart says to you, "Your face, Lord, | do I seek."

⁹ Hide not your face from me. Turn not your servant away in | anger,*

O you who have been my help. Cast me not off; forsake me not, O God of my sal- | vation!

¹⁰ For my father and my mother have for- | saken me,*

but the Lord will | take me in.

¹¹ Teach me your way, | O Lord,*

and lead me on a level path because of my | enemies.

¹² Give me not up to the will of my adver- | saries;*

for false witnesses have risen against me, and they breathe out | violence.

¹³ I believe that I shall look upon the goodness | of the Lord*

in the land of the | living!

¹⁴ Wait | for the Lord;*

be strong, and let your heart take courage; wait | for the Lord!

Psalm 37:3–7a, 27–28a, 39–40a   *Delight yourself in the Lord*

³ Trust in the Lord, | and do good;*

dwell in the land and befriend | faithfulness.

⁴ Delight yourself | in the Lord,*

and he will give you the desires | of your heart.

⁵ Commit your way | to the Lord;*

trust in him, and | he will act.

⁶ He will bring forth your righteousness | as the light,*

and your justice as the | noonday.

⁷ᵃ Be still be- | fore the Lord*

and wait patiently | for him.

²⁷ Turn away from evil | and do good;*

so shall you dwell for- | ever.

²⁸ᵃ For the Lord loves justice; he will not for- | sake his saints.*

They are preserved for- | ever.   ►

39 The salvation of the righteous is | from the LORD;*
>   he is their stronghold in the time of | trouble.
40a The LORD | helps them*
>   and de- | livers them.

Psalm 119:81–83   *My soul longs for Your salvation*

81 My soul longs for your sal- | vation;*
>   I hope | in your word.
82 My eyes long for your | promise;*
>   I ask, "When will you | comfort me?"
83 For I have become like a wineskin | in the smoke,*
>   yet I have not forgotten your | statutes.

ADDITIONAL PSALMODY

Psalm 40:1–4a	*I waited for the Lord, and He delivered me*
Psalm 42	*Hope in God; for I shall again praise Him*
Psalm 43	*Let Your light and Your truth lead me*
Psalm 46:10–11	*Be still, and know that I am God*
Psalm 62:1–2, 5–8, 11–12a	*Wait in silence for the Lord*
Psalm 73:21–26	*You guide me with Your counsel*
Psalm 119:89–94	*I am Yours; save me*
Psalm 119:105–109	*Your word is a lamp to my feet*
Psalm 119:169–176	*Let my soul live and praise You*
Psalm 130:5–7	*I wait for the Lord, and in His word I hope*

READINGS

James 5:7–11   *Be patient until the coming of the Lord*

7Be patient, therefore, brothers, until the coming of the Lord. See how the farmer waits for the precious fruit of the earth, being patient about it, until it receives the early and the late rains. 8You also, be patient. Establish your hearts, for the coming of the Lord is at hand. 9Do not grumble against one another, brothers, so that you may not be judged; behold, the Judge is standing at the door. 10As an example of suffering and patience, brothers, take the prophets who spoke in the name of the Lord. ¹¹Behold, we consider those blessed who remained steadfast. You have heard of the steadfastness of Job, and you have seen the purpose of the Lord, how the Lord is compassionate and merciful.

Ecclesiastes 7:8b   *The patient spirit*

⁸ᵇThe patient in spirit is better than the proud in spirit.

Lamentations 3:25–26   *The Lord is good to those who wait*

²⁵ The LORD is good to those who wait for him,
    to the soul who seeks him.
²⁶ It is good that one should wait quietly
    for the salvation of the LORD.

ADDITIONAL READINGS

Gen. 16:1–6	*The impatience of Sarai and Abram*
1 Sam. 13:8–14	*The folly of Saul's impatience*
Is. 40:27–31	*Those who wait for the Lord shall renew their strength*
Rom. 5:1–5	*Tribulation works patience*
2 Cor. 4:16–18	*We do not lose heart*
Eph. 4:1–2a	*Walk in a manner of your calling with all patience*
Phil. 4:4–13	*Content in every circumstance*
Col. 1:9–14	*May you be strengthened for endurance and patience*
Heb. 6:10–12	*The faithful and patient saints inherited the promise*
2 Peter 3:8–9	*The Lord is patient toward you*

PRAYERS

Almighty God, our heavenly Father, we give You thanks that by the patient suffering and death of Your Son You rescued us from all faithlessness. Deliver __name__ from the sin of impatience. By Your Word and Spirit, teach __him/her__ to commend __himself/herself__ to You and to trust that in all things You work for __his/her__ eternal good. ▶

343

Strengthen _him/her_ to bear all crosses, adversities, and trials with patience and fervent trust in _his/her_ Savior as _he/she_ awaits Your deliverance and peace; through Jesus Christ, Your Son, our Lord, who lives and reigns with You and the Holy Spirit, one God, now and forever. (807)

O God, by the patient endurance of Your only-begotten Son You beat down the pride of the old enemy. Help us to treasure rightly in our hearts what our Lord has of His goodness borne for our sake that following His blessed example we may bear with patience all that is adverse to us; through Jesus Christ, Your Son, our Lord, who lives and reigns with You and the Holy Spirit, one God, now and forever. (199, 217)

O Lord, give us an abiding trust in Your good will that no impatience or suffering of mind or body may weaken our faith in You. Teach us to say, "Thy will be done," and to accept Your holy and gracious will in all things. Out of the shadows of our doubts and fears, bring the light of Your great mercy toward us; through Jesus Christ, Your Son, our Lord, who lives and reigns with You and the Holy Spirit, one God, now and forever. (808)

HYMNS
From God Can Nothing Move Me
LSB 713

The Lord my life arranges;
Who can His work destroy?
In His good time He changes
All sorrow into joy.
So let me then be still:
My body, soul, and spirit
His tender care inherit
According to His will. (st. 3)

Each day at His good pleasure
    God's gracious will is done.
He sent His greatest treasure
    In Jesus Christ, His Son.
    He ev'ry gift imparts.
The bread of earth and heaven
Are by His kindness given.
    Praise Him with thankful hearts! (st. 4)

Yet even though I suffer
    The world's unpleasantness,
And though the days grow rougher
    And bring me great distress,
    That day of bliss divine,
Which knows no end or measure,
And Christ, who is my pleasure,
    Forever shall be mine. (st. 6)

Stanzas 3–4 © 2006 Concordia Publishing House
Stanza 6 © 1978 Lutheran Book of Worship

If Thou But Trust in God to Guide Thee   *LSB 750*

What can these anxious cares avail thee,
    These never-ceasing moans and sighs?
What can it help if thou bewail thee
    O'er each dark moment as it flies?
Our cross and trials do but press
The heavier for our bitterness.

Be patient and await His leisure
    In cheerful hope, with heart content
To take whate'er thy Father's pleasure
    And His discerning love hath sent,
Nor doubt our inmost wants are known
To Him who chose us for His own. (sts. 2–3)

ADDITIONAL HYMNS

All Depends on Our Possessing	*LSB 732*
Entrust Your Days and Burdens	*LSB 754:3–4*
I Leave All Things to God's Direction	*LSB 719*
I Walk in Danger All the Way	*LSB 716:2, 5*
What Is the World to Me	*LSB 730*

For Those Whose Relatives Have Left the Faith

When a person renounces the Christian faith by word or action, Christian family and friends are deeply concerned about the spiritual welfare of their loved one. The pastor will remind them of Christ's faithfulness to His promises made to all who have been baptized. The pastor will encourage them to witness faithfully to their loved one, pray for him or her, and trust in the power of God's Word to work repentance and restoration to the faith.

PSALMODY

Psalm 53   *The fool says there is no God*

[1] The fool says in his heart, "There | is no God."*
> They are corrupt, doing abominable iniquity; there is none | who does good.

[2] God looks down from heaven on the chil- | dren of man*
> to see if there are any who understand, who seek | after God.

[3] They have all fallen away; together they have be- | come corrupt;*
> there is none who does good, not | even one.

[4] Have those who work evil no | knowledge,*
> who eat up my people as they eat bread, and do not call up- | on God?

⁵ There they are, in great terror, where there is no | terror!*
   For God scatters the bones of him who encamps against you;
   you put them to shame, for God has re- | jected them.
⁶ Oh, that salvation for Israel would come out of | Zion!*
   When God restores the fortunes of his people, let Jacob re-
   joice, let Israel | be glad.

Psalm 119:41–48   *I will speak of Your testimonies*

⁴¹ Let your steadfast love come to me, | O Lord,*
   your salvation according to your | promise;
⁴² then shall I have an answer for him who | taunts me,*
   for I trust | in your word.
⁴³ And take not the word of truth utterly out | of my mouth,*
   for my hope is in your | just decrees.
⁴⁴ I will keep your law con- | tinually,*
   forever and | ever,
⁴⁵ and I shall walk in a | wide place,*
   for I have sought your | precepts.
⁴⁶ I will also speak of your testimonies be- | fore kings*
   and shall not be | put to shame,
⁴⁷ for I find my delight in your com- | mandments,*
   which | I love.
⁴⁸ I will lift up my hands toward your commandments, | which I love,*
   and I will meditate on your | statutes.

Psalm 115   *Not to us, but to Your name give glory*

¹ Not to us, O Lord, not to us, but to your name give | glory,*
   for the sake of your steadfast love and your | faithfulness!
² Why should the | nations say,*
   "Where | is their God?"
³ Our God is in the | heavens;*
   he does all that he | pleases.

▶

⁴ Their idols are sil- | ver and gold,*
    the work of | human hands.
⁵ They have mouths, but | do not speak;*
    eyes, but | do not see.
⁶ They have ears, but | do not hear;*
    noses, but | do not smell.
⁷ They have hands, but do not feel; feet, but | do not walk;*
    and they do not make a sound | in their throat.
⁸ Those who make them be- | come like them;*
    so do all who | trust in them.
⁹ O Israel, trust | in the LORD!*
    He is their help | and their shield.
¹⁰ O house of Aaron, trust | in the LORD!*
    He is their help | and their shield.
¹¹ You who fear the LORD, trust | in the LORD!*
    He is their help | and their shield.
¹² The LORD has remembered us; he will | bless us;*
    he will bless the house of Israel; he will bless the house
    of | Aaron;
¹³ he will bless those who | fear the LORD,*
    both the small | and the great.
¹⁴ May the LORD give you | increase,*
    you and your | children!
¹⁵ May you be blessed | by the LORD,*
    who made | heaven and earth!
¹⁶ The heavens are the LORD's | heavens,*
    but the earth he has given to the chil- | dren of man.
¹⁷ The dead do not | praise the LORD,*
    nor do any who go down into | silence.
¹⁸ But we will | bless the LORD*
    from this time forth and forevermore. | Praise the LORD!

ADDITIONAL PSALMODY

Psalm 1	*The way of the righteous*
Psalm 14	*Are there any who seek after God?*
Psalm 25	*The Lord instructs sinners in the way*
Psalm 27:11–14	*Teach me Your way, O Lord*
Psalm 33:6–22	*The Lord brings the nations to nothing*
Psalm 43	*Let Your light and truth lead me*
Psalm 67	*May Your way be known on earth*
Psalm 85	*Restore us again, O God*
Psalm 119:129–136	*Your words give light and understanding*

READINGS

Ezekiel 34:11–24   *The Lord will search for His sheep*

¹¹"Thus says the Lord GOD: Behold, I, I myself will search for my sheep and will seek them out. ¹²As a shepherd seeks out his flock when he is among his sheep that have been scattered, so will I seek out my sheep, and I will rescue them from all places where they have been scattered on a day of clouds and thick darkness. ¹³And I will bring them out from the peoples and gather them from the countries, and will bring them into their own land. And I will feed them on the mountains of Israel, by the ravines, and in all the inhabited places of the country. ¹⁴I will feed them with good pasture, and on the mountain heights of Israel shall be their grazing land. There they shall lie down in good grazing land, and on rich pasture they shall feed on the mountains of Israel. ¹⁵I myself will be the shepherd of my sheep, and I myself will make them lie down, declares the Lord GOD. ¹⁶I will seek the lost, and I will bring back the strayed, and I will bind up the injured, and I will strengthen the weak, and the fat and the strong I will destroy. I will feed them in justice.

¹⁷"As for you, my flock, thus says the Lord GOD: Behold, I judge between sheep and sheep, between rams and male goats. ¹⁸Is it not enough for you to feed on the good pasture, that you must tread down with your feet the rest of your pasture; and to drink of clear water, that you must muddy the rest of the water with your feet? ¹⁹And ▶

must my sheep eat what you have trodden with your feet, and drink what you have muddied with your feet?

20"Therefore, thus says the Lord GOD to them: Behold, I, I myself will judge between the fat sheep and the lean sheep. 21Because you push with side and shoulder, and thrust at all the weak with your horns, till you have scattered them abroad, 22I will rescue my flock; they shall no longer be a prey. And I will judge between sheep and sheep. 23And I will set up over them one shepherd, my servant David, and he shall feed them: he shall feed them and be their shepherd. 24And I, the LORD, will be their God, and my servant David shall be prince among them. I am the LORD; I have spoken."

John 6:66–69   *Jesus has the words of eternal life*

66After this many of [Jesus'] disciples turned back and no longer walked with him. 67So Jesus said to the Twelve, "Do you want to go away as well?" 68Simon Peter answered him, "Lord, to whom shall we go? You have the words of eternal life, 69and we have believed, and have come to know, that you are the Holy One of God."

1 Timothy 6:3–12   *Take hold of eternal life*

3If anyone teaches a different doctrine and does not agree with the sound words of our Lord Jesus Christ and the teaching that accords with godliness, 4he is puffed up with conceit and understands nothing. He has an unhealthy craving for controversy and for quarrels about words, which produce envy, dissension, slander, evil suspicions, 5and constant friction among people who are depraved in mind and deprived of the truth, imagining that godliness is a means of gain. 6Now there is great gain in godliness with contentment, 7for we brought nothing into the world, and we cannot take anything out of the world. 8But if we have food and clothing, with these we will be content. 9But those who desire to be rich fall into temptation, into a snare, into many senseless and harmful desires that plunge people into ruin and destruction. 10For the love of money is a root of all kinds of evils. It is through this craving that some have wandered away from the faith and pierced themselves with many pangs.

¹¹But as for you, O man of God, flee these things. Pursue righteousness, godliness, faith, love, steadfastness, gentleness. ¹²Fight the good fight of the faith. Take hold of the eternal life to which you were called and about which you made the good confession in the presence of many witnesses.

1 Peter 3:14–17 *Do not be afraid to defend the faith*

¹⁴But even if you should suffer for righteousness' sake, you will be blessed. Have no fear of them, nor be troubled, ¹⁵but in your hearts regard Christ the Lord as holy, always being prepared to make a defense to anyone who asks you for a reason for the hope that is in you; ¹⁶yet do it with gentleness and respect, having a good conscience, so that, when you are slandered, those who revile your good behavior in Christ may be put to shame. ¹⁷For it is better to suffer for doing good, if that should be God's will, than for doing evil.

Acts 4:12 *There is salvation in Jesus alone*

¹²There is salvation in no one else, for there is no other name under heaven given among men by which we must be saved.

ADDITIONAL READINGS

Luke 15:1–7	*Parable of the lost sheep*
Luke 15:11–32	*Parable of the prodigal son*
John 8:31–36	*The truth of Jesus will set free*
John 10:1–18	*Jesus is the Good Shepherd*
John 14:1–7	*Jesus is the way, the truth, and the life*
2 Cor. 4:1–6	*The light of the Gospel*
Col. 2:8–15	*Let no one take you captive by human wisdom*
2 Tim. 2:14–19	*God's firm foundation stands*
2 Peter 1:16–20	*We do not follow myths*
1 John 4:1–6	*Test the spirits*
Jude 17–23	*Persevere in the true faith*

PRAYERS

For the return of the wayward and erring

Almighty, merciful, and most gracious God and Father, we implore You to turn the heart of __name__, who has forsaken the faith once delivered to Your Church and wandered from it. Mercifully visit __him/her__ and turn __him/her__ again that in singleness of heart __he/she__ may take pleasure in Your Word and be made wise to salvation through faith in Christ Jesus, our Lord, who lives and reigns with You and the Holy Spirit, one God, now and forever. (112 alt.)

For the family

Almighty and merciful God, we fervently pray for __name__, who has turned away from You. Send Your holy angels to watch over __him/her__, and deliver __him/her__ by Your mighty Word. Comfort and uphold __his/her__ family that, committing their loved one into Your hands, they may know the consolation of Your love and not be afraid; through Jesus Christ, Your Son, our Lord, who lives and reigns with You and the Holy Spirit, one God, now and forever. (809)

HYMNS

O Dearest Jesus, What Law Hast Thou Broken   *LSB 439*

What punishment so strange is suffered yonder!
The Shepherd dies for sheep that loved to wander;
The Master pays the debt His servants owe Him,
Who would not know Him. (st. 4)

Lord, 'Tis Not That I Did Choose Thee
LSB 573

Lord, 'tis not that I did choose Thee;
    That, I know, could never be;
For this heart would still refuse Thee
    Had Thy grace not chosen me.
Thou hast from the sin that stained me
    Washed and cleansed and set me free
And unto this end ordained me,
    That I ever live to Thee.

It was grace in Christ that called me,
    Taught my darkened heart and mind;
Else the world had yet enthralled me,
    To Thy heav'nly glories blind.
Now I worship none above Thee;
    For Thy grace alone I thirst,
Knowing well that, if I love Thee,
    Thou, O Lord, didst love me first. (sts. 1–2)

ADDITIONAL HYMNS

Christ, the Word of God Incarnate	*LSB 540:4*
I Bind unto Myself Today	*LSB 604*
Jesus Sinners Doth Receive	*LSB 609:1–3*
Not unto Us	*LSB 558:3*
The King of Love My Shepherd Is	*LSB 709:3*

Occult Practices and Demonic Affliction

Those engaged in occult activities and other satanic arts align themselves with the spiritual forces opposed to the one true God. Such practices endanger the body as well as the soul. In these situations, the pastor's only weapon is the name of Jesus Christ invoked in prayer, recalling the Lord's defeat of Satan and all his works and all his ways. Remembrance of Holy Baptism through the use of Individual Confession and Absolution (pages 28–30) is strongly encouraged. In cases where the individual is unrepentant and demonic possession is suspected, counsel from other experienced pastors should be sought.

PSALMODY

Psalm 91 *The serpent you will trample underfoot*

1 He who dwells in the shelter of the | Most High*
   will abide in the shadow of the Al- | mighty.

2 I will say to the Lord, "My refuge and my | fortress,*
   my God, in | whom I trust."

3 For he will deliver you from the snare of the | fowler*
   and from the deadly | pestilence.

4 He will cover you with his pinions, and under his wings you will find | refuge;*
   his faithfulness is a shield and | buckler.

5 You will not fear the terror | of the night,*
   nor the arrow that | flies by day,

6 nor the pestilence that stalks in | darkness,*
   nor the destruction that wastes at | noonday.

7 A thousand may fall at your side, ten thousand at your | right hand,*
   but it will not come | near you.

8 You will only look | with your eyes*
   and see the recompense of the | wicked.

9 Because you have made the Lord your | dwelling place—*
   the Most High, who is my | refuge—

¹⁰ no evil shall be allowed to be- | fall you,*
      no plague come | near your tent.

¹¹ For he will command his angels con- | cerning you*
      to guard you in | all your ways.

¹² On their hands they will | bear you up,*
      lest you strike your foot a- | gainst a stone.

¹³ You will tread on the lion and the | adder;*
      the young lion and the serpent you will trample | underfoot.

¹⁴ "Because he holds fast to me in love, I will de- | liver him;*
      I will protect him, because he | knows my name.

¹⁵ When he calls to me, I will answer him; I will be with him
in | trouble;*
      I will rescue him and | honor him.

¹⁶ With long life I will sat- | isfy him*
      and show him my sal- | vation."

Psalm 107:1–2, 10–15   *The Lord brought them out of darkness*

¹ Oh give thanks to the LORD, for | he is good,*
      for his steadfast love endures for- | ever!

² Let the redeemed of the LORD | say so,*
      whom he has redeemed from | trouble.

¹⁰ Some sat in darkness and in the shad- | ow of death,*
      prisoners in affliction | and in irons,

¹¹ for they had rebelled against the | words of God,*
      and spurned the counsel of the | Most High.

¹² So he bowed their hearts down with hard | labor;*
      they fell down, with | none to help.

¹³ Then they cried to the LORD in their | trouble,*
      and he delivered them from | their distress.

¹⁴ He brought them out of darkness and the shad- | ow of death,*
      and burst their | bonds apart.

¹⁵ Let them thank the LORD for his | steadfast love,*
      for his wondrous works to the chil- | dren of men!

Psalm 143

Deliver me from my enemies, O Lord

¹ Hear my prayer, O Lᴏʀᴅ; give ear to my pleas for | mercy!*
   In your faithfulness answer me, in your | righteousness!

² Enter not into judgment with your | servant,*
   for no one living is righteous be- | fore you.

³ For the enemy has pursued my soul; he has crushed my life | to the ground;*
   he has made me sit in darkness like | those long dead.

⁴ Therefore my spirit faints with- | in me;*
   my heart within me | is appalled.

⁵ I remember the days of old; I meditate on all that | you have done;*
   I ponder the work | of your hands.

⁶ I stretch out my | hands to you;*
   my soul thirsts for you like a | parched land.

⁷ Answer me quickly, O Lᴏʀᴅ! My | spirit fails!*
   Hide not your face from me, lest I be like those who go down | to the pit.

⁸ Let me hear in the morning of your steadfast love, for in | you I trust.*
   Make me know the way I should go, for to you I lift | up my soul.

⁹ Deliver me from my enemies, | O Lᴏʀᴅ!*
   I have fled to you for | refuge!

¹⁰ Teach me to do your will, for you | are my God!*
   Let your good Spirit lead me on | level ground!

¹¹ For your name's sake, O Lᴏʀᴅ, pre- | serve my life!*
   In your righteousness bring my soul out of | trouble!

¹² And in your steadfast love you will cut off my | enemies,*
   and you will destroy all the adversaries of my soul, for I am your | servant.

ADDITIONAL PSALMODY

Psalm 3	*Arise, O Lord, and save me*
Psalm 27:1–5	*The Lord is my light and my salvation*
Psalm 38:1–6, 21–22	*Make haste to help me, O Lord*
Psalm 46	*God utters His voice, the earth melts*
Psalm 70	*Hasten to me, O God*
Psalm 141	*Give ear to my voice when I call to You*

READINGS

Ephesians 6:10–18   *Our warfare is against the forces of evil*

¹⁰Be strong in the Lord and in the strength of his might. ¹¹Put on the whole armor of God, that you may be able to stand against the schemes of the devil. ¹²For we do not wrestle against flesh and blood, but against the rulers, against the authorities, against the cosmic powers over this present darkness, against the spiritual forces of evil in the heavenly places. ¹³Therefore take up the whole armor of God, that you may be able to withstand in the evil day, and having done all, to stand firm. ¹⁴Stand therefore, having fastened on the belt of truth, and having put on the breastplate of righteousness, ¹⁵and, as shoes for your feet, having put on the readiness given by the gospel of peace. ¹⁶In all circumstances take up the shield of faith, with which you can extinguish all the flaming darts of the evil one; ¹⁷and take the helmet of salvation, and the sword of the Spirit, which is the word of God, ¹⁸praying at all times in the Spirit, with all prayer and supplication. To that end keep alert with all perseverance, making supplication for all the saints.

Matthew 4:1–11   *Jesus defeats Satan in His temptation*

¹Then Jesus was led up by the Spirit into the wilderness to be tempted by the devil. ²And after fasting forty days and forty nights, he was hungry. ³And the tempter came and said to him, "If you are the Son of God, command these stones to become loaves of bread." ⁴But he answered, "It is written,

▶

> "'Man shall not live by bread alone,
> but by every word that comes from the mouth of God.'"

⁵Then the devil took him to the holy city and set him on the pinnacle of the temple ⁶and said to him, "If you are the Son of God, throw yourself down, for it is written,

> "'He will command his angels concerning you,'

and

> "'On their hands they will bear you up,
> lest you strike your foot against a stone.'"

⁷Jesus said to him, "Again it is written, 'You shall not put the Lord your God to the test.'" ⁸Again, the devil took him to a very high mountain and showed him all the kingdoms of the world and their glory. ⁹And he said to him, "All these I will give you, if you will fall down and worship me." ¹⁰Then Jesus said to him, "Be gone, Satan! For it is written,

> "'You shall worship the Lord your God
> and him only shall you serve.'"

¹¹Then the devil left him, and behold, angels came and were ministering to him.

ADDITIONAL READINGS

1 Sam. 28:7–17	*Saul and the medium of Endor*
Is. 8:16–20	*Should not people inquire of their God?*
Mark 16:15–18	*In My name they will cast out demons*
Luke 10:17–20	*Satan fell like lightning from heaven*
Luke 11:14–23	*Jesus, the stronger one*
Acts 19:18–20	*Renouncing satanic arts*
Rom. 8:28–39	*All things work together for good*
Col. 2:8–15	*Christ's triumph over Satan imparted through Baptism*
Heb. 4:14–16	*Let us approach the throne of grace*
1 Peter 5:6–11	*Resist the devil*

PRAYERS

Almighty and most merciful God, Father, Son, and Holy Spirit, since You have called __name__ by Your name in the waters of Holy Baptism, deliver __him/her__ from the oppression of Satan and his evil host. Break and hinder every evil plan and purpose of the devil, the world, and __his__ own sinful nature that does not want __him/her__ to live in the true faith and the freedom that comes from Christ's righteousness. Do not allow __him/her__ to be severed from You, but strengthen __him/her__ against every assault of the evil one; for You live and reign, one God, now and forever. (810)

Almighty God, You justify the ungodly and desire not the death of the sinner. We humbly ask You to assist __name__ by Your heavenly aid and to shield __him/her__ always from the evil foe. Grant that __he/she__ may not be separated from You by any temptation but, trusting in Your mercy, may serve You without ceasing; through Jesus Christ, Your Son, our Lord, who lives and reigns with You and the Holy Spirit, one God, now and forever. (811)

For the return of the wayward and erring

Almighty and most gracious God and Father, we implore You to turn the heart of __name__, who is in doubt or temptation through the corruption of Your truth. Mercifully visit __him/her__ and restore __him/her__ again that in gladness of heart __he/she__ may take pleasure in Your Word and be made wise to salvation through faith in Christ Jesus, our Lord, who lives and reigns with You and the Holy Spirit, one God, now and forever. (112 alt.)

For the family

Almighty and merciful God, we fervently pray for __name__, who is severely attacked by the powers of darkness. Send Your holy angels to watch over __him/her__, and deliver __him/her__ by Your mighty ▶

Word. Comfort and uphold _his/her_ family that, committing their loved one into Your hands, they may know the consolation of Your love and not be afraid; through Jesus Christ, Your Son, our Lord, who lives and reigns with You and the Holy Spirit, one God, now and forever. (809)

The following prayer is by Martin Luther. The pastor may lay his hands on the head of the one for whom the prayer is offered as it is spoken.

O God, almighty Father, You told us through Your Son, "Truly, truly, I say to you, whatever you ask of the Father in My name, He will give it to you." He has commanded and encouraged us to pray in His name, "Ask, and you will receive," and has also said, "Call upon Me in the day of trouble; I will deliver you, and you shall glorify Me." We unworthy sinners, relying on these Your words and command, pray for Your mercy with such faith as we can muster. Graciously free _name_ from all evil, and undo the work that Satan has done in _him/her_, to the honor of Your name and the strengthening of the faith of believers; through the same Jesus Christ, Your Son, our Lord, who lives and reigns with You and the Holy Spirit, one God, now and forever. (812)

HYMNS

A Mighty Fortress Is Our God

LSB 656

With might of ours can naught be done,
    Soon were our loss effected;
But for us fights the valiant One,
    Whom God Himself elected.
Ask ye, Who is this?
Jesus Christ it is,
    Of Sabaoth Lord,
    And there's none other God;
He holds the field forever.

Though devils all the world should fill,
    All eager to devour us,
We tremble not, we fear no ill;
    They shall not overpow'r us.
This world's prince may still
Scowl fierce as he will,
    He can harm us none.
    He's judged; the deed is done;
One little word can fell him. (sts. 2–3)

I Bind unto Myself Today

LSB 604

I bind unto myself today
    The strong name of the Trinity
By invocation of the same,
    The Three in One and One in Three.

I bind this day to me forever,
    By pow'r of faith, Christ's incarnation,
His Baptism in the Jordan River,
    His cross of death for my salvation,
His bursting from the spicèd tomb,
    His riding up the heav'nly way,
His coming at the day of doom,
    I bind unto myself today.

I bind unto myself today
    The pow'r of God to hold and lead,
His eye to watch, His might to stay,
    His ear to hearken to my need,
The wisdom of my God to teach,
    His hand to guide, His shield to ward,
The Word of God to give me speech,
    His heav'nly host to be my guard.

▶

Against the demon snares of sin,
    The vice that gives temptation force,
The natural lusts that war within,
    The hostile foes that mar my course;
Or few or many, far or nigh,
    In ev'ry place and in all hours,
Against their fierce hostility,
    I bind to me those holy pow'rs. (sts. 1–4)

ADDITIONAL HYMNS

God's Own Child, I Gladly Say It	LSB 594:2–3
Jesus, Priceless Treasure	LSB 743:2–3
Rise! To Arms! With Prayer Employ You	LSB 668:1
Through Jesus' Blood and Merit	LSB 746
Triune God, Be Thou Our Stay	LSB 505

Addiction

Addictions (e.g., alcohol, drugs, gambling, pornography) become a substitute for God as the object of the addiction becomes the center of one's life and enslaves that person into a bondage from which he cannot free himself. In addition, the addiction frustrates and angers the addict's family and friends who also need the encouragement and comfort of God's Word. In his ministry to the addict, the pastor will call the addict to repentance and a lively trust in the freeing Gospel of Jesus Christ. The pastor will encourage the addict to rely on the strength of Christ and will shepherd him or her to live in the newness of life given in Holy Baptism. In his ministry to the members of the addict's family, the pastor will encourage patience and perseverance, appropriate confrontation and forgiveness, and, above all, reliance on the sure mercy of God to provide for their every need.

When visiting someone undergoing treatment, the rite of Visiting the Sick and Distressed (pages 31–38) may be used.

PSALMODY

Psalm 6
O Lord, deliver my life

¹ O Lord, rebuke me not in your | anger,*
    nor discipline me | in your wrath.

² Be gracious to me, O Lord, for I am | languishing;*
    heal me, O Lord, for my bones are | troubled.

³ My soul also is greatly | troubled.*
    But you, O Lord— | how long?

⁴ Turn, O Lord, deliv- | er my life;*
    save me for the sake of your | steadfast love.

⁵ For in death there is no remem- | brance of you;*
    in Sheol who will | give you praise?

⁶ I am weary with my moaning; every night I flood my | bed with tears;*
    I drench my couch with my | weeping.
       ►

⁷ My eye wastes away be- | cause of grief;*
>   it grows weak because of | all my foes.
⁸ Depart from me, all you workers of | evil,*
>   for the LORD has heard the sound of my | weeping.
⁹ The LORD has | heard my plea;*
>   the LORD ac- | cepts my prayer.
¹⁰ All my enemies shall be ashamed and greatly | troubled;*
>   they shall turn back and be put to shame in a | moment.

Psalm 69:1–5, 16–18   *The wrongs I have done are not hidden*

¹ Save me, | O God!*
>   For the waters have come up | to my neck.
² I sink in deep mire, where there is no | foothold;*
>   I have come into deep waters, and the flood sweeps | over me.
³ I am weary with my crying out; my | throat is parched.*
>   My eyes grow dim with waiting | for my God.
⁴ More in number than the hairs | of my head*
>   are those who hate me with- | out cause;
> mighty are those who would destroy me, those who attack | me
> with lies.*
>   What I did not steal must I | now restore?
⁵ O God, you know my | folly;*
>   the wrongs I have done are not hid- | den from you.
¹⁶ Answer me, O LORD, for your steadfast | love is good;*
>   according to your abundant mercy, | turn to me.
¹⁷ Hide not your face from your servant; for I am | in distress;*
>   make haste to | answer me.
¹⁸ Draw near to my soul, re- | deem me;*
>   ransom me because of my | enemies!

Psalm 70 *I am poor and needy, O God*

¹ Make haste, O God, to de- | liver me!*
O Lord, make haste to | help me!

² Let them be put to shame and confusion who | seek my life!*
Let them be turned back and brought to dishonor who de- | sire my hurt!

³ Let them turn back because | of their shame*
who say, "A- | ha, Aha!"

⁴ May all who seek you rejoice and be | glad in you!*
May those who love your salvation say evermore, | "God is great!"

⁵ But I am poor and needy; hasten to me, | O God!*
You are my help and my deliverer; O Lord, do | not delay!

ADDITIONAL PSALMODY

Psalm 20:1–2	*May the Lord answer, protect, and support you*
Psalm 31	*Be a rock of refuge for me*
Psalm 51:1–12	*Forgive, renew, and strengthen me*
Psalm 55:1, 16–17, 22	*Cast your burden on the Lord*
Psalm 71:1–5, 12	*Deliver me and rescue me*
Psalm 102:1–7, 11–17	*Do not hide Your face in the day of distress*
Psalm 121	*My help comes from the Lord*
Psalm 130	*Out of the depths I cry to You, O Lord*
Psalm 143	*Teach me to do Your will, for You are my God*

READINGS

Romans 13:11b–14 *Let us cast off the works of darkness*

¹¹ᵇThe hour has come for you to wake from sleep. For salvation is nearer to us now than when we first believed. ¹²The night is far gone; the day is at hand. So then let us cast off the works of darkness and put on the armor of light. ¹³Let us walk properly as in the daytime, not in orgies and drunkenness, not in sexual immorality and sensuality, not in quarreling and jealousy. ¹⁴But put on the Lord Jesus Christ, and make no provision for the flesh, to gratify its desires.

Romans 7:15–25   *I do not do what I want*

¹⁵I do not understand my own actions. For I do not do what I want, but I do the very thing I hate. ¹⁶Now if I do what I do not want, I agree with the law, that it is good. ¹⁷So now it is no longer I who do it, but sin that dwells within me. ¹⁸For I know that nothing good dwells in me, that is, in my flesh. For I have the desire to do what is right, but not the ability to carry it out. ¹⁹For I do not do the good I want, but the evil I do not want is what I keep on doing. ²⁰Now if I do what I do not want, it is no longer I who do it, but sin that dwells within me.

²¹So I find it to be a law that when I want to do right, evil lies close at hand. ²²For I delight in the law of God, in my inner being, ²³but I see in my members another law waging war against the law of my mind and making me captive to the law of sin that dwells in my members. ²⁴Wretched man that I am! Who will deliver me from this body of death? ²⁵Thanks be to God through Jesus Christ our Lord! So then, I myself serve the law of God with my mind, but with my flesh I serve the law of sin.

Colossians 3:12–17   *Let the peace of Christ rule in your hearts*

¹²Put on then, as God's chosen ones, holy and beloved, compassion, kindness, humility, meekness, and patience, ¹³bearing with one another and, if one has a complaint against another, forgiving each other; as the Lord has forgiven you, so you also must forgive. ¹⁴And above all these put on love, which binds everything together in perfect harmony. ¹⁵And let the peace of Christ rule in your hearts, to which indeed you were called in one body. And be thankful. ¹⁶Let the word of Christ dwell in you richly, teaching and admonishing one another in all wisdom, singing psalms and hymns and spiritual songs, with thankfulness in your hearts to God. ¹⁷And whatever you do, in word or deed, do everything in the name of the Lord Jesus, giving thanks to God the Father through him.

ADDITIONAL READINGS

Prov. 7:6–27	*Sexual addiction leads to death*
Luke 15:11–32	*Parable of the prodigal son*
Luke 21:34–36	*Do not be weighed down with drunkenness*
John 8:34–36	*The Son makes us free*
Rom. 6:1–14	*Dead to sin and alive to God in Christ*
1 Cor. 6:9–11	*Drunkards will not inherit the Kingdom*
1 Cor. 9:24–27	*I discipline my body and keep it under control*
Gal. 5:16–25	*The works of the flesh and the fruit of the Spirit*
Eph. 5:8–21	*Be filled with the Spirit*
Col. 3:1–10	*Set your mind on things above*

PRAYERS

For the individual

Gracious God, You are the strength of all who put their trust in You. We pray for __name__, who is enslaved by __alcohol / drugs / gambling / pornography / other__. Deliver __him/her__ from all that would hold __him/her__ captive that by Your grace __he/she__ may walk in the newness of life; through Jesus Christ, Your Son, our Lord, who lives and reigns with You and the Holy Spirit, one God, now and forever. (813)

For a recovering addict

Loving Father, You sent Your Son to proclaim liberty to the captives and freedom to the oppressed. Sustain __name__ as __he/she__ recovers from addiction to __alcohol / drugs / gambling / pornography / other__. Strengthen __him/her__ by Your Holy Spirit that, the bonds of __his/her__ addiction being broken, __he/she__ may be restored to fullness of life in Christ, who lives and reigns with You and the Holy Spirit, one God, now and forever. (814)

For the family

Heavenly Father, shed the light of Your mercy upon the family and loved ones of __name__, and dispel the dark night of __his/her__ addiction. Turn sorrow into joy, pain into gladness, and worry and anxiety into a ▶

confident hope in You and in Your gracious promises. Bring healing to this family and to _ name _ that _ his/her _ dependency may be given over to You. Grant that _ his/her _ sin be forgiven and that a renewal of love and unity take place; through Jesus Christ, Your Son, our Lord, who lives and reigns with You and the Holy Spirit, one God, now and forever. (815)

HYMN

One Thing's Needful
LSB 536

One thing's needful; Lord, this treasure
> Teach me highly to regard.
All else, though it first give pleasure,
> Is a yoke that presses hard!
Beneath it the heart is still fretting and striving,
No true, lasting happiness ever deriving.
> This one thing is needful; all others are vain—
> I count all but loss that I Christ may obtain! (st. 1)

Wisdom's highest, noblest treasure,
> Jesus, is revealed in You.
Let me find in You my pleasure,
> And my wayward will subdue,
Humility there and simplicity reigning,
In paths of true wisdom my steps ever training.
> If I learn from Jesus this knowledge divine,
> The blessing of heavenly wisdom is mine. (st. 3)

Nothing have I, Christ, to offer,
> You alone, my highest good.
Nothing have I, Lord, to proffer
> But Your crimson-colored blood.
Your death on the cross has death wholly defeated
And thereby my righteousness fully completed;
> Salvation's white raiments I there did obtain,
> And in them in glory with You I shall reign. (st. 4)

Therefore You alone, my Savior,
    Shall be all in all to me;
Search my heart and my behavior,
    Root out all hypocrisy.
Through all my life's pilgrimage, guard and uphold me,
In loving forgiveness, O Jesus, enfold me.
    This one thing is needful; all others are vain—
    I count all but loss that I Christ may obtain! (st. 5)

ADDITIONAL HYMNS

All for Christ I Have Forsaken	*LSB 753*
Come unto Me, Ye Weary	*LSB 684*
I Am Trusting Thee, Lord Jesus	*LSB 729*
I Heard the Voice of Jesus Say	*LSB 699*
Rise, My Soul, to Watch and Pray	*LSB 663*
Today Your Mercy Calls Us	*LSB 915*

Homosexuality

Like all sins, homosexual lust lives in the flesh and mind and may or may not manifest itself through indecent, ungodly behavior. Those who struggle with homosexuality need to hear God's judgment against this distortion of His gift of sexuality. It is imperative, however, that the pastor clearly distinguish between God's condemnation of homosexual lust and behavior and His relentless love for all sinners. Using this clear word of God, the pastor will call for repentance and proclaim the saving Gospel, which alone has the power to overcome sin and produce fruits of repentance. Families of homosexuals also need the light and strength of the Gospel as they seek to support their loved one while yet speaking the truth of God's Word.

PSALMODY

Psalm 51:1–12   *Create in me a clean heart, O God*

¹ Have mercy on me, O God, according to your | steadfast love;*
    according to your abundant mercy blot out my trans- | gressions.

² Wash me thoroughly from my in- | iquity,*
    and cleanse me | from my sin!

³ For I know my trans- | gressions,*
    and my sin is ever be- | fore me.

⁴ Against you, you only, have I sinned and done what is evil | in your sight,*
    so that you may be justified in your words and blameless in your | judgment.

⁵ Behold, I was brought forth in in- | iquity,*
    and in sin did my mother con- | ceive me.

⁶ Behold, you delight in truth in the inward | being,*
    and you teach me wisdom in the | secret heart.

⁷ Purge me with hyssop, and I | shall be clean;*
    wash me, and I shall be whit- | er than snow.

⁸ Let me hear joy and | gladness;*
    let the bones that you have bro- | ken rejoice.
⁹ Hide your face | from my sins,*
    and blot out all my in- | iquities.
¹⁰ Create in me a clean heart, | O God,*
    and renew a right spirit with- | in me.
¹¹ Cast me not away from your | presence,*
    and take not your Holy Spirit | from me.
¹² Restore to me the joy of your sal- | vation,*
    and uphold me with a willing | spirit.

Psalm 32   *You forgave the iniquity of my sin*

¹ Blessèd is the one whose transgression is for- | given,*
    whose sin is | covered.
² Blessèd is the man against whom the LORD counts no in- | iquity,*
    and in whose spirit there is | no deceit.
³ For when I kept silent, my bones wast- | ed away*
    through my groaning | all day long.
⁴ For day and night your hand was heavy up- | on me;*
    my strength was dried up as by the heat of | summer.
⁵ I acknowledged my sin to you, and I did not cover my in- | iquity;*
    I said, "I will confess my transgressions to the LORD," and
    you forgave the iniquity | of my sin.
⁶ Therefore let everyone who is godly offer prayer to you at a time
when you | may be found;*
    surely in the rush of great waters, they shall not | reach him.
⁷ You are a hiding place for me; you preserve me from | trouble;*
    you surround me with shouts of de- | liverance.
⁸ I will instruct you and teach you in the way | you should go;*
    I will counsel you with my eye up- | on you.
⁹ Be not like a horse or a mule, without under- | standing,*
    which must be curbed with bit and bridle, or it will not
    stay | near you.

►

¹⁰ Many are the sorrows of the | wicked,*
    but steadfast love surrounds the one who trusts | in the LORD.
¹¹ Be glad in the LORD, and rejoice, O | righteous,*
    and shout for joy, all you up- | right in heart!

Psalm 38:1–11, 18, 21–22   *Do not forsake me, O Lord*

¹ O LORD, rebuke me not in your | anger,*
    nor discipline me | in your wrath!
² For your arrows have sunk | into me,*
    and your hand has come | down on me.
³ There is no soundness in my flesh because of your
    indig- | nation;*
    there is no health in my bones because | of my sin.
⁴ For my iniquities have gone o- | ver my head;*
    like a heavy burden, they are too heav- | y for me.
⁵ My wounds stink and | fester*
    because of my | foolishness,
⁶ I am utterly bowed down and | prostrate;*
    all the day I go about | mourning.
⁷ For my sides are filled with | burning,*
    and there is no soundness | in my flesh.
⁸ I am feeble | and crushed;*
    I groan because of the tumult | of my heart.
⁹ O Lord, all my longing is be- | fore you;*
    my sighing is not hid- | den from you.
¹⁰ My heart throbs; my strength | fails me,*
    and the light of my eyes—it also has | gone from me.
¹¹ My friends and companions stand aloof | from my plague,*
    and my nearest kin stand | far off.
¹⁸ I confess my in- | iquity;*
    I am sorry | for my sin.
²¹ Do not forsake me, | O LORD!*
    O my God, be not | far from me!

²² Make haste to | help me,*
O Lord, my sal- | vation!

ADDITIONAL PSALMODY

Psalm 1	*Blessed are the righteous*
Psalm 6	*Heal me, O Lord, for I am troubled*
Psalm 25:1–12, 16–18	*Consider my affliction, and forgive all my sins*
Psalm 34:1–8, 17–20, 22	*The Lord is near to the brokenhearted*
Psalm 69:1–3, 5, 16–18a	*Save me, O God, for I am sinking*
Psalm 130	*I wait for the Lord and hope in His word*
Psalm 139	*The Lord knows all, even my heart*
Psalm 141:1–4, 8	*I seek refuge in the Lord*
Psalm 143:1–2, 6–8, 10–11	*Make me know the way I should go*

READINGS
1 Corinthians 6:9–11, 15–20   *The body is a temple*

⁹Do you not know that the unrighteous will not inherit the kingdom of God? Do not be deceived: neither the sexually immoral, nor idolaters, nor adulterers, nor men who practice homosexuality, ¹⁰nor thieves, nor the greedy, nor drunkards, nor revilers, nor swindlers will inherit the kingdom of God. ¹¹And such were some of you. But you were washed, you were sanctified, you were justified in the name of the Lord Jesus Christ and by the Spirit of our God.

¹⁵Do you not know that your bodies are members of Christ? Shall I then take the members of Christ and make them members of a prostitute? Never! ¹⁶Or do you not know that he who is joined to a prostitute becomes one body with her? For, as it is written, "The two will become one flesh." ¹⁷But he who is joined to the Lord becomes one spirit with him. ¹⁸Flee from sexual immorality. Every other sin a person commits is outside the body, but the sexually immoral person sins against his own body. ¹⁹Or do you not know that your body is a temple of the Holy Spirit within you, whom you have from God? You are not your own, ²⁰for you were bought with a price. So glorify God in your body.

2 Peter 2:4–10a   *The impenitence of Sodom and Gomorrah*

⁴If God did not spare angels when they sinned, but cast them into hell and committed them to chains of gloomy darkness to be kept until the judgment; ⁵if he did not spare the ancient world, but preserved Noah, a herald of righteousness, with seven others, when he brought a flood upon the world of the ungodly; ⁶if by turning the cities of Sodom and Gomorrah to ashes he condemned them to extinction, making them an example of what is going to happen to the ungodly; ⁷and if he rescued righteous Lot, greatly distressed by the sensual conduct of the wicked ⁸(for as that righteous man lived among them day after day, he was tormenting his righteous soul over their lawless deeds that he saw and heard); ⁹then the Lord knows how to rescue the godly from trials, and to keep the unrighteous under punishment until the day of judgment, ¹⁰and especially those who indulge in the lust of defiling passion and despise authority.

John 3:19–21   *People loved darkness rather than light*

¹⁹[Jesus said:] "This is the judgment: the light has come into the world, and people loved the darkness rather than the light because their deeds were evil. ²⁰For everyone who does wicked things hates the light and does not come to the light, lest his deeds should be exposed. ²¹But whoever does what is true comes to the light, so that it may be clearly seen that his deeds have been carried out in God."

ADDITIONAL READINGS

PRAYERS

For the individual

Almighty God, in Your righteous judgment, You have condemned our sin and declared us all to be unrighteous; yet, in Your gracious mercy You have inflicted the punishment for our sin on Your beloved Son, Jesus Christ, who was given into death for our offenses. Look with compassion upon _name_, who struggles with homosexuality. Grant _him/her_ grace daily to turn to You in contrition and repentance, to receive with a thankful heart the forgiveness won for _him/her_ by Christ, and to desire earnestly to turn away from sin and walk in the way of truth. Strengthen _his/her_ faith, and sustain _him/her_ always by Your Holy Spirit; through Jesus Christ, Your Son, our Lord, who lives and reigns with You and the Holy Spirit, one God, now and forever. (816)

For the family

Heavenly Father, look with favor upon the family and loved ones of _name_, and comfort them with Your Word. Grant them Your grace that they may witness to the truth of Your Word as they entrust _name_ to Your care. Sustain them in the hope of the Gospel that, facing the future with confidence, they may support their loved one and encourage _him/her_ to live according to Your Word; through Jesus Christ, Your Son, our Lord, who lives and reigns with You and the Holy Spirit, one God, now and forever. (817)

HYMNS

Create in Me
LSB 192/956

Create in me a clean heart, O God,
    and renew a right spirit within me.
Cast me not away from Thy presence,
    and take not Thy Holy Spirit from me.
Restore unto me the joy of Thy salvation,
    and uphold me with Thy free spirit. Amen.

Psalm 51:10–12

I Heard the Voice of Jesus Say

LSB 699

I heard the voice of Jesus say,
    "Come unto Me and rest;
Lay down, thou weary one, lay down
    Thy head upon My breast."
I came to Jesus as I was,
    So weary, worn, and sad;
I found in Him a resting place,
    And He has made me glad.

I heard the voice of Jesus say,
    "Behold, I freely give
The living water; thirsty one,
    Stoop down and drink and live."
I came to Jesus, and I drank
    Of that life-giving stream;
My thirst was quenched, my soul revived,
    And now I live in Him.

I heard the voice of Jesus say,
    "I am this dark world's light.
Look unto Me; thy morn shall rise
    And all thy day be bright."
I looked to Jesus, and I found
    In Him my star, my sun;
And in that light of life I'll walk
    Till trav'ling days are done.

ADDITIONAL HYMNS

Come unto Me, Ye Weary	*LSB 684*
I Am Trusting Thee, Lord Jesus	*LSB 729*
One Thing's Needful	*LSB 536:1, 3–5*
Rise, My Soul, to Watch and Pray	*LSB 663*
Today Your Mercy Calls Us	*LSB 915*

HOME AND FAMILY

Marriage

Marriage, the union of a man and a woman, reflects the mystical union between Christ and His bride, the Church. Graciously established by the creator in the beginning, marriage is an essential foundation stone for a healthy society and Church. In the midst of a fallen world that ignores this truth, the Church is called to support and encourage all married couples.

PSALMODY

Psalm 127   *Unless the Lord builds the house*

¹ Unless the LORD builds the house, those who build it la- | bor in vain.*

    Unless the LORD watches over the city, the watchman stays a- | wake in vain.

² It is in vain that you rise up early and go late to rest, eating the bread of | anxious toil;*

    for he gives to his be- | lovèd sleep.

³ Behold, children are a heritage | from the LORD,*

    the fruit of the womb | a reward.

⁴ Like arrows in the hand of a | warrior*

    are the children | of one's youth.

⁵ Blessèd is the man who fills his quiver | with them!*

    He shall not be put to shame when he speaks with his enemies | in the gate.

Psalm 128 *Blessed is everyone who fears the Lord*

¹ Blessèd is everyone who | fears the LORD,*
   who walks | in his ways!
² You shall eat the fruit of the labor | of your hands;*
   you shall be blessed, and it shall be | well with you.
³ Your wife will be like a fruitful vine with- | in your house;*
   your children will be like olive shoots around your | table.
⁴ Behold, thus shall the | man be blessed*
   who | fears the LORD.
⁵ The LORD bless you from | Zion!*
   May you see the prosperity of Jerusalem all the days | of
   your life!
⁶ May you see your children's | children!*
   Peace be upon | Israel!

Psalm 133 *Dwelling together in unity*

¹ Behold, how good and pleas- | ant it is*
   when brothers dwell in | unity!
² It is like the precious oil on the head, running down on the beard,
   on the beard of | Aaron,*
   running down on the collar | of his robes!
³ It is like the dew of Hermon, which falls on the mountains of | Zion!*
   For there the LORD has commanded the blessing, life
   for- | evermore.

ADDITIONAL PSALMODY

Psalm 67	*May God be gracious to us*
Psalm 125	*The Lord surrounds His people*
Psalm 126	*Restore our fortunes, O Lord*

READINGS
Mark 10:6–9 *Jesus teaches about marriage*

⁶[Jesus said:] "From the beginning of creation, 'God made them male and female.' ⁷'Therefore a man shall leave his father and mother and hold fast to his wife, ⁸and they shall become one flesh.' So they are no longer two but one flesh. ⁹What therefore God has joined together, let not man separate."

Ephesians 5:22–33 *The bridegroom Christ and His Church*

²²Wives, submit to your own husbands, as to the Lord. ²³For the husband is the head of the wife even as Christ is the head of the church, his body, and is himself its Savior. ²⁴Now as the church submits to Christ, so also wives should submit in everything to their husbands.

²⁵Husbands, love your wives, as Christ loved the church and gave himself up for her, ²⁶that he might sanctify her, having cleansed her by the washing of water with the word, ²⁷so that he might present the church to himself in splendor, without spot or wrinkle or any such thing, that she might be holy and without blemish. ²⁸In the same way husbands should love their wives as their own bodies. He who loves his wife loves himself. ²⁹For no one ever hated his own flesh, but nourishes and cherishes it, just as Christ does the church, ³⁰because we are members of his body. ³¹"Therefore a man shall leave his father and mother and hold fast to his wife, and the two shall become one flesh." ³²This mystery is profound, and I am saying that it refers to Christ and the church. ³³However, let each one of you love his wife as himself, and let the wife see that she respects her husband.

1 Corinthians 12:31b—13:13 *The greatest of these is love*

¹²:³¹ᵇI will show you a still more excellent way.

¹³:¹If I speak in the tongues of men and of angels, but have not love, I am a noisy gong or a clanging cymbal. ²And if I have prophetic powers, and understand all mysteries and all knowledge, ▶

and if I have all faith, so as to remove mountains, but have not love, I am nothing. ³If I give away all I have, and if I deliver up my body to be burned, but have not love, I gain nothing.

⁴Love is patient and kind; love does not envy or boast; it is not arrogant ⁵or rude. It does not insist on its own way; it is not irritable or resentful; ⁶it does not rejoice at wrongdoing, but rejoices with the truth. ⁷Love bears all things, believes all things, hopes all things, endures all things.

⁸Love never ends. As for prophecies, they will pass away; as for tongues, they will cease; as for knowledge, it will pass away. ⁹For we know in part and we prophesy in part, ¹⁰but when the perfect comes, the partial will pass away. ¹¹When I was a child, I spoke like a child, I thought like a child, I reasoned like a child. When I became a man, I gave up childish ways. ¹²For now we see in a mirror dimly, but then face to face. Now I know in part; then I shall know fully, even as I have been fully known.

¹³So now faith, hope, and love abide, these three; but the greatest of these is love.

ADDITIONAL READINGS

Gen. 1:26–31   *Male and female are created in God's image*
Gen. 2:18–25   *The two become one flesh*
Song of Songs 2:10–13   *The lover and his beloved*
John 15:9–12   *Love one another as I have loved you*
Eph. 4:25—5:2   *Walk in love, as Christ loved us*
1 Peter 2:21—3:7   *Husbands and wives learn from Christ's submission*
1 John 4:7–12   *If God so loved us, we also ought to love one another*

PRAYERS

Most gracious God, we give thanks for the joy and blessings that You have granted _name_ and _name_ . Assist them always with Your grace that with true fidelity and steadfast love they may ever honor and keep their promises, grow in love toward You and for each other, and come at last to the eternal joys that You have promised; through Jesus Christ, Your Son, our Lord, who lives and reigns with You and the Holy Spirit, one God, now and forever. (818)

Heavenly Father, look in favor upon Your servants _name_ and _name_. Consecrate and sanctify their marriage by Your holy Word that they may live in steadfast love and faithfulness to one another. Grant them grace ever to remember with gladness that You have joined them together in this holy union; through Jesus Christ, Your Son, our Lord, who lives and reigns with You and the Holy Spirit, one God, now and forever. (819)

For resolution of marital problems

Heavenly Father, receive our thanks and praise for the wisdom and guidance of Your holy Word. Grant wisdom to _name_ and _name_ as they struggle to resolve the problems and conflicts afflicting their marriage. Fill their hearts with an understanding of Your truth and love, and guide them by Your Holy Spirit that they might be reconciled to one another, even as they are reconciled in Your Son, Jesus Christ, our Lord, who lives and reigns with You and the Holy Spirit, one God, now and forever. (820)

Lord God, through our Baptism into Christ You have bound us together in a common faith and life. Help us in the midst of our struggles to confront one another without hatred or bitterness and to work toward mutual forbearance and respect; through Jesus Christ, Your Son, our Lord, who lives and reigns with You and the Holy Spirit, one God, now and forever. (821)

HYMN

O Father, All Creating

LSB 858

O Father, all creating,
   Whose wisdom, love, and pow'r
First bound two lives together
   In Eden's primal hour,
Today to these Your children
   Your earliest gifts renew:
A home by You made happy,
   A love by You kept true. (st. 1)

O Spirit of the Father,
   Breathe on them from above,
So searching in Your pureness,
   So tender in Your love
That, guarded by Your presence
   And kept from strife and sin,
Their hearts may heed Your guidance
   And know You dwell within. (st. 3)

Unless You build it, Father,
   The house is built in vain;
Unless You, Savior, bless it,
   The joy will turn to pain.
But nothing breaks the union
   Of hearts in You made one;
The love Your Spirit hallows
   Is endless love begun. (st. 4)

ADDITIONAL HYMNS

Gracious Savior, Grant Your Blessing   LSB 860:1–4
Lord, When You Came as Welcome Guest   LSB 859
Love in Christ Is Strong and Living   LSB 706
O Christ, Our Hope, Our Hearts' Desire   LSB 553:1–2, 4

Rearing Children

Children are gifts from the Lord. Christian parents are given the joyful calling of rearing their children in the faith and instructing them for loving service in the world. The sins both of parents and children obscure the awareness and the understanding of their divinely ordered relationships and hinder the fulfillment of their duties. Pastoral care will seek to help all in the household recognize the gifts they have in each other and strengthen them in their various callings as baptized children of the heavenly Father.

PSALMODY

Psalm 103:11–18   *As a father shows compassion to his children*

¹¹ For as high as the heavens are a- | bove the earth,*
    so great is his steadfast love toward those who | fear him;
¹² as far as the east is | from the west,*
    so far does he remove our transgres- | sions from us.
¹³ As a father shows compassion to his | children,*
    so the LORD shows compassion to those who | fear him.
¹⁴ For he | knows our frame;*
    he remembers that | we are dust.
¹⁵ As for man, his days | are like grass;*
    he flourishes like a flower | of the field;
¹⁶ for the wind passes over it, and | it is gone,*
    and its place knows | it no more.
¹⁷ But the steadfast love of the LORD is from everlasting to everlasting on those who | fear him,*
    and his righteousness to children's | children,
¹⁸ to those who keep his | covenant*
    and remember to do his com- | mandments.

Psalm 78:1–7 *Fathers will tell their children of the Lord*

¹ Give ear, O my people, to my | teaching;*
    incline your ears to the words | of my mouth!
² I will open my mouth in a | parable;*
    I will utter dark sayings | from of old,
³ things that we have | heard and known,*
    that our fathers have | told us.
⁴ We will not hide them from their children, but tell to the coming
    generation the glorious deeds of the LORD, | and his might,*
    and the wonders that | he has done.
⁵ He established a testimony in Jacob and appointed a law in | Israel,*
    which he commanded our fathers to teach to their | children,
⁶ that the next generation might know them, the children | yet
    unborn,*
    and arise and tell them to their | children,
⁷ so that they should set their | hope in God*
    and not forget the works of God, but keep his com- | mandments.

ADDITIONAL PSALMODY

Psalm 127   *Unless the Lord builds the house*
Psalm 133   *When brothers dwell in unity*

READINGS

Mark 10:13–16 *Let the children come to Me*

¹³They were bringing children to him that he might touch them, and
the disciples rebuked them. ¹⁴But when Jesus saw it, he was indignant
and said to them, "Let the children come to me; do not hinder them,
for to such belongs the kingdom of God. ¹⁵Truly, I say to you, whoever does not receive the kingdom of God like a child shall not enter
it." ¹⁶And he took them in his arms and blessed them, laying his
hands on them.

Deuteronomy 11:18–21 *Teach My Word to your children*

[18]You shall therefore lay up these words of mine in your heart and in your soul, and you shall bind them as a sign on your hand, and they shall be as frontlets between your eyes. [19]You shall teach them to your children, talking of them when you are sitting in your house, and when you are walking by the way, and when you lie down, and when you rise. [20]You shall write them on the doorposts of your house and on your gates, [21]that your days and the days of your children may be multiplied in the land that the LORD swore to your fathers to give them, as long as the heavens are above the earth.

Ephesians 6:1–4 *Children, honor; fathers, do not provoke*

[1]Children, obey your parents in the Lord, for this is right. [2]"Honor your father and mother" (this is the first commandment with a promise), [3]"that it may go well with you and that you may live long in the land." [4]Fathers, do not provoke your children to anger, but bring them up in the discipline and instruction of the Lord.

ADDITIONAL READINGS

Gen. 4:1–16	*Cain and Abel*
Prov. 22:6	*Train up a child in the way he should go*
Matt. 18:21–35	*Forgive your brother from your heart*
Luke 11:11–13	*If you know how to give good gifts to your children*
Col. 3:20–21	*Do not provoke your children*
Heb. 12:5–11	*As earthly fathers discipline their children*

PRAYERS

For parents

Lord and Giver of life, look with kindness upon the father and mother of _ name of child(ren) _ and upon all parents. Let them ever rejoice in the gift You have given them. Enable them to be teachers and examples of righteousness for their children. Strengthen them in their own Baptism that they may share eternally with their children the ▶

385

salvation You have given them; through Jesus Christ, Your Son, our Lord, who lives and reigns with You and the Holy Spirit, one God, now and forever. (506 alt.)

For parents facing challenges

Almighty God, heavenly Father, You have blessed us with the joy and care of children. As __name(s) of parent(s)__ rear(s) __their/his/her__ child(ren), give __them/him/her__ calm strength and patient wisdom that __they/he/she__ may teach __them/him/her__ to love whatever is just and true and good, following the example of our Savior; through Jesus Christ, Your Son, our Lord, who lives and reigns with You and the Holy Spirit, one God, now and forever. (246 alt.)

Lord God, from whom every family in heaven and earth is named, receive our thanks for the blessings You have bestowed upon __name(s) of parent(s)__, to whom You have entrusted the care of __name(s) of child(ren)__. Forgive __their/his/her__ shortcomings and failures as (a) parent(s), and grant __them/him/her__ Your grace that __they/he/she__ might faithfully bring up __their/his/her__ child(ren) in Your nurture and instruction; through Jesus Christ, Your Son, our Lord, who lives and reigns with You and the Holy Spirit, one God, now and forever. (822)

For children in crisis

Father in heaven, You see Your children growing up in a sinful and corrupt world. Give __name(s)__ strength to remain steadfast in __his/her/their__ holy faith, and keep __him/her/them__ in Your tender care. Show __him/her/them__ the truth of Your Word, shield __him/her/them__ from all evil, and lead __him/her/them__ in the way __he/she/they__ should go; through Jesus Christ, Your Son, our Lord, who lives and reigns with You and the Holy Spirit, one God, now and forever. (823)

Almighty God, our heavenly Father, be a source of strength and hope for _____name of child_____. Protect _____him/her_____ from all danger, call _____him/her_____ to repentance, and grant _____him/her_____ Your forgiveness and love. Guide _____him/her_____ by Your Word into paths of righteousness and life, and send Your holy angel to watch over _____him/her_____, that the evil one may have no power over _____him/her_____; through Jesus Christ, Your Son, our Lord, who lives and reigns with You and the Holy Spirit, one God, now and forever. (250 alt.)

For guidance

God our Father, Your Son grew in wisdom and stature and in favor with God and all people. Bless, guide, and govern _____name_____ by Your Holy Spirit that _____he/she_____ may grow in grace and in the knowledge of Your Word. Grant that _____he/she_____ may serve You well and usefully, developing _____his/her_____ talents not for _____his/her_____ own sake but for the glory of God and the welfare of _____his/her_____ neighbor. Protect and defend _____him/her_____ from all danger and harm, giving Your holy angel charge over _____him/her_____; through Jesus Christ, Your Son, our Lord, who lives and reigns with You and the Holy Spirit, one God, now and forever. (247 alt.)

Sibling rivalry

Dear Lord, You know how easily tempted we are to fight with our brothers and sisters. Remind _____name_____ and _____name_____ of how much You love them. Forgive them their sins, and strengthen them in Your love. As You have forgiven them, help them to forgive and love each other; through Jesus Christ, Your Son, our Lord, who lives and reigns with You and the Holy Spirit, one God, now and forever. (824)

HYMNS
Oh, Blest the House
LSB 862

Oh, blest the parents who give heed
Unto their children's foremost need
And weary not of care or cost.
May none to them and heav'n be lost! (st. 3)

Lord Jesus Christ, the Children's Friend
LSB 866

Lord Jesus Christ, the children's friend,
To each of them Your presence send;
Call them by name and keep them true
In loving faith, dear Lord, to You. (st. 1)

For by Your Word we clearly see
That we have sinned continually;
But show us too, forgiving Lord,
Your saving Gospel's great reward. (st. 4)

That all of us, Your children dear,
By Christ redeemed, may Christ revere;
Lead us in joy that all we do
Will witness to our love for You. (st. 5)

Then guard and keep us to the end,
Secure in You, our gracious friend,
That in Your heav'nly family
We sing Your praise eternally. (st. 6)

© 1982 Concordia Publishing House

ADDITIONAL HYMNS

Let Children Hear the Mighty Deeds   LSB 867
Our Father, by Whose Name   LSB 863
Shepherd of Tender Youth   LSB 864

Ministering to the Elderly

The blessing of extended years is a gift from God, bringing with it joys as well as challenges. While the elderly may experience an increasing number of losses as their lives progress, pastoral care will point them to the Lord's steadfast love for them in Christ Jesus and to His ongoing purposes for them as baptized children of their heavenly Father.

As the circumstance warrants, see the sections Times of Illness (pages 195–204), Chronic Illness (pages 205–212), End of Life Decisions (pages 221–227), Ministering to Caregivers (pages 228–233), and Ministering to the Dying (pages 234–246) for additional resources.

The Blessing of a Home (pages 148–158) may be used when the elderly are moving into a new home or assisted living or nursing home facility.

PSALMODY

Psalm 71:17–21   *God will not forsake us in old age*

¹⁷ O God, from my youth you have | taught me,*
     and I still proclaim your | wondrous deeds.
¹⁸ So even to old age and gray hairs, O God, do not for- | sake me,*
     until I proclaim your might to another generation, your
     power to all | those to come.
¹⁹ Your righteousness, O God, reaches the high | heavens.*
     You who have done great things, O God, who is | like you?
²⁰ You who have made me see many troubles and calamities will
     revive | me again;*
     from the depths of the earth you will bring me | up again.
²¹ You will increase my | greatness*
     and comfort | me again.

Psalm 90:1–2, 7–10, 14–17 *Our dwelling place in all generations*

¹ Lord, you have been our | dwelling place*
    in all gener- | ations.

² Before the mountains were brought forth, or ever you had
formed the earth | and the world,*
    from everlasting to everlasting | you are God.

⁷ For we are brought to an end by your | anger;*
    by your wrath we | are dismayed.

⁸ You have set our iniquities be- | fore you,*
    our secret sins in the light of your | presence.

⁹ For all our days pass away un- | der your wrath;*
    we bring our years to an end | like a sigh.

¹⁰ The years of our life are seventy, or even by reason of
strength | eighty;*
    yet their span is but toil and trouble; they are soon gone, and
we | fly away.

¹⁴ Satisfy us in the morning with your | steadfast love,*
    that we may rejoice and be glad | all our days.

¹⁵ Make us glad for as many days as you have af- | flicted us,*
    and for as many years as we have seen | evil.

¹⁶ Let your work be shown to your | servants,*
    and your glorious power to their | children.

¹⁷ Let the favor of the Lord our God be upon us, and establish the
work of our hands up- | on us;*
    yes, establish the work | of our hands!

ADDITIONAL PSALMODY

Psalm 27:4–5   *Dwell in the house of the Lord all my life*
Psalm 31:1–5, 14–15a, 24   *I trust in You, O Lord*

READINGS

Isaiah 46:3–4   *Carried from the womb to old age*

³ Listen to me, O house of Jacob,
     all the remnant of the house of Israel,
who have been borne by me from before your birth,
     carried from the womb;
⁴ even to your old age I am he,
     and to gray hairs I will carry you.
I have made, and I will bear;
     I will carry and will save.

Philippians 4:4–9   *Be anxious for nothing*

⁴Rejoice in the Lord always; again I will say, Rejoice. ⁵Let your reasonableness be known to everyone. The Lord is at hand; ⁶do not be anxious about anything, but in everything by prayer and supplication with thanksgiving let your requests be made known to God. ⁷And the peace of God, which surpasses all understanding, will guard your hearts and your minds in Christ Jesus.

⁸Finally, brothers, whatever is true, whatever is honorable, whatever is just, whatever is pure, whatever is lovely, whatever is commendable, if there is any excellence, if there is anything worthy of praise, think about these things. ⁹What you have learned and received and heard and seen in me—practice these things, and the God of peace will be with you.

ADDITIONAL READINGS

2 Cor. 12:9–10   *Christ's grace is sufficient for us*
Heb. 12:1–3   *Surrounded by a cloud of witnesses*

PRAYERS

For the aged in a variety of distresses

Gracious Father, in Your mercy look on __name__, whose increasing years brings __him/her__ __weakness / anxiety / distress / loneliness__. Provide __him/her__ with a home where love and respect, concern and understanding are shown. Grant __him/her__ a willing heart to accept help and, as __his/her__ strength wanes, increase __his/her__ faith and the assurance of Your love through Jesus Christ, __his/her__ Savior, who lives and reigns with You and the Holy Spirit, one God, now and forever. (251 alt.)

Moving from one's own home

Lord Jesus Christ, the same yesterday, today, and forever, Your coming was welcomed and praised by Simeon and Anna in their old age. Keep __name__, we pray, as __he/she/they__ moves from __his/her/their__ own home in order to receive the added care that __he/she/they__ now requires. Comfort __him/her/them__ at this time of loss and keep alive in __him/her/their__ the memories of the Lord's faithfulness in this place. Bless __him/her/them__ in __his/her/their__ new surroundings, and enable __him/her/them__ to find companionship in the communion of saints; through Jesus Christ, our Lord, who lives and reigns with the Father and the Holy Spirit, one God, now and forever. (825)

Mourning a spouse who confessed Christ

Lord God, heavenly Father, in Your wisdom You called __name of deceased__ from this vale of tears to Yourself in heaven. Comfort __name of surviving spouse__ with the sure and certain hope of the resurrection to eternal life and a blessed reunion in heaven. Relieve __her/him__ of the loneliness that brings sadness and give __her/him__ joy in the fellowship of Your Church; through Jesus Christ, Your Son, our Lord, who lives and reigns with You and the Holy Spirit, one God, now and forever. (826)

Mourning a spouse who may not have been a confessing Christian

Heavenly Father, look in mercy upon __*name*__ , who sorrows over the death of __*name of deceased*__ . Comfort __*her/him*__ with the assurance that You have not forsaken __*her/him*__ , relieve __*her/him*__ of the loneliness that refuses to subside, and strengthen __*her/his*__ confession of Your saving name, that __*she/he*__ may one day enter Your eternal kingdom; through Jesus Christ, Your Son, our Lord, who lives and reigns with You and the Holy Spirit, one God, now and forever. (827)

Birthday celebration

We give You thanks, O Lord, for the many blessings You have given to Your servant __*name*__ , especially for bestowing on __*her/him*__ length of days in this present life. Grant that __*she/he*__ may always know Your loving-kindness, abide in the confession of Your name, and put __*her/his*__ trust each day in Your gracious care and protection; through Jesus Christ, Your Son, our Lord, who lives and reigns with You and the Holy Spirit, one God, now and forever. (828)

HYMNS

Praise to the Lord, the Almighty
LSB 790

Praise to the Lord, who o'er all things is wondrously reigning
And, as on wings of an eagle, uplifting, sustaining.
　　Have you not seen
　　All that is needful has been
Sent by His gracious ordaining? (st. 2)

Praise to the Lord, who has fearfully, wondrously, made you,
Health has bestowed and, when heedlessly falling, has stayed you.
　　What need or grief
　　Ever has failed of relief?
Wings of His mercy did shade you. (st. 3)

▶

Praise to the Lord! O let all that is in me adore Him!
All that has life and breath, come now with praises before Him!
    Let the Amen
    Sound from His people again;
Gladly forever adore Him! (st. 5)

My Faith Looks Up to Thee
LSB 702

May Thy rich grace impart
Strength to my fainting heart;
    My zeal inspire!
As Thou hast died for me,
Oh, may my love to Thee
Pure, warm, and changeless be,
    A living fire!

While life's dark maze I tread
And griefs around me spread,
    Be Thou my guide;
Bid darkness turn to day,
Wipe sorrow's tears away,
Nor let me ever stray
    From Thee aside.

When ends life's transient dream,
When death's cold, sullen stream
    Shall o'er me roll,
Blest Savior, then, in love,
Fear and distrust remove;
O bear me safe above,
    A ransomed soul! (sts. 2–4)

ADDITIONAL HYMNS

Draw Us to Thee   *LSB 701*
Great Is Thy Faithfulness   *LSB 809*

Abuse

Empathy, compassion, and patience will characterize the pastor's approach in dealing with the physical, emotional, and spiritual damage that may be present in victims of abuse. Because the effects of abuse often linger, the pastor will recognize the need for ongoing care marked by patient use of the Gospel to heal, to release from bondage to anger, shame, and fear, and to restore to a life of faith and love.

The pastor may want to suggest that the emotional scars from abuse may well require the assistance of other professional help as well.

PSALMODY

Psalm 13 *Will You forget me forever?*

¹ How long, O Lord? Will you forget me for- | ever?*
How long will you hide your | face from me?

² How long must I take counsel in my soul and have sorrow in my heart | all the day?*
How long shall my enemy be exalted | over me?

³ Consider and answer me, O | Lord my God;*
light up my eyes, lest I sleep the | sleep of death,   ►

⁴ lest my enemy say, "I have prevailed | over him,"*
   lest my foes rejoice because I am | shaken.
⁵ But I have trusted in your | steadfast love;*
   my heart shall rejoice in your sal- | vation.
⁶ I will sing | to the LORD,*
   because he has dealt bountifully | with me.

Psalm 31:1–4, 9, 15–16   *My soul and body are in grief*

¹ In you, O LORD, do I take refuge; let me never be | put to shame;*
   in your righteousness de- | liver me!
² Incline your ear to me; rescue me | speedily!*
   Be a rock of refuge for me, a strong fortress to | save me!
³ For you are my rock and my | fortress;*
   and for your name's sake you lead me and | guide me;
⁴ you take me out of the net they have hidden | for me,*
   for you are my | refuge.
⁹ Be gracious to me, O LORD, for I am | in distress;*
   my eye is wasted from grief; my soul and my body | also.
¹⁵ My times are | in your hand;*
   rescue me from the hand of my enemies and from my
   perse- | cutors!
¹⁶ Make your face shine on your | servant;*
   save me in your | steadfast love!

ADDITIONAL PSALMODY

Psalm 6:4–10   *The Lord has heard my plea*
Psalm 70   *O Lord, make haste to help me!*
Psalm 71:1–6, 12   *You have given the command to save me*
Psalm 91   *I will be with you in trouble*
Psalm 140:1–4, 6, 12–13   *Deliver me from evil and violent men*

READINGS
Romans 8:26–30, 37–39   *Nothing shall separate us*

[26]The Spirit helps us in our weakness. For we do not know what to pray for as we ought, but the Spirit himself intercedes for us with groanings too deep for words. [27]And he who searches hearts knows what is the mind of the Spirit, because the Spirit intercedes for the saints according to the will of God. [28]And we know that for those who love God all things work together for good, for those who are called according to his purpose. [29]For those whom he foreknew he also predestined to be conformed to the image of his Son, in order that he might be the firstborn among many brothers. [30]And those whom he predestined he also called, and those whom he called he also justified, and those whom he justified he also glorified.

[37]No, in all these things we are more than conquerors through him who loved us. [38]For I am sure that neither death nor life, nor angels nor rulers, nor things present nor things to come, nor powers, [39]nor height nor depth, nor anything else in all creation, will be able to separate us from the love of God in Christ Jesus our Lord.

Hebrews 4:14–16   *Jesus sympathizes with our weaknesses*

[14]Since then we have a great high priest who has passed through the heavens, Jesus, the Son of God, let us hold fast our confession. [15]For we do not have a high priest who is unable to sympathize with our weaknesses, but one who in every respect has been tempted as we are, yet without sin. [16]Let us then with confidence draw near to the throne of grace, that we may receive mercy and find grace to help in time of need.

ADDITIONAL READINGS

Lam. 3:22–26	*The steadfast love of the Lord never ceases*
John 16:33	*Christ has overcome the world*
1 Peter 2:19–24	*Christ also suffered for you*
1 Peter 5:6–7	*Cast all your anxieties on Him*

PRAYERS

Lord God, You promise to help and comfort those who call upon You in the day of trouble. Grant to __ *name* __ Your deliverance in Christ Jesus that by the power of Your Holy Spirit __ *he/she* __ may not be overcome in adversity but be strengthened to live confidently in Your love and peace. Make __ *him/her* __ to know that in all things You work for the good of those who love You and that nothing can separate __ *him/her* __ from Your love, which is in Christ Jesus, our Lord, who lives and reigns with You and the Holy Spirit, one God, now and forever. (829)

For the physically abused

Father in heaven, look with tenderness on __ *name* __, who has been physically abused. Extend Your healing hand that __ *he/she* __ may be made whole. Remove the damage __ *he/she* __ has suffered in mind, heart, and spirit. By the guidance of Your Spirit, lead __ *him/her* __ to trust in Your steadfast mercy that __ *he/she* __ may live at peace with everyone; through Jesus Christ, Your Son, our Lord, who lives and reigns with You and the Holy Spirit, one God, now and forever. (830)

For the sexually abused

Merciful Father, the physical and emotional pain caused by the sin against __ *name's* __ body is deep and severe. You know what __ *he/she* __ has experienced and what is needed for healing, and You alone can provide it. Through Your promises to __ *name* __ in Holy Baptism, cleanse __ *him/her* __ from __ *his/her* __ shame, and make all things new, that __ *he/she* __ may be strengthened to live a fulfilling life in You; through the same Jesus Christ, Your Son, our Lord, who lives and reigns with You and the Holy Spirit, one God, now and forever. (831)

HYMNS
Jesus, Grant That Balm and Healing
LSB 421

Ev'ry wound that pains or grieves me
 By Your wounds, Lord, is made whole;
When I'm faint, Your cross revives me,
 Granting new life to my soul.
Yes, Your comfort renders sweet
Ev'ry bitter cup I meet;
 For Your all-atoning passion
 Has procured my soul's salvation. (st. 4)

Thee We Adore, O Hidden Savior
LSB 640

Fountain of goodness, Jesus, Lord and God:
Cleanse us, unclean, with Thy most cleansing blood;
Increase our faith and love, that we may know
The hope and peace which from Thy presence flow. (st. 4)

ADDITIONAL HYMNS
All for Christ I Have Forsaken	*LSB 753*
Christ, the Life of All the Living	*LSB 420:5*
Since Our Great High Priest, Christ Jesus	*LSB 529:2*

Separation and Divorce

Separation and divorce embody the essence of the fall and its effect in the realm of marriage. The experience is traumatic, representing a "living death" that elicits a vast array of emotions and leads to grieving over the loss of spouse and family, friends, status, income, and the like. Children will especially need help to understand and accept the breakdown and to express and deal with their emotions of fear and abandonment. The promise of God's love and care for them in Christ cannot be emphasized enough.

For additional resources, see the section on Marriage (pages 377–382) and Reconciliation with Other Christians (pages 327–333).

PSALMODY
Psalm 71:1–3, 20–21, 23–24a   *The Lord will revive me again*

¹ In you, O LORD, do I take | refuge;*
    let me never be | put to shame!

² In your righteousness deliver me and | rescue me;*
    incline your ear to me, and | save me!

³ Be to me a rock of refuge, to which I may contin- | ually come;*
    you have given the command to save me, for you are my
    rock and my | fortress.

²⁰ You who have made me see many troubles and calamities will
    revive | me again;*
    from the depths of the earth you will bring me | up again.

²¹ You will increase my | greatness*
    and comfort | me again.

²³ My lips will shout for joy, when I sing prais- | es to you;*
    my soul also, which you | have redeemed.

²⁴ And my tongue will talk of your | righteous help*
    all | the day long.

Psalm 32:1–7   *I will confess my transgressions to the Lord*

¹ Blessèd is the one whose transgression is for- | given,*
    whose sin is | covered.

² Blessèd is the man against whom the LORD counts no in- | iquity,*
    and in whose spirit there is | no deceit.

³ For when I kept silent, my bones wast- | ed away*
    through my groaning | all day long.

⁴ For day and night your hand was heavy up- | on me;*
    my strength was dried up as by the heat of | summer.

⁵ I acknowledged my sin to you, and I did not cover my in- | iquity;*
    I said, "I will confess my transgressions to the LORD," and
    you forgave the iniquity | of my sin.

⁶ Therefore let everyone who is godly offer prayer to you at a time
    when you | may be found;*
    surely in the rush of great waters, they shall not | reach him.

⁷ You are a hiding place for me; you preserve me from | trouble;*
    you surround me with shouts of de- | liverance.

Psalm 27:1–5, 7–10, 14   *The Lord will take me in*

¹ The LORD is my light and my salvation; whom | shall I fear?*
    The LORD is the stronghold of my life; of whom shall I | be
    afraid?

² When evildoers assail me to eat | up my flesh,*
    my adversaries and foes, it is they who stum- | ble and fall.

³ Though an army encamp against me, my heart | shall not fear;*
    though war arise against me, yet I will be | confident.

⁴ One thing have I asked of the LORD, that will I seek | after:*
    that I may dwell in the house of the LORD all the days of my
    life, to gaze upon the beauty of the LORD and to inquire in
    his | temple.

⁵ For he will hide me in his shelter in the day of | trouble;*
    he will conceal me under the cover of his tent; he will lift me
    high up- | on a rock. ►

⁷ Hear, O Lᴏʀᴅ, when I | cry aloud;*
    be gracious to me and | answer me!
⁸ You have said, | "Seek my face."*
    My heart says to you, "Your face, Lᴏʀᴅ, | do I seek."
⁹ Hide not your face from me. Turn not your servant away in | anger,*
    O you who have been my help. Cast me not off; forsake me
    not, O God of my sal- | vation!
¹⁰ For my father and my mother have for- | saken me,*
    but the Lᴏʀᴅ will | take me in.
¹⁴ Wait | for the Lᴏʀᴅ;*
    be strong, and let your heart take courage; wait | for the Lᴏʀᴅ!

ADDITIONAL PSALMODY

Psalm 6:1–4	*Save me for the sake of Your steadfast love*
Psalm 25:1–2a, 4–5, 15–18	*Bring me out of my distress*
Psalm 31:1–5, 9–15a	*My strength fails because of my iniquity*
Psalm 42:1–5	*Hope in God; for I shall again praise Him*

READINGS

Philippians 4:6–9   *The peace of God*

⁶Do not be anxious about anything, but in everything by prayer and supplication with thanksgiving let your requests be made known to God. ⁷And the peace of God, which surpasses all understanding, will guard your hearts and your minds in Christ Jesus.

    ⁸Finally, brothers, whatever is true, whatever is honorable, whatever is just, whatever is pure, whatever is lovely, whatever is commendable, if there is any excellence, if there is anything worthy of praise, think about these things. ⁹What you have learned and received and heard and seen in me—practice these things, and the God of peace will be with you.

Colossians 3:12–15 *Forgive each other*

¹²Put on then, as God's chosen ones, holy and beloved, compassion, kindness, humility, meekness, and patience, ¹³bearing with one another and, if one has a complaint against another, forgiving each other; as the Lord has forgiven you, so you also must forgive. ¹⁴And above all these put on love, which binds everything together in perfect harmony. ¹⁵And let the peace of Christ rule in your hearts, to which indeed you were called in one body. And be thankful.

1 John 4:7–11, 19 *If God so loved us, we also ought to love*

⁷Beloved, let us love one another, for love is from God, and whoever loves has been born of God and knows God. ⁸Anyone who does not love does not know God, because God is love. ⁹In this the love of God was made manifest among us, that God sent his only Son into the world, so that we might live through him. ¹⁰In this is love, not that we have loved God but that he loved us and sent his Son to be the propitiation for our sins. ¹¹Beloved, if God so loved us, we also ought to love one another.

¹⁹We love because he first loved us.

ADDITIONAL READINGS

Luke 7:36–50 *Jesus forgives the woman who anoints His feet*
John 8:3–11 *Jesus forgives the woman caught in adultery*
John 15:7–12 *Abide in My love*
Eph. 4:31—5:2 *Be kind to one another*

PRAYERS

For those who are separated

Father of mercies and God of all consolation, come to the aid of ___*names*___ . Turn them from their sin that they may live for You alone. Give them the power of Your Holy Spirit that they may attend to Your Word, confess their sins, receive Your forgiveness, and grow into ►

the fullness of Your Son, Jesus Christ, our Lord, who lives and reigns with You and the Holy Spirit, one God, now and forever. (832)

For an abandoned spouse

God of all comfort, You have promised that You will never leave us comfortless. Comfort _ name _, who has been abandoned. Grant _ him/her _ Your Holy Spirit that, clinging to the truth of Your Word, _ he/she _ may trust in the promise that You will be with _ him/her _ always, that you will provide for _ him/her _, and that nothing will separate _ him/her _ from Your love, which is in Christ Jesus, our Lord, who lives and reigns with You and the Holy Spirit, one God, now and forever. (833)

For those who are divorced

Look with mercy, O Lord, on Your servants _ name _ and _ name _, for whom the bond of wedded love and faithfulness has been broken. Where they have sinned, grant them repentance that they may receive Your forgiveness and live in the mercy of Your healing power; through Jesus Christ, our Lord, who lives and reigns with You and the Holy Spirit, one God, now and forever. (245)

Lord of mercy and compassion, be with _ name _ and _ name _. Break down their bitterness and hatred, and grant them repentance and forgiveness that, acknowledging their sin and trusting in Your mercy, they may walk in the newness of life; through Your Son, Jesus Christ, our Lord, who lives and reigns with You and the Holy Spirit, one God, now and forever. (834)

For parents who have divorced

Heavenly Father, guide _ name _ and _ name _ to be faithful parents even though they have divorced. Help them by Your gracious mercy that they may cooperate in caring for their children and in bringing them up in the nurture and admonition of the Lord; through Jesus

Christ, Your Son, our Lord, who lives and reigns with You and the Holy Spirit, one God, now and forever. (835)

For the children

Heavenly Father, comfort _name(s) of child(ren)_ , whose parents are _separated / getting a divorce / divorced_ . Help _them/him/her_ to know that You love _them/him/her_ . Help _them/him/her_ to trust in Jesus, who promises never to leave _them/him/her_ . Preserve _them/him/her_ from the temptation to blame _themselves/ himself/herself_ for _their/his/her_ parents' sins. Lead _them/him/her_ to forgive _their/his/her_ father and mother, and teach _them/him/her_ to honor them at all times; through Jesus Christ, Your Son, our Lord, who lives and reigns with You and the Holy Spirit, one God, now and forever. (836)

O Lord Jesus, though our fathers and mothers may forsake us, You will take care of us. Your suffering and death is our comfort and strength when we are filled with sadness and confusion. Comfort and strengthen _name(s) of child(ren)_ , whose parents are _separated / getting a divorce / divorced_ . Help _them/him/her_ not to be afraid but to cast every care upon You because You care for _them/him/her_ . Keep _their/his/her_ faith firmly grounded in Your Word of mercy, that _they/he/she_ may face the days ahead with forgiveness, love, and honor for _their/his/her_ parents; for You live and reign with the Father and the Holy Spirit, one God, now and forever. (837)

For the entire family or other family members

Lord God, heavenly Father, it is Your will that those whom You have joined together in one flesh never be separated. We acknowledge that the devastation of sin wreaks havoc upon our lives, our marriages, and our families, so that our only hope of salvation is in Your mercy in Christ Jesus, our Lord. Deliver this family from all bitterness and resentment. Strengthen them to live by faith in Your mercy toward us, ▶

so that they may live at peace with one another and serve each other faithfully; through Jesus Christ, Your Son, our Lord, who lives and reigns with You and the Holy Spirit, one God, now and forever. (838)

HYMNS

In Thee Is Gladness
LSB 818

In Thee is gladness
Amid all sadness,
Jesus, sunshine of my heart.
By Thee are given
The gifts of heaven,
Thou the true Redeemer art.
Our souls Thou wakest,
Our bonds Thou breakest;
Who trusts Thee surely
Has built securely;
He stands forever: Alleluia!
Our hearts are pining
To see Thy shining,
Dying or living
To Thee are cleaving;
Naught can us sever: Alleluia!

Since He is ours,
We fear no powers,
Not of earth nor sin nor death.
He sees and blesses
In worst distresses;
He can change them with a breath.
Wherefore the story
Tell of His glory
With hearts and voices;
All heav'n rejoices

In Him forever: Alleluia!
  We shout for gladness,
  Triumph o'er sadness,
  Love Him and praise Him
  And still shall raise Him
Glad hymns forever: Alleluia!

Son of God, Eternal Savior

LSB 842

Son of God, eternal Savior,
  Source of life and truth and grace,
Word made flesh, whose birth among us
  Hallows all our human race,
You our Head, who, throned in glory,
  For Your own will ever plead:
Fill us with Your love and pity,
  Heal our wrongs, and help our need. (st. 1)

Come, O Christ, and reign among us,
  King of love and Prince of Peace;
Hush the storm of strife and passion,
  Bid its cruel discords cease.
By Your patient years of toiling,
  By Your silent hours of pain,
Quench our fevered thirst of pleasure,
  Stem our selfish greed of gain. (st. 3)

Son of God, eternal Savior,
  Source of life and truth and grace,
Word made flesh, whose birth among us
  Hallows all our human race:
By Your praying, by Your willing
  That Your people should be one,
Grant, O grant our hope's fruition:
  Here on earth Your will be done. (st. 4)

Lord of Glory, You Have Bought Us
LSB 851

Lord of glory, You have bought us
    With Your lifeblood as the price,
Never grudging for the lost ones
    That tremendous sacrifice.
Give us faith to trust You boldly,
    Hope, to stay our souls on You;
But, oh, best of all Your graces,
    With Your love our love renew. (st. 4)

ADDITIONAL HYMNS

"Forgive Our Sins as We Forgive"	LSB 843
How Clear Is Our Vocation, Lord	LSB 853
Lord, Help Us Walk Your Servant Way	LSB 857
O God of Mercy, God of Might	LSB 852:1–3

At the Restoration of Peace in the Home

These resources are intended for use when peace has been restored in the home following any form of conflict or turmoil, be it separation or divorce, the rebellion of children, even various crises such as fire, accident, or other disruptive events. As peace is graciously restored by the Lord, faith bears the fruit of thanksgiving and praise and calls upon the Giver to nurture the harmony He has granted.

PSALMODY

Psalm 28:6–9   *The Lord has heard my pleas for mercy*

⁶ Blessèd | be the LORD!*
　　For he has heard the voice of my pleas for | mercy.
⁷ The LORD is my strength and my shield; in him my heart trusts,
　　and | I am helped;*
　　my heart exults, and with my song I give | thanks to him.
⁸ The LORD is the strength of his | people;*
　　he is the saving refuge of his a- | nointed.
⁹ Oh, save your people and bless your | heritage!*
　　Be their shepherd and carry them for- | ever.

Psalm 85:1–2, 7–13   *You forgave the iniquity of Your people*

¹ LORD, you were favorable | to your land;*
　　you restored the fortunes of | Jacob.
² You forgave the iniquity of your | people;*
　　you covered | all their sin.
⁷ Show us your steadfast love, | O LORD,*
　　and grant us your sal- | vation.
⁸ Let me hear what God the | LORD will speak,*
　　for he will speak peace to his people, to his saints;
　　but let them not turn back to | folly.
⁹ Surely his salvation is near to those who | fear him,*
　　that glory may dwell | in our land.

▶

¹⁰ Steadfast love and faith- | fulness meet;*
　　righteousness and peace kiss each | other.
¹¹ Faithfulness springs up | from the ground,*
　　and righteousness looks down | from the sky.
¹² Yes, the LORD will give | what is good,*
　　and our land will yield its | increase.
¹³ Righteousness will go be- | fore him*
　　and make his foot- | steps a way.

ADDITIONAL PSALMODY

Psalm 25:4–10   *The Lord teaches the humble His way*
Psalm 34:1–6, 17–19, 22   *Let us exalt the Lord together*
Psalm 133   *The blessedness of brotherly unity*
Psalm 147:1–3, 12–15, 20b   *The Lord makes peace in your borders*

READINGS

Matthew 5:1–9, 13–16   *The Beatitudes*

¹Seeing the crowds, [Jesus] went up on the mountain, and when he sat down, his disciples came to him.

　²And he opened his mouth and taught them, saying:

³ "Blessed are the poor in spirit, for theirs is the kingdom of heaven.

⁴ "Blessed are those who mourn, for they shall be comforted.

⁵ "Blessed are the meek, for they shall inherit the earth.

⁶ "Blessed are those who hunger and thirst for righteousness, for they shall be satisfied.

⁷ "Blessed are the merciful, for they shall receive mercy.

⁸ "Blessed are the pure in heart, for they shall see God.

⁹ "Blessed are the peacemakers, for they shall be called sons of God.

　¹³"You are the salt of the earth, but if salt has lost its taste, how shall its saltiness be restored? It is no longer good for anything except to be thrown out and trampled under people's feet.

　¹⁴"You are the light of the world. A city set on a hill cannot be hidden. ¹⁵Nor do people light a lamp and put it under a basket, but on

a stand, and it gives light to all in the house. ¹⁶In the same way, let your light shine before others, so that they may see your good works and give glory to your Father who is in heaven."

2 Corinthians 5:17–19 *God reconciled us to Himself*

¹⁷If anyone is in Christ, he is a new creation. The old has passed away; behold, the new has come. ¹⁸All this is from God, who through Christ reconciled us to himself and gave us the ministry of reconciliation; ¹⁹that is, in Christ God was reconciling the world to himself, not counting their trespasses against them, and entrusting to us the message of reconciliation.

ADDITIONAL READINGS

Is. 26:3–4	*God keeps His own in perfect peace*
John 14:27	*Jesus gives us His peace*
John 15:8–12	*Love one another as I have loved you*
Rom. 14:17–19	*The kingdom is righteousness, peace, and joy*
Gal. 5:22–24	*The fruit of the Spirit is love, joy, peace*
Eph. 2:11–21	*Christ Himself is our peace*

PRAYERS

Gracious God and Father, we give You thanks and praise for healing the brokenhearted and binding up their wounds, especially for restoring ___ names ___ to peace with one another. You have heard their humble prayers and blessed them according to Your faithful promises. Strengthen them in Your mercy and forgiveness in Christ. Keep them in His love that, delivered from all strife and turmoil, they may live in peace and finally receive eternal rest with You in heaven; through Jesus Christ, Your Son, our Lord, who lives and reigns with You and the Holy Spirit, one God, now and forever. (839)

O God, from whom come all holy desires, all good counsels, and all just works, give to us, Your servants, that peace which the world ▶

cannot give, that our hearts may be set to obey Your commandments and also that we, being defended from the fear of our enemies, may live in peace and quietness; through Jesus Christ, Your Son, our Lord, who lives and reigns with You and the Holy Spirit, one God, now and forever. (410)

HYMNS

Our Father, Who from Heaven Above
LSB 766

Give us this day our daily bread,
And let us all be clothed and fed.
    Save us from hardship, war, and strife;
    In plague and famine, spare our life,
That we in honest peace may live,
To care and greed no entrance give.

Forgive our sins, Lord, we implore,
That they may trouble us no more;
    We, too, will gladly those forgive
    Who hurt us by the way they live.
Help us in our community
To serve each other willingly. (sts. 5–6)

Stanza 5 © 1980 Concordia Publishing House

Sing Praise to God, the Highest Good
LSB 819

Sing praise to God, the highest good,
    The author of creation,
The God of love who understood
    Our need for His salvation.
With healing balm our souls He fills
And ev'ry faithless murmur stills:
    To God all praise and glory!

What God's almighty pow'r has made,
    In mercy He is keeping.
By morning glow or evening shade
    His eye is never sleeping.
Within the kingdom of His might
All things are just and good and right:
    To God all praise and glory!

We sought the Lord in our distress;
    O God, in mercy hear us.
Our Savior saw our helplessness
    And came with peace to cheer us.
For this we thank and praise the Lord,
Who is by one and all adored:
    To God all praise and glory! (sts. 1–3)

ADDITIONAL HYMNS

All Praise to Thee, for Thou, O King Divine	*LSB 815*
Draw Us to Thee	*LSB 701*
Love Divine, All Loves Excelling	*LSB 700:1, 3–4*
Our Father, by Whose Name	*LSB 863*
Rise, Shine, You People	*LSB 825*

Moving

Any number of issues and concerns arise as a family moves and relocates to a new home. Some people may be saddened over leaving familiar surroundings, friendships, and acquaintances. Feelings about their new dwelling and its environment may range from joyful expectation to anxious uncertainty. The ministry of the Word will proclaim the Lord's gracious promise to be with and bless His baptized people in all of life's circumstances. The pastor will also help the family find a Lutheran congregation in their new location.

The rite for Farewell and Godspeed to Members (*LSB Agenda,* page 34) may be used to bid farewell on the last Sunday that the members attend worship before moving.

PSALMODY

Psalm 139:1–10   *Where shall I go from Your Spirit?*

¹ O Lᴏʀᴅ, you have searched me and | known me!*
  ² You know when I sit down and when I rise up; you discern my thoughts | from afar.
³ You search out my path and my | lying down*
  and are acquainted with | all my ways.
⁴ Even before a word is | on my tongue,*
  behold, O Lᴏʀᴅ, you know it alto- | gether.
⁵ You hem me in, behind | and before,*
  and lay your hand up- | on me.
⁶ Such knowledge is too wonder- | ful for me;*
  it is high; I cannot | attain it.
⁷ Where shall I go from your | Spirit?*
  Or where shall I flee from your | presence?
⁸ If I ascend to heaven, | you are there!*
  If I make my bed in Sheol, | you are there!
⁹ If I take the wings of the | morning*
  and dwell in the uttermost parts | of the sea,

¹⁰ even there your hand shall | lead me,*
   and your right hand shall | hold me.

Psalm 91:1–2, 9–12   *The Lord's angels will guard you*

¹ He who dwells in the shelter of the | Most High*
   will abide in the shadow of the Al- | mighty.
² I will say to the LORD, "My refuge and my | fortress,*
   my God, in | whom I trust."
⁹ Because you have made the LORD your | dwelling place—*
   the Most High, who is my | refuge—
¹⁰ no evil shall be allowed to be- | fall you,*
   no plague come | near your tent.
¹¹ For he will command his angels con- | cerning you*
   to guard you in | all your ways.
¹² On their hands they will | bear you up,*
   lest you strike your foot a- | gainst a stone.

Psalm 121   *The Lord will keep you from all evil*

¹ I lift up my eyes | to the hills.*
   From where does my | help come?
² My help comes | from the LORD,*
   who made | heaven and earth.
³ He will not let your | foot be moved;*
   he who keeps you will not | slumber.
⁴ Behold, he who keeps | Israel*
   will neither slum- | ber nor sleep.
⁵ The LORD is your | keeper;*
   the LORD is your shade on your | right hand.
⁶ The sun shall not strike | you by day,*
   nor the | moon by night.
⁷ The LORD will keep you from all | evil;*
   he will | keep your life.
⁸ The LORD will keep your going out and your | coming in*
   from this time forth and for- | evermore.

ADDITIONAL PSALMODY

Psalm 36:5–10   *How precious is Your steadfast love*
Psalm 112:1–7   *Blessed is the man who fears the Lord*
Psalm 118:1, 14–16, 25, 29   *O Lord, we pray, give us success*

READINGS

Matthew 6:19–21, 25–33   *Seek the kingdom of God*

[19][Jesus said:] "Do not lay up for yourselves treasures on earth, where moth and rust destroy and where thieves break in and steal, [20]but lay up for yourselves treasures in heaven, where neither moth nor rust destroys and where thieves do not break in and steal. [21]For where your treasure is, there your heart will be also.

[25]"Therefore I tell you, do not be anxious about your life, what you will eat or what you will drink, nor about your body, what you will put on. Is not life more than food, and the body more than clothing? [26]Look at the birds of the air: they neither sow nor reap nor gather into barns, and yet your heavenly Father feeds them. Are you not of more value than they? [27]And which of you by being anxious can add a single hour to his span of life? [28]And why are you anxious about clothing? Consider the lilies of the field, how they grow: they neither toil nor spin, [29]yet I tell you, even Solomon in all his glory was not arrayed like one of these. [30]But if God so clothes the grass of the field, which today is alive and tomorrow is thrown into the oven, will he not much more clothe you, O you of little faith? [31]Therefore do not be anxious, saying, 'What shall we eat?' or 'What shall we drink?' or 'What shall we wear?' [32]For the Gentiles seek after all these things, and your heavenly Father knows that you need them all. [33]But seek first the kingdom of God and his righteousness, and all these things will be added to you."

Mark 10:28–30 *Blessings a hundredfold in the age to come*

²⁸Peter began to say to [Jesus], "See, we have left everything and followed you." ²⁹Jesus said, "Truly, I say to you, there is no one who has left house or brothers or sisters or mother or father or children or lands, for my sake and for the gospel, ³⁰who will not receive a hundredfold now in this time, houses and brothers and sisters and mothers and children and lands, with persecutions, and in the age to come eternal life."

Proverbs 24:3–4 *Wisdom builds the house*

³ By wisdom a house is built,
    and by understanding it is established;
⁴ by knowledge the rooms are filled
    with all precious and pleasant riches.

ADDITIONAL READINGS

Is. 32:17–18	*God's people will abide in peaceful dwellings*
Is. 46:3–4, 9–10	*God declares the end from the beginning*
Matt. 7:24–25	*The wise man built his house on the rock*
Luke 2:39–40	*The holy family in Nazareth*
Luke 10:38–42	*Jesus at the home of Martha and Mary*

PRAYERS

Lord God, Your gracious presence attends Your people wherever they go. Be with *name(s)*, whose *life is / lives are* in transition as *he/she/they* move(s) from a familiar home to a new community. Support *him/her/them* in times of challenge or loneliness, and surround *him/her/them* with caring Christian people so that *he/she/they* may find welcome and peace in *his/her/their* new location and joy in Your ongoing kindness and love; through Jesus Christ, our Lord, who lives and reigns with You and the Holy Spirit, one God, now and forever. (253 alt.)

For moving from a home

Lord God, You have called Your servants to ventures of which we cannot see the ending, by paths as yet untrodden, through perils unknown. Give us faith to go out with good courage, not knowing where we go but only that Your hand is leading us and Your love supporting us; through Jesus Christ, Your Son, our Lord, who lives and reigns with You and the Holy Spirit, one God, now and forever. (193)

For moving to a new home

Heavenly Father, we implore You to visit the home in which Your servant(s) (___name(s)___) will live. Drive the evil one far from ___him/her/them___. Let Your holy angels encamp around ___him/her/them___ day and night. Defend ___him/her/them___ from all danger, and graciously bless ___him/her/them___, that ___his/her/their___ home may be a place where Your name is praised forevermore; through Jesus Christ, Your Son, our Lord, who lives and reigns with You and the Holy Spirit, one God, now and forever. (840)

For the children who are moving

Heavenly Father, You watched over Your beloved Son as Joseph took Him and His mother to live in Egypt. Be with ___name(s) of child(ren)___ as ___he/she/they___ move(s) with ___his/her/their___ parents to ___his/her/their___ new home. Bring ___him/her/them___ safely to ___his/her/their___ destination, provide for all ___his/her/their___ needs, and surround ___him/her/them___ with faithful friends; through Jesus Christ, Your Son, our Lord, who lives and reigns with You and the Holy Spirit, one God, now and forever. (841)

HYMNS

Jesus, Lead Thou On

LSB 718

Jesus, lead Thou on
Till our rest is won;
    And although the way be cheerless,
    We will follow calm and fearless.
Guide us by Thy hand
To our fatherland. (st. 1)

If the way be drear,
If the foe be near,
    Let not faithless fears o'ertake us;
    Let not faith and hope forsake us;
For through many a woe
To our home we go. (st. 2)

Jesus, lead Thou on
Till our rest is won.
    Heav'nly leader, still direct us,
    Still support, console, protect us,
Till we safely stand
In our fatherland. (st. 4)

To God the Holy Spirit Let Us Pray

LSB 768

To God the Holy Spirit let us pray
For the true faith needed on our way
That He may defend us when life is ending
And from exile home we are wending.
    Lord, have mercy! (st. 1)

►

Shine in our hearts, O Spirit, precious light;
Teach us Jesus Christ to know aright
That we may abide in the Lord who bought us,
Till to our true home He has brought us.

Lord, have mercy! (st. 4)

ADDITIONAL HYMNS

Consider How the Birds Above	LSB 736
Evening and Morning	LSB 726
Have No Fear, Little Flock	LSB 735
I Lie, O Lord, within Your Care	LSB 885
I'm But a Stranger Here	LSB 748
Lord, Take My Hand and Lead Me	LSB 722
Rejoice, My Heart, Be Glad and Sing	LSB 737:1–4, 7

Children in Transition

Children usually leave their parental home to establish their own lives as part of the earthly journey ordained by God. Both parents and their offspring need to be strengthened in this truth and pointed to the Lord's promise to guide and care for His people. More unsettling and grievous is the situation when there is a child whose faith in Christ is languishing, or whose life is immoral, or who has completely denied the faith. Trusting upon God's abiding promises to our children in Holy Baptism and calling upon Him in intercessory prayer for this type of child are vital.

PSALMODY

Psalm 119:9–16 *How can a young man keep his way pure?*

⁹ How can a young man keep his | way pure?*
    By guarding it according | to your word.
¹⁰ With my whole heart I | seek you;*
    let me not wander from your com- | mandments!
¹¹ I have stored up your word | in my heart,*
    that I might not sin a- | gainst you.
¹² Blessèd are you, | O Lord;*
    teach me your | statutes!
¹³ With my lips | I declare*
    all the just decrees | of your mouth.
¹⁴ In the way of your testimonies | I delight*
    as much as in all | riches.
¹⁵ I will meditate on your | precepts*
    and fix my eyes | on your ways.
¹⁶ I will delight in your | statutes;*
    I will not for- | get your word.

Psalm 28:1–2, 7–9   *Save and bless Your heritage*

¹ To you, O Lord, I call; my rock, be not | deaf to me,*
> lest, if you be silent to me, I become like those who go down | to the pit.

² Hear the voice of my pleas for mercy, when I cry to | you for help,*
> when I lift up my hands toward your most holy sanctu- | ary.

⁷ The Lord is my strength and my shield; in him my heart trusts, and | I am helped;*
> my heart exults, and with my song I give | thanks to him.

⁸ The Lord is the strength of his | people;*
> he is the saving refuge of his a- | nointed.

⁹ Oh, save your people and bless your | heritage!*
> Be their shepherd and carry them for- | ever.

Psalm 121   *The Lord will keep you from all evil*

¹ I lift up my eyes | to the hills.*
> From where does my | help come?

² My help comes | from the Lord,*
> who made | heaven and earth.

³ He will not let your | foot be moved;*
> he who keeps you will not | slumber.

⁴ Behold, he who keeps | Israel*
> will neither slum- | ber nor sleep.

⁵ The Lord is your | keeper;*
> the Lord is your shade on your | right hand.

⁶ The sun shall not strike | you by day,*
> nor the | moon by night.

⁷ The Lord will keep you from all | evil;*
> he will | keep your life.

⁸ The Lord will keep your going out and your | coming in*
> from this time forth and for- | evermore.

ADDITIONAL PSALMODY

Psalm 25:1–10   *Remember not the sins of my youth*
Psalm 46   *Be still, and know that I am God*
Psalm 111   *The Lord remembers His covenant forever*
Psalm 139:7–18   *How precious to me are Your thoughts, O God!*

READINGS

Exodus 33:14–17   *The Lord goes with His people*

¹⁴[The Lord] said, "My presence will go with you, and I will give you rest." ¹⁵And he said to him, "If your presence will not go with me, do not bring us up from here. ¹⁶For how shall it be known that I have found favor in your sight, I and your people? Is it not in your going with us, so that we are distinct, I and your people, from every other people on the face of the earth?"

¹⁷And the LORD said to Moses, "This very thing that you have spoken I will do, for you have found favor in my sight, and I know you by name."

2 Timothy 3:14–17   *From childhood you have known the Scriptures*

¹⁴Continue in what you have learned and have firmly believed, knowing from whom you learned it ¹⁵and how from childhood you have been acquainted with the sacred writings, which are able to make you wise for salvation through faith in Christ Jesus. ¹⁶All Scripture is breathed out by God and profitable for teaching, for reproof, for correction, and for training in righteousness, ¹⁷that the man of God may be competent, equipped for every good work.

Proverbs 3:1–7   *My son, do not forget my teaching*

¹ My son, do not forget my teaching,
     but let your heart keep my commandments,
² for length of days and years of life
     and peace they will add to you.

▶

³ Let not steadfast love and faithfulness forsake you;
  bind them around your neck;
  write them on the tablet of your heart.
⁴ So you will find favor and good success
  in the sight of God and man.
⁵ Trust in the LORD with all your heart,
  and do not lean on your own understanding.
⁶ In all your ways acknowledge him,
  and he will make straight your paths.
⁷ Be not wise in your own eyes;
  fear the LORD, and turn away from evil.

Romans 12:1–2 *Do not be conformed to this world*

¹I appeal to you therefore, brothers, by the mercies of God, to present your bodies as a living sacrifice, holy and acceptable to God, which is your spiritual worship. ²Do not be conformed to this world, but be transformed by the renewal of your mind, that by testing you may discern what is the will of God, what is good and acceptable and perfect.

ADDITIONAL READINGS

Gen. 31:48–49	*The Lord watch between you and me*
Ex. 34:4–7a	*The Lord is merciful and gracious*
Ezek. 18:30–32	*God has no pleasure in the death of anyone*
Matt. 28:20b	*Christ promises to be with us always*
Luke 12:22–32	*Seek His kingdom*
Luke 15:11–32	*The parable of the prodigal son*
Rom. 8:26–30	*The Spirit intercedes for us*
Heb. 4:14–16	*Grace to help in time of need*
James 4:13–15	*If the Lord wills, we will live and do this*

PRAYERS

Going away to college

Lord God, heavenly Father, Your Son grew and became strong, filled with wisdom. Grant Your favor to   _name_ , who departs for college, and assure   _him/her_   of Your loving presence and protection. Bless   _his/her_   studies that   _he/she_   may diligently apply   _himself/ herself_   to wisdom and increase in knowledge and understanding for faithful and loving service in the world. Lead   _him/her_   to Your house regularly that   _he/she_   may be strengthened through Your holy Word and Supper to live each day in the promises of   _his/her_   Baptism; through Jesus Christ, Your Son, our Lord, who lives and reigns with You and the Holy Spirit, one God, now and forever. (842)

Moving out on one's own

Almighty God, gracious Father, the promise of Your presence is sure and certain to us in Holy Baptism. Be with Your   _son/daughter   name_   and lead   _him/her_   forth in Your peace. Guide and direct   _him/her_ , protect and defend   _him/her_ . Grant   _him/her_   Your Holy Spirit that   _he/she_   may remain steadfast in the faith and come at last to eternal life in Your heavenly kingdom; through Jesus Christ, Your Son, our Lord, who lives and reigns with You and the Holy Spirit, one God, now and forever. (843)

Entering military service

O Lord of hosts, stretch forth Your almighty arm to strengthen and protect   _name_ , who now begins service in the armed forces of our country. Bless   _his/her_   training that   _he/she_   may apply   _himself/ herself_   with all diligence. Support   _him/her_   in times of war, and in times of peace keep   _him/her_   from all evil, giving   _him/her_   courage and loyalty and granting that in all things   _he/she_   may serve honestly and without reproach; through Jesus Christ, Your Son, our Lord, who lives and reigns with You and the Holy Spirit, one God, now and forever. (844)

For a wayward child

Almighty God, merciful and most gracious Father, we earnestly implore You to turn the hearts of all who have forsaken the faith once delivered to Your Church, especially those who have wandered from it or are in doubt or temptation through the corruption of Your truth. In mercy, rescue _name_. Bring _him/her_ to repentance and turn _him/her_ again to delight in Your Word and be made wise to salvation through faith in Your Son, Jesus Christ, our Lord, who lives and reigns with You and the Holy Spirit, one God, now and forever. (845)

HYMNS

Go, My Children, with My Blessing

LSB 922

Go, My children, with My blessing,
  Never alone.
Waking, sleeping, I am with you;
  You are My own.
 In My love's baptismal river
 I have made you Mine forever.
Go, My children, with My blessing—
  You are My own. (st. 1)

Go, My children, sins forgiven,
  At peace and pure.
Here you learned how much I love you,
  What I can cure.
 Here you heard My dear Son's story;
 Here you touched Him, saw His glory.
Go, My children, sins forgiven,
  At peace and pure. (st. 2)

I the Lord will bless and keep you
And give you peace;
I the Lord will smile upon you
And give you peace:
I the Lord will be your Father,
Savior, Comforter, and Brother.
Go, My children; I will keep you
And give you peace. (st. 4)

© 1983 Concordia Publishing House

Jesus Sinners Doth Receive   LSB 609

Jesus sinners doth receive;
Oh, may all this saying ponder
Who in sin's delusions live
And from God and heaven wander!
Here is hope for all who grieve:
Jesus sinners doth receive. (st. 1)

Sheep that from the fold did stray
No true shepherd e'er forsaketh;
Weary souls that lost their way
Christ, the Shepherd, gently taketh
In His arms that they may live:
Jesus sinners doth receive. (st. 3)

ADDITIONAL HYMNS

Christ Be My Leader	LSB 861
Father Welcomes	LSB 605
I Am Jesus' Little Lamb	LSB 740
I Lie, O Lord, within Your Care	LSB 885
Jesus Loves Me	LSB 588
Jesus Sinners Doth Receive	LSB 609
Lord, Help Us Ever to Retain	LSB 865
Lord, Take My Hand and Lead Me	LSB 722
Now the Light Has Gone Away	LSB 887:1–3, 5

Separation during Times of War or Emergency

The burdens of separation that war and national emergency bring are borne both by those who are called upon to serve their country and by loved ones awaiting their return. Throughout the days of separation and the days of "not knowing," God's people are comforted by His ever-watchful presence. They confess—even in times of separation—the oneness they have in Christ, which will be made complete in the resurrection on the day of His glorious coming.

PSALMODY

Psalm 91   *His angels will guard you in the battle*

¹ He who dwells in the shelter of the | Most High*
    will abide in the shadow of the Al- | mighty.

² I will say to the Lord, "My refuge and my | fortress,*
    my God, in | whom I trust."

³ For he will deliver you from the snare of the | fowler*
    and from the deadly | pestilence.

⁴ He will cover you with his pinions, and under his wings you will find | refuge;*
    his faithfulness is a shield and | buckler.

⁵ You will not fear the terror | of the night,*
    nor the arrow that | flies by day,

⁶ nor the pestilence that stalks in | darkness,*
    nor the destruction that wastes at | noonday.

⁷ A thousand may fall at your side, ten thousand at your | right hand,*
    but it will not come | near you.

⁸ You will only look | with your eyes*
    and see the recompense of the | wicked.

⁹ Because you have made the Lord your | dwelling place—*
    the Most High, who is my | refuge—

¹⁰ no evil shall be allowed to be- | fall you,*
>> no plague come | near your tent.

¹¹ For he will command his angels con- | cerning you*
>> to guard you in | all your ways.

¹² On their hands they will | bear you up,*
>> lest you strike your foot a- | gainst a stone.

¹³ You will tread on the lion and the | adder;*
>> the young lion and the serpent you will trample | underfoot.

¹⁴ "Because he holds fast to me in love, I will de- | liver him;*
>> I will protect him, because he | knows my name.

¹⁵ When he calls to me, I will answer him; I will be with him
in | trouble;*
>> I will rescue him and | honor him.

¹⁶ With long life I will sat- | isfy him*
>> and show him my sal- | vation."

Psalm 46   *The Lord of hosts is with us*

¹ God is our ref- | uge and strength,*
>> a very present help in | trouble.

² Therefore we will not fear though the | earth gives way,*
>> though the mountains be moved into the heart | of the sea,

³ though its waters | roar and foam,*
>> though the mountains tremble at its | swelling.

⁴ There is a river whose streams make glad the cit- | y of God,*
>> the holy habitation of the | Most High.

⁵ God is in the midst of her; she shall | not be moved;*
>> God will help her when | morning dawns.

⁶ The nations rage, the kingdoms | totter;*
>> he utters his voice, the | earth melts.

⁷ The LORD of hosts is | with us;*
>> the God of Jacob is our | fortress.

⁸ Come, behold the works | of the LORD,*
>> how he has brought desolations | on the earth.   ▶

⁹ He makes wars cease to the end | of the earth;*

    he breaks the bow and shatters the spear; he burns the
chariots | with fire.

¹⁰ "Be still, and know that | I am God.*

    I will be exalted among the nations, I will be exalted | in the
earth!"

¹¹ The LORD of hosts is | with us;*

    the God of Jacob is our | fortress.

ADDITIONAL PSALMODY

Psalm 37:3–7a   *Be still and wait patiently for the Lord*
Psalm 121   *The Lord is your keeper*

READINGS

Romans 8:38–39   *Nothing can separate us from God's love*

³⁸I am sure that neither death nor life, nor angels nor rulers, nor things
present nor things to come, nor powers, ³⁹nor height nor depth, nor
anything else in all creation, will be able to separate us from the love
of God in Christ Jesus our Lord.

John 10:27–29   *I give them eternal life, and they will never perish*

²⁷[Jesus said:] "My sheep hear my voice, and I know them, and they
follow me. ²⁸I give them eternal life, and they will never perish, and
no one will snatch them out of my hand. ²⁹My Father, who has given
them to me, is greater than all, and no one is able to snatch them out
of the Father's hand."

Lamentations 3:22–27   *The Lord is good to those who wait for Him*

²² The steadfast love of the LORD never ceases;

    his mercies never come to an end;

²³ they are new every morning;

    great is your faithfulness.

²⁴ "The LORD is my portion," says my soul,
    "therefore I will hope in him."
²⁵ The LORD is good to those who wait for him,
    to the soul who seeks him.
²⁶ It is good that one should wait quietly
    for the salvation of the LORD.
²⁷ It is good for a man that he bear
    the yoke in his youth.

ADDITIONAL READINGS

Phil. 4:19–20	*God supplies your every need*
Col. 1:10–14	*May you be strengthened*
2 Thess. 3:3	*The Lord is faithful and will guard you*

PRAYERS

Lord Jesus, You have promised to be with us always, even to the very end of the age. Mercifully watch over those we love, especially __name__, who is now separated from us by __war / disaster / other circumstances__. Protect __him/her__ in this time of danger and trial. Teach __him/her__ and us to know that in the communion of Your holy Church You are always near and that we are ever one in You; through Jesus Christ, Your Son, our Lord, who lives and reigns with You and the Holy Spirit, one God, now and forever. (846)

Almighty God, merciful Father, by Your holy Word and Sacraments You have created Your Church in this world to be a godly communion and family. Guide and bless __name__ that wherever __he/she__ is called to serve __he/she__ may find a place of solace and pleasant fellowship among Your faithful people; through Jesus Christ, Your Son, our Lord, who lives and reigns with You and the Holy Spirit, one God, now and forever. (847)

HYMNS

If God Himself Be for Me

LSB 724

If God Himself be for me,
    I may a host defy;
For when I pray, before me
    My foes, confounded, fly.
If Christ, my head and master,
    Befriend me from above,
What foe or what disaster
    Can drive me from His love? (st. 1)

He canceled my offenses,
    Delivered me from death;
He is the Lord who cleanses
    My soul from sin through faith.
In Him I can be cheerful,
    Courageous on my way;
In Him I am not fearful
    Of God's great Judgment Day. (st. 4)

No danger, thirst, or hunger,
    No pain or poverty,
No earthly tyrant's anger
    Shall ever vanquish me.
Though earth should break asunder,
    My fortress You shall be;
No fire or sword or thunder
    Shall sever You from me. (st. 8)

My heart with joy is springing;
    I am no longer sad.
My soul is filled with singing;
    Your sunshine makes me glad.

The sun that cheers my spirit
    Is Jesus Christ, my King;
The heav'n I shall inherit
    Makes me rejoice and sing. (st. 10)

Now the Light Has Gone Away
LSB 887

Let my near and dear ones be
Always near and dear to Thee;
O bring me and all I love
To Thy happy home above. (st. 3)

ADDITIONAL HYMNS

Children of the Heavenly Father	*LSB 725*
Eternal Father, Strong to Save	*LSB 717*
From God Can Nothing Move Me	*LSB 713*
In God, My Faithful God	*LSB 745*
In the Very Midst of Life	*LSB 755*
Jesus Christ, My Sure Defense	*LSB 741*
Jesus Loves Me	*LSB 588*
Lord, Help Us Ever to Retain	*LSB 865*
Lord, It Belongs Not to My Care	*LSB 757*
Lord, Take My Hand and Lead Me	*LSB 722*
On Eagles' Wings	*LSB 727*
Through Jesus' Blood and Merit	*LSB 746*

✠ VOCATION

Understanding One's Vocation

Vocation is the setting in which the Christian is called to live by faith in Christ and in love toward others. The Table of Duties in Luther's Small Catechism, which describes the various estates in which Christians serve their neighbors, can be helpful to the pastor in strengthening the faithful to carry out their vocations. Christians rely on the grace of God alone in their vocation so that they may serve with joy under the cross. The cultivation of a Christian understanding and sense of vocation is crucial in addressing any number of work-related situations and concerns.

PSALMODY
Psalm 127:1–2   *Unless the Lord builds the house*

¹ Unless the LORD builds the house, those who build it la- | bor in vain.*

>   Unless the LORD watches over the city, the watchman stays a- | wake in vain.

² It is in vain that you rise up early and go late to rest, eating the bread of | anxious toil;*

>   for he gives to his be- | lovèd sleep.

Psalm 145:15–21   *The eyes of all look to the Lord*

15 The eyes of all | look to you,*
     and you give them their food in due | season.
16 You open | your hand;*
     you satisfy the desire of every | living thing.
17 The LORD is righteous in | all his ways*
     and kind in | all his works.
18 The LORD is near to all who | call on him,*
     to all who call on | him in truth.
19 He fulfills the desire of those who | fear him;*
     he also hears their cry and | saves them.
20 The LORD preserves all who | love him,*
     but all the wicked he | will destroy.
21 My mouth will speak the praise | of the LORD,*
     and let all flesh bless his holy name forever and | ever.

ADDITIONAL PSALMODY

Psalm 1   *The blessed man walks in the counsel of the Lord*
Psalm 139   *I am fearfully and wonderfully made*

READINGS

Ecclesiastes 2:24–26   *Finding fulfillment in one's work*

24There is nothing better for a person than that he should eat and drink and find enjoyment in his toil. This also, I saw, is from the hand of God, 25for apart from him who can eat or who can have enjoyment? 26For to the one who pleases him God has given wisdom and knowledge and joy, but to the sinner he has given the business of gathering and collecting, only to give to one who pleases God. This also is vanity and a striving after wind.

Genesis 1:26–28   *Created in God's image to have dominion*

26Then God said, "Let us make man in our image, after our likeness. ▶

435

And let them have dominion over the fish of the sea and over the birds of the heavens and over the livestock and over all the earth and over every creeping thing that creeps on the earth."

²⁷So God created man in his own image,
in the image of God he created him;
male and female he created them.

²⁸And God blessed them. And God said to them, "Be fruitful and multiply and fill the earth and subdue it and have dominion over the fish of the sea and over the birds of the heavens and over every living thing that moves on the earth."

Genesis 3:15–19   *The toil of work under the curse of the fall*

¹⁵ "I will put enmity between you and the woman,
and between your offspring and her offspring;
he shall bruise your head,
and you shall bruise his heel."
¹⁶ To the woman he said,
"I will surely multiply your pain in childbearing;
in pain you shall bring forth children.
Your desire shall be for your husband,
and he shall rule over you."
¹⁷ And to Adam he said,
"Because you have listened to the voice of your wife
and have eaten of the tree
of which I commanded you,
'You shall not eat of it,'
cursed is the ground because of you;
in pain you shall eat of it all the days of your life;
¹⁸ thorns and thistles it shall bring forth for you;
and you shall eat the plants of the field.
¹⁹ By the sweat of your face
you shall eat bread,

till you return to the ground,
    for out of it you were taken;
for you are dust,
    and to dust you shall return."

ADDITIONAL READINGS

Prov. 6:6–11	*The lesson of the ant*
Eccl. 3	*There is a time for everything*
Eccl. 5:18–20	*To rejoice in one's toil is God's gift*
Eph. 6:5–9	*For workers and masters*
2 Thess. 3:6–12	*Work quietly and earn a living*

PRAYERS

Almighty God, look with favor upon __name__ in __his/her__ vocation as __name of vocation__. Give __him/her__ wisdom, courage, and patience to serve in sacrificial love, and strengthen __him/her__ in this calling; through Jesus Christ, Your Son, our Lord, who lives and reigns with You and the Holy Spirit, one God, now and forever. (848)

Lord God Almighty, You have blessed __name__ with various and unique gifts. Grant __him/her__ the grace to use them always to Your honor and glory; through Jesus Christ, Your Son, our Lord, who lives and reigns with You and the Holy Spirit, one God, now and forever. (849)

O God, by the patient suffering of Your only-begotten Son You have beaten down the pride of the old enemy. Now help us, we humbly pray, rightly to treasure in our hearts all that our Lord has of His goodness borne for our sake that following His blessed example we may bear with patience all that is adverse to us; through Jesus Christ, our Lord. (199, 217)

Lord God, You have called Your servants to ventures of which we cannot see the ending, by paths as yet untrodden, through perils ▶

unknown. Give us faith to go out with good courage, not knowing where we go but only that Your hand is leading us and Your love supporting us; through Jesus Christ, Your Son, our Lord, who lives and reigns with You and the Holy Spirit, one God, now and forever. (193)

HYMNS

Salvation unto Us Has Come
LSB 555

Faith clings to Jesus' cross alone
    And rests in Him unceasing;
And by its fruits true faith is known,
    With love and hope increasing.
For faith alone can justify;
Works serve our neighbor and supply
    The proof that faith is living. (st. 9)

Forth in Thy Name, O Lord, I Go
LSB 854

Forth in Thy name, O Lord, I go,
    My daily labor to pursue,
Thee, only Thee, resolved to know
    In all I think or speak or do. (st. 1)

The task Thy wisdom has assigned,
    O let me cheerfully fulfill;
In all my works Thy presence find,
    And prove Thy good and perfect will. (st. 2)

Give me to bear Thine easy yoke,
    And ev'ry moment watch and pray,
And still to things eternal look,
    And hasten to Thy glorious day. (st. 4)

ADDITIONAL HYMNS

Church of God, Elect and Glorious — *LSB 646*
For All the Faithful Women — *LSB 855:1, 9, 3*

Beginning a New Job

God has established the occupational and economic realm as one of the structures of human life. Work is, therefore, a gift of God. Entering the work world and beginning a new job can be exciting and exhilarating. It can also be an occasion for fear and apprehension. Quite often, it is not only young high school or college graduates who undertake new employment but also individuals who are embarking on a new career or who are forced to change jobs.

PSALMODY

Psalm 104:1–2, 14–15, 23–24, 27–30   *Mankind looks to God*

¹ Bless the LORD, | O my soul!*

O LORD my God, you are | very great!

You are clothed with splendor and | majesty,*

²covering yourself with light as with a garment, stretching out the heavens | like a tent.

¹⁴ You cause the grass to grow for the livestock and plants for man to | cultivate,*

that he may bring forth food from the earth ¹⁵and wine to gladden the | heart of man,

▶

439

oil to make his | face shine*
    and bread to strengthen | man's heart.

23 Man goes out | to his work*
    and to his labor until the | evening.

24 O LORD, how manifold are your works! In wisdom have you | made
    them all;*
    the earth is full of your | creatures.

27 These all | look to you,*
    to give them their food in due | season.

28 When you give it to them, they gath- | er it up;*
    when you open your hand, they are filled with | good things.

29 When you hide your face, they | are dismayed;*
    when you take away their breath, they die and return | to
    their dust.

30 When you send forth your Spirit, they are cre- | ated,*
    and you renew the face | of the ground.

Psalm 128   *You shall eat the fruit of your hands*

1 Blessèd is everyone who | fears the LORD,*
    who walks | in his ways!

2 You shall eat the fruit of the labor | of your hands;*
    you shall be blessed, and it shall be | well with you.

3 Your wife will be like a fruitful vine with- | in your house;*
    your children will be like olive shoots around your | table.

4 Behold, thus shall the | man be blessed*
    who | fears the LORD.

5 The LORD bless you from | Zion!*
    May you see the prosperity of Jerusalem all the days | of
    your life!

6 May you see your children's | children!*
    Peace be upon | Israel!

ADDITIONAL PSALMODY

Psalm 16:1–8   *The Lord preserves those who take refuge in Him*
Psalm 25:1, 5, 12   *Lead me in Your truth and teach me*
Psalm 127:1–2   *Without the Lord our work is in vain*

READINGS

Genesis 2:15–17, 19–20a   *God established work*

¹⁵The LORD God took the man and put him in the garden of Eden to work it and keep it. ¹⁶And the LORD God commanded the man, saying, "You may surely eat of every tree of the garden, ¹⁷but of the tree of the knowledge of good and evil you shall not eat, for in the day that you eat of it you shall surely die."

¹⁹So out of the ground the LORD God formed every beast of the field and every bird of the heavens and brought them to the man to see what he would call them. And whatever the man called every living creature, that was its name. ²⁰The man gave names to all livestock and to the birds of the heavens and to every beast of the field.

Matthew 6:25–33   *Seek first the kingdom of God*

²⁵[Jesus said:] "Therefore I tell you, do not be anxious about your life, what you will eat or what you will drink, nor about your body, what you will put on. Is not life more than food, and the body more than clothing? ²⁶Look at the birds of the air: they neither sow nor reap nor gather into barns, and yet your heavenly Father feeds them. Are you not of more value than they? ²⁷And which of you by being anxious can add a single hour to his span of life? ²⁸And why are you anxious about clothing? Consider the lilies of the field, how they grow: they neither toil nor spin, ²⁹yet I tell you, even Solomon in all his glory was not arrayed like one of these. ³⁰But if God so clothes the grass of the field, which today is alive and tomorrow is thrown into the oven, will he not much more clothe you, O you of little faith? ³¹Therefore do not be anxious, saying, 'What shall we eat?' or ▶

'What shall we drink?' or 'What shall we wear?' ³²For the Gentiles seek after all these things, and your heavenly Father knows that you need them all. ³³But seek first the kingdom of God and his righteousness, and all these things will be added to you."

ADDITIONAL READINGS

Deut. 8:1–18	*Do not forget the Lord your God*
Luke 12:13–21	*The parable of the rich fool*
Eph. 6:5–8	*Honoring the employer*
Phil. 4:4–9	*Be anxious for nothing*
2 Thess. 3:6–12	*God's will is that we work*

PRAYERS

Eternal God, be present with ___name___ and bless ___him/her___ as ___he/she___ begins ___his/her___ new job. Protect ___him/her___ in danger and fear. Grant ___him/her___ diligence and faithfulness that ___he/she___ may meet the needs of others with competence and compassion; through Jesus Christ, Your Son, our Lord, who lives and reigns with You and the Holy Spirit, one God, now and forever. (850)

Lord God, You have called Your servants to ventures of which we cannot see the ending, by paths as yet untrodden, through perils unknown. Give us faith to go out with good courage, not knowing where we go but only that Your hand is leading us and Your love supporting us; through Jesus Christ, Your Son, our Lord, who lives and reigns with You and the Holy Spirit, one God, now and forever. (193)

Direct us, O Lord, in all our doings with Your most gracious favor, and further us with Your continual help, that in all our works begun, continued, and ended in You we may glorify Your holy name and finally, by Your mercy, obtain eternal salvation; through Jesus Christ, Your Son, our Lord, who lives and reigns with You and the Holy Spirit, one God, now and forever. (188)

HYMN

With the Lord Begin Your Task

LSB 869

With the Lord begin your task;
    Jesus will direct it.
For His aid and counsel ask;
    Jesus will perfect it.
Ev'ry morn with Jesus rise,
    And when day is ended,
In His name then close your eyes;
    Be to Him commended. (st. 1)

If your task be thus begun
    With the Savior's blessing,
Safely then your course will run,
    Toward the promise pressing.
Good will follow ev'rywhere
    While you here must wander;
You at last the joy will share
    In the mansions yonder. (st. 4)

Thus, Lord Jesus, ev'ry task
    Be to You commended;
May Your will be done, I ask,
    Until life is ended.
Jesus, in Your name begun
    Be the day's endeavor;
Grant that it may well be done
    To Your praise forever. (st. 5)

© 1941 Concordia Publishing House

ADDITIONAL HYMNS

Church of God, Elect and Glorious — *LSB 646*
For All the Faithful Women — *LSB 855:1, 9, 3*
For the Fruits of His Creation — *LSB 894:2*

Trouble at Work

The workplace is not immune to the ravages of sin. Trouble at one's place of employment ranges from everyday conflict with fellow workers or employers to more serious problems that threaten termination of employment. Pastoral care will seek to strengthen the faithful to rely on God's Word for help and guidance, commending their workplace troubles to the Lord.

PSALMODY

Psalm 37:1–11   *Commit your way to the Lord*

¹ Fret not yourself because of evil- | doers;*
   be not envious of wrong- | doers!
² For they will soon fade | like the grass*
   and wither like the | green herb.
³ Trust in the LORD, | and do good;*
   dwell in the land and befriend | faithfulness.
⁴ Delight yourself | in the LORD,*
   and he will give you the desires | of your heart.
⁵ Commit your way | to the LORD;*
   trust in him, and | he will act.
⁶ He will bring forth your righteousness | as the light,*
   and your justice as the | noonday.

444

⁷ Be still before the LORD and wait patiently | for him;*
  fret not yourself over the one who prospers in his way,
  over the man who carries out evil de- | vices!
⁸ Refrain from anger, and for- | sake wrath!*
  Fret not yourself; it tends only to | evil.
⁹ For the evildoers shall be | cut off,*
  but those who wait for the LORD shall inher- | it the land.
¹⁰ In just a little while, the wicked will | be no more;*
  though you look carefully at his place, he will | not be there.
¹¹ But the meek shall inher- | it the land*
  and delight themselves in a- | bundant peace.

Psalm 90:1–2, 12–17   *Establish the work of our hands*

¹ Lord, you have been our | dwelling place*
  in all gener- | ations.
² Before the mountains were brought forth, or ever you had
  formed the earth | and the world,*
  from everlasting to everlasting | you are God.
¹² So teach us to number | our days*
  that we may get a heart of | wisdom.
¹³ Return, O LORD! | How long?*
  Have pity on your | servants!
¹⁴ Satisfy us in the morning with your | steadfast love,*
  that we may rejoice and be glad | all our days.
¹⁵ Make us glad for as many days as you have af- | flicted us,*
  and for as many years as we have seen | evil.
¹⁶ Let your work be shown to your | servants,*
  and your glorious power to their | children.
¹⁷ Let the favor of the Lord our God be upon us, and establish the
  work of our hands up- | on us;*
  yes, establish the work | of our hands!

ADDITIONAL PSALMODY

Psalm 27	*He will hide me in the day of trouble*
Psalm 91:1–2, 14–16	*God is my refuge and fortress*
Psalm 101	*Ponder the way that is blameless*
Psalm 124	*The Lord on our side*

READINGS
Matthew 5:44–48   *Love those who do not love you*

⁴⁴[Jesus said:] "I say to you, Love your enemies and pray for those who persecute you, ⁴⁵so that you may be sons of your Father who is in heaven. For he makes his sun rise on the evil and on the good, and sends rain on the just and on the unjust. ⁴⁶For if you love those who love you, what reward do you have? Do not even the tax collectors do the same? ⁴⁷And if you greet only your brothers, what more are you doing than others? Do not even the Gentiles do the same? ⁴⁸You therefore must be perfect, as your heavenly Father is perfect."

1 Peter 3:13–17   *It is better to suffer for doing good*

¹³Now who is there to harm you if you are zealous for what is good? ¹⁴But even if you should suffer for righteousness' sake, you will be blessed. Have no fear of them, nor be troubled, ¹⁵but in your hearts regard Christ the Lord as holy, always being prepared to make a defense to anyone who asks you for a reason for the hope that is in you; ¹⁶yet do it with gentleness and respect, having a good conscience, so that, when you are slandered, those who revile your good behavior in Christ may be put to shame. ¹⁷For it is better to suffer for doing good, if that should be God's will, than for doing evil.

ADDITIONAL READINGS

Prov. 12:14–20	*Those who plan peace have joy*
Rom. 12:14–21	*If possible, live peaceably with all*
James 3:13–18	*The wisdom from above is peaceable*
1 Peter 5:5–11	*Humble yourselves under God's mighty hand*

446

PRAYERS

Almighty God, You are a very present help in time of trouble. Strengthen _name_ as _he/she_ faces difficulty in the workplace. Uphold _him/her_ with Your love, and give _him/her_ Your peace. Help and guide _his/her_ actions that _he/she_ may be delivered by Your great mercy; through Jesus Christ, Your Son, our Lord, who lives and reigns with You and the Holy Spirit, one God, now and forever. (851)

Almighty God, You have bound us together in a common life. Help us in the midst of our struggles for truth to confront one another without hatred or bitterness and to work together with mutual patience and respect; through Jesus Christ, our Lord, who lives and reigns with You and the Holy Spirit, one God, now and forever. (852)

O God, the author of peace and lover of concord, defend _name_ from all the assaults of _his/her_ enemies that trusting in Your defense _he/she_ may rejoice in Your abiding presence; through Jesus Christ, Your Son, our Lord, who lives and reigns with You and the Holy Spirit, one God, now and forever. (853)

HYMNS

Praise the Almighty

LSB 797

Blessèd, oh, blessèd are they forever
    Whose help is from the Lord Most High,
Whom from salvation can nothing sever,
    And who in hope to Christ draw nigh.
To all who trust in Him, our Lord
Will aid and counsel now afford.
    Alleluia, alleluia!

Penitent sinners, for mercy crying,
    Pardon and peace from Him obtain;
Ever the wants of the poor supplying,
    Their faithful God He will remain.
He helps His children in distress,
The widows and the fatherless.
    Alleluia, alleluia! (sts. 3–4)

Come, My Soul, with Every Care   *LSB 779*

Come, my soul, with ev'ry care,
Jesus loves to answer prayer;
He Himself has bid thee pray,
Therefore will not turn away. (st. 1)

Show me what is mine to do;
Ev'ry hour my strength renew.
Let me live a life of faith;
Let me die Thy people's death. (st. 6)

In God, My Faithful God   *LSB 745*

In God, my faithful God,
I trust when dark my road;
Great woes may overtake me,
Yet He will not forsake me.
My troubles He can alter;
His hand lets nothing falter. (st. 1)

"So be it," then, I say
With all my heart each day.
Dear Lord, we all adore You,
We sing for joy before You.
Guide us while here we wander
Until we praise You yonder. (st. 5)

ADDITIONAL HYMNS

All Praise to Thee, My God, This Night	*LSB 883:2*
Christ, Mighty Savior	*LSB 881:4–5*
Eternal Spirit of the Living Christ	*LSB 769*
God, Who Made the Earth and Heaven	*LSB 877:1–2*
How Clear Is Our Vocation, Lord	*LSB 853*
Lord, Help Us Walk Your Servant Way	*LSB 857*
Lord, Support Us All Day Long	*LSB 884:1–2, 4*
Praise to the Lord, the Almighty	*LSB 790:2–4*
What a Friend We Have in Jesus	*LSB 770*

The Unemployed

Loss of a job may present a challenge to a person's faith as well as his or her understanding of vocation. Anxiety and fear of the future often surface, calling into question the Lord's gracious providence. Questions of worth, competence, and the ability to care for one's family may arise as well. The pastor will support and encourage the unemployed by directing him or her to God's promises to give daily bread and His presence with His people in all the circumstances of life. The pastor will use this occasion to deepen the understanding in his parishioner that one's vocation is determined not by the work done but by our calling to live by faith in Christ.

PSALMODY

Psalm 37:3–7a, 23–24, 39–40   *The Lord delivers us*

³ Trust in the Lᴏʀᴅ, | and do good;*
    dwell in the land and befriend | faithfulness.
⁴ Delight yourself | in the Lᴏʀᴅ,*
    and he will give you the desires | of your heart. ▶

⁵ Commit your way | to the LORD;*
      trust in him, and | he will act.
⁶ He will bring forth your righteousness | as the light,*
      and your justice as the | noonday.
⁷ Be still be- | fore the LORD*
      and wait patiently | for him.
²³ The steps of a man are established | by the LORD,*
      when he delights | in his way;
²⁴ though he fall, he shall not be cast | headlong,*
      for the LORD up- | holds his hand.
³⁹ The salvation of the righteous is | from the LORD;*
      he is their stronghold in the time of | trouble.
⁴⁰ The LORD helps them and de- | livers them;*
      he delivers them from the wicked and saves them,
      because they take ref- | uge in him.

Psalm 34:1–10   *I sought the Lord, and He answered me*

¹ I will bless the LORD at | all times;*
      his praise shall continually be | in my mouth.
² My soul makes its boast | in the LORD;*
      let the humble hear | and be glad.
³ Oh, magnify the | LORD with me,*
      and let us exalt his name to- | gether!
⁴ I sought the LORD, and he | answered me*
      and delivered me from | all my fears.
⁵ Those who look to him are | radiant,*
      and their faces shall never | be ashamed.
⁶ This poor man cried, and the LORD | heard him*
      and saved him out of all his | troubles.
⁷ The angel of the LORD encamps around those who | fear him,*
      and de- | livers them.
⁸ Oh, taste and see that the | LORD is good!*
      Blessèd is the man who takes ref- | uge in him!

⁹ Oh, fear the LORD, | you his saints,*
 for those who fear him | have no lack!
¹⁰ The young lions suffer want and | hunger;*
 but those who seek the LORD lack | no good thing.

Psalm 13 *How long will You forget me?*

¹ How long, O LORD? Will you forget me for- | ever?*
 How long will you hide your | face from me?
² How long must I take counsel in my soul and have sorrow in my
 heart | all the day?*
 How long shall my enemy be exalted | over me?
³ Consider and answer me, O | LORD my God;*
 light up my eyes, lest I sleep the | sleep of death,
⁴ lest my enemy say, "I have prevailed | over him,"*
 lest my foes rejoice because I am | shaken.
⁵ But I have trusted in your | steadfast love;*
 my heart shall rejoice in your sal- | vation.
⁶ I will sing | to the LORD,*
 because he has dealt bountifully | with me.

ADDITIONAL PSALMODY

Psalm 27:1, 5, 14 *Be strong and take courage in the Lord*
Psalm 33:13–22 *The Lord sees us, and we hope in Him*

READINGS
Philippians 4:11b–13, 19–20 *I have learned to be content*

¹¹ᵇI have learned in whatever situation I am to be content. ¹²I know how
to be brought low, and I know how to abound. In any and every circumstance, I have learned the secret of facing plenty and hunger, abundance and need. ¹³I can do all things through him who strengthens me.

¹⁹And my God will supply every need of yours according to his
riches in glory in Christ Jesus. ²⁰To our God and Father be glory forever and ever. Amen.

Hebrews 13:5–6 *The Lord is my helper*

⁵Keep your life free from love of money, and be content with what you have, for he has said, "I will never leave you nor forsake you." ⁶So we can confidently say,

> "The Lord is my helper;
>> I will not fear;
> what can man do to me?"

1 Timothy 6:6–8 *Great gain in godliness with contentment*

⁶Now there is great gain in godliness with contentment, ⁷for we brought nothing into the world, and we cannot take anything out of the world. ⁸But if we have food and clothing, with these we will be content.

ADDITIONAL READINGS

Matt. 6:25–34 *Do not be anxious*
Matt. 7:7–11 *God gives good things to His children*

PRAYERS

Heavenly Father, during His earthly ministry, Your Son had nowhere to lay His head. Look with pity on __name__, who seeks work but is unable to find any. Of Your tender mercy raise up opportunities for employment that in peace and thankfulness _he/she_ may earn a just wage, serve _his/her_ neighbor in love, and find the contentment that You promise; for the sake of Him by whose poverty we are made rich, even Jesus Christ, our Lord, who lives and reigns with You and the Holy Spirit, one God, now and forever. (854)

O God, support __name__ in the day of _his/her_ trouble and need. Give _him/her_ faith to cast _his/her_ cares on You, and preserve _him/her_ from all bitterness and resentment. According to Your goodness increase the opportunity for _his/her_ employment that with a thankful heart _he/she_ may earn a just wage and be of service to others; through Jesus Christ, Your Son, our Lord, who lives and reigns with You and the Holy Spirit, one God, now and forever. (290 alt.)

Heavenly Father, we commend to Your care those who suffer want and anxiety from lack of work. Grant that the wealth and resources of this rich land be profitably used so that all persons may find suitable and fulfilling employment and receive just payment for their labor; through Jesus Christ, our Lord. (289)

HYMNS

All Depends on Our Possessing
LSB 732

All depends on our possessing
God's abundant grace and blessing,
    Though all earthly wealth depart.
They who trust with faith unshaken
By their God are not forsaken
    And will keep a dauntless heart.

He who to this day has fed me
And to many joys has led me
    Is and ever shall be mine.
He who ever gently schools me,
He who daily guides and rules me
    Will remain my help divine. (sts. 1–2)

Entrust Your Days and Burdens
LSB 754

Entrust your days and burdens
    To God's most loving hand;
He cares for you while ruling
    The sky, the sea, the land.
For He who guides the tempests
    Along their thund'rous ways
Will find for you a pathway
    And guide you all your days.

▶

Rely on God your Savior
    And find your life secure.
Make His work your foundation
    That your work may endure.
No anxious thought, no worry,
    No self-tormenting care
Can win your Father's favor;
    His heart is moved by prayer.

Take heart, have hope, my spirit,
    And do not be dismayed;
God helps in ev'ry trial
    And makes you unafraid.
Await His time with patience
    Through darkest hours of night
Until the sun you hoped for
    Delights your eager sight.

Leave all to His direction;
    His wisdom rules for you
In ways to rouse your wonder
    At all His love can do.
Soon He, His promise keeping,
    With wonder-working pow'rs
Will banish from your spirit
    What gave you troubled hours. (sts. 1–4)

ADDITIONAL HYMNS

Consider How the Birds Above	LSB 736
Eternal Spirit of the Living Christ	LSB 769
I Trust, O Lord, Your Holy Name	LSB 734
In God, My Faithful God	LSB 745:1
My Soul, Now Praise Your Maker	LSB 820:1, 3–4
On My Heart Imprint Your Image	LSB 422

Our Father, Who from Heaven Above *LSB 766: 4–6, 9*
Who Trusts in God a Strong Abode *LSB 714*

At the Time of Retirement

Christians understand retirement as an opportunity to serve their families, neighbors, and church in new ways. Retirees may struggle with uncertainties about the future, the loss of a sense of usefulness, or how they may serve in changing circumstances. When speaking about retirement, the pastor should lead those he serves in thanksgiving to God for His past faithfulness to them and emphasize the joys of new work and service in Christ Jesus.

PSALMODY

Psalm 71:17–19 *From youth to old age, the Lord has taught me*

¹⁷ O God, from my youth you have | taught me,*
    and I still proclaim your | wondrous deeds.
¹⁸ So even to old age and gray hairs, O God, do not for- | sake me,*
    until I proclaim your might to another generation,
        your power to all | those to come.
¹⁹ Your righteousness, O God, reaches the high | heavens.*
    You who have done great things, O God, who is | like you?

Psalm 27:4–5 *That I may dwell in the house of the Lord*

⁴ One thing have I asked of the LORD, that will I seek | after:*
    that I may dwell in the house of the LORD all the days of my
    life, to gaze upon the beauty of the LORD and to inquire in
    his | temple.
⁵ For he will hide me in his shelter in the day of | trouble;*
    he will conceal me under the cover of his tent; he will lift me
    high up- | on a rock.

Psalm 92:1, 4, 12–15   *It is good to give thanks to the Lord*

¹ It is good to give thanks | to the LORD,*
    to sing praises to your name, | O Most High.
⁴ For you, O LORD, have made me glad | by your work;*
    at the works of your hands I | sing for joy.
¹² The righteous flourish like the | palm tree*
    and grow like a cedar in | Lebanon.
¹³ They are planted in the house | of the LORD;*
    they flourish in the courts | of our God.
¹⁴ They still bear fruit in | old age;*
    they are ever full of | sap and green,
¹⁵ to declare that the LORD is | upright;*
    he is my rock, and there is no unrighteousness | in him.

ADDITIONAL PSALMODY

Psalm 121   *The Lord will keep you always*
Psalm 139   *The Lord knows even my heart*

READINGS

Isaiah 46:3–4   *Carried by the Lord from the womb to old age*

³ "Listen to me, O house of Jacob,
    all the remnant of the house of Israel,
who have been borne by me from before your birth,
    carried from the womb;
⁴ even to your old age I am he,
    and to gray hairs I will carry you.
I have made, and I will bear;
    I will carry and will save."

Philippians 3:12–14   *I press on toward the goal in Christ Jesus*

¹²Not that I have already obtained this or am already perfect, but I press on to make it my own, because Christ Jesus has made me his own. ¹³Brothers, I do not consider that I have made it my own. But

one thing I do: forgetting what lies behind and straining forward to what lies ahead, [14]I press on toward the goal for the prize of the upward call of God in Christ Jesus.

ADDITIONAL READINGS

Eccl. 3:1–8	*A time for everything*
Luke 2:25–40	*Simeon and Anna wait patiently*
Phil. 4:4–9	*Let your requests be made known to God*
Col. 3:12–17	*Let Christ's peace rule your hearts*

PRAYERS

Heavenly Father, we give thanks for __*name*__ and for __*his/her*__ (__*number of years*__) years of service (at __*place of work*__). Prosper __*his/her*__ deeds done according to Your will, and bless __*him/her*__ as __*he/she*__ retires. Grant that __*he/she*__ may be open to the new opportunities that You now permit __*him/her*__ to enjoy, to the glory of Your holy name; through Jesus Christ, Your Son, our Lord, who lives and reigns with You and the Holy Spirit, one God, now and forever. (855)

Almighty God, grant __*name*__ in __*his/her*__ retirement the grace to ask what You would have __*him/her*__ to do, that the Spirit of wisdom may guide __*him/her*__. Spare __*him/her*__ from false choices. Grant that in Your light __*he/she*__ may see light and in Your straight path may not be made to stumble; through Jesus Christ, Your Son, our Lord, who lives and reigns with You and the Holy Spirit, one God, now and forever. (856)

HYMN

Across the Sky the Shades of Night

LSB 899

We gather up in this brief hour
    The mem'ry of Your mercies:
Your wondrous goodness, love, and pow'r
    Our grateful song rehearses;
For You have been our strength and stay
In many a dark and dreary day
    Of sorrow and reverses.

▶

457

We now remember, as we pray,
    Our dear ones in Your caring
Who brightly shine in endless day,
    Past death and all despairing.
At our life's end, Lord, as Your own,
Bring us with them around Your throne,
    The joys of heaven sharing.

Then, gracious God, in years to come,
    We pray Your hand may guide us,
And, onward through our journey home,
    Your mercy walk beside us
Until at last our ransomed life
Is safe from peril, toil, and strife
    When heav'n itself shall hide us. (sts. 3–5)

Stanza 4 © 2006 Concordia Publishing House

ADDITIONAL HYMNS

For All the Faithful Women	*LSB 855:3–4*
For the Fruits of His Creation	*LSB 894*
Forth in Thy Name, O Lord, I Go	*LSB 854:1, 3, 5*
Guide Me, O Thou Great Redeemer	*LSB 918*
Not unto Us	*LSB 558*
Now Thank We All Our God	*LSB 895*
O God, Our Help in Ages Past	*LSB 733*
There Is a Time for Everything	*LSB 762:1, 4*

TIMES OF CELEBRATION

Birthdays

Birthdays give the Christian opportunity to confess that "God has made me and all creatures . . . and still takes care of [me]." Birthday celebrations are well served by the proclamation of this truth and of the Gospel of Christ's redemption of those whom He has made. The sacrifice of prayer, praise, and thanksgiving extols the Lord's name and petitions Him to strengthen the faithful that they may serve and obey Him throughout their days.

PSALMODY

Psalm 100

Make a joyful noise

¹ Make a joyful noise to the Lord, | all the earth!*
　　²Serve the Lord with gladness! Come into his presence
　　with | singing!
³ Know that the Lord, | he is God!*
　　It is he who made us, and we are his; we are his people, and
　　the sheep of his | pasture.
⁴ Enter his gates with thanksgiving, and his | courts with praise!*
　　Give thanks to him; | bless his name!
⁵ For the Lord is good; his steadfast love endures for- | ever,*
　　and his faithfulness to all gener- | ations.

Psalm 139:1–6, 13–17   *I am fearfully and wonderfully made*

¹ O LORD, you have searched me and | known me!*
> ²You know when I sit down and when I rise up; you discern
> my thoughts | from afar.

³ You search out my path and my | lying down*
> and are acquainted with | all my ways.

⁴ Even before a word is | on my tongue,*
> behold, O LORD, you know it alto- | gether.

⁵ You hem me in, behind | and before,*
> and lay your hand up- | on me.

⁶ Such knowledge is too wonder- | ful for me;*
> it is high; I cannot | attain it.

¹³ For you formed my | inward parts;*
> you knitted me together in my | mother's womb.

¹⁴ I praise you, for I am fearfully and wonder- | fully made.*
> Wonderful are your works; my soul knows it | very well.

¹⁵ My frame was not hid- | den from you,*
> when I was being made in secret, intricately woven in the
> depths | of the earth.

¹⁶ Your eyes saw my unformed substance; in your book were
written, every | one of them,*
> the days that were formed for me, when as yet there
> were | none of them.

¹⁷ How precious to me are your thoughts, | O God!*
> How vast is the | sum of them!

Psalm 90:1–2, 10a, 12, 14, 16–17   *Teach us to number our days*

¹ Lord, you have been our | dwelling place*
> in all gener- | ations.

² Before the mountains were brought forth, or ever you had formed
the earth | and the world,*
> from everlasting to everlasting | you are God.

¹⁰ The years of our life are | seventy,*
  or even by reason of strength | eighty.
¹² So teach us to number | our days*
  that we may get a heart of | wisdom.
¹⁴ Satisfy us in the morning with your | steadfast love,*
  that we may rejoice and be glad | all our days.
¹⁶ Let your work be shown to your | servants,*
  and your glorious power to their | children.
¹⁷ Let the favor of the Lord our God be upon us, and establish the
  work of our hands up- | on us;*
  yes, establish the work | of our hands!

ADDITIONAL PSALMODY

Psalm 71:1, 5–6, 15–23	*Even in my old age, do not forsake me*
Psalm 103	*God is compassionate*
Psalm 118:1–4, 25–29	*God's steadfast love endures forever*
Psalm 145	*One generation declares to the next*

READINGS

Ecclesiastes 11:5, 8a, 9a; 12:1a   *Rejoicing in God's gift of life*

⁵ As you do not know the way the spirit comes to the bones in the
  womb of a woman with child, so you do not know the work of
  God who makes everything.
⁸ So if a person lives many years, let him rejoice in them all.
⁹ Rejoice, O young man, in your youth, and let your heart cheer
  you in the days of your youth.
^{12:1}Remember also your Creator in the days of your youth.

Isaiah 46:3–4, 8a, 9   *Even in your old age God will carry you*

³ "Listen to me, O house of Jacob,
  all the remnant of the house of Israel,
  who have been borne by me from before your birth,
  carried from the womb;   ▶

⁴ even to your old age I am he,
  and to gray hairs I will carry you.
I have made, and I will bear;
  I will carry and will save.
⁸ Remember this and stand firm,
  ⁹remember the former things of old;
for I am God, and there is no other;
  I am God, and there is none like me."

Colossians 3:17 · *Do everything in the name of Christ*

¹⁷And whatever you do, in word or deed, do everything in the name of the Lord Jesus, giving thanks to God the Father through him.

ADDITIONAL READINGS

Prov. 3:1–6 · *Length of days and years of life*
Prov. 9:10–11 · *God multiplies our days*
Phil. 4:4–7 · *Rejoice in the Lord always*
1 Thess. 5:16–18 · *Rejoice always*

PRAYERS

Heavenly Father, our times are in Your hands. Look with favor, we pray, on Your servant _ name _ as _ he/she _ begins another year. Grant that _ he/she _ may grow in wisdom and grace, and strengthen _ his/her _ trust in Your goodness all the days of _ his/her _ life; through Jesus Christ, Your Son, our Lord, who lives and reigns with You and the Holy Spirit, one God, now and forever. (306 alt.)

For birthdays of the elderly

Gracious Lord, we thank and praise You for Your continued goodness to Your servant _ name _, whom You have blessed with length of days in this present life. Grant that _ he/she _ may continue to know Your loving-kindness, abide in the confession of Your care and protection, and in all things glorify Your holy name; through Jesus

Christ, Your Son, our Lord, who lives and reigns with You and the Holy Spirit, one God, now and forever. (307 alt.)

For the birthday of a child

Heavenly Father, You have promised to send Your holy angels to guard and keep Your children. We thank and praise You for the gift of life and for the protection and care You have provided _ name _ as _ he/she _ celebrates _ his/her _ _____ birthday. Grant that _ he/she _ may grow in grace and serve You faithfully all the days of _ his/her _ life and finally come to the fullness of Your joys in heaven; through Jesus Christ, Your Son, our Lord, who lives and reigns with You and the Holy Spirit, one God, now and forever. (308 alt.)

HYMN

O Morning Star, How Fair and Bright   LSB 395

Almighty Father, in Your Son
You loved us when not yet begun
    Was this old earth's foundation!
Your Son has ransomed us in love
To live in Him here and above:
      This is Your great salvation.
        Alleluia!
      Christ the living,
    To us giving
      Life forever,
Keeps us Yours and fails us never!

O let the harps break forth in sound!
Our joy be all with music crowned,
    Our voices gladly blending!
For Christ goes with us all the way—
Today, tomorrow, ev'ry day!
    His love is never ending!

►

463

Sing out! Ring out!
Jubilation!
Exultation!
Tell the story!
Great is He, the King of Glory!

What joy to know, when life is past,
The Lord we love is first and last,
The end and the beginning!
He will one day, oh, glorious grace,
Transport us to that happy place
Beyond all tears and sinning!
Amen! Amen!
Come, Lord Jesus!
Crown of gladness!
We are yearning
For the day of Your returning! (sts. 4–6)

© *1978 Lutheran Book of Worship*

ADDITIONAL HYMNS

Abide, O Dearest Jesus	*LSB 919*
Abide with Me	*LSB 878*
Across the Sky the Shades of Night	*LSB 899:3, 5*
Alleluia! Let Praises Ring	*LSB 822*
Evening and Morning	*LSB 726*
Now Greet the Swiftly Changing Year	*LSB 896*
Now Thank We All Our God	*LSB 895*
Praise to the Lord, the Almighty	*LSB 790*
Tell Out, My Soul, the Greatness of the Lord	*LSB 935*
We All Believe in One True God	*LSB 954*

Anniversaries

For Christians, anniversary celebrations are centered on the enduring love and mercy of God in Christ Jesus. The past is remembered to identify God's gracious blessings and to offer Him due thanks and praise. The pastor, honored to rejoice with those who are celebrating, will exhort them to commit their future to the Lord and to trust in Him alone.

PSALMODY

Psalm 67 *God shall bless us*

¹ May God be gracious to us and | bless us*
    and make his face to shine up- | on us,
² that your way may be | known on earth,*
    your saving power among all | nations.
³ Let the peoples praise you, | O God;*
    let all the peoples | praise you!
⁴ Let the nations be glad and | sing for joy,*
    for you judge the peoples with equity and guide the nations
    up- | on earth.
⁵ Let the peoples praise you, | O God;*
    let all the peoples | praise you!
⁶ The earth has yielded its | increase;*
    God, our God, shall | bless us.
⁷ God shall | bless us;*
    let all the ends of the earth | fear him!

Psalm 118:1–4, 25–29 *God makes His light to shine upon us*

¹ Oh give thanks to the LORD, for | he is good;*
    for his steadfast love endures for- | ever!
² Let | Israel say,*
    "His steadfast love endures for- | ever."
³ Let the house of | Aaron say,*
    "His steadfast love endures for- | ever."

▶

⁴ Let those who fear the | Lᴏʀᴅ say,*
    "His steadfast love endures for- | ever."
²⁵ Save us, we pray, | O Lᴏʀᴅ!*
    O Lᴏʀᴅ, we pray, give | us success!
²⁶ Blessèd is he who comes in the name | of the Lᴏʀᴅ!*
    We bless you from the house | of the Lᴏʀᴅ.
²⁷ The Lᴏʀᴅ is God, and he has made his light to shine up- | on us.*
    Bind the festal sacrifice with cords, up to the horns of
    the | altar!
²⁸ You are my God, and I will give | thanks to you;*
    you are my God; I will ex- | tol you.
²⁹ Oh give thanks to the Lᴏʀᴅ, for | he is good;*
    for his steadfast love endures for- | ever!

ADDITIONAL PSALMODY

Psalm 36:5–10	*God's steadfast love endures*
Psalm 92:1–5, 12–15	*The righteous shall flourish like the palm tree*
Psalm 127	*God builds the house*
Psalm 128	*May you see your children's children*
Psalm 150	*Let everything that has breath praise the Lord*

READINGS

Genesis 2:18–24   *The institution of marriage*

¹⁸Then the Lᴏʀᴅ God said, "It is not good that the man should be alone; I will make him a helper fit for him." ¹⁹So out of the ground the Lᴏʀᴅ God formed every beast of the field and every bird of the heavens and brought them to the man to see what he would call them. And whatever the man called every living creature, that was its name. ²⁰The man gave names to all livestock and to the birds of the heavens and to every beast of the field. But for Adam there was not found a helper fit for him. ²¹So the Lᴏʀᴅ God caused a deep sleep to fall upon the man, and while he slept took one of his ribs and closed up its place with flesh. ²²And the rib that the Lᴏʀᴅ God had taken from

the man he made into a woman and brought her to the man. ²³Then the man said,

> "This at last is bone of my bones
> > and flesh of my flesh;
> she shall be called Woman,
> > because she was taken out of Man."

²⁴Therefore a man shall leave his father and his mother and hold fast to his wife, and they shall become one flesh.

Isaiah 12:2–6 *Give thanks to the Lord*

> ² "Behold, God is my salvation;
> > I will trust, and will not be afraid;
> for the LORD GOD is my strength and my song,
> > and he has become my salvation."

> ³ With joy you will draw water from the wells of salvation. ⁴And you will say in that day:

> "Give thanks to the LORD,
> > call upon his name,
> make known his deeds among the peoples,
> > proclaim that his name is exalted.

> ⁵ "Sing praises to the LORD, for he has done gloriously;
> > let this be made known in all the earth.
> ⁶ Shout, and sing for joy, O inhabitant of Zion,
> > for great in your midst is the Holy One of Israel."

Luke 1:46–55 *The Magnificat*

> ⁴⁶ Mary said, "My soul magnifies the Lord,
> > ⁴⁷and my spirit rejoices in God my Savior,
> ⁴⁸ for he has looked on the humble estate of his servant.
> > For behold, from now on all generations will call me blessed; ▶

[49] for he who is mighty has done great things for me,
and holy is his name.
[50] And his mercy is for those who fear him
from generation to generation.
[51] He has shown strength with his arm;
he has scattered the proud in the thoughts of their hearts;
[52] he has brought down the mighty from their thrones
and exalted those of humble estate;
[53] he has filled the hungry with good things,
and the rich he has sent empty away.
[54] He has helped his servant Israel,
in remembrance of his mercy,
[55] as he spoke to our fathers,
to Abraham and to his offspring forever."

ADDITIONAL READINGS

Gen. 1:26–31	*God created them male and female*
Is. 61:10–11	*God causes righteousness and praise*
Matt. 19:4–6	*No longer two but one flesh*
John 15:1–5	*The vine and the branches*
1 Cor. 12:31b—13:13	*The more excellent way of love*
Eph. 3:14–21	*Christ dwells in us through faith*
Eph. 5:21–33	*Husbands and wives in Christ*

PRAYERS

For a marriage anniversary

Lord God, heavenly Father, we give thanks for the joy and blessings that You have granted *name* and *name* during the _____ years of their marriage. Assist them always by Your grace that with true fidelity and steadfast love they may ever honor and keep their promises, grow in love toward You and for each other, and come at last to the eternal joys that You have promised; through Jesus Christ, Your Son, our Lord, who lives and reigns with You and the Holy Spirit, one God, now and forever. (243 alt.)

General occasion

Almighty God, every good and perfect gift comes from You, the Father of lights. Receive our thanks and praise for the tender mercies You have shown to Your humble servant(s) __name(s)__ , who rejoice(s) on the anniversary of ___name of occasion___ . Grant __him/her/them__ Your Holy Spirit that, acknowledging Your goodness, __he/she/they__ may magnify Your holy name and continue to serve You in joy and gladness all the days of __his/her/their__ life; through Jesus Christ, Your Son, our Lord, who lives and reigns with You and the Holy Spirit, one God, now and forever. (857)

HYMNS

Hymns marked with an asterisk (*) are especially appropriate for the anniversary of a marriage.

*O Father, All Creating   LSB 858

O Father, all creating,
    Whose wisdom, love, and pow'r
First bound two lives together
    In Eden's primal hour,
Today to these Your children
    Your earliest gifts renew:
A home by You made happy,
    A love by You kept true. (st. 1)

Go, My Children, with My Blessing   LSB 922

I the Lord will bless and keep you
        And give you peace;
I the Lord will smile upon you
        And give you peace:
    I the Lord will be your Father,
    Savior, Comforter, and Brother.
Go, My children; I will keep you
        And give you peace. (st. 4)   © 1983 Concordia Publishing House

469

My Soul, Now Praise Your Maker

LSB 820

My soul, now praise your Maker!
    Let all within me bless His name
Who makes you full partaker
    Of mercies more than you dare claim.
Forget Him not whose meekness
    Still bears with all your sin,
Who heals your ev'ry weakness,
    Renews your life within;
Whose grace and care are endless
    And saved you through the past;
Who leaves no suff'rer friendless
    But rights the wronged at last. (st. 1)

He offers all His treasure
    Of justice, truth, and righteousness,
His love beyond all measure,
    His yearning pity o'er distress;
Nor treats us as we merit
    But sets His anger by.
The poor and contrite spirit
    Finds His compassion nigh;
And high as heav'n above us,
    As dawn from close of day,
So far, since He has loved us,
    He puts our sins away. (st. 2)

His grace remains forever,
    And children's children yet shall prove
That God forsakes them never
    Who in true fear shall seek His love.
In heav'n is fixed His dwelling,
    His rule is over all;
O hosts with might excelling,

With praise before Him fall.
Praise Him forever reigning,
    All you who hear His Word—
Our life and all sustaining.
    My soul, O praise the Lord! (st. 4)

ADDITIONAL HYMNS

All Glory Be to God Alone	*LSB 948*
*Go, My Children, with My Blessing	*LSB 922:1, 5, 4*
Kyrie! God, Father	*LSB 942*
Lift Every Voice and Sing	*LSB 964:3*
My Soul Rejoices	*LSB 933*
Now Thank We All Our God	*LSB 895*
O God, Our Help in Ages Past	*LSB 733*
*Oh, Blest the House	*LSB 862:2, 5*

Anniversary of a Baptism

The Sacrament of Holy Baptism forms and shapes the Christian life as each day the child of God repents, turns to Christ in faith, and lives in the newness of life by the Holy Spirit. At an anniversary of one's Baptism, the pastor will seek to emphasize the nature of this heavenly washing, its benefits and power, and the significance of baptizing with water. When possible, it is fitting that baptismal sponsors be included in the celebration. Use of the Apostles' Creed (the baptismal creed) is urged. If a baptismal candle was given at the time of the Baptism, it may be lighted.

PSALMODY

Psalm 84   *A day in Your courts is better than a thousand elsewhere*

¹ How lovely is your | dwelling place,*
    O | LORD of hosts!

² My soul longs, yes, faints for the courts | of the LORD;*
    my heart and flesh sing for joy to the | living God.

³ Even the sparrow finds a home, and the swallow a nest for
    herself, where she may | lay her young,*
    at your altars, O LORD of hosts, my King | and my God.

⁴ Blessèd are those who dwell | in your house,*
    ever sing- | ing your praise!

⁵ Blessèd are those whose strength is | in you,*
    in whose heart are the highways to | Zion.

⁶ As they go through the Valley of Baca they make it a | place of
    springs;*
    the early rain also covers | it with pools.

⁷ They go from | strength to strength;*
    each one appears before God in | Zion.

⁸ O LORD God of hosts, | hear my prayer;*
    give ear, O God of | Jacob!

⁹ Behold our shield, | O God;*
    look on the face of your a- | nointed!

¹⁰ For a day in your courts is better than a thousand | elsewhere.*
 I would rather be a doorkeeper in the house of my God than
 dwell in the tents of | wickedness.

¹¹ For the LORD God is a sun and shield; the LORD bestows favor
 and | honor.*
 No good thing does he withhold from those who walk
 up- | rightly.

¹² O | LORD of hosts,*
 blessèd is the one who | trusts in you!

Psalm 118:1–4, 14–16, 19–21, 26–29   *God's light shines*

¹ Oh give thanks to the LORD, for | he is good;*
 for his steadfast love endures for- | ever!

² Let | Israel say,*
 "His steadfast love endures for- | ever."

³ Let the house of | Aaron say,*
 "His steadfast love endures for- | ever."

⁴ Let those who fear the | LORD say,*
 "His steadfast love endures for- | ever."

¹⁴ The LORD is my strength | and my song;*
 he has become my sal- | vation.

¹⁵ Glad songs of salvation are in the tents of the | righteous:*
 "The right hand of the LORD does | valiantly,

¹⁶ the right hand of the | LORD exalts,*
 the right hand of the LORD does | valiantly!"

¹⁹ Open to me the gates of | righteousness,*
 that I may enter through them and give thanks | to the LORD.

²⁰ This is the gate | of the LORD;*
 the righteous shall enter | through it.

²¹ I thank you that you have | answered me*
 and have become my sal- | vation.

²⁶ Blessèd is he who comes in the name | of the LORD!*
 We bless you from the house | of the LORD.

▶

²⁷ The LORD is God, and he has made his light to shine up- | on us.*
    Bind the festal sacrifice with cords, up to the horns of
    the | altar!
²⁸ You are my God, and I will give | thanks to you;*
    you are my God; I will ex- | tol you.
²⁹ Oh give thanks to the LORD, for | he is good;*
    for his steadfast love endures for- | ever!

ADDITIONAL PSALMODY

Psalm 1   *The Lord knows the way of the righteous*
Psalm 100   *We are the sheep of God's pasture*
Psalm 135:1–4, 13–14, 19–21   *God has compassion on His servants*

READINGS
Romans 6:3–11   *Buried with Christ in Holy Baptism*

³Do you not know that all of us who have been baptized into Christ
Jesus were baptized into his death? ⁴We were buried therefore with him
by baptism into death, in order that, just as Christ was raised from the
dead by the glory of the Father, we too might walk in newness of life.
    ⁵For if we have been united with him in a death like his, we shall
certainly be united with him in a resurrection like his. ⁶We know that
our old self was crucified with him in order that the body of sin might
be brought to nothing, so that we would no longer be enslaved to sin.
⁷For one who has died has been set free from sin. ⁸Now if we have
died with Christ, we believe that we will also live with him. ⁹We know
that Christ being raised from the dead will never die again; death no
longer has dominion over him. ¹⁰For the death he died he died to sin,
once for all, but the life he lives he lives to God. ¹¹So you also must
consider yourselves dead to sin and alive to God in Christ Jesus.

John 3:1–8   *Born of water and the Spirit*

¹Now there was a man of the Pharisees named Nicodemus, a ruler of
the Jews. ²This man came to Jesus by night and said to him, "Rabbi,

we know that you are a teacher come from God, for no one can do these signs that you do unless God is with him." ³Jesus answered him, "Truly, truly, I say to you, unless one is born again he cannot see the kingdom of God." ⁴Nicodemus said to him, "How can a man be born when he is old? Can he enter a second time into his mother's womb and be born?" ⁵Jesus answered, "Truly, truly, I say to you, unless one is born of water and the Spirit, he cannot enter the kingdom of God. ⁶That which is born of the flesh is flesh, and that which is born of the Spirit is spirit. ⁷Do not marvel that I said to you, 'You must be born again.' ⁸The wind blows where it wishes, and you hear its sound, but you do not know where it comes from or where it goes. So it is with everyone who is born of the Spirit.'"

Galatians 3:26–29 *You have put on Christ*

²⁶In Christ Jesus you are all sons of God, through faith. ²⁷For as many of you as were baptized into Christ have put on Christ. ²⁸There is neither Jew nor Greek, there is neither slave nor free, there is neither male nor female, for you are all one in Christ Jesus. ²⁹And if you are Christ's, then you are Abraham's offspring, heirs according to promise.

ADDITIONAL READINGS

Jer. 17:7–8	*Like a tree planted by water*
Ezek. 36:24–28	*I will sprinkle clean water on you*
Matt. 28:16–20	*Baptizing them in the triune name*
Mark 16:15–16	*Whoever believes and is baptized will be saved*
Rom. 8:14–17	*You have received the Spirit of adoption as sons*
Eph. 1:13–14	*Sealed with the promised Holy Spirit*
Eph. 4:1–6	*One Lord, one faith, one Baptism*
Eph. 4:21–24	*Put off your old self; put on the new self*
Col. 2:9–15	*Buried and raised with Christ in Baptism*
Col. 3:1–10	*Put on the new self*
1 Peter 2:2–3	*Like newborn infants*

PRAYERS

Gracious Lord, we give thanks that in Holy Baptism we receive forgiveness of sins, deliverance from death and the devil, and eternal salvation. We ask You continually to bless _name_ and all baptized children with Your Word and Spirit. On this anniversary of _his/her_ Baptism, grant that _he/she_ may faithfully take to heart the grace You have given _him/her_, boldly confess _his/her_ Savior, and share in the heavenly joy of all Your saints; through Jesus Christ, Your Son, our Lord, who lives and reigns with You and the Holy Spirit, one God, now and forever. (176 alt.)

Almighty God, through the washing of water with the Word we are united with Christ Jesus in His death and resurrection. Grant that _name_, who has been baptized and redeemed from the old life of sin, may be renewed in Your Holy Spirit and live before You in righteousness and purity forever; through Jesus Christ, Your Son, our Lord, who lives and reigns with You and the Holy Spirit, one God, now and forever. (858)

HYMN

All Christians Who Have Been Baptized   LSB 596

In Baptism we now put on Christ—
    Our shame is fully covered
With all that He once sacrificed
    And freely for us suffered.
For here the flood of His own blood
Now makes us holy, right, and good
    Before our heav'nly Father.

O Christian, firmly hold this gift
    And give God thanks forever!
It gives the power to uplift
    In all that you endeavor.

When nothing else revives your soul,
Your Baptism stands and makes you whole
    And then in death completes you.

So use it well! You are made new—
    In Christ a new creation!
As faithful Christians, live and do
    Within your own vocation,
Until that day when you possess
His glorious robe of righteousness
    Bestowed on you forever! (sts. 4–6)

© 2004 Concordia Publishing House

ADDITIONAL HYMNS

Baptized into Your Name Most Holy	*LSB 590*
God's Own Child, I Gladly Say It	*LSB 594*
O Gracious Lord, with Love Draw Near	*LSB 599*
Once in the Blest Baptismal Waters	*LSB 598*
This Is the Spirit's Entry Now	*LSB 591*

For Answered Prayer

Our heavenly Father always hears and answers the prayers of His children in times of both sorrow and joy. While Christians living under the cross suffer distress and hardship, they are also rescued and delivered in the Lord's time and way and are blessed with joy and gladness in Him. It is pleasing to our heavenly Father when His people gratefully acknowledge His love and bless Him for His goodness and mercy, giving Him all honor and glory.

PSALMODY

Psalm 28:6–9
The Lord has heard the voice of my plea

⁶ Blessèd | be the LORD!*
    For he has heard the voice of my pleas for | mercy.
⁷ The LORD is my strength and my shield; in him my heart trusts,
    and | I am helped;*
        my heart exults, and with my song I give | thanks to him.
⁸ The LORD is the strength of his | people;*
    he is the saving refuge of his a- | nointed.
⁹ Oh, save your people and bless your | heritage!*
    Be their shepherd and carry them for- | ever.

Psalm 116:1–2, 17–19
God inclines His ear to us

¹ I love the LORD, because | he has heard*
    my voice and my pleas for | mercy.
² Because he inclined his | ear to me,*
    therefore I will call on him as long | as I live.
¹⁷ I will offer to you the sacrifice of thanks- | giving*
    and call on the name | of the LORD.
¹⁸ I will pay my vows | to the LORD*
    in the presence of all his | people,
¹⁹ in the courts of the house | of the LORD,*
    in your midst, O Jerusalem. | Praise the LORD!

ADDITIONAL PSALMODY

Psalm 50:14–15   *Call upon Me in the day of trouble*
Psalm 86:1–13   *In the day of trouble I will call upon You*
Psalm 100   *God's steadfast love endures forever*
Psalm 136:1–4, 23–26   *Give thanks for God's steadfast love*

READINGS
Luke 17:11–19   *Jesus hears the prayer of the Samaritan*

¹¹On the way to Jerusalem he was passing along between Samaria and Galilee. ¹²And as he entered a village, he was met by ten lepers, who stood at a distance ¹³and lifted up their voices, saying, "Jesus, Master, have mercy on us." ¹⁴When he saw them he said to them, "Go and show yourselves to the priests." And as they went they were cleansed. ¹⁵Then one of them, when he saw that he was healed, turned back, praising God with a loud voice; ¹⁶and he fell on his face at Jesus' feet, giving him thanks. Now he was a Samaritan. ¹⁷Then Jesus answered, "Were not ten cleansed? Where are the nine? ¹⁸Was no one found to return and give praise to God except this foreigner?" ¹⁹And he said to him, "Rise and go your way; your faith has made you well."

Jonah 2:2, 7–9   *The Lord answered me in my distress*

² I called out to the LORD, out of my distress,
     and he answered me;
out of the belly of Sheol I cried,
     and you heard my voice.
⁷ When my life was fainting away,
     I remembered the LORD,
and my prayer came to you,
     into your holy temple.
⁸ Those who pay regard to vain idols
     forsake their hope of steadfast love.
⁹ But I with the voice of thanksgiving
     will sacrifice to you;

►

what I have vowed I will pay.
    Salvation belongs to the LORD!

ADDITIONAL READINGS

Matt. 7:7–11	*Ask, and it shall be given to you*
Luke 11:5–13	*Boldness in prayer*
John 14:13–14	*Jesus' promise to answer prayer in His name*
Phil. 4:4–7	*Let your requests be made known to God*
1 Thess. 5:16–18	*Give thanks in all circumstances*
1 John 5:13–15	*The confidence that we have toward God*

PRAYER

Almighty God, heavenly Father, You have promised to hear the petitions of those who ask in Your Son's name. We humbly thank You for having heard the prayer of Your servant __name__ and for answering __him/her__ according to Your will. Continue to supply __his/her__ need from Your bountiful hand, that __he/she__ may evermore praise and glorify Your holy name; through Jesus Christ, our Lord, who lives and reigns with You and the Holy Spirit, one God, now and forever. (859)

HYMNS

Sing Praise to God, the Highest Good   *LSB 819*

We sought the Lord in our distress;
    O God, in mercy hear us.
Our Savior saw our helplessness
    And came with peace to cheer us.
For this we thank and praise the Lord,
Who is by one and all adored:
    To God all praise and glory! (st. 3)

My Soul, Now Praise Your Maker

LSB 820

My soul, now praise your Maker!
    Let all within me bless His name
Who makes you full partaker
    Of mercies more than you dare claim.
Forget Him not whose meekness
    Still bears with all your sin,
Who heals your ev'ry weakness,
    Renews your life within;
Whose grace and care are endless
    And saved you through the past;
Who leaves no suff'rer friendless
    But rights the wronged at last. (st. 1)

ADDITIONAL HYMNS

For the Fruits of His Creation	LSB 894
From All That Dwell Below the Skies	LSB 816
Give Thanks with a Grateful Heart	LSB 806
God Moves in a Mysterious Way	LSB 765
In Holy Conversation	LSB 772
Now Thank We All Our God	LSB 895
O Bless the Lord, My Soul	LSB 814
Oh, That I Had a Thousand Voices	LSB 811:1, 3
Praise God, from Whom All Blessings Flow	LSB 805
Praise, My Soul, the King of Heaven	LSB 793
Voices Raised to You We Offer	LSB 795:1, 3, 5
What God Ordains Is Always Good	LSB 760:1–2, 4

At the Time of Engagement

The engagement of a man and a woman in preparation for holy matrimony is a blessing from God. It is a sacred bond that gives witness to their love for each other and their sincere desire and commitment to be united as husband and wife and become one flesh. Like marriage itself, engagement "is not to be entered into inadvisedly or lightly, but reverently [and] deliberately" (Marriage rite). As the pastor proclaims these truths, he will rejoice with the couple and exhort them to look to the strength that the Lord supplies, grounding their hopes for the future on His gracious promises in Jesus Christ.

PSALMODY

Psalm 145:1–5, 18–21   *The Lord preserves all who love Him*

¹ I will extol you, my | God and King,*
　　and bless your name forever and | ever.
² Every day I will | bless you*
　　and praise your name forever and | ever.
³ Great is the LORD, and greatly | to be praised,*
　　and his greatness is un- | searchable.
⁴ One generation shall commend your works to an- | other,*
　　and shall declare your | mighty acts.
⁵ On the glorious splendor of your | majesty,*
　　and on your wondrous works, I will | meditate.
¹⁸ The LORD is near to all who | call on him,*
　　to all who call on | him in truth.
¹⁹ He fulfills the desire of those who | fear him;*
　　he also hears their cry and | saves them.
²⁰ The LORD preserves all who | love him,*
　　but all the wicked he | will destroy.
²¹ My mouth will speak the praise | of the LORD,*
　　and let all flesh bless his holy name forever and | ever.

Psalm 127 *Unless the Lord builds the house*

¹ Unless the LORD builds the house, those who build it la- | bor in vain.*

    Unless the LORD watches over the city, the watchman stays a- | wake in vain.

² It is in vain that you rise up early and go late to rest, eating the bread of | anxious toil;*

    for he gives to his be- | lovèd sleep.

³ Behold, children are a heritage | from the LORD,*

    the fruit of the womb | a reward.

⁴ Like arrows in the hand of a | warrior*

    are the children | of one's youth.

⁵ Blessèd is the man who fills his quiver | with them!*

    He shall not be put to shame when he speaks with his enemies | in the gate.

ADDITIONAL PSALMODY

Psalm 67	*God, our God, shall bless us*
Psalm 115:12–15, 18b	*God will bless those who fear Him*
Psalm 128	*Wife and children are gifts from God*
Psalm 148:1–4, 7a, 12–14	*Praise the Lord for His goodness*

READINGS

Genesis 1:26–28 *Created in God's likeness*

²⁶Then God said, "Let us make man in our image, after our likeness. And let them have dominion over the fish of the sea and over the birds of the heavens and over the livestock and over all the earth and over every creeping thing that creeps on the earth."

²⁷ So God created man in his own image,
    in the image of God he created him;
    male and female he created them.

▶

²⁸And God blessed them. And God said to them, "Be fruitful and multiply and fill the earth and subdue it and have dominion over the fish of the sea and over the birds of the heavens and over every living thing that moves on the earth."

Song of Songs 2:10–13a, 16a

My beloved is mine, and I am his

¹⁰ My beloved speaks and says to me:
> "Arise, my love, my beautiful one, and come away,
¹¹ for behold, the winter is past;
> the rain is over and gone.
¹² The flowers appear on the earth,
> the time of singing has come,
> and the voice of the turtledove is heard in our land.
¹³ The fig tree ripens its figs,
> and the vines are in blossom;
> they give forth fragrance."
¹⁶ My beloved is mine, and I am his.

1 John 4:7–16

Love one another

⁷Beloved, let us love one another, for love is from God, and whoever loves has been born of God and knows God. ⁸Anyone who does not love does not know God, because God is love. ⁹In this the love of God was made manifest among us, that God sent his only Son into the world, so that we might live through him. ¹⁰In this is love, not that we have loved God but that he loved us and sent his Son to be the propitiation for our sins. ¹¹Beloved, if God so loved us, we also ought to love one another. ¹²No one has ever seen God; if we love one another, God abides in us and his love is perfected in us.

¹³By this we know that we abide in him and he in us, because he has given us of his Spirit. ¹⁴And we have seen and testify that the Father has sent his Son to be the Savior of the world. ¹⁵Whoever confesses that Jesus is the Son of God, God abides in him, and he in God. ¹⁶So we

have come to know and to believe the love that God has for us. God is love, and whoever abides in love abides in God, and God abides in him.

ADDITIONAL READINGS

Gen. 2:18, 21–22	*The Lord God brought the woman to the man*
Matt. 7:24–27	*Build your house on the rock*
Mark 10:6–9	*A man shall leave his father and mother*
John 15:9–12	*Abide in Christ's love*
1 Cor. 12:31b—13:13	*The more excellent way of love*
Eph. 5:1–2, 21–33	*Walk in love as Christ loved us*
Col. 3:12–19	*Put on love, which binds everything together*

PRAYERS

Almighty God, the source of all goodness, we thank You for leading __name__ and __name__ to each other to enter the bonds of wedded love. Bless them as they prepare for their marriage. Grant that they may look forward to their wedding day with holy joy and experience there a foretaste of that bliss which You have prepared for all Your saints at the marriage feast of the Lamb in His kingdom, which has no end; through the same Jesus Christ, Your Son, our Lord, who lives and reigns with You and the Holy Spirit, one God, now and forever. (860)

Lord God, we humbly implore You to give to __name__ and __name__ the rich blessings of Your fatherly hand during their engagement. Make them pure in heart and chaste in body, that together they may walk in the ways of Your holy Word and receive Your gifts with thanksgiving; through Jesus Christ, Your Son, our Lord, who lives and reigns with You and the Holy Spirit, one God, now and forever. (861)

HYMN

O Father, All Creating

LSB 858

O Father, all creating,
    Whose wisdom, love, and pow'r
First bound two lives together
    In Eden's primal hour,
Today to these Your children
    Your earliest gifts renew:
A home by You made happy,
    A love by You kept true. (st. 1)

O Spirit of the Father,
    Breathe on them from above,
So searching in Your pureness,
    So tender in Your love
That, guarded by Your presence
    And kept from strife and sin,
Their hearts may heed Your guidance
    And know You dwell within. (st. 3)

ADDITIONAL HYMNS

Gracious Savior, Grant Your Blessing   *LSB 860:4*
Lord, When You Came as Welcome Guest   *LSB 859:1–3*
Where Charity and Love Prevail   *LSB 845*

At the Wedding Reception

The pastor's attendance at the reception for the newly married is a witness in itself similar to that given by our Lord when He blessed a wedding at Cana in Galilee with His presence. In view of the sacred union of husband and wife created by God, it is a unique time to rejoice and give thanks for the blessings of marriage sanctified by the Gospel of our Lord Jesus Christ.

PSALMODY

Psalm 128 *God blesses His faithful through families*

¹ Blessèd is everyone who | fears the LORD,*
    who walks | in his ways!
² You shall eat the fruit of the labor | of your hands;*
    you shall be blessed, and it shall be | well with you.
³ Your wife will be like a fruitful vine with- | in your house;*
    your children will be like olive shoots around your | table.
⁴ Behold, thus shall the | man be blessed*
    who | fears the LORD.
⁵ The LORD bless you from | Zion!*
    May you see the prosperity of Jerusalem all the days | of
    your life!
⁶ May you see your children's | children!*
    Peace be upon | Israel!

Psalm 98:1–6 *God has done marvelous things*

¹ Oh sing to the LORD a new song, for he has done | marvelous
things!*
    His right hand and his holy arm have worked salva- | tion for
    him.
² The LORD has made known his sal- | vation;*
    he has revealed his righteousness in the sight of
    the | nations.

▶

3 He has remembered his steadfast love and faithfulness to the
   house of | Israel.*
        All the ends of the earth have seen the salvation | of our God.
4 Make a joyful noise to the Lord, | all the earth;*
        break forth into joyous song and sing | praises!
5 Sing praises to the Lord | with the lyre,*
        with the lyre and the sound of | melody!
6 With trumpets and the sound | of the horn*
        make a joyful noise before the | King, the Lord!

ADDITIONAL PSALMODY

Psalm 96:1–6   *Declare God's glory among the nations*
Psalm 100   *God's steadfast love endures forever*

READINGS

John 15:9   *Abide in My love*

9As the Father has loved me, so have I loved you. Abide in my love.

Hebrews 13:20–21   *The great Shepherd will equip you*

20Now may the God of peace who brought again from the dead our
Lord Jesus, the great shepherd of the sheep, by the blood of the eternal covenant, 21equip you with everything good that you may do his
will, working in us that which is pleasing in his sight, through Jesus
Christ, to whom be glory forever and ever. Amen.

ADDITIONAL READINGS

Zeph. 3:14, 17   *Rejoice, for the Lord your God is in your midst*
John 2:1–12   *Jesus also was invited to the wedding*
1 Cor. 13:13   *The greatest of these is love*
Phil. 4:4–7   *Rejoice in the Lord*
1 Thess. 5:16–18   *Rejoice always*

PRAYERS

Heavenly Father, Your Son used the joy of the marriage feast as a sign of the joy of Your kingdom. Be present with _name_ and _name_, whom You have united as husband and wife, and sanctify them with Your love. Bless our celebration, and bring us all at last to the joy of feasting with You in Your eternal kingdom; through Jesus Christ, our Lord, who lives and reigns with You and the Holy Spirit, one God, now and forever. (312 alt.)

Eternal God, our creator and redeemer, as You gladdened the wedding at Cana in Galilee by the presence of Your Son, so bring Your joy to this wedding by His presence now. Look in favor on _name_ and _name_, and grant that they, rejoicing in all Your gifts, may at length celebrate the marriage feast that has no end with Christ, our Lord, who lives and reigns with You and the Holy Spirit, one God, now and forever. (862)

The following table prayer may also be said:

The eyes of all look to You, O Lord, and You give them their food at the proper time; You open Your hand and satisfy the desires of every living thing.   *Psalm 145:15–16*

Lord God, heavenly Father, bless us and these Your gifts which we receive from Your bountiful goodness, through Jesus Christ, our Lord. Amen. (445)

HYMN

O Father, All Creating

LSB 858

With good wine, Lord, at Cana
    The wedding feast You blessed.
Grant also these Your presence,
    And be their dearest guest.
Their store of earthly gladness
    Transform to heav'nly wine,
And teach them, in the testing,
    To know the gift divine. (st. 2)

Unless You build it, Father,
    The house is built in vain;
Unless You, Savior, bless it,
    The joy will turn to pain.
But nothing breaks the union
    Of hearts in You made one;
The love Your Spirit hallows
    Is endless love begun. (st. 4)

ADDITIONAL HYMNS

Be Present at Our Table, Lord	LSB 775
Come, Lord Jesus, Be Our Guest	LSB 776
Feed Thy Children, God Most Holy	LSB 774
Gracious Savior, Grant Your Blessing	LSB 860:3–5
Lord, When You Came as Welcome Guest	LSB 859:1–2, 4

At Family Reunions
or Other Celebrations

Family reunions provide Christians with an opportunity to give thanks to the Father "from whom every family in heaven and on earth is named" (Eph. 3:15) for the bounty of His blessings in body and soul. These gatherings celebrate the bonds of kinship and family that bind generation to generation. Recalling our Father's past mercies, we look forward in hope to that day when all who confess Christ will be gathered together in our eternal home.

PSALMODY

Psalm 68:4–6, 19, 35   *God protects His people*

⁴ Sing to God, sing praises | to his name;*
    lift up a song to him who rides through the deserts; his name
    is the LORD; exult be- | fore him!
⁵ Father of the fatherless and protector of | widows*
    is God in his holy habi- | tation.
⁶ God settles the solitary in a home; he leads out the prisoners to
    pros- | perity,*
    but the rebellious dwell in a | parched land.
¹⁹ Blessèd be the Lord, who daily | bears us up;*
    God is our sal- | vation.
³⁵ Awesome is God from his sanctu- | ary;*
    the God of Israel—he is the one who gives power and
    strength to his people. Blessèd | be God!

Psalm 147:1, 12–15, 19–20   *God watches over His people*

¹ Praise the LORD! For it is good to sing praises | to our God;*
    for it is pleasant, and a song of praise is | fitting.
¹² Praise the LORD, O Je- | rusalem!*
    Praise your God, O | Zion!   ▶

¹³ For he strengthens the bars | of your gates;*
    he blesses your children with- | in you.
¹⁴ He makes peace in your | borders;*
    he fills you with the finest | of the wheat.
¹⁵ He sends out his command | to the earth;*
    his word runs | swiftly.
¹⁹ He declares his word to | Jacob,*
    his statutes and just decrees to | Israel.
²⁰ He has not dealt thus with any other | nation;*
    they do not know his just decrees. | Praise the LORD!

ADDITIONAL PSALMODY

Psalm 78:1–7	*Tell the coming generation*
Psalm 90:1–2, 14–17	*Establish the work of our hands*
Psalm 111	*The fear of the Lord is the beginning of wisdom*
Psalm 121	*The Lord will keep you now and forevermore*
Psalm 133	*Dwelling in unity*

READINGS
Joshua 24:14–15   *We will serve the Lord*

¹⁴Now therefore fear the LORD and serve him in sincerity and in faithfulness. Put away the gods that your fathers served beyond the River and in Egypt, and serve the LORD. ¹⁵And if it is evil in your eyes to serve the LORD, choose this day whom you will serve, whether the gods your fathers served in the region beyond the River, or the gods of the Amorites in whose land you dwell. But as for me and my house, we will serve the LORD.

John 15:8–12   *Love one another*

⁸[Jesus said:] "By this my Father is glorified, that you bear much fruit and so prove to be my disciples. ⁹As the Father has loved me, so have I loved you. Abide in my love. ¹⁰If you keep my commandments, you will abide in my love, just as I have kept my Father's

commandments and abide in his love. [11]These things I have spoken to you, that my joy may be in you, and that your joy may be full.

[12]"This is my commandment, that you love one another as I have loved you."

Ephesians 3:14–21 *Knowing the love of Christ*

[14]For this reason I bow my knees before the Father, [15]from whom every family in heaven and on earth is named, [16]that according to the riches of his glory he may grant you to be strengthened with power through his Spirit in your inner being, [17]so that Christ may dwell in your hearts through faith—that you, being rooted and grounded in love, [18]may have strength to comprehend with all the saints what is the breadth and length and height and depth, [19]and to know the love of Christ that surpasses knowledge, that you may be filled with all the fullness of God.

[20]Now to him who is able to do far more abundantly than all that we ask or think, according to the power at work within us, [21]to him be glory in the church and in Christ Jesus throughout all generations, forever and ever. Amen.

3 John 4 *Walking in God's truth*

[4]I have no greater joy than to hear that my children are walking in the truth.

ADDITIONAL READINGS

Gen. 33:1–4 (5–7)	*The reunion of Jacob and Esau*
Job 42:10–12a	*Job's family eats bread with him in his house*
Rom. 15:5–7	*Live in harmony that you may glorify Him*
Phil. 1:9–11	*May your love abound more and more*
Col. 3:12–17	*Let the peace of Christ rule in your hearts*
1 John 3:1–2	*We are God's children*

PRAYERS

Lord God, heavenly Father, You guided and blessed the holy families of old by Your Word and Spirit. We thank You for guiding this family to be together. Remind them of the unity You have given them in Christ Jesus, help them to know and appreciate one another, and strengthen among them the bonds of love and care, that they may encourage, comfort, and support one another in Christ Jesus, our Lord, who lives and reigns with You and the Holy Spirit, one God, now and forever. (863)

Almighty God, Father in heaven, You set the solitary in families. Bless the _name_ family for whom we pray. Fill them with faith in Your Son and strengthen their love for each other. Show them the wonders of Your grace and Your abundant goodness toward them, that they may thank and glorify You and declare Your praise in all the world; through Jesus Christ, Your Son, our Lord, who lives and reigns with You and the Holy Spirit, one God, now and forever. (864)

HYMNS

Our Father, Who from Heaven Above
LSB 766

Our Father, who from heav'n above
Bids all of us to live in love
    As members of one family
    And pray to You in unity,
Teach us no thoughtless words to say
But from our inmost hearts to pray. (st. 1)

Give us this day our daily bread,
And let us all be clothed and fed.
    Save us from hardship, war, and strife;
    In plague and famine, spare our life,
That we in honest peace may live,
To care and greed no entrance give. (st. 5)

Forgive our sins, Lord, we implore,
That they may trouble us no more;
    We, too, will gladly those forgive
    Who hurt us by the way they live.
Help us in our community
To serve each other willingly. (st. 6)

Stanza 5 © 1980 Concordia Publishing House

Blest Be the Tie That Binds
LSB 649

Blest be the tie that binds
    Our hearts in Christian love;
The fellowship of kindred minds
    Is like to that above. (st. 1)

We share our mutual woes,
    Our mutual burdens bear,
And often for each other flows
    The sympathizing tear. (st. 3)

When here our pathways part,
    We suffer bitter pain;
Yet, one in Christ and one in heart,
    We hope to meet again. (st. 4)

ADDITIONAL HYMNS

All People That on Earth Do Dwell	LSB 791
Be Present at Our Table, Lord	LSB 775
Come, Lord Jesus, Be Our Guest	LSB 776
Feed Thy Children, God Most Holy	LSB 774
Great Is Thy Faithfulness	LSB 809
Praise God, from Whom All Blessings Flow	LSB 805
To God the Holy Spirit Let Us Pray	LSB 768:1–2, 4

Graduation

Graduations are milestones that mark the faithfulness of the Lord in the lives of His children. The graduate may react in a variety of ways—sadness at parting, satisfaction at completion of a program, excitement as well as concern for the future. When parents have played a supportive role in reaching this milestone, the pastor will want to recognize their unique contribution also.

PSALMODY

Psalm 25:1–2a, 10–14   *Steadfast love and faithfulness*

¹ To you, O LORD, I lift | up my soul.*
   ²O my God, in you I trust; let me not be | put to shame.
¹⁰ All the paths of the LORD are steadfast love and | faithfulness,*
   for those who keep his covenant and his testi- | monies.
¹¹ For your name's sake, | O LORD,*
   pardon my guilt, for | it is great.
¹² Who is the man who | fears the LORD?*
   Him will he instruct in the way that | he should choose.
¹³ His soul shall abide in well- | being,*
   and his offspring shall inher- | it the land.
¹⁴ The friendship of the LORD is for those who | fear him,*
   and he makes known to them his | covenant.

Psalm 111:1–4, 7–10   *Great are the works of the Lord*

¹ Praise the LORD! I will give thanks to the LORD with my | whole heart,*
   in the company of the upright, in the congre- | gation.
² Great are the works | of the LORD,*
   studied by all who de- | light in them.
³ Full of splendor and majesty | is his work,*
   and his righteousness endures for- | ever.

⁴ He has caused his wondrous works to be re- | membered;*
    the LORD is gracious and | merciful.
⁷ The works of his hands are faith- | ful and just;*
    all his precepts are | trustworthy;
⁸ they are established forever and | ever,*
    to be performed with faithfulness and up- | rightness.
⁹ He sent redemption to his people; he has commanded his
covenant for- | ever.*
    Holy and awesome | is his name!
¹⁰ The fear of the LORD is the beginning of wisdom; all those who
practice it have a good under- | standing.*
    His praise endures for- | ever!

ADDITIONAL PSALMODY

Psalm 86:8–13a   *Teach me to walk in Your truth*
Psalm 115:1, 11–14a, 15, 18b   *The Lord has remembered us*
Psalm 119:33–38, 40   *Teach me the way of Your statutes*

READINGS

Proverbs 3:13–23   *Nothing can compare with wisdom*

¹³ Blessed is the one who finds wisdom,
    and the one who gets understanding,
¹⁴ for the gain from her is better than gain from silver
    and her profit better than gold.
¹⁵ She is more precious than jewels,
    and nothing you desire can compare with her.
¹⁶ Long life is in her right hand;
    in her left hand are riches and honor.
¹⁷ Her ways are ways of pleasantness,
    and all her paths are peace.
¹⁸ She is a tree of life to those who lay hold of her;
    those who hold her fast are called blessed.

►

¹⁹ The LORD by wisdom founded the earth;
    by understanding he established the heavens;
²⁰ by his knowledge the deeps broke open,
    and the clouds drop down the dew.
²¹ My son, do not lose sight of these—
    keep sound wisdom and discretion,
²² and they will be life for your soul
    and adornment for your neck.
²³ Then you will walk on your way securely,
    and your foot will not stumble.

Matthew 6:25–33   *Do not be anxious about your life*

²⁵[Jesus said:] "Therefore I tell you, do not be anxious about your life, what you will eat or what you will drink, nor about your body, what you will put on. Is not life more than food, and the body more than clothing? ²⁶Look at the birds of the air: they neither sow nor reap nor gather into barns, and yet your heavenly Father feeds them. Are you not of more value than they? ²⁷And which of you by being anxious can add a single hour to his span of life? ²⁸And why are you anxious about clothing? Consider the lilies of the field, how they grow: they neither toil nor spin, ²⁹yet I tell you, even Solomon in all his glory was not arrayed like one of these. ³⁰But if God so clothes the grass of the field, which today is alive and tomorrow is thrown into the oven, will he not much more clothe you, O you of little faith? ³¹Therefore do not be anxious, saying, 'What shall we eat?' or 'What shall we drink?' or 'What shall we wear?' ³²For the Gentiles seek after all these things, and your heavenly Father knows that you need them all. ³³But seek first the kingdom of God and his righteousness, and all these things will be added to you."

2 Timothy 1:3–7   *From childhood you have learned the faith*

³I thank God whom I serve, as did my ancestors, with a clear conscience, as I remember you constantly in my prayers night and day.

[4]As I remember your tears, I long to see you, that I may be filled with joy. [5]I am reminded of your sincere faith, a faith that dwelt first in your grandmother Lois and your mother Eunice and now, I am sure, dwells in you as well. [6]For this reason I remind you to fan into flame the gift of God, which is in you through the laying on of my hands, [7]for God gave us a spirit not of fear but of power and love and self-control.

ADDITIONAL READINGS

1 Kings 3:10–15	*Solomon blessed with wisdom*
Prov. 3:1–8	*In all your ways acknowledge God*
1 Cor. 1:20–25	*Christ, the power and wisdom of God*
Eph. 5:15–20	*Walk wisely*
James 3:17–18	*The wisdom from above*

PRAYERS

At a graduation

Lord God, heavenly Father, You provide schools and teachers for faithful instruction and dedicated learning. Receive our thanks for the knowledge gained by those who are now graduating. As they continue to learn and grow, grant them Your Holy Spirit that their talents and abilities may be used for Your glory and as a blessing to others; through Jesus Christ, our Lord. (309)

For an elementary school graduate

Lord God, heavenly Father, You provided Your servant St. Timothy with faithful instruction in Your Word during his childhood, establishing for him a foundation of knowledge that served him throughout his life. Receive our thanks for the knowledge provided for *name* by parents, teachers, and Your Church. As *he/she* continues to learn, grant *him/her* Your Holy Spirit that *his/her* understanding of Your gifts and talents will increase, leading into the vocation in which You would have *him/her* serve; through Jesus Christ, Your Son, our Lord, who lives and reigns with You and the Holy Spirit, one God, now and forever. (865)

For a high school graduate

Heavenly Father, we thank You for graciously bringing _name_ to this point of formal education. For all the efforts of parents and teachers through these years we praise You. We ask wisdom and guidance for _name_ as _he/she_ makes decisions about _his/her_ life that will have implications for years to come. Give _him/her_ a rich measure of Your Spirit as fields of study and opportunities for employment become available. Help _him/her_ accurately assess the gifts and abilities You have given and bless the choices that _he/she_ makes. May _he/she_ ever grow closer to You in faith and with _his/her_ life honor the name of Your only Son, Jesus Christ, our Lord, who lives and reigns with You and the Holy Spirit, one God, now and forever. (866)

For a college or university graduate

Lord Jesus Christ, in love You gave Yourself on the cross that we may have life abundantly. Hear our prayer for _name_, and receive our thanksgiving for the _name of degree_ that has been conferred on _him/her_. Guide _him/her_ in making decisions about vocation and family. Let Your Word dwell richly in _him/her_ as You nurture the faith given _him/her_ in Baptism and strengthened by Your Holy Supper. Let what has been learned be employed in mature Christian service, and grant _him/her_ wisdom to discern what is false and to hold on to what is true; for You live and reign with the Father and the Holy Spirit, one God, now and forever. (867)

HYMN

One Thing's Needful   LSB 536

Wisdom's highest, noblest treasure,
    Jesus, is revealed in You.
Let me find in You my pleasure,
    And my wayward will subdue,

Humility there and simplicity reigning,
In paths of true wisdom my steps ever training.
> If I learn from Jesus this knowledge divine,
> The blessing of heavenly wisdom is mine.

Nothing have I, Christ, to offer,
> You alone, my highest good.
Nothing have I, Lord, to proffer
> But Your crimson-colored blood.
Your death on the cross has death wholly defeated
And thereby my righteousness fully completed;
> Salvation's white raiments I there did obtain,
> And in them in glory with You I shall reign.

Therefore You alone, my Savior,
> Shall be all in all to me;
Search my heart and my behavior,
> Root out all hypocrisy.
Through all my life's pilgrimage, guard and uphold me,
In loving forgiveness, O Jesus, enfold me.
> This one thing is needful; all others are vain—
> I count all but loss that I Christ may obtain! (sts. 3–5)

ADDITIONAL HYMNS

Christ Be My Leader	*LSB 861*
Earth and All Stars	*LSB 817:5–7*
Lord, Help Us Ever to Retain	*LSB 865*
Not unto Us	*LSB 558*
Oh, That I Had a Thousand Voices	*LSB 811:1–2, 5*
Praise God, from Whom All Blessings Flow	*LSB 805*
Shepherd of Tender Youth	*LSB 864:1, 4*

MISCELLANEOUS SITUATIONS

The Poor, Hungry, and Neglected

The Lord affirms that we do not live by bread alone but by every word that proceeds from the mouth of God. Those who suffer poverty or hunger, or are neglected in any way, often fear the future and can be tempted to doubt the promise that God will provide for their daily bread. They may even be tempted to be angry with Him. The certainty of God's gracious presence and provision is threatened by such loneliness and despair. The pastor will remind the one in need that because God gave us His Son, He also promises with Him to give us all that we need to support us in this body and life. Additionally, the pastor will encourage the congregation to reach out with charity to those who have a genuine temporal need.

PSALMODY
Psalm 34:1–3, 8–10, 15, 17–19   *Oh, taste and see*

¹ I will bless the LORD at | all times;*
　　his praise shall continually be | in my mouth.
² My soul makes its boast | in the LORD;*
　　let the humble hear | and be glad.
³ Oh, magnify the | LORD with me,*
　　and let us exalt his name to- | gether!
⁸ Oh, taste and see that the | LORD is good!*
　　Blessèd is the man who takes ref- | uge in him!

⁹ Oh, fear the LORD, | you his saints,*
  for those who fear him | have no lack!
¹⁰ The young lions suffer want and | hunger;*
  but those who seek the LORD lack | no good thing.
¹⁵ The eyes of the LORD are toward the | righteous*
  and his ears | toward their cry.
¹⁷ When the righteous cry for help, the | LORD hears*
  and delivers them out of all their | troubles.
¹⁸ The LORD is near to the broken- | hearted*
  and saves the crushed in | spirit.
¹⁹ Many are the afflictions of the | righteous,*
  but the LORD delivers him out | of them all.

Psalm 142   *I pour out my complaint before the Lord*

¹ With my voice I cry out | to the LORD;*
  with my voice I plead for mercy | to the LORD.
² I pour out my complaint be- | fore him;*
  I tell my trouble be- | fore him.
³ When my spirit faints within me, you | know my way!*
  In the path where I walk they have hidden a | trap for me.
⁴ Look to the right and see: there is none who takes notice | of me;*
  no refuge remains to me; no one cares | for my soul.
⁵ I cry to you, | O LORD;*
  I say, "You are my refuge, my portion in the land of the | living."
⁶ Attend to my cry, for I am brought | very low!*
  Deliver me from my persecutors, for they are too | strong for me!
⁷ Bring me out of prison, that I may give thanks | to your name!*
  The righteous will surround me, for you will deal
  bountifully | with me.

ADDITIONAL PSALMODY

Psalm 23   *The Lord is my shepherd*
Psalm 37:3–8, 23–28a   *Commit your way to the Lord*
Psalm 91:1–2, 9–12, 14–16   *He calls to Me; I will answer him*

READINGS

Isaiah 43:1–3a *Fear not; I have created and redeemed you*

¹ But now thus says the LORD,
    he who created you, O Jacob,
    he who formed you, O Israel:
"Fear not, for I have redeemed you;
    I have called you by name, you are mine.
² When you pass through the waters, I will be with you;
    and through the rivers, they shall not overwhelm you;
when you walk through fire you shall not be burned,
    and the flame shall not consume you.
³ For I am the LORD your God,
    the Holy One of Israel, your Savior."

Philippians 4:11–13 *In whatever situation I am content*

¹¹Not that I am speaking of being in need, for I have learned in whatever situation I am to be content. ¹²I know how to be brought low, and I know how to abound. In any and every circumstance, I have learned the secret of facing plenty and hunger, abundance and need. ¹³I can do all things through him who strengthens me.

ADDITIONAL READINGS

Matt. 6:25–34   *Seek first His kingdom*
Matt. 25:31–46   *Service to Christ's suffering brothers*
James 5:7–11   *Patience and steadfastness in suffering*

PRAYERS

Almighty and gracious God, look upon Your child __*name*__ in __*his/her*__ suffering and mercifully provide for __*his/her*__ needs. Keep __*him/her*__ from discouragement and bitterness. Be a refuge to __*him/her*__ and to all who are __*poor / hungry / neglected*__ that they may be delivered and preserved according to Your promises in Christ

Jesus, who lives and reigns with You and the Holy Spirit, one God, now and forever. (868)

Almighty God, You graciously give Your children all that they need to support this body and life. Grant Your grace to _name_ at this time. Open Your hand and satisfy _his/her_ needs.

Specific needs may be mentioned here.

Do not let _him/her_ fall into despair, resentment, or the mire of self-pity. Renew in _him/her_ hope and faith. Give _him/her_ the assurance of Your presence and the courage to face the trials of the days to come; through Jesus Christ, our Lord. (869)

HYMNS

Hail to the Lord's Anointed
LSB 398

He comes with rescue speedy
    To those who suffer wrong,
To help the poor and needy
    And bid the weak be strong;
To give them songs for sighing,
    Their darkness turn to light,
Whose souls, condemned and dying,
    Were precious in His sight. (st. 2)

What Is the World to Me
LSB 730

What is the world to me
    With all its vaunted pleasure
When You, and You alone,
    Lord Jesus, are my treasure!
You only, dearest Lord,
    My soul's delight shall be;
You are my peace, my rest.
    What is the world to me! (st. 1)

►

The world seeks after wealth
    And all that mammon offers
Yet never is content
    Though gold should fill its coffers.
I have a higher good,
    Content with it I'll be:
My Jesus is my wealth.
    What is the world to me! (st. 3)

What is the world to me!
    My Jesus is my treasure,
My life, my health, my wealth,
    My friend, my love, my pleasure,
My joy, my crown, my all,
    My bliss eternally.
Once more, then, I declare:
    What is the world to me! (st. 4)

ADDITIONAL HYMNS

All Depends on Our Possessing	*LSB 732:1–4*
Children of the Heavenly Father	*LSB 725:4*
Consider How the Birds Above	*LSB 736*
Hark the Glad Sound	*LSB 349:3*
How Firm a Foundation	*LSB 728:2–3*
O Jesus Christ, Thy Manger Is	*LSB 372:3–4*

Those in Prison

In ministering to those in prison, the pastor's chief task is to lead them to repentance, faith, and new life in Christ. Those who may have been unjustly imprisoned need to be comforted and strengthened in the knowledge that the Lord mercifully cares for His people and controls all things according to His gracious will. The families of prisoners must also be served since they too suffer along with their incarcerated loved ones.

PSALMODY

Psalm 130 *With the Lord there is forgiveness*

¹ Out | of the depths*
   I cry to you, | O Lᴏʀᴅ!
² O Lord, | hear my voice!*
   Let your ears be attentive to the voice of my pleas for | mercy!
³ If you, O Lᴏʀᴅ, should mark in- | iquities,*
   O Lord, | who could stand?
⁴ But with you there is for- | giveness,*
   that you | may be feared.
⁵ I wait for the Lᴏʀᴅ, my | soul waits,*
   and in his | word I hope;
⁶ my soul waits for the Lord more than watchmen for the | morning,*
   more than watchmen for the | morning.
⁷ O Israel, hope in the Lᴏʀᴅ! For with the Lᴏʀᴅ there is | steadfast love,*
   and with him is plentiful re- | demption.
⁸ And he will redeem | Israel*
   from all his in- | iquities.

ADDITIONAL PSALMODY

Psalm 23 *The Lord is my shepherd*
Psalm 25:1–7 *Remember not the sins of my youth*

Psalm 121   *My help comes from the Lord*
Psalm 146:5–10   *The Lord lifts up those who are bowed down*

READINGS

1 John 1:5—2:2   *He is faithful and just to forgive us our sins*

[5]This is the message we have heard from him and proclaim to you, that God is light, and in him is no darkness at all. [6]If we say we have fellowship with him while we walk in darkness, we lie and do not practice the truth. [7]But if we walk in the light, as he is in the light, we have fellowship with one another, and the blood of Jesus his Son cleanses us from all sin. [8]If we say we have no sin, we deceive ourselves, and the truth is not in us. [9]If we confess our sins, he is faithful and just to forgive us our sins and to cleanse us from all unrighteousness. [10]If we say we have not sinned, we make him a liar, and his word is not in us.

[2:1]My little children, I am writing these things to you so that you may not sin. But if anyone does sin, we have an advocate with the Father, Jesus Christ the righteous. [2]He is the propitiation for our sins, and not for ours only but also for the sins of the whole world.

1 Peter 5:6–11   *Humble yourselves under God's mighty hand*

[6]Humble yourselves, therefore, under the mighty hand of God so that at the proper time he may exalt you, [7]casting all your anxieties on him, because he cares for you. [8]Be sober-minded; be watchful. Your adversary the devil prowls around like a roaring lion, seeking someone to devour. [9]Resist him, firm in your faith, knowing that the same kinds of suffering are being experienced by your brotherhood throughout the world. [10]And after you have suffered a little while, the God of all grace, who has called you to his eternal glory in Christ, will himself restore, confirm, strengthen, and establish you. [11]To him be the dominion forever and ever. Amen.

Luke 23:39–43   *Jesus forgives the criminal crucified with Him*

³⁹One of the criminals who were hanged railed at him, saying, "Are you not the Christ? Save yourself and us!" ⁴⁰But the other rebuked him, saying, "Do you not fear God, since you are under the same sentence of condemnation? ⁴¹And we indeed justly, for we are receiving the due reward of our deeds; but this man has done nothing wrong." ⁴²And he said, "Jesus, remember me when you come into your kingdom." ⁴³And he said to him, "Truly, I say to you, today you will be with me in Paradise."

ADDITIONAL READINGS

Gen. 39	*Joseph is unjustly accused*
Matt. 11:25–30	*Christ promises rest to those heavy laden*
John 3:14–18a	*Whoever believes in God's Son has eternal life*
Rom. 8:28–39	*All things work together for good*
Rom. 13:1–5	*Submit to the authorities instituted by God*
Heb. 13:1–3	*The imprisoned are not to be forgotten*

PRAYERS

For the prisoner

Lord Jesus Christ, for our sake You were condemned as a criminal. Visit this prison with Your justice and mercy. Remember _name_ and all prisoners. As You once forgave the repentant thief from the cross, so assure _name_ that all _his/her_ sins are forgiven. Protect _him/her_ from every evil of body and soul, and deliver _him/her_ from discouragement and despair. Give _him/her_ hope for the future and amendment of life, and help _him/her_ serve _his/her_ sentence with patience and trust in You. Enlighten all who work in this institution that they may be humane and compassionate; through Jesus Christ, our Lord, who lives and reigns with You and the Holy Spirit, one God, now and forever. (295 alt.)

O Lord, You desire all to be saved and to come to the knowledge of the truth. By Your Spirit lead _name_ to acknowledge _his/her_ sin, receive Your forgiveness, and live in the freedom of Your Gospel. Sustain _him/her_ with Your mercy that _he/she_ might bear with patience _his/her_ time of imprisonment. Guard _him/her_ from every evil of body and soul. Be with _his/her_ family, and keep them united in the bonds of love. Hear us for the sake of Your Son, Jesus Christ, our Lord, who lives and reigns with You and the Holy Spirit, one God, now and forever. (870)

For the family

Merciful God and Father, remember Your servant _name of person incarcerated_ and _his/her_ family as they deal with _his/her_ imprisonment. Relieve and comfort them with the truth that You will not forsake them but are at work in all things for the good of Your people and the glory of Your name. Guide them by Your Holy Spirit, and help them to entrust their lives to Your care and keeping, not doubting Your love but clinging in faith to Your promise of deliverance to all who call upon You; through Jesus Christ, our Lord, who lives and reigns with You and the Holy Spirit, one God, now and forever. (871)

For a Christian facing execution

Heavenly Father, Your Son, our Lord Jesus Christ, has destroyed death and brought life and immortality to light through the Gospel. We ask You to be present with _name_, whose life in this world is coming to an end. In mercy forgive _him/her_ all _his/her_ sins and strengthen _him/her_ in _his/her_ Baptism. Bring _him/her_ by Your Spirit to true repentance and a firm faith in Your promise of eternal life for all who trust in Christ. Remove all fear and doubt, and comfort _him/her_ with the knowledge that at the moment of _his/her_ departure, _he/she_ will be with Christ and that on the day of the resurrection of all flesh, _he/she_ shall be raised to life everlasting and stand before You in the righteousness of Christ; through the same

Jesus Christ, our Lord, who lives and reigns with You and the Holy Spirit, one God, now and forever. (872)

Upon release from prison

Gracious Lord, we give You thanks that you have sustained _name_ during _his/her_ time of imprisonment. As _he/she_ is now released, grant _him/her_ grace to trust in Your righteousness alone and face the future in the confidence of the forgiveness of sins. Be with _him/her_ now as _he/she_ is reunited with family and friends. Direct and guide _his/her_ steps that _he/she_ may resist temptation, walk in the way of Your Word, and live in the communion of Your Church. Establish _him/her_ in a place of suitable employment, and bless _his/her_ work that _he/she_ may serve You in newness of life; through Jesus Christ, Your Son, our Lord, who lives and reigns with You and the Holy Spirit, one God, now and forever. (873)

HYMN

In Adam We Have All Been One

LSB 569

In Adam we have all been one,
    One huge rebellious man;
We all have fled that evening voice
    That sought us as we ran.

We fled Thee, and in losing Thee
    We lost our brother too;
Each singly sought and claimed his own;
    Each man his brother slew.

But Thy strong love, it sought us still
    And sent Thine only Son
That we might hear His Shepherd's voice
    And, hearing Him, be one. (sts. 1–3)

© 1969 Concordia Publishing House

511

ADDITIONAL HYMNS

Baptismal Waters Cover Me	*LSB 616*
Come, Thou Precious Ransom, Come	*LSB 350:1–2*
Hark the Glad Sound	*LSB 349:2*
I Leave All Things to God's Direction	*LSB 719:1–3*
Lord, to You I Make Confession	*LSB 608*
O Dearest Jesus, What Law Hast Thou Broken	*LSB 439:1, 3–5*
To Thee, Omniscient Lord of All	*LSB 613*

Times of Catastrophe

The effects of humanity's sin on all of creation are especially evident during times of catastrophe or natural disaster. Questions abound; doubts multiply; anxiety and fear unsettle God's people. The pastor brings God's Word, which points to Christ, who conquered sin and death and who is present in His Gospel at all times to calm, comfort, and strengthen His people.

PSALMODY

Psalm 77:1–2, 7–15   *Seek the Lord in the day of trouble*

¹ I cry a- | loud to God,*
> aloud to God, and he will | hear me.

² In the day of my trouble I | seek the Lord;*
> in the night my hand is stretched out without wearying;
> my soul refuses to be | comforted.

⁷ "Will the Lord spurn for- | ever,*
> and never again be | favorable?

⁸ Has his steadfast love for- | ever ceased?*
> Are his promises at an end | for all time?

⁹ Has God forgotten to be | gracious?*
> Has he in anger shut up his com- | passion?"

¹⁰ Then I said, "I will ap- | peal to this,*
     to the years of the right hand of the | Most High."
¹¹ I will remember the deeds | of the LORD;*
     yes, I will remember your won- | ders of old.
¹² I will ponder | all your work,*
     and meditate on your | mighty deeds.
¹³ Your way, O God, is | holy.*
     What god is great | like our God?
¹⁴ You are the God who works | wonders;*
     you have made known your might among the | peoples.
¹⁵ You with your arm redeemed your | people,*
     the children of Jacob and | Joseph.

Psalm 46   *Though the earth gives way, God is our refuge*

¹ God is our ref- | uge and strength,*
     a very present help in | trouble.
² Therefore we will not fear though the | earth gives way,*
     though the mountains be moved into the heart | of the sea,
³ though its waters | roar and foam,*
     though the mountains tremble at its | swelling.
⁴ There is a river whose streams make glad the cit- | y of God,*
     the holy habitation of the | Most High.
⁵ God is in the midst of her; she shall | not be moved;*
     God will help her when | morning dawns.
⁶ The nations rage, the kingdoms | totter;*
     he utters his voice, the | earth melts.
⁷ The LORD of hosts is | with us;*
     the God of Jacob is our | fortress.
⁸ Come, behold the works | of the LORD,*
     how he has brought desolations | on the earth.
⁹ He makes wars cease to the end | of the earth;*
     he breaks the bow and shatters the spear; he burns the
     chariots | with fire.

▶

[10] "Be still, and know that | I am God.*
    I will be exalted among the nations, I will be exalted | in the
    earth!"
[11] The LORD of hosts is | with us;*
    the God of Jacob is our | fortress.

ADDITIONAL PSALMODY

Psalm 5	*Let all who take refuge in You rejoice*
Psalm 31:1–5	*Into Your hand I commit my spirit*
Psalm 42:1–6a	*I shall again praise God*
Psalm 91	*My refuge and my fortress*

READINGS

2 Corinthians 4:17–18   *Our afflictions prepare us for glory*

[17]For this slight momentary affliction is preparing for us an eternal
weight of glory beyond all comparison, [18]as we look not to the things
that are seen but to the things that are unseen. For the things that are
seen are transient, but the things that are unseen are eternal.

1 Peter 4:12–13   *Christ shares in your fiery trial*

[12]Beloved, do not be surprised at the fiery trial when it comes upon
you to test you, as though something strange were happening to you.
[13]But rejoice insofar as you share Christ's sufferings, that you may
also rejoice and be glad when his glory is revealed.

ADDITIONAL READINGS

Deut. 33:25b–27a	*Underneath us are God's everlasting arms*
Is. 45:1–12	*God's activity in history reveals His power*
Matt. 24:6–8	*War, famine, and earthquakes*
Luke 13:1–5	*The call to repentance*
Rom. 8:14–24	*Heirs with Christ, provided we suffer with Him*
2 Cor. 12:9	*Christ's power is made perfect in weakness*
1 Peter 1:3–9	*Trials test the genuineness of faith*

PRAYERS

After a catastrophe

Almighty God, merciful Father, Your thoughts are not our thoughts, and Your ways are not our ways. In Your wisdom You have permitted this disastrous _fire / flood / earthquake / plane crash / terrorist attack / other_ to befall us. Keep (_name(s)_ and) all of us from despair and do not let our faith fail us, but sustain and comfort us. Direct all efforts to attend the injured, console the bereaved, and protect the helpless. Deliver any who are still in danger, and bring hope and healing that we may find relief and restoration; through Jesus Christ, Your Son, our Lord, who lives and reigns with You and the Holy Spirit, one God, now and forever. (292)

During an epidemic or ongoing stress

Almighty God, heavenly Father, give us grace to trust You during this time of illness and distress. In mercy put an end to the _epidemic / plague / other_ that afflicts us. Grant relief to those who suffer, and comfort all who mourn. Sustain all medical personnel in their labors, and cause Your people ever to serve You in righteousness and holiness; through Jesus Christ, Your Son, our Lord, who lives and reigns with You and the Holy Spirit, one God, now and forever. (291)

Following an act of terrorism or persecution

Gracious God, heavenly Father, You know the shock and sorrow that the events of these days have spread across the land. We are helpless before the evil that afflicts us and therefore cry out to You for comfort, shelter, and protection. Mercifully embrace the frightened in Your love, empower the weak with Your strength, restrain the wicked by Your might, and preserve the righteous in Your grace, giving us Your peace and turning tragedy to triumph; through Jesus Christ, Your Son, our Lord, who lives and reigns with You and the Holy Spirit, one God, now and forever. (874)

For rescue workers

Merciful Father, we commend to Your keeping all who work to bring rescue and relief (especially ___names___). Give them courage in danger, skill in difficulty, and compassion in service. Sustain them with bodily strength and calmness of mind that they may perform their work to the well-being of those in need so that lives may be saved and communities restored; through Jesus Christ, Your Son, our Lord, who lives and reigns with You and the Holy Spirit, one God, now and forever. (875)

HYMN

Jesus, Priceless Treasure
LSB 743

In Thine arms I rest me;
Foes who would molest me
 Cannot reach me here.
Though the earth be shaking,
Ev'ry heart be quaking,
 Jesus calms my fear.
  Lightnings flash
  And thunders crash;
Yet, though sin and hell assail me,
Jesus will not fail me. (st. 2)

Satan, I defy thee;
Death, I now decry thee;
 Fear, I bid thee cease.
World, thou shalt not harm me
Nor thy threats alarm me
 While I sing of peace.
  God's great pow'r
  Guards ev'ry hour;
Earth and all its depths adore Him,
Silent bow before Him. (st. 3)

Hence, all fear and sadness!
For the Lord of gladness,
    Jesus, enters in.
Those who love the Father,
Though the storms may gather,
    Still have peace within.
        Yea, whate'er
        I here must bear,
Thou art still my purest pleasure,
Jesus, priceless treasure! (st. 6)

ADDITIONAL HYMNS

A Mighty Fortress Is Our God	*LSB 656/657*
Eternal Father, Strong to Save	*LSB 717*
Evening and Morning	*LSB 726*
I Know My Faith Is Founded	*LSB 587*
I Trust, O Lord, Your Holy Name	*LSB 734*
Jesus Lives! The Victory's Won	*LSB 490*
There Is a Time for Everything	*LSB 762*
When Aimless Violence Takes Those We Love	*LSB 764*
Why Should Cross and Trial Grieve Me	*LSB 756*

Missing Persons

In cases of missing persons, families will experience initial shock, which may be followed by sadness, impatience, anger, and fear. Immediate resolution of the situation may not occur. The pastor will care for the family members throughout their suffering, providing the comfort of the Gospel and the certainty of Christ's presence and salvation for them and their loved one. It may be desirable for the family itself to gather for regular prayer and readings from Holy Scripture.

PSALMODY

Psalm 27 *The Lord is my salvation; whom shall I fear?*

1 The Lord is my light and my salvation; whom | shall I fear?*
   The Lord is the stronghold of my life; of whom shall I | be afraid?

2 When evildoers assail me to eat | up my flesh,*
   my adversaries and foes, it is they who stum- | ble and fall.

3 Though an army encamp against me, my heart | shall not fear;*
   though war arise against me, yet I will be | confident.

4 One thing have I asked of the Lord, that will I seek | after:*
   that I may dwell in the house of the Lord all the days of my life, to gaze upon the beauty of the Lord and to inquire in his | temple.

5 For he will hide me in his shelter in the day of | trouble;*
   he will conceal me under the cover of his tent; he will lift me high up- | on a rock.

6 And now my head shall be lifted up above my enemies all around me, and I will offer in his tent sacrifices with | shouts of joy;*
   I will sing and make melody | to the Lord.

7 Hear, O Lord, when I | cry aloud;*
   be gracious to me and | answer me!

8 You have said, | "Seek my face."*
   My heart says to you, "Your face, Lord, | do I seek."

⁹ Hide not your face from me. Turn not your servant away in | anger,*

O you who have been my help. Cast me not off; forsake me
not, O God of my sal- | vation!

¹⁰ For my father and my mother have for- | saken me,*

but the LORD will | take me in.

¹¹ Teach me your way, | O LORD,*

and lead me on a level path because of my | enemies.

¹² Give me not up to the will of my adver- | saries;*

for false witnesses have risen against me, and they breathe
out | violence.

¹³ I believe that I shall look upon the goodness | of the LORD*

in the land of the | living!

¹⁴ Wait | for the LORD;*

be strong, and let your heart take courage; wait | for the LORD!

Psalm 121 *The Lord will keep you from all evil*

¹ I lift up my eyes | to the hills.*

From where does my | help come?

² My help comes | from the LORD,*

who made | heaven and earth.

³ He will not let your | foot be moved;*

he who keeps you will not | slumber.

⁴ Behold, he who keeps | Israel*

will neither slum- | ber nor sleep.

⁵ The LORD is your | keeper;*

the LORD is your shade on your | right hand.

⁶ The sun shall not strike | you by day,*

nor the | moon by night.

⁷ The LORD will keep you from all | evil;*

he will | keep your life.

⁸ The LORD will keep you going out and your | coming in*

from this time forth and for- | evermore.

ADDITIONAL PSALMODY

Psalm 31:9, 17, 23–24	*The Lord preserves the faithful*
Psalm 42	*Why is my soul downcast?*
Psalm 46:1–7, 10–11	*God is our refuge and strength*
Psalm 62	*Wait for God alone*
Psalm 71:1–3, 20	*Rescue me and save me*
Psalm 91:1–6, 11–13	*God is my fortress*
Psalm 105:1–4	*Seek the Lord and His strength*
Psalm 139:1–18	*The Lord sees and knows all, even my heart*
Psalm 143	*Hide not Your face from me*

READINGS

Isaiah 53:3–6   *Surely He has borne our griefs*

³ He was despised and rejected by men;
   a man of sorrows, and acquainted with grief;
and as one from whom men hide their faces
   he was despised, and we esteemed him not.
⁴ Surely he has borne our griefs
   and carried our sorrows;
yet we esteemed him stricken,
   smitten by God, and afflicted.
⁵ But he was wounded for our transgressions;
   he was crushed for our iniquities;
upon him was the chastisement that brought us peace,
   and with his stripes we are healed.
⁶ All we like sheep have gone astray;
   we have turned every one to his own way;
and the LORD has laid on him
   the iniquity of us all.

Romans 8:31–39   *If God is for us, who can be against us?*

³¹What then shall we say to these things? If God is for us, who can be against us? ³²He who did not spare his own Son but gave him up

for us all, how will he not also with him graciously give us all things? [33]Who shall bring any charge against God's elect? It is God who justifies. [34]Who is to condemn? Christ Jesus is the one who died—more than that, who was raised—who is at the right hand of God, who indeed is interceding for us. [35]Who shall separate us from the love of Christ? Shall tribulation, or distress, or persecution, or famine, or nakedness, or danger, or sword? [36]As it is written,

> "For your sake we are being killed all the day long;
>> we are regarded as sheep to be slaughtered."

[37]No, in all these things we are more than conquerors through him who loved us. [38]For I am sure that neither death nor life, nor angels nor rulers, nor things present nor things to come, nor powers, [39]nor height nor depth, nor anything else in all creation, will be able to separate us from the love of God in Christ Jesus our Lord.

ADDITIONAL READINGS

Is. 40:25–31	*They shall renew their strength*
Is. 43:1–3a	*Fear not, for I have redeemed you*
Lam. 3:21–33, 55–58	*The steadfast love of the Lord*
Luke 15:11–32	*Parable of the prodigal son*
John 10:1–18	*The Good Shepherd lays down His life*
John 14:1–6	*Let not your hearts be troubled*
2 Cor. 4:6–9	*We are afflicted in every way, but not crushed*

PRAYERS

For the family

Almighty Father, You did not withhold Your Son but delivered Him up for us all that we might know the certainty that nothing will separate us from Your love. Be present with _____name of family_____ and, according to Your gracious will, bring _____name of missing person_____ back to them. As their confidence in You is tested and while peril and questions surround them, make them more than conquerors through ▶

521

faith in Christ that they may bear up under this burden and be at peace; through Jesus Christ, Your Son, our Lord, who lives and reigns with You and the Holy Spirit, one God, now and forever. (876)

For the missing person

O Lord Jesus Christ, in the waters of Holy Baptism You have found us by Your grace and have generously poured out on us Your new and abundant life. Bring _ name _ safely home and back into our midst again. In any danger, protect _ him/her _. In any conflict, give reconciliation. In any fear, give _ him/her _ Your peace; for You live and reign with the Father and the Holy Spirit, one God, now and forever. (296)

HYMN

When in the Hour of Deepest Need
LSB 615

When in the hour of deepest need
We know not where to look for aid;
When days and nights of anxious thought
No help or counsel yet have brought,

Then is our comfort this alone
That we may meet before Your throne;
To You, O faithful God, we cry
For rescue in our misery.

For You have promised, Lord, to heed
Your children's cries in time of need
Through Him whose name alone is great,
Our Savior and our advocate. (sts. 1–3)

ADDITIONAL HYMNS

Children of the Heavenly Father	*LSB 725*
Christ, the Word of God Incarnate	*LSB 540:4*
Grant Peace, We Pray, in Mercy, Lord	*LSB 777/778*

Victims of Violence

Victims of violence have had a physical encounter with evil and the powers of darkness. The horrors suffered may scar them deeply, and their lives may be paralyzed by fear, shame, and anger. The return to a feeling of well-being and protection may be long in coming, requiring extended pastoral and perhaps professional care. The Lord promises to provide healing and peace through the word of the Gospel and the support and fellowship of the Church.

PSALMODY

Psalm 34:1–8   *I sought the Lord, and He answered me*

¹ I will bless the LORD at | all times;*
  his praise shall continually be | in my mouth.
² My soul makes its boast | in the LORD;*
  let the humble hear | and be glad.
³ Oh, magnify the | LORD with me,*
  and let us exalt his name to- | gether!
⁴ I sought the LORD, and he | answered me*
  and delivered me from | all my fears.
⁵ Those who look to him are | radiant,*
  and their faces shall never | be ashamed.
⁶ This poor man cried, and the LORD | heard him*
  and saved him out of all his | troubles.
⁷ The angel of the LORD encamps around those who | fear him,*
  and de- | livers them.
⁸ Oh, taste and see that the | LORD is good!*
  Blessèd is the man who takes ref- | uge in him!

Psalm 139:7–12   *The Lord is with you wherever you go*

⁷ Where shall I go from your | Spirit?*
　　Or where shall I flee from your | presence?
⁸ If I ascend to heaven, | you are there!*
　　If I make my bed in Sheol, | you are there!
⁹ If I take the wings of the | morning*
　　and dwell in the uttermost parts | of the sea,
¹⁰ even there your hand shall | lead me,*
　　and your right hand shall | hold me.
¹¹ If I say, "Surely the darkness shall | cover me,*
　　and the light about me | be night,"
¹² even the darkness is not | dark to you;*
　　the night is bright as the day, for darkness is as | light with you.

ADDITIONAL PSALMODY

Psalm 27	*The Lord is my light and salvation*
Psalm 36	*Your love extends to the heavens*
Psalm 43	*Vindicate and defend me, Lord*
Psalm 51:7–8a, 10–12	*Create in me a new heart*
Psalm 86	*Save Your servant, who trusts in You*

READINGS

Isaiah 41:10–13   *Fear not; the Lord helps you*

¹⁰ Fear not, for I am with you;
　　be not dismayed, for I am your God;
　I will strengthen you, I will help you,
　　I will uphold you with my righteous right hand.
¹¹ Behold, all who are incensed against you
　　shall be put to shame and confounded;
　those who strive against you
　　shall be as nothing and shall perish.
¹² You shall seek those who contend with you,
　　but you shall not find them;

those who war against you
shall be as nothing at all.
¹³ For I, the LORD your God,
hold your right hand;
it is I who say to you, "Fear not,
I am the one who helps you."

1 Peter 5:6–11 *The Lord will restore, strengthen, and establish you*

⁶Humble yourselves, therefore, under the mighty hand of God so that at the proper time he may exalt you, ⁷casting all your anxieties on him, because he cares for you. ⁸Be sober-minded; be watchful. Your adversary the devil prowls around like a roaring lion, seeking someone to devour. ⁹Resist him, firm in your faith, knowing that the same kinds of suffering are being experienced by your brotherhood throughout the world. ¹⁰And after you have suffered a little while, the God of all grace, who has called you to his eternal glory in Christ, will himself restore, confirm, strengthen, and establish you. ¹¹To him be the dominion forever and ever. Amen.

ADDITIONAL READINGS

Jer. 29:11–14a	*I know the plans I have for you*
2 Cor. 4:16–18	*Our afflictions prepare us for eternal glory*
Heb. 13:5b–6	*I will never leave you nor forsake you*

PRAYERS

For those physically attacked or raped

Almighty God, You are a fortress of defense in the time of trouble. We thank You for preserving __name's__ life in the midst of the danger and violence __he/she__ has suffered. Look upon __him/her__ in mercy and grant __him/her__ Your peace that __he/she__ may cling to You in faith and not be ashamed or afraid; through Jesus Christ, Your Son, our Lord, who lives and reigns with You and the Holy Spirit, one God, now and forever. (877)

For those robbed

Father of mercies and God of all grace, look upon Your servant
_ name _, who has suffered the loss of material goods through the
wickedness of others. Comfort _him/her_ with Your tender conso-
lations and draw _him/her_ closer to You in faith that _he/she_ may
set _his/her_ mind on things above and on the treasures laid up in
heaven where neither moth nor rust destroys and where thieves do not
break in and steal; through Jesus Christ, Your Son, our Lord, who
lives and reigns with You and the Holy Spirit, one God, now and forever. (878)

For continued protection

O God, You see that of ourselves we have no strength. By Your
mighty power defend us from all adversities that may happen to the
body and from all evil thoughts that may assault and hurt the soul;
through Jesus Christ, Your Son, our Lord, who lives and reigns with
You and the Holy Spirit, one God, now and forever. (L24)

Merciful and everlasting God the Father, You did not spare Your own
Son but delivered Him up for us all that He might bear our sins on the
cross. Grant that our hearts may be so fixed with steadfast faith in
our Savior that we may not fear the power of any adversaries; through
Jesus Christ, our Lord, who lives and reigns with You and the Holy
Spirit, one God, now and forever. (L31 alt.)

HYMNS
Jesus, Priceless Treasure
LSB 743

In Thine arms I rest me;
Foes who would molest me
    Cannot reach me here.
Though the earth be shaking,
Ev'ry heart be quaking,

Jesus calms my fear.
Lightnings flash
And thunders crash;
Yet, though sin and hell assail me,
Jesus will not fail me. (st. 2)

Jesus, Grant That Balm and Healing   *LSB 421*

Jesus, grant that balm and healing
In Your holy wounds I find,
Ev'ry hour that I am feeling
Pains of body and of mind.
Should some evil thought within
Tempt my treach'rous heart to sin,
Show the peril, and from sinning
Keep me from its first beginning. (st. 1)

Ev'ry wound that pains or grieves me
By Your wounds, Lord, is made whole;
When I'm faint, Your cross revives me,
Granting new life to my soul.
Yes, Your comfort renders sweet
Ev'ry bitter cup I meet;
For Your all-atoning passion
Has procured my soul's salvation. (st. 4)

Dear Christians, One and All, Rejoice   *LSB 556*

To me He said: "Stay close to Me,
I am your rock and castle.
Your ransom I Myself will be;
For you I strive and wrestle.
For I am yours, and you are Mine,
And where I am you may remain;
The foe shall not divide us." (st. 7)

ADDITIONAL HYMNS

Christ, the Life of All the Living	*LSB 420:1, 5–6*
I Lie, O Lord, within Your Care	*LSB 885*
I Walk in Danger All the Way	*LSB 716:5–6*
Jesus, I Will Ponder Now	*LSB 440:5*
Jesus, in Your Dying Woes	*LSB 447:10–12*
Lamb of God, Pure and Holy	*LSB 434*
Lord of Our Life	*LSB 659:1, 3–4*
O God, Forsake Me Not	*LSB 731:1, 4*
O Perfect Life of Love	*LSB 452:1, 3, 5*
When Aimless Violence Takes Those We Love	*LSB 764:1, 3–5*

Persecution of Christians

Persecution and reproach may come to those who bear the name of Christ. At such times Christians may be tempted to doubt their faith and confession of faith in Christ. The pastor will assure them that suffering for Christ's sake testifies that they belong to Him and are being made perfect in Him through weakness.

PSALMODY
Psalm 31:9–10, 14–16, 19–20   *Be gracious to me*

⁹ Be gracious to me, O LORD, for I am | in distress;*
>   my eye is wasted from grief; my soul and my body | also.

¹⁰ For my life is spent with sorrow, and my years with | sighing;*
>   my strength fails because of my iniquity, and my bones | waste away.

¹⁴ But I trust in you, | O LORD;*
>   I say, "You | are my God."

¹⁵ My times are | in your hand;*
  rescue me from the hand of my enemies and from my
  perse- | cutors!
¹⁶ Make your face shine on your | servant;*
  save me in your | steadfast love!
¹⁹ Oh, how abundant is your goodness, which you have stored up
  for those who | fear you*
    and worked for those who take refuge in you, in the sight of
    the children of | mankind!
²⁰ In the cover of your presence you hide them from the | plots of
  men;*
    you store them in your shelter from the | strife of tongues.

Psalm 69:6–12, 16–18 — *Those who hope in the Lord*

⁶ Let not those who hope in you be put to shame through me,
  O Lord | GOD of hosts;*
    let not those who seek you be brought to dishonor through
    me, O God of | Israel.
⁷ For it is for your sake that I have | borne reproach,*
  that dishonor has covered | my face.
⁸ I have become a stranger to my | brothers,*
  an alien to my | mother's sons.
⁹ For zeal for your house has con- | sumed me,*
    and the reproaches of those who reproach you have fall- | en
    on me.
¹⁰ When I wept and humbled my soul with | fasting,*
  it became | my reproach.
¹¹ When I made sackcloth my | clothing,*
  I became a byword | to them.
¹² I am the talk of those who sit | in the gate,*
  and the drunkards make songs a- | bout me.
¹⁶ Answer me, O LORD, for your steadfast | love is good;*
  according to your abundant mercy, | turn to me. ▶

¹⁷ Hide not your face from your servant; for I am | in distress;*
    make haste to | answer me.
¹⁸ Draw near to my soul, re- | deem me;*
    ransom me because of my | enemies!

ADDITIONAL PSALMODY

Psalm 35	*Vindicate me, O Lord*
Psalm 71	*Let me never be put to shame*
Psalm 119:81–88	*My soul longs for Your salvation*
Psalm 143	*Deliver me from my enemies*

READINGS
1 Kings 19:1–2, 9–18   *The Lord sustains Elijah*

¹Ahab told Jezebel all that Elijah had done, and how he had killed all the prophets with the sword. ²Then Jezebel sent a messenger to Elijah, saying, "So may the gods do to me and more also, if I do not make your life as the life of one of them by this time tomorrow."

⁹There he came to a cave and lodged in it. And behold, the word of the LORD came to him, and he said to him, "What are you doing here, Elijah?" ¹⁰He said, "I have been very jealous for the LORD, the God of hosts. For the people of Israel have forsaken your covenant, thrown down your altars, and killed your prophets with the sword, and I, even I only, am left, and they seek my life, to take it away." ¹¹And he said, "Go out and stand on the mount before the LORD." And behold, the LORD passed by, and a great and strong wind tore the mountains and broke in pieces the rocks before the LORD, but the LORD was not in the wind. And after the wind an earthquake, but the LORD was not in the earthquake. ¹²And after the earthquake a fire, but the LORD was not in the fire. And after the fire the sound of a low whisper. ¹³And when Elijah heard it, he wrapped his face in his cloak and went out and stood at the entrance of the cave. And behold, there came a voice to him and said, "What are you doing here, Elijah?" ¹⁴He said, "I have been very jealous for the LORD, the God of hosts.

For the people of Israel have forsaken your covenant, thrown down your altars, and killed your prophets with the sword, and I, even I only, am left, and they seek my life, to take it away." ¹⁵And the LORD said to him, "Go, return on your way to the wilderness of Damascus. And when you arrive, you shall anoint Hazael to be king over Syria. ¹⁶And Jehu the son of Nimshi you shall anoint to be king over Israel, and Elisha the son of Shaphat of Abel-meholah you shall anoint to be prophet in your place. ¹⁷And the one who escapes from the sword of Hazael shall Jehu put to death, and the one who escapes from the sword of Jehu shall Elisha put to death. ¹⁸Yet I will leave seven thousand in Israel, all the knees that have not bowed to Baal, and every mouth that has not kissed him.'"

Acts 7:2a, 52–60   *Stephen's martyrdom*

²And Stephen said: "Brothers and fathers, hear me. . . . ⁵²Which of the prophets did not your fathers persecute? And they killed those who announced beforehand the coming of the Righteous One, whom you have now betrayed and murdered, ⁵³you who received the law as delivered by angels and did not keep it."

⁵⁴Now when they heard these things they were enraged, and they ground their teeth at him. ⁵⁵But he, full of the Holy Spirit, gazed into heaven and saw the glory of God, and Jesus standing at the right hand of God. ⁵⁶And he said, "Behold, I see the heavens opened, and the Son of Man standing at the right hand of God." ⁵⁷But they cried out with a loud voice and stopped their ears and rushed together at him. ⁵⁸Then they cast him out of the city and stoned him. And the witnesses laid down their garments at the feet of a young man named Saul. ⁵⁹And as they were stoning Stephen, he called out, "Lord Jesus, receive my spirit." ⁶⁰And falling to his knees he cried out with a loud voice, "Lord, do not hold this sin against them." And when he had said this, he fell asleep.

ADDITIONAL READINGS

Matt. 5:11–12	*Blessed are the persecuted*
Matt. 5:43–48	*Pray for those who persecute you*
John 15:18–21; 16:33	*Peace for persecuted disciples*
Phil. 1:12–14, 27–30	*Paul imprisoned for Christ*
2 Tim. 3:10–17	*All who desire to live in Christ will be persecuted*
2 Tim. 4:14–18	*Paul rescued from "the lion's mouth"*
Heb. 11:32–40	*The example of the faithful people of old*
1 Peter 4:12–14, 16	*Do not be surprised at the fiery trial*

PRAYERS

Lord Jesus Christ, before whom all in heaven and earth shall bow, grant courage that __*name*__ may confess Your saving name in the face of any opposition from a world hostile to the Gospel. Help __*him/her*__ to remember the long line of Your faithful witnesses who endured persecution and even faced death rather than dishonor You. By Your Spirit, strengthen __*him/her*__ to confess You before all, knowing that You will confess __*him/her*__ before Your Father in heaven; for You live and reign with the Father and the Holy Spirit, one God, now and forever. (111 alt.)

Almighty God, Your Son, Jesus Christ, chose to suffer pain before going up to joy and crucifixion before entering into glory. Mercifully grant that __*name*__, walking in the way of the cross, may find this path to be the way of life and peace; through Jesus Christ, our Lord, who lives and reigns with You and the Holy Spirit, one God, now and forever. (879)

For enemies and persecutors

Almighty, everlasting God, through Your only Son, our blessed Lord, You commanded us to love our enemies, to do good to those who hate us, and to pray for those who persecute us. Therefore, we earnestly implore You that by Your gracious working our enemies may be led to true repentance, may have the same love toward us as we have toward them, and may be of one accord and of one mind and heart with us and with Your whole Church; through Jesus Christ, our Lord, who lives and reigns with You and the Holy Spirit, one God, now and forever. (110)

HYMN

If God Himself Be for Me

LSB 724

If God Himself be for me,
    I may a host defy;
For when I pray, before me
    My foes, confounded, fly.
If Christ, my head and master,
    Befriend me from above,
What foe or what disaster
    Can drive me from His love? (st. 1)

Who clings with resolution
    To Him whom Satan hates
Must look for persecution;
    For him the burden waits
Of mock'ry, shame, and losses
    Heaped on his blameless head;
A thousand plagues and crosses
    Will be his daily bread. (st. 6)

My heart with joy is springing;
    I am no longer sad.
My soul is filled with singing;
    Your sunshine makes me glad.
The sun that cheers my spirit
    Is Jesus Christ, my King;
The heav'n I shall inherit
    Makes me rejoice and sing. (st. 10)

ADDITIONAL HYMNS

A Mighty Fortress Is Our God	*LSB 656/657*
From God Can Nothing Move Me	*LSB 713:6*
In Thee Is Gladness	*LSB 818*
Jesus, Priceless Treasure	*LSB 743:1–3*
What Is the World to Me	*LSB 730*

OTHER RESOURCES

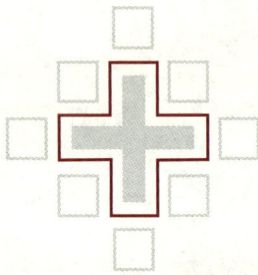

COLLECTS OF THE DAY AND READINGS

The following pages contain the collects and appointed readings according to the outline above.

During The Time of Christmas and The Time of Easter, the same collects are used for both the Three-Year Lectionary and One-Year Lectionary. For the second half of the Church Year, the collects vary between lectionaries, and so each are included in their own section.

For the Feasts, Festivals, and Occasions, the collects and readings are the same for both the Three-Year Lectionary and One-Year Lectionary.

SUNDAYS AND SEASONS

The Time of Christmas

First Sunday in Advent

Stir up Your power, O Lord, and come, that by Your protection we may be rescued from the threatening perils of our sins and saved by Your mighty deliverance; for You live and reign with the Father and the Holy Spirit, one God, now and forever. (L01)

A Isaiah 2:1–5
  Psalm 122 (v. 6)
  Romans 13:(8–10) 11–14
  Matthew 21:1–11
   or Matthew 24:36–44

C Jeremiah 33:14–16
  Psalm 25:1–10 (v. 6)
  1 Thessalonians 3:9–13
  Luke 19:28–40
   or Luke 21:25–36

B Isaiah 64:1–9
  Psalm 80:1–7 (v. 7)
  1 Corinthians 1:3–9
  Mark 11:1–10
   or Mark 13:24–37

1Yr. Jeremiah 23:5–8
  Psalm 24 (v. 7)
  Romans 13:(8–10) 11–14
  Matthew 21:1–9

Second Sunday in Advent

Stir up our hearts, O Lord, to make ready the way of Your only-begotten Son, that by His coming we may be enabled to serve You with pure minds; through the same Jesus Christ, our Lord, who lives and reigns with You and the Holy Spirit, one God, now and forever. (L02)

A Isaiah 11:1–10
  Psalm 72:1–7 (v. 18)
  Romans 15:4–13
  Matthew 3:1–12

C Malachi 3:1–7b
  Psalm 66:1–12 (v. 12b)
  Philippians 1:2–11
  Luke 3:1–14 (15–20)

B Isaiah 40:1–11
  Psalm 85 (v. 9)
  2 Peter 3:8–14
  Mark 1:1–8

1Yr. Malachi 4:1–6
  Psalm 50:1–15 (v. 15)
  Romans 15:4–13
  Luke 21:25–36

Third Sunday in Advent

Lord Jesus Christ, we implore You to hear our prayers and to lighten the darkness of our hearts by Your gracious visitation; for You live and reign with the Father and the Holy Spirit, one God, now and forever. (L03)

A   Isaiah 35:1–10
Psalm 146 (v. 5)
James 5:7–11
Matthew 11:2–15

C   Zephaniah 3:14–20
Psalm 85 (v. 2)
Philippians 4:4–7
Luke 7:18–28 (29–35)

B   Isaiah 61:1–4, 8–11
Psalm 126 (v. 5)
1 Thessalonians 5:16–24
John 1:6–8, 19–28

1Yr.   Isaiah 40:1–8 (9–11)
Psalm 85 (v. 9)
1 Corinthians 4:1–5
Matthew 11:2–10 (11)

Fourth Sunday in Advent

Stir up Your power, O Lord, and come and help us by Your might, that the sins which weigh us down may be quickly lifted by Your grace and mercy; for You live and reign with the Father and the Holy Spirit, one God, now and forever. (L04)

A   Isaiah 7:10–17
Psalm 24 (v. 7)
Romans 1:1–7
Matthew 1:18–25

C   Micah 5:2–5a
Psalm 80:1–7 (v. 7)
Hebrews 10:5–10
Luke 1:39–45 (46–56)

B   2 Samuel 7:1–11, 16
Psalm 89:1–5 (19–29) (v. 8)
Romans 16:25–27
Luke 1:26–38

1Yr.   Deuteronomy 18:15–19
Psalm 111 (v. 9)
Philippians 4:4–7
John 1:19–28
or Luke 1:39–56

The Nativity of Our Lord
Christmas Eve

O God, You make us glad with the yearly remembrance of the birth of Your only-begotten Son, Jesus Christ. Grant that as we joyfully receive Him as our Redeemer, we may with sure confidence behold Him when He comes to be our Judge; through the same Jesus Christ, our Lord, who lives and reigns with You and the Holy Spirit, one God, now and forever. (L05)

ABC, 1Yr. Isaiah 7:10–14
Psalm 110:1–4 (v. 2a)
1 John 4:7–16
Matthew 1:18–25

The Nativity of Our Lord
Christmas Midnight

O God, You make this most holy night to shine with the brightness of the true Light. Grant that as we have known the mysteries of that Light on earth we may also come to the fullness of His joys in heaven; through the same Jesus Christ, Your Son, our Lord, who lives and reigns with You and the Holy Spirit, one God, now and forever. (L06)

ABC, 1Yr. Isaiah 9:2–7
Psalm 96 (v. 2)
Titus 2:11–14
Luke 2:1–14 (15–20)

The Nativity of Our Lord
Christmas Dawn

Most merciful God, You gave Your eternal Word to become incarnate of the pure Virgin. Grant Your people grace to put away fleshly lusts, that they may be ready for Your visitation; through Jesus Christ, our Lord, who lives and reigns with You and the Holy Spirit, one God, now and forever. (L07)

ABC   Isaiah 62:10–12
Psalm 98 (v. 2)
Titus 3:4–7
Luke 2:(1–14) 15–20

1Yr.   Micah 5:2–5a
Psalm 80:1–7 (v. 7)
Titus 3:4–7
Luke 2:(1–14) 15–20

The Nativity of Our Lord

Christmas Day

Almighty God, grant that the birth of Your only-begotten Son in the flesh may set us free from the bondage of sin; through Jesus Christ, Your Son, our Lord, who lives and reigns with You and the Holy Spirit, one God, now and forever. (L08)

ABC   Isaiah 52:7–10
Psalm 2 (v. 7)
Hebrews 1:1–6 (7–12)
John 1:1–14 (15–18)

1Yr.   Exodus 40:17–21, 34–38
Psalm 2 (v. 7)
Titus 3:4–7
John 1:1–14 (15–18)

First Sunday after Christmas

O God, our Maker and Redeemer, You wonderfully created us and in the incarnation of Your Son yet more wondrously restored our human nature. Grant that we may ever be alive in Him who made Himself to be like us; through Jesus Christ, our Lord, who lives and reigns with You and the Holy Spirit, one God, now and forever. (L09)

A   Isaiah 63:7–14
Psalm 111 (v. 9a, b)
Galatians 4:4–7
Matthew 2:13–23

C   Exodus 13:1–3a, 11–15
Psalm 111 (v. 9a, b)
Colossians 3:12–17
Luke 2:22–40

B   Isaiah 61:10—62:3
Psalm 111 (v. 9a, b)
Galatians 4:4–7
Luke 2:22–40

1Yr.   Isaiah 11:1–5
     or 2 Samuel 7:1–16
Psalm 89:1–8 (v. 8)
Galatians 4:1–7
Luke 2:(22–32) 33–40

Second Sunday after Christmas

Almighty God, You have poured into our hearts the true Light of Your incarnate Word. Grant that this Light may shine forth in our lives; through the same Jesus Christ, Your Son, our Lord, who lives and reigns with You and the Holy Spirit, one God, now and forever. (L10)

ABC	1 Kings 3:4–15	1Yr.	Genesis 46:1–7
	Psalm 119:97–104 (v. 99)		Psalm 77:11–20 (v. 13)
	Ephesians 1:3–14		1 Peter 4:12–19
	Luke 2:40–52		Matthew 2:13–23

The Epiphany of Our Lord

O God, by the leading of a star You made known Your only-begotten Son to the Gentiles. Lead us, who know You by faith, to enjoy in heaven the fullness of Your divine presence; through the same Jesus Christ, our Lord, who lives and reigns with You and the Holy Spirit, one God, now and forever. (L11)

ABC	Isaiah 60:1–6	1Yr.	Isaiah 60:1–6
	Psalm 72:1–11 (12–15) (v. 18)		Psalm 24 (v. 7)
	Ephesians 3:1–12		Ephesians 3:1–12
	Matthew 2:1–12		Matthew 2:1–12

The Baptism of Our Lord

Father in heaven, at the Baptism of Jesus in the Jordan River You proclaimed Him Your beloved Son and anointed Him with the Holy Spirit. Make all who are baptized in His name faithful in their calling as Your children and inheritors with Him of everlasting life; through the same Jesus Christ, our Lord, who lives and reigns with You and the Holy Spirit, one God, now and forever. (L12)

A	Isaiah 42:1–9	B	Genesis 1:1–5	C	Isaiah 43:1–7
	Psalm 29 (v. 3)		Psalm 29 (v. 3)		Psalm 29 (v. 3)
	Romans 6:1–11		Romans 6:1–11		Romans 6:1–11
	Matthew 3:13–17		Mark 1:4–11		Luke 3:15–22

1Yr. Joshua 3:1–3, 7–8, 13–17
      or Isaiah 42:1–7
      Psalm 85 (v. 9)
      1 Corinthians 1:26–31
      Matthew 3:13–17

First Sunday after the Epiphany (One-Year Lectionary)

O Lord, mercifully receive the prayers of Your people who call upon You and grant that they both perceive and know what things they ought to do and also may have grace and power faithfully to fulfill the same; through Jesus Christ, Your Son, our Lord, who lives and reigns with You and the Holy Spirit, one God, now and forever. (L13)

1Yr. 1 Kings 8:6–13
      Psalm 50:1–15 (v. 15)
      Romans 12:1–5
      Luke 2:41–52

Second Sunday after the Epiphany

Almighty and everlasting God, who governs all things in heaven and on earth, mercifully hear the prayers of Your people and grant us Your peace through all our days; through Jesus Christ, Your Son, our Lord, who lives and reigns with You and the Holy Spirit, one God, now and forever. (L14)

A   Isaiah 49:1–7
    Psalm 40:1–11 (v. 3)
    1 Corinthians 1:1–9
    John 1:29–42a

C   Isaiah 62:1–5
    Psalm 128 (v. 5)
    1 Corinthians 12:1–11
    John 2:1–11

B   1 Samuel 3:1–10 (11–20)
    Psalm 139:1–10 (v. 14)
    1 Corinthians 6:12–20
    John 1:43–51

1Yr. Exodus 33:12–23
      or Amos 9:11–15
      Psalm 67 (v. 1)
      or Psalm 111 (v. 9)
      Ephesians 5:22–33
      or Romans 12:6–16
      John 2:1–11

Third Sunday after the Epiphany

Almighty and everlasting God, mercifully look upon our infirmities and stretch forth the hand of Your majesty to heal and defend us; through Jesus Christ, Your Son, our Lord, who lives and reigns with You and the Holy Spirit, one God, now and forever. (L15)

A   Isaiah 9:1–4
      Psalm 27:1–9 (10–14) (v. 1)
      1 Corinthians 1:10–18
      Matthew 4:12–25

C   Nehemiah 8:1–3, 5–6, 8–10
      Psalm 19:(1–6) 7–14 (v. 14)
      1 Corinthians 12:12–31a
      Luke 4:16–30

B   Jonah 3:1–5, 10
      Psalm 62 (v. 8)
      1 Corinthians 7:29–31 (32–35)
      Mark 1:14–20

1 Yr.   2 Kings 5:1–15a
      Psalm 110:1–4 (v. 2a)
      Romans 1:8–17
      or Romans 12:16–21
      Matthew 8:1–13

Fourth Sunday after the Epiphany

Almighty God, You know we live in the midst of so many dangers that in our frailty we cannot stand upright. Grant strength and protection to support us in all dangers and carry us through all temptations; through Jesus Christ, Your Son, our Lord, who lives and reigns with You and the Holy Spirit, one God, now and forever. (L16)

A   Micah 6:1–8
      Psalm 15 (Ps. 16:1)
      1 Corinthians 1:18–31
      Matthew 5:1–12

C   Jeremiah 1:4–10 (17–19)
      Psalm 71:1–6 (7–11) (v. 12)
      1 Corinthians 12:31b—13:13
      Luke 4:31–44

B   Deuteronomy 18:15–20
      Psalm 111 (v. 3)
      1 Corinthians 8:1–13
      Mark 1:21–28

1Yr.   Jonah 1:1–17
      Psalm 96 (v. 2)
      Romans 8:18–23
      or Romans 13:8–10
      Matthew 8:23–27

Fifth Sunday after the Epiphany

O Lord, keep Your family the Church continually in the true faith that, relying on the hope of Your heavenly grace, we may ever be defended by Your mighty power; through Jesus Christ, Your Son, our Lord, who lives and reigns with You and the Holy Spirit, one God, now and forever. (L17)

A	Isaiah 58:3–9a	C	Isaiah 6:1–8 (9–13)
	Psalm 112:1–9 (v. 4)		Psalm 138 (v. 5)
	1 Corinthians 2:1–12 (13–16)		1 Corinthians 14:12b–20
	Matthew 5:13–20		Luke 5:1–11
B	Isaiah 40:21–31	1Yr.	Genesis 18:20–33
	Psalm 147:1–11 (v. 5)		Psalm 80:1–7 (v. 7)
	1 Corinthians 9:16–27		Colossians 3:12–17
	Mark 1:29–39		Matthew 13:24–30 (36–43)

Sixth Sunday after the Epiphany / Septuagesima

O Lord, graciously hear the prayers of Your people that we who justly suffer the consequence of our sin may be mercifully delivered by Your goodness to the glory of Your name; through Jesus Christ, Your Son, our Lord, who lives and reigns with You and the Holy Spirit, one God, now and forever. (L18)

A	Deuteronomy 30:15–20	C	Jeremiah 17:5–8
	Psalm 119:1–8 (v. 1)		Psalm 1 (v. 2)
	1 Corinthians 3:1–9		1 Corinthians 15:(1–11) 12–20
	Matthew 5:21–37		Luke 6:17–26
B	2 Kings 5:1–14	1Yr.	Exodus 17:1–7
	Psalm 30 (v. 2)		Psalm 95:1–9 (v. 6)
	1 Corinthians 10:(19–30) 31—11:1		1 Corinthians 9:24—10:5
	Mark 1:40–45		Matthew 20:1–16

Seventh Sunday after the Epiphany / Sexagesima

O God, the strength of all who put their trust in You, mercifully grant that by Your power we may be defended against all adversity; through Jesus Christ, Your Son, our Lord, who lives and reigns with You and the Holy Spirit, one God, now and forever. (L19)

A   Leviticus 19:1–2, 9–18
      Psalm 119:33–40 (v. 35)
      1 Corinthians 3:10–23
      Matthew 5:38–48

C   Genesis 45:3–15
      Psalm 103:1–13 (v. 8)
      1 Corinthians 15:21–26, 30–42
      Luke 6:27–38

B   Isaiah 43:18–25
      Psalm 41 (v. 4)
      2 Corinthians 1:18–22
      Mark 2:1–12

1Yr.   Isaiah 55:10–13
      Psalm 84 (v. 4)
      2 Corinthians 11:19—12:9
      or Hebrews 4:9–13
      Luke 8:4–15

Eighth Sunday after the Epiphany / Quinquagesima

O Lord, mercifully hear our prayers and having set us free from the bonds of our sins deliver us from every evil; through Jesus Christ, Your Son, our Lord, who lives and reigns with You and the Holy Spirit, one God, now and forever. (L20)

A   Isaiah 49:8–16a
      Psalm 115:(1–8) 9–18 (v. 1)
      1 Corinthians 4:1–13
      Matthew 6:24–34

C   Jeremiah 7:1–7 (8–15)
      Psalm 92 (v. 4)
      1 Corinthians 15:42–52 (53–58)
      Luke 6:39–49

B   Hosea 2:14–20
      Psalm 103:1–13 (v. 22)
      2 Corinthians 2:12—3:6
      Mark 2:(13–17) 18–22

1Yr.   1 Samuel 16:1–13
      or Isaiah 35:3–7
      Psalm 89:18–29 (v. 20)
      or Psalm 146 (v. 2)
      1 Corinthians 13:1–13
      Luke 18:31–43

The Transfiguration of Our Lord

O God, in the glorious transfiguration of Your beloved Son You confirmed the mysteries of the faith by the testimony of Moses and Elijah. In the voice that came from the bright cloud You wonderfully foreshowed our adoption by grace. Mercifully make us co-heirs with the King in His glory and bring us to the fullness of our inheritance in heaven; through the same Jesus Christ, our Lord, who lives and reigns with You and the Holy Spirit, one God, now and forever. (L21)

A	Exodus 24:8–18	C	Deuteronomy 34:1–12
	Psalm 2:6–12 (v. 6)		Psalm 99 (v. 9)
	2 Peter 1:16–21		Hebrews 3:1–6
	Matthew 17:1–9		Luke 9:28–36
B	2 Kings 2:1–12	1Yr.	Exodus 34:29–35
	or Exodus 34:29–35		*or* Exodus 3:1–14
	Psalm 50:1–6 (v. 2)		Psalm 2 (v. 7)
	2 Corinthians 3:12–13 (14–18); 4:1–6		2 Peter 1:16–21
	Mark 9:2–9		Matthew 17:1–9

The Time of Easter

Ash Wednesday

Almighty and everlasting God, You despise nothing You have made and forgive the sins of all who are penitent. Create in us new and contrite hearts that lamenting our sins and acknowledging our wretchedness we may receive from You full pardon and forgiveness; through Jesus Christ, Your Son, our Lord, who lives and reigns with You and the Holy Spirit, one God, now and forever. (L22)

ABC	Joel 2:12–19	1Yr.	Joel 2:12–19
	Psalm 51:1–13 (14–19) (v. 17)		*or* Jonah 3:1–10
	2 Corinthians 5:20b—6:10		Psalm 51:1–13 (14–19) (v. 17)
	Matthew 6:1–6, 16–21		2 Peter 1:2–11
			Matthew 6:(1–6) 16–21

First Sunday in Lent

O Lord God, You led Your ancient people through the wilderness and brought them to the promised land. Guide the people of Your Church that following our Savior we may walk through the wilderness of this world toward the glory of the world to come; through Jesus Christ, Your Son, our Lord, who lives and reigns with You and the Holy Spirit, one God, now and forever. (L23)

A   Genesis 3:1–21
Psalm 32:1–7 (v. 7a)
Romans 5:12–19
Matthew 4:1–11

B   Genesis 22:1–18
Psalm 25:1–10 (v. 14)
James 1:12–18
Mark 1:9–15

C   Deuteronomy 26:1–11
Psalm 91:1–13 (v. 1)
Romans 10:8b–13
Luke 4:1–13

1Yr.   Genesis 3:1–21
   or 1 Samuel 17:40–51
Psalm 32 (v. 7)
   or Psalm 118:1–13 (v. 5)
2 Corinthians 6:1–10
   or Hebrews 4:14–16
Matthew 4:1–11

Second Sunday in Lent

O God, You see that of ourselves we have no strength. By Your mighty power defend us from all adversities that may happen to the body and from all evil thoughts that may assault and hurt the soul; through Jesus Christ, Your Son, our Lord, who lives and reigns with You and the Holy Spirit, one God, now and forever. (L24)

A   Genesis 12:1–9
Psalm 121 (v. 8)
Romans 4:1–8, 13–17
John 3:1–17

B   Genesis 17:1–7, 15–16
Psalm 22:23–31 (v. 22)
Romans 5:1–11
Mark 8:27–38

C   Jeremiah 26:8–15
Psalm 4 (v. 8)
Philippians 3:17—4:1
Luke 13:31–35

1Yr.   Genesis 32:22–32
Psalm 121 (vv. 1–2)
1 Thessalonians 4:1–7
   or Romans 5:1–5
Matthew 15:21–28

Third Sunday in Lent

O God, whose glory it is always to have mercy, be gracious to all who have gone astray from Your ways and bring them again with penitent hearts and steadfast faith to embrace and hold fast the unchangeable truth of Your Word; through Jesus Christ, Your Son, our Lord, who lives and reigns with You and the Holy Spirit, one God, now and forever. (L25)

A Exodus 17:1–7
   Psalm 95:1–9 (v. 6)
   Romans 5:1–8
   John 4:5–26 (27–30, 39–42)

B Exodus 20:1–17
   Psalm 19 (v. 8)
   1 Corinthians 1:18–31
   John 2:13–22 (23–25)

C Ezekiel 33:7–20
   Psalm 85 (v. 8)
   1 Corinthians 10:1–13
   Luke 13:1–9

1Yr. Exodus 8:16–24
      or Jeremiah 26:1–15
      Psalm 136:1–16 (v. 26)
      or Psalm 4 (v. 8)
      Ephesians 5:1–9
      Luke 11:14–28

Fourth Sunday in Lent

Almighty God, our heavenly Father, Your mercies are new every morning; and though we deserve only punishment, You receive us as Your children and provide for all our needs of body and soul. Grant that we may heartily acknowledge Your merciful goodness, give thanks for all Your benefits, and serve You in willing obedience; through Jesus Christ, Your Son, our Lord, who lives and reigns with You and the Holy Spirit, one God, now and forever. (L26)

A Isaiah 42:14–21
   Psalm 142 (v. 5)
   Ephesians 5:8–14
   John 9:1–41
   or John 9:1–7, 13–17, 34–39

B Numbers 21:4–9
   Psalm 107:1–9 (v. 19)
   Ephesians 2:1–10
   John 3:14–21

C Isaiah 12:1–6
   Psalm 32 (v. 11)
   2 Corinthians 5:16–21
   Luke 15:1–3, 11–32

1Yr. Exodus 16:2–21
      or Isaiah 49:8–13
      Psalm 132:8–18 (v. 13)
      Galatians 4:21–31
      or Acts 2:41–47
      John 6:1–15

Fifth Sunday in Lent

Almighty God, by Your great goodness mercifully look upon Your people that we may be governed and preserved evermore in body and soul; through Jesus Christ, Your Son, our Lord, who lives and reigns with You and the Holy Spirit, one God, now and forever. (L27)

A   Ezekiel 37:1–14
Psalm 130 (v. 7)
Romans 8:1–11
John 11:1–45 (46–53)
   or John 11:17–27, 38–53

C   Isaiah 43:16–21
Psalm 126 (v. 3)
Philippians 3:(4b–7) 8–14
Luke 20:9–20

B   Jeremiah 31:31–34
Psalm 119:9–16 (v. 10)
Hebrews 5:1–10
Mark 10:(32–34) 35–45

1Yr.   Genesis 22:1–14
Psalm 43 (v. 5)
Hebrews 9:11–15
John 8:(42–45) 46–59

Palm Sunday / Sunday of the Passion

Almighty and everlasting God, You sent Your Son, our Savior Jesus Christ, to take upon Himself our flesh and to suffer death upon the cross. Mercifully grant that we may follow the example of His great humility and patience and be made partakers of His resurrection; through the same Jesus Christ, our Lord, who lives and reigns with You and the Holy Spirit, one God, now and forever. (L28)

A   John 12:12–19 (Procession)
Isaiah 50:4–9a
Psalm 118:19–29 (v. 26)
   or Psalm 31:9–16 (v. 5)
Philippians 2:5–11
Matthew 26:1—27:66
   or Matthew 27:11–66
   or John 12:20–43

B   John 12:12–19 (Procession)
Zechariah 9:9–12
Psalm 118:19–29 (v. 26)
   or Psalm 31:9–16 (v. 5)
Philippians 2:5–11
Mark 14:1—15:47
   or Mark 15:1–47
   or John 12:20–43

C   John 12:12–19 (Procession)
Deuteronomy 32:36–39
Psalm 118:19–29 (v. 26)
   or Psalm 31:9–16 (v. 5)
Philippians 2:5–11
Luke 22:1—23:56
   or Luke 23:1–56
   or John 12:20–43

1Yr.   Matthew 21:1–9 (Procession)
   or John 12:12–19 (Procession)
Zechariah 9:9–12
Psalm 118:19–29 (v. 26)
   or Psalm 31:9–16 (v. 5)
Philippians 2:5–11
Matthew 26:1—27:66
   or Matthew 27:11–54

Monday in Holy Week

Almighty God, grant that in the midst of our failures and weaknesses we may be restored through the passion and intercession of Your only-begotten Son, who lives and reigns with You and the Holy Spirit, one God, now and forever. (L29)

ABC   Isaiah 50:5–10
Psalm 36:5–10 (v. 9)
Hebrews 9:11–15
Matthew 26:1—27:66
   or John 12:1–23

1Yr.   Isaiah 50:5–10
Psalm 36:5–10 (v. 9)
1 Peter 2:21–24
John 12:1–36 (37–43)

Tuesday in Holy Week

Almighty and everlasting God, grant us by Your grace so to pass through this holy time of our Lord's passion that we may obtain the forgiveness of our sins; through Jesus Christ, Your Son, our Lord, who lives and reigns with You and the Holy Spirit, one God, now and forever. (L30)

ABC   Isaiah 49:1–7
Psalm 71:1–14 (v. 12)
1 Corinthians 1:18–25 (26–31)
Mark 14:1—15:47
   or John 12:23–50

1Yr.   Jeremiah 11:18–20
Psalm 54 (v. 4)
1 Timothy 6:12–14
Mark 14:1—15:47

Wednesday in Holy Week

Merciful and everlasting God, You did not spare Your only Son but delivered Him up for us all to bear our sins on the cross. Grant that our hearts may be so fixed with steadfast faith in Him that we fear not the power of sin, death, and the devil; through the same Jesus Christ, our Lord, who lives and reigns with You and the Holy Spirit, one God, now and forever. (L31)

ABC	Isaiah 62:11—63:7	1Yr.	Isaiah 62:11—63:7
	Psalm 70 (v. 5)		Psalm 70 (v. 5)
	Romans 5:6–11		Revelation 1:5b–7
	Luke 22:1—23:56		Luke 22:1—23:56
	or John 13:16–38		

Holy (Maundy) Thursday

O Lord, in this wondrous Sacrament You have left us a remembrance of Your passion. Grant that we may so receive the sacred mystery of Your body and blood that the fruits of Your redemption may continually be manifest in us; for You live and reign with the Father and the Holy Spirit, one God, now and forever. (L32)

A	Exodus 24:3–11	1Yr.	Exodus 12:1–14
	Psalm 116:12–19 (v. 17)		*or* Exodus 24:3–11
	Hebrews 9:11–22		Psalm 116:12–19 (v. 17)
	Matthew 26:17–30		1 Corinthians 11:23–32
			John 13:1–15 (34–35)

B	Exodus 24:3–11	ABC (alt.)	Exodus 12:1–14
	Psalm 116:12–19 (v. 17)		Psalm 116:12–19 (v. 17)
	1 Corinthians 10:16–17		1 Corinthians 11:23–32
	Mark 14:12–26		John 13:1–17, 31b–35

C	Jeremiah 31:31–34
	Psalm 116:12–19 (v. 17)
	Hebrews 10:15–25
	Luke 22:7–20

Good Friday

Almighty God, graciously behold this Your family for whom our
Lord Jesus Christ was willing to be betrayed and delivered into the
hands of sinful men to suffer death upon the cross; through the same
Jesus Christ, Your Son, our Lord, who lives and reigns with You and
the Holy Spirit, one God, now and forever. (L33)

ABC	Isaiah 52:13—53:12	1Yr.	Isaiah 52:13—53:12
	Psalm 22 (v. 1)		Psalm 22 (v. 1)
	or Psalm 31 (v. 1)		*or* Psalm 31 (v. 1)
	Hebrews 4:14–16; 5:7–9		2 Corinthians 5:14–21
	John 18:1—19:42		John 18:1—19:42
	or John 19:17–30		

Holy Saturday

O God, creator of heaven and earth, grant that as the crucified body
of Your dear Son was laid in the tomb and rested on this holy Sabbath, so we may await with Him the coming of the third day, and rise
with Him to newness of life, who lives and reigns with You and the
Holy Spirit, one God, now and forever. (L34)

ABC	Daniel 6:1–24	1Yr.	Daniel 6:1–24
	Psalm 16 (v. 10)		Psalm 16 (v. 10)
	1 Peter 4:1–8		1 Peter 3:17–22
	Matthew 27:57–66		Matthew 27:57–66

The Resurrection of Our Lord
Vigil of Easter

O God, You made this most holy night to shine with the glory of the
Lord's resurrection. Preserve in us the spirit of adoption which You
have given so that, made alive in body and soul, we may serve You
purely; through Jesus Christ, Your Son, our Lord, who lives and
reigns with You and the Holy Spirit, one God, now and forever. (466)

See the readings appointed in the LSB Altar Book, *pages 537–541
and page 549.*

The Resurrection of Our Lord
Easter Sunrise

Almighty God, through Your only-begotten Son, Jesus Christ, You overcame death and opened to us the gate of everlasting life. We humbly pray that we may live before You in righteousness and purity forever; through the same Jesus Christ, our Lord, who lives and reigns with You and the Holy Spirit, one God, now and forever. (L35)

A Exodus 14:10—15:1
 Psalm 118:15–29 (v. 1)
  or The Song of Moses and Israel
 1 Corinthians 15:1–11
 John 20:1–18

C Job 19:23–27
 Psalm 118:15–29 (v. 1)
 1 Corinthians 15:51–57
 John 20:1–18

B Exodus 15:1–11
 Psalm 118:15–29 (v. 1)
 1 Corinthians 5:6b–8
 John 20:1–18

1Yr. Isaiah 25:6–9
  or Exodus 14:10—15:1
 Psalm 16 (v. 11)
  or The Song of Moses and Israel
 1 Corinthians 15:1–11
  or 1 Corinthians 15:12–25
 John 20:1–18

The Resurrection of Our Lord
Easter Day

Almighty God the Father, through Your only-begotten Son, Jesus Christ, You have overcome death and opened the gate of everlasting life to us. Grant that we, who celebrate with joy the day of our Lord's resurrection, may be raised from the death of sin by Your life-giving Spirit; through Jesus Christ, our Lord, who lives and reigns with You and the Holy Spirit, one God, now and forever. (L36)

OR

O God, for our redemption You gave Your only-begotten Son to the death of the cross and by His glorious resurrection delivered us from the power of the enemy. Grant that all our sin may be drowned through daily repentance and that day by day we may arise to live be-

554

fore You in righteousness and purity forever; through Jesus Christ, our Lord, who lives and reigns with You and the Holy Spirit, one God, now and forever. (L37)

A Acts 10:34–43
  or Jeremiah 31:1–6
  Psalm 16 (v. 10)
  Colossians 3:1–4
  Matthew 28:1–10

C Isaiah 65:17–25
  Psalm 16 (v. 10)
  1 Corinthians 15:19–26
  Luke 24:1–12

B Isaiah 25:6–9
  Psalm 16 (v. 10)
  1 Corinthians 15:1–11
  Mark 16:1–8

1Yr. Job 19:23–27
  Psalm 118:15–29 (v. 1)
  1 Corinthians 5:6–8
  or 1 Corinthians 15:51–57
  Mark 16:1–8

The Resurrection of Our Lord

Easter Evening / Easter Monday

O God, in the paschal feast You restore all creation. Continue to send Your heavenly gifts upon Your people that they may walk in perfect freedom and receive eternal life; through Jesus Christ, Your Son, our Lord, who lives and reigns with You and the Holy Spirit, one God, now and forever. (L38)

ABC Exodus 15:1–18
  or Daniel 12:1c–3
  Psalm 100 (v. 5)
  Acts 10:34–43
  or 1 Corinthians 5:6b–8
  Luke 24:13–35 (36–49)

1Yr. Exodus 15:1–18
  Psalm 100 (v. 5)
  Acts 10:34–43
  Luke 24:13–35

The Resurrection of Our Lord
Easter Tuesday

Almighty God, through the resurrection of Your Son You have secured peace for our troubled consciences. Grant us this peace evermore that trusting in the merit of Your Son we may come at last to the perfect peace of heaven; through the same Jesus Christ, Your Son, our Lord, who lives and reigns with You and the Holy Spirit, one God, now and forever. (L39)

ABC		1Yr.	
	Daniel 3:8–28		Daniel 3:8–28
	Psalm 2 (v. 7)		Psalm 2 (v. 7)
	Acts 13:26–33		Acts 13:26–33
	Luke 24:36–49		Luke 24:36–48 (49)

The Resurrection of Our Lord
Easter Wednesday

Almighty God, by the glorious resurrection of Your Son, Jesus Christ, You destroyed death and brought life and immortality to light. Grant that we who have been raised with Him may abide in His presence and rejoice in the hope of eternal glory; through the same Jesus Christ, our Lord, who lives and reigns with You and the Holy Spirit, one God, now and forever. (L40)

ABC, 1Yr.	
	Acts 3:13–15, 17–19
	Psalm 61 (vv. 6–7)
	Colossians 3:1–7
	or 1 Corinthians 11:23–26
	John 21:1–14

Second Sunday of Easter

Almighty God, grant that we who have celebrated the Lord's resurrection may by Your grace confess in our life and conversation that Jesus is Lord and God; through the same Jesus Christ, Your Son, who lives and reigns with You and the Holy Spirit, one God, now and forever. (L41)

A	Acts 5:29–42	C	Acts 5:12–20 (21–32)
	Psalm 148 (v. 13)		Psalm 148 (v. 13)
	1 Peter 1:3–9		Revelation 1:4–18
	John 20:19–31		John 20:19–31
B	Acts 4:32–35	1Yr.	Ezekiel 37:1–14
	Psalm 148 (v. 13)		Psalm 33 (v. 6)
	1 John 1:1—2:2		1 John 5:4–10
	John 20:19–31		John 20:19–31

Third Sunday of Easter

O God, through the humiliation of Your Son You raised up the fallen world. Grant to Your faithful people, rescued from the peril of everlasting death, perpetual gladness and eternal joys; through Jesus Christ, our Lord, who lives and reigns with You and the Holy Spirit, one God, now and forever. (L42)

A	Acts 2:14a, 36–41	C	Acts 9:1–22
	Psalm 116:1–14 (v. 5)		Psalm 30 (vv. 11a, 12b)
	1 Peter 1:17–25		Revelation 5:(1–7) 8–14
	Luke 24:13–35		John 21:1–14 (15–19)
B	Acts 3:11–21	1Yr.	Ezekiel 34:11–16
	Psalm 4 (v. 7)		Psalm 23 (v. 6)
	1 John 3:1–7		1 Peter 2:21–25
	Luke 24:36–49		John 10:11–16

Fourth Sunday of Easter (Three-Year Lectionary)

Almighty God, merciful Father, since You have wakened from death the Shepherd of Your sheep, grant us Your Holy Spirit that when we hear the voice of our Shepherd we may know Him who calls us each by name and follow where He leads; through the same Jesus Christ, Your Son, our Lord, who lives and reigns with You and the Holy Spirit, one God, now and forever. (L43)

A	Acts 2:42–47	B	Acts 4:1–12	C	Acts 20:17–35
	Psalm 23 (v. 1)		Psalm 23 (v. 6)		Psalm 23 (v. 4)
	1 Peter 2:19–25		1 John 3:16–24		Revelation 7:9–17
	John 10:1–10		John 10:11–18		John 10:22–30

Fourth Sunday of Easter (One-Year Lectionary)

Almighty God, You show those in error the light of Your truth so that they may return to the way of righteousness. Grant faithfulness to all who are admitted into the fellowship of Christ's Church that they may avoid whatever is contrary to their confession and follow all such things as are pleasing to You; through Jesus Christ, Your Son, our Lord, who lives and reigns with You and the Holy Spirit, one God, now and forever. (L44)

1Yr.	Isaiah 40:25–31
	or Lamentations 3:22–33
	Psalm 147:1–11 (v. 5)
	1 Peter 2:11–20
	or 1 John 3:1–3
	John 16:16–22

Fifth Sunday of Easter

O God, You make the minds of Your faithful to be of one will. Grant that we may love what You have commanded and desire what You promise, that among the many changes of this world our hearts may be fixed where true joys are found; through Jesus Christ, Your Son, our Lord, who lives and reigns with You and the Holy Spirit, one God, now and forever. (L45)

A	Acts 6:1–9; 7:2a, 51–60	C	Acts 11:1–18
	Psalm 146 (v. 2)		Psalm 148 (v. 13)
	1 Peter 2:2–10		Revelation 21:1–7
	John 14:1–14		John 16:12–22
			or John 13:31–35
B	Acts 8:26–40	1Yr.	Isaiah 12:1–6
	Psalm 150 (v. 6)		Psalm 66:1–8 (v. 5)
	1 John 4:1–11 (12–21)		James 1:16–21
	John 15:1–8		John 16:5–15

Sixth Sunday of Easter

O God, the giver of all that is good, by Your holy inspiration grant that we may think those things that are right and by Your merciful guiding accomplish them; through Jesus Christ, Your Son, our Lord, who lives and reigns with You and the Holy Spirit, one God, now and forever. (L46)

A	Acts 17:16–31	C	Acts 16:9–15
	Psalm 66:8–20 (v. 8)		Psalm 67 (v. 3)
	1 Peter 3:13–22		Revelation 21:9–14, 21–27
	John 14:15–21		John 16:23–33
			or John 5:1–9
B	Acts 10:34–48	1Yr.	Numbers 21:4–9
	Psalm 98 (v. 2)		Psalm 107:1–9 (v. 19)
	1 John 5:1–8		1 Timothy 2:1–6
	John 15:9–17		*or* James 1:22–27
			John 16:23–30 (31–33)

The Ascension of Our Lord

Almighty God, as Your only-begotten Son, our Lord Jesus Christ, ascended into the heavens, so may we also ascend in heart and mind and continually dwell there with Him, who lives and reigns with You and the Holy Spirit, one God, now and forever. (L47)

ABC	Acts 1:1–11	1Yr.	2 Kings 2:5–15
	Psalm 47 (v. 5)		Psalm 110 (v. 1)
	Ephesians 1:15–23		Acts 1:1–11
	Luke 24:44–53		Mark 16:14–20
			or Luke 24:44–53

Seventh Sunday of Easter

O King of glory, Lord of hosts, uplifted in triumph far above all heavens, leave us not without consolation but send us the Spirit of truth whom You promised from the Father; for You live and reign with Him and the Holy Spirit, one God, now and forever. (L48)

A	Acts 1:12–26	C	Acts 1:12–26
	Psalm 68:1–10 (v. 32)		Psalm 133 (v. 1)
	1 Peter 4:12–19; 5:6–11		Revelation 22:1–6 (7–11) 12–20
	John 17:1–11		John 17:20–26

B	Acts 1:12–26	1Yr.	Ezekiel 36:22–28
	Psalm 1 (v. 6)		Psalm 51:1–12 (v. 10)
	1 John 5:9–15		1 Peter 4:7–11 (12–14)
	John 17:11b–19		John 15:26—16:4

Pentecost

Pentecost Eve

Almighty and ever-living God, You fulfilled Your promise by sending the gift of the Holy Spirit to unite disciples of all nations in the cross and resurrection of Your Son, Jesus Christ. By the preaching of the Gospel spread this gift to the ends of the earth; through the same Jesus Christ, our Lord, who lives and reigns with You and the Holy Spirit, one God, now and forever. (L49)

ABC	Exodus 19:1–9	1Yr.	Joel 3:1–5
	Psalm 113 (v. 3)		Psalm 85 (v. 11)
	Romans 8:12–17 (22–27)		Romans 8:12–17
	John 14:8–21		John 14:15–21

Pentecost

The Day of Pentecost

O God, on this day You once taught the hearts of Your faithful people by sending them the light of Your Holy Spirit. Grant us in our day by the same Spirit to have a right understanding in all things and evermore to rejoice in His holy consolation; through Jesus Christ,

Your Son, our Lord, who lives and reigns with You and the Holy
Spirit, one God, now and forever. (L50)

A	Numbers 11:24–30	C	Genesis 11:1–9
	Psalm 25:1–15 (v. 4)		Psalm 143 (v. 10)
	Acts 2:1–21		Acts 2:1–21
	John 7:37–39		John 14:23–31
B	Ezekiel 37:1–14	1Yr.	Genesis 11:1–9
	Psalm 139:1–12 (13–16) (v. 17)		Psalm 143 (v. 11)
	Acts 2:1–21		Acts 2:1–21
	John 15:26–27; 16:4b–15		John 14:23–31

Pentecost

Pentecost Evening / Pentecost Monday

O God, who gave Your Holy Spirit to the apostles, grant us that same
Spirit that we may live in faith and abide in peace; through Jesus
Christ, Your Son, our Lord, who lives and reigns with You and the
Holy Spirit, one God, now and forever. (L51)

ABC, 1Yr.	Isaiah 57:15–21
	Psalm 43 (v. 3)
	Acts 10:34a, 42–48
	John 3:16–21

Pentecost

Pentecost Tuesday

Almighty and ever-living God, You fulfilled Your promise by sending the gift of the Holy Spirit to unite disciples of all nations in the
cross and resurrection of Your Son, Jesus Christ. By the preaching of
the Gospel spread this gift to the ends of the earth; through the same
Jesus Christ, our Lord, who lives and reigns with You and the Holy
Spirit, one God, now and forever. (L49)

ABC	Isaiah 32:14–20	1Yr.	Isaiah 32:14–20
	Psalm 27 (v. 1)		Psalm 85 (v. 10)
	Acts 8:14–17		Acts 8:14–17
	John 10:1–10		John 10:1–10

The Time of the Church
SERIES A

The Holy Trinity

Almighty and everlasting God, You have given us grace to acknowledge the glory of the eternal Trinity by the confession of a true faith and to worship the Unity in the power of the Divine Majesty. Keep us steadfast in this faith and defend us from all adversities; for You, O Father, Son, and Holy Spirit, live and reign, one God, now and forever. (L52)

> A Genesis 1:1—2:4a
> Psalm 8 (v. 9)
> Acts 2:14a, 22–36
> Matthew 28:16–20

Sunday on May 24–28 (Proper 3)

Eternal God, You counsel us not to be anxious about earthly things. Keep alive in us a proper yearning for those heavenly treasures awaiting all who trust in Your mercy, that we may daily rejoice in Your salvation and serve You with constant devotion; through Jesus Christ, Your Son, our Lord, who lives and reigns with You and the Holy Spirit, one God, now and forever. (A61)

> A Isaiah 49:8–16a
> Psalm 115:(1–8) 9–18 (v. 1)
> Romans 1:8–17
> Matthew 6:24–34

Sunday on May 29—June 4 (Proper 4)

Lord of all power and might, author and giver of all good things, instill in our hearts the love of Your name, impress on our minds the teachings of Your Word, and increase in our lives all that is holy and just; through Jesus Christ, Your Son, our Lord, who lives and reigns with You and the Holy Spirit, one God, now and forever. (A62)

> A Deuteronomy 11:18–21, 26–28
> Psalm 4 (v. 8)
> Romans 3:21–28
> Matthew 7:15–29

Sunday on June 5–11 (Proper 5)

Almighty and most merciful God, You sent Your Son, Jesus Christ, to seek and to save the lost. Graciously open our ears and our hearts to hear His call and to follow Him by faith that we may feast with Him forever in His kingdom; through the same Jesus Christ, our Lord, who lives and reigns with You and the Holy Spirit, one God, now and forever. (A63)

A Hosea 5:15—6:6
Psalm 119:65–72 (v. 65)
Romans 4:13–25
Matthew 9:9–13

Sunday on June 12–18 (Proper 6)

Almighty, eternal God, in the Word of Your apostles and prophets You have proclaimed to us Your saving will. Grant us faith to believe Your promises that we may receive eternal salvation; through Jesus Christ, our Lord, who lives and reigns with You and the Holy Spirit, one God, now and forever. (A64)

A Exodus 19:2–8
Psalm 100 (v. 5)
Romans 5:6–15
Matthew 9:35—10:8 (9–20)

Sunday on June 19–25 (Proper 7)

O God, because Your abiding presence always goes with us, keep us aware of Your daily mercies that we may live secure and content in Your eternal love; through Jesus Christ, Your Son, our Lord, who lives and reigns with You and the Holy Spirit, one God, now and forever. (A65)

A Jeremiah 20:7–13
Psalm 91:1–10 (11–16) (v. 1)
Romans 6:12–23
Matthew 10:5a, 21–33

Sunday on June 26—July 2 (Proper 8)

Almighty God, by the working of Your Holy Spirit, grant that we may gladly hear Your Word proclaimed among us and follow its directing; through Jesus Christ, Your Son, our Lord, who lives and reigns with You and the Holy Spirit, one God, now and forever. (A66)

> A Jeremiah 28:5–9
> Psalm 119:153–160 (v. 154)
> Romans 7:1–13
> Matthew 10:34–42

Sunday on July 3–9 (Proper 9)

Gracious God, our heavenly Father, Your mercy attends us all our days. Be our strength and support amid the wearisome changes of this world, and at life's end grant us Your promised rest and the full joys of Your salvation; through Jesus Christ, Your Son, our Lord, who lives and reigns with You and the Holy Spirit, one God, now and forever. (A67)

> A Zechariah 9:9–12
> Psalm 145:1–14 (v. 19)
> Romans 7:14–25a
> Matthew 11:25–30

Sunday on July 10–16 (Proper 10)

Blessed Lord, since You have caused all Holy Scriptures to be written for our learning, grant that we may so hear them, read, mark, learn, and inwardly digest them that we may embrace and ever hold fast the blessed hope of everlasting life; through Jesus Christ, Your Son, our Lord, who lives and reigns with You and the Holy Spirit, one God, now and forever. (A68)

> A Isaiah 55:10–13
> Psalm 65:(1–8) 9–13 (v. 5)
> Romans 8:12–17
> Matthew 13:1–9, 18–23

Sunday on July 17–23 (Proper 11)

O God, so rule and govern our hearts and minds by Your Holy Spirit that, ever mindful of Your final judgment, we may be stirred up to holiness of living here and dwell with You in perfect joy hereafter; through Jesus Christ, Your Son, our Lord, who lives and reigns with You and the Holy Spirit, one God, now and forever. (A69)

> A   Isaiah 44:6–8
>   Psalm 119:57–64 (v. 89)
>   Romans 8:18–27
>   Matthew 13:24–30, 36–43

Sunday on July 24–30 (Proper 12)

Almighty and everlasting God, give us an increase of faith, hope, and love, that, receiving what You have promised, we may love what You have commanded; through Jesus Christ, Your Son, our Lord, who lives and reigns with You and the Holy Spirit, one God, now and forever. (A70)

> A   Deuteronomy 7:6–9
>   Psalm 125 (v. 2)
>   Romans 8:28–39
>   Matthew 13:44–52

Sunday on July 31—August 6 (Proper 13)

Heavenly Father, though we do not deserve Your goodness, still You provide for all our needs of body and soul. Grant us Your Holy Spirit that we may acknowledge Your gifts, give thanks for all Your benefits, and serve You in willing obedience; through Jesus Christ, Your Son, our Lord, who lives and reigns with You and the Holy Spirit, one God, now and forever. (A71)

> A   Isaiah 55:1–5
>   Psalm 136:1–9 (23–26) (v. 26)
>   Romans 9:1–5 (6–13)
>   Matthew 14:13–21

Sunday on August 7–13 (Proper 14)

Almighty and most merciful God, preserve us from all harm and danger that we, being ready in both body and soul, may cheerfully accomplish what You want done; through Jesus Christ, Your Son, our Lord, who lives and reigns with You and the Holy Spirit, one God, now and forever. (A72)

> A   Job 38:4–18
> Psalm 18:1–6 (7–16) (v. 46)
> Romans 10:5–17
> Matthew 14:22–33

Sunday on August 14–20 (Proper 15)

Almighty and everlasting Father, You give Your children many blessings even though we are undeserving. In every trial and temptation grant us steadfast confidence in Your loving-kindness and mercy; through Jesus Christ, Your Son, our Lord, who lives and reigns with You and the Holy Spirit, one God, now and forever. (A73)

> A   Isaiah 56:1, 6–8
> Psalm 67 (v. 5)
> Romans 11:1–2a, 13–15, 28–32
> Matthew 15:21–28

Sunday on August 21–27 (Proper 16)

Almighty God, whom to know is everlasting life, grant us to know Your Son, Jesus, to be the way, the truth, and the life that we may boldly confess Him to be the Christ and steadfastly walk in the way that leads to life eternal; through the same Jesus Christ, our Lord, who lives and reigns with You and the Holy Spirit, one God, now and forever. (A74)

> A   Isaiah 51:1–6
> Psalm 138 (v. 8a)
> Romans 11:33—12:8
> Matthew 16:13–20

Sunday on August 28—September 3 (Proper 17)

Almighty God, Your Son willingly endured the agony and shame of the cross for our redemption. Grant us courage to take up our cross daily and follow Him wherever He leads; through the same Jesus Christ, our Lord, who lives and reigns with You and the Holy Spirit, one God, now and forever. (A75)

> A Jeremiah 15:15–21
> Psalm 26 (v. 8)
> Romans 12:9–21
> Matthew 16:21–28

Sunday on September 4–10 (Proper 18)

O God, from whom all good proceeds, grant to us, Your humble servants, Your holy inspiration, that we may set our minds on the things that are right and, by Your merciful guiding, accomplish them; through Jesus Christ, Your Son, our Lord, who lives and reigns with You and the Holy Spirit, one God, now and forever. (A76)

> A Ezekiel 33:7–9
> Psalm 32:1–7 (v. 1)
> Romans 13:1–10
> Matthew 18:1–20

Sunday on September 11–17 (Proper 19)

O God, our refuge and strength, the author of all godliness, hear the devout prayers of Your Church, especially in times of persecution, and grant that what we ask in faith we may obtain; through Jesus Christ, our Lord, who lives and reigns with You and the Holy Spirit, one God, now and forever. (A77)

> A Genesis 50:15–21
> Psalm 103:1–12 (v. 13)
> Romans 14:1–12
> Matthew 18:21–35

Sunday on September 18–24 (Proper 20)

Lord God, heavenly Father, since we cannot stand before You relying on anything we have done, help us trust in Your abiding grace and live according to Your Word; through Jesus Christ, Your Son, our Lord, who lives and reigns with You and the Holy Spirit, one God, now and forever. (A78)

> A Isaiah 55:6–9
> Psalm 27:1–9 (v. 4a)
> Philippians 1:12–14, 19–30
> Matthew 20:1–16

Sunday on September 25—October 1 (Proper 21)

Almighty God, You exalted Your Son to the place of all honor and authority. Enlighten our minds by Your Holy Spirit that, confessing Jesus as Lord, we may be led into all truth; through the same Jesus Christ, our Lord, who lives and reigns with You and the Holy Spirit, one God, now and forever. (A79)

> A Ezekiel 18:1–4, 25–32
> Psalm 25:1–10 (v. 4)
> Philippians 2:1–4 (5–13) 14–18
> Matthew 21:23–27 (28–32)

Sunday on October 2–8 (Proper 22)

Gracious God, You gave Your Son into the hands of sinful men who killed Him. Forgive us when we reject Your unfailing love, and grant us the fullness of Your salvation; through Jesus Christ, Your Son, our Lord, who lives and reigns with You and the Holy Spirit, one God, now and forever. (A80)

> A Isaiah 5:1–7
> Psalm 80:7–19 (v. 7)
> Philippians 3:4b–14
> Matthew 21:33–46

Sunday on October 9–15 (Proper 23)

Almighty God, You invite us to trust in You for our salvation. Deal with us not in the severity of Your judgment but by the greatness of Your mercy; through Jesus Christ, Your Son, our Lord, who lives and reigns with You and the Holy Spirit, one God, now and forever. (A81)

A Isaiah 25:6–9
Psalm 23 (v. 5a)
Philippians 4:4–13
Matthew 22:1–14

Sunday on October 16–22 (Proper 24)

O God, the protector of all who trust in You, have mercy on us that with You as our ruler and guide we may so pass through things temporal that we lose not the things eternal; through Jesus Christ, Your Son, our Lord, who lives and reigns with You and the Holy Spirit, one God, now and forever. (A82)

A Isaiah 45:1–7
Psalm 96:1–9 (10–13) (v. 9a)
1 Thessalonians 1:1–10
Matthew 22:15–22

Sunday on October 23–29 (Proper 25)

O God, You have commanded us to love You above all things and our neighbors as ourselves. Grant us the Spirit to think and do what is pleasing in Your sight, that our faith in You may never waver and our love for one another may not falter; through Jesus Christ, Your Son, our Lord, who lives and reigns with You and the Holy Spirit, one God, now and forever. (A83)

A Leviticus 19:1–2, 15–18
Psalm 1 (v. 1a)
1 Thessalonians 2:1–13
Matthew 22:34–46

Sunday on October 30—November 5 (Proper 26)

Merciful and gracious Lord, You cause Your Word to be proclaimed in every generation. Stir up our hearts and minds by Your Holy Spirit that we may receive this proclamation with humility and finally be exalted at the coming of Your Son, our Savior, Jesus Christ, who lives and reigns with You and the Holy Spirit, one God, now and forever. (A84)

A Micah 3:5–12
Psalm 43 (v. 3)
1 Thessalonians 4:1–12
Matthew 23:1–12

Sunday on November 6–12 (Proper 27)

Lord God, heavenly Father, send forth Your Son to lead home His bride, the Church, that with all the company of the redeemed we may finally enter into His eternal wedding feast; through the same Jesus Christ, our Lord, who lives and reigns with You and the Holy Spirit, one God, now and forever. (A85)

A Amos 5:18–24
Psalm 70 (v. 4)
1 Thessalonians 4:13–18
Matthew 25:1–13

Sunday on November 13–19 (Proper 28)

Almighty and ever-living God, You have given exceedingly great and precious promises to those who trust in You. Dispel from us the works of darkness and grant us to live in the light of Your Son, Jesus Christ, that our faith may never be found wanting; through the same Jesus Christ, our Lord, who lives and reigns with You and the Holy Spirit, one God, now and forever. (A86)

A Zephaniah 1:7–16
Psalm 90:1–12 (v. 17)
1 Thessalonians 5:1–11
Matthew 25:14–30

Sunday on November 20–26 (Proper 29)

Eternal God, merciful Father, You have appointed Your Son as judge of the living and the dead. Enable us to wait for the day of His return with our eyes fixed on the kingdom prepared for Your own from the foundation of the world; through Jesus Christ, our Lord, who lives and reigns with You and the Holy Spirit, one God, now and forever. (A87)

A   Ezekiel 34:11–16, 20–24
       Psalm 95:1–7a (v. 7a)
       1 Corinthians 15:20–28
       Matthew 25:31–46

The Time of the Church
Series B

The Holy Trinity

Almighty and everlasting God, You have given us grace to acknowledge the glory of the eternal Trinity by the confession of a true faith and to worship the Unity in the power of the Divine Majesty. Keep us steadfast in this faith and defend us from all adversities; for You, O Father, Son, and Holy Spirit, live and reign, one God, now and forever. (L52)

> B Isaiah 6:1–8
> Psalm 29 (v. 2)
> Acts 2:14a, 22–36
> John 3:1–17

Sunday on May 24–28 (Proper 3)

Merciful Father, You have given Your only Son as the sacrifice for sinners. Grant us grace to receive the fruits of His redeeming work with thanksgiving and daily to follow in His way; through Jesus Christ, our Lord, who lives and reigns with You and the Holy Spirit, one God, now and forever. (B61)

> B Hosea 2:14–20
> Psalm 103:1–13 (v. 22)
> Acts 2:14a, 36–47
> Mark 2:(13–17) 18–22

Sunday on May 29—June 4 (Proper 4)

Eternal God, Your Son Jesus Christ is our true Sabbath rest. Help us to keep each day holy by receiving His Word of comfort that we may find our rest in Him, who lives and reigns with You and the Holy Spirit, one God, now and forever. (B62)

> B Deuteronomy 5:12–15
> Psalm 81:1–10 (v. 13)
> 2 Corinthians 4:5–12
> Mark 2:23–28 (3:1–6)

Sunday on June 5–11 (Proper 5)

Almighty and eternal God, Your Son Jesus triumphed over the prince of demons and freed us from bondage to sin. Help us to stand firm against every assault of Satan, and enable us always to do Your will; through Jesus Christ, our Lord, who lives and reigns with You and the Holy Spirit, one God, now and forever. (B63)

> B Genesis 3:8–15
> Psalm 130 (v. 7)
> 2 Corinthians 4:13—5:1
> Mark 3:20–35

Sunday on June 12–18 (Proper 6)

Blessed Lord, since You have caused all Holy Scriptures to be written for our learning, grant that we may so hear them, read, mark, learn, and inwardly digest them that we may embrace and ever hold fast the blessed hope of everlasting life; through Jesus Christ, Your Son, our Lord, who lives and reigns with You and the Holy Spirit, one God, now and forever. (B64)

> B Ezekiel 17:22–24
> Psalm 1 (v. 6)
> 2 Corinthians 5:1–10 (11–17)
> Mark 4:26–34

Sunday on June 19–25 (Proper 7)

Almighty God, in Your mercy guide the course of this world so that Your Church may joyfully serve You in godly peace and quietness; through Jesus Christ, Your Son, our Lord, who lives and reigns with You and the Holy Spirit, one God, now and forever. (B65)

> B Job 38:1–11
> Psalm 124 (v. 8)
> 2 Corinthians 6:1–13
> Mark 4:35–41

Sunday on June 26—July 2 (Proper 8)

Heavenly Father, during His earthly ministry Your Son Jesus healed the sick and raised the dead. By the healing medicine of the Word and Sacraments pour into our hearts such love toward You that we may live eternally; through the same Jesus Christ, our Lord, who lives and reigns with You and the Holy Spirit, one God, now and forever. (B66)

B Lamentations 3:22–33
Psalm 30 (v. 10)
2 Corinthians 8:1–9, 13–15
Mark 5:21–43

Sunday on July 3–9 (Proper 9)

O God, Your almighty power is made known chiefly in showing mercy. Grant us the fullness of Your grace that we may be called to repentance and made partakers of Your heavenly treasures; through Your Son, Jesus Christ, our Lord, who lives and reigns with You and the Holy Spirit, one God, now and forever. (B67)

B Ezekiel 2:1–5
Psalm 123 (v. 1)
2 Corinthians 12:1–10
Mark 6:1–13

Sunday on July 10–16 (Proper 10)

O Lord, You granted Your prophets strength to resist the temptations of the devil and courage to proclaim repentance. Give us pure hearts and minds to follow Your Son faithfully even into suffering and death; through the same Jesus Christ, our Lord, who lives and reigns with You and the Holy Spirit, one God, now and forever. (B68)

B Amos 7:7–15
Psalm 85:(1–7) 8–13 (v. 7)
Ephesians 1:3–14
Mark 6:14–29

Sunday on July 17–23 (Proper 11)

Heavenly Father, though we do not deserve Your goodness, still You provide for all our needs of body and soul. Grant us Your Holy Spirit that we may acknowledge Your gifts, give thanks for all Your benefits, and serve You in willing obedience; through Jesus Christ, Your Son, our Lord, who lives and reigns with You and the Holy Spirit, one God, now and forever. (B69)

B Jeremiah 23:1–6
Psalm 23 (v. 6)
Ephesians 2:11–22
Mark 6:30–44

Sunday on July 24–30 (Proper 12)

Almighty and most merciful God, the protector of all who trust in You, strengthen our faith and give us courage to believe that in Your love You will rescue us from all adversities; through Jesus Christ, Your Son, our Lord, who lives and reigns with You and the Holy Spirit, one God, now and forever. (B70)

B Genesis 9:8–17
Psalm 136:1–9 (v. 26)
Ephesians 3:14–21
Mark 6:45–56

Sunday on July 31—August 6 (Proper 13)

Merciful Father, You gave Your Son Jesus as the heavenly bread of life. Grant us faith to feast on Him in Your Word and Sacraments that we may be nourished unto life everlasting; through the same Jesus Christ, our Lord, who lives and reigns with You and the Holy Spirit, one God, now and forever. (B71)

B Exodus 16:2–15
Psalm 145:10–21 (v. 15)
Ephesians 4:1–16
John 6:22–35

Sunday on August 7–13 (Proper 14)

Gracious Father, Your blessed Son came down from heaven to be the true bread that gives life to the world. Grant that Christ, the bread of life, may live in us and we in Him, who lives and reigns with You and the Holy Spirit, one God, now and forever. (B72)

> B   1 Kings 19:1–8
> Psalm 34:1–8 (v. 3)
> Ephesians 4:17—5:2
> John 6:35–51

Sunday on August 14–20 (Proper 15)

Almighty God, whom to know is everlasting life, grant us to know Your Son, Jesus, to be the way, the truth, and the life, that we may steadfastly follow His steps in the way that leads to life eternal; through Jesus Christ, our Lord, who lives and reigns with You and the Holy Spirit, one God, now and forever. (B73)

> B   Proverbs 9:1–10
> *or* Joshua 24:1–2a, 14–18
> Psalm 34:12–22 (v. 11)
> Ephesians 5:6–21
> John 6:51–69

Sunday on August 21–27 (Proper 16)

Almighty and merciful God, defend Your Church from all false teaching and error that Your faithful people may confess You to be the only true God and rejoice in Your good gifts of life and salvation; through Jesus Christ, Your Son, our Lord, who lives and reigns with You and the Holy Spirit, one God, now and forever. (B74)

> B   Isaiah 29:11–19
> Psalm 14 (v. 7a)
> Ephesians 5:22–33
> Mark 7:1–13

Sunday on August 28—September 3 (Proper 17)

O God, the source of all that is just and good, nourish in us every virtue and bring to completion every good intent that we may grow in grace and bring forth the fruit of good works; through Jesus Christ, Your Son, our Lord, who lives and reigns with You and the Holy Spirit, one God, now and forever. (B75)

> B   Deuteronomy 4:1–2, 6–9
> Psalm 119:129–136 (v. 132)
> Ephesians 6:10–20
> Mark 7:14–23

Sunday on September 4–10 (Proper 18)

O Lord, let Your merciful ears be open to the prayers of Your humble servants and grant that what they ask may be in accord with Your gracious will; through Jesus Christ, Your Son, our Lord, who lives and reigns with You and the Holy Spirit, one God, now and forever. (B76)

> B   Isaiah 35:4–7a
> Psalm 146 (v. 2)
> James 2:1–10, 14–18
> Mark 7:(24–30) 31–37

Sunday on September 11–17 (Proper 19)

Lord Jesus Christ, our support and defense in every need, continue to preserve Your Church in safety, govern her by Your goodness, and bless her with Your peace; for You live and reign with the Father and the Holy Spirit, one God, now and forever. (B77)

> B   Isaiah 50:4–10
> Psalm 116:1–9 (v. 5)
> James 3:1–12
> Mark 9:14–29

Sunday on September 18–24 (Proper 20)

O God, whose strength is made perfect in weakness, grant us humility and childlike faith that we may please You in both will and deed; through Jesus Christ, Your Son, our Lord, who lives and reigns with You and the Holy Spirit, one God, now and forever. (B78)

> B Jeremiah 11:18–20
> Psalm 54 (v. 4)
> James 3:13—4:10
> Mark 9:30–37

Sunday on September 25—October 1 (Proper 21)

Everlasting Father, source of every blessing, mercifully direct and govern us by Your Holy Spirit that we may complete the works You have prepared for us to do; through Jesus Christ, Your Son, our Lord, who lives and reigns with You and the Holy Spirit, one God, now and forever. (B79)

> B Numbers 11:4–6, 10–16, 24–29
> Psalm 104:27–35 (v. 24)
> James 5:(1–12) 13–20
> Mark 9:38–50

Sunday on October 2–8 (Proper 22)

Merciful Father, Your patience and loving-kindness toward us have no end. Grant that by Your Holy Spirit we may always think and do those things that are pleasing in Your sight; through Jesus Christ, Your Son, our Lord, who lives and reigns with You and the Holy Spirit, one God, now and forever. (B80)

> B Genesis 2:18–25
> Psalm 128 (v. 1)
> Hebrews 2:1–13 (14–18)
> Mark 10:2–16

Sunday on October 9–15 (Proper 23)

Lord Jesus Christ, whose grace always precedes and follows us, help us to forsake all trust in earthly gain and to find in You our heavenly treasure; for You live and reign with the Father and the Holy Spirit, one God, now and forever. (B81)

> B Amos 5:6–7, 10–15
> Psalm 90:12–17 (v. 1)
> Hebrews 3:12–19
> Mark 10:17–22

Sunday on October 16–22 (Proper 24)

O God, Your divine wisdom sets in order all things in heaven and on earth. Put away from us all things hurtful and give us those things that are beneficial for us; through Jesus Christ, Your Son, our Lord, who lives and reigns with You and the Holy Spirit, one God, now and forever. (B82)

> B Ecclesiastes 5:10–20
> Psalm 119:9–16 (v. 14)
> Hebrews 4:1–13 (14–16)
> Mark 10:23–31

Sunday on October 23–29 (Proper 25)

O God, the helper of all who call on You, have mercy on us and give us eyes of faith to see Your Son that we may follow Him on the way that leads to eternal life; through the same Jesus Christ, Your Son, our Lord, who lives and reigns with You and the Holy Spirit, one God, now and forever. (B83)

> B Jeremiah 31:7–9
> Psalm 126 (v. 5)
> Hebrews 7:23–28
> Mark 10:46–52

Sunday on October 30—November 5 (Proper 26)

Lord Jesus Christ, our great High Priest, cleanse us by the power of Your redeeming blood that in purity and peace we may worship and adore Your holy name; for You live and reign with the Father and the Holy Spirit, one God, now and forever. (B84)

> B Deuteronomy 6:1–9
> Psalm 119:1–8 (v. 5)
> Hebrews 9:11–14 (15–22)
> Mark 12:28–37

Sunday on November 6–12 (Proper 27)

Almighty and ever-living God, You have given exceedingly great and precious promises to those who trust in You. Grant us so firmly to believe in Your Son Jesus that our faith may never be found wanting; through the same Jesus Christ, our Lord, who lives and reigns with You and the Holy Spirit, one God, now and forever. (B85)

> B 1 Kings 17:8–16
> Psalm 146 (v. 9a)
> Hebrews 9:24–28
> Mark 12:38–44

Sunday on November 13–19 (Proper 28)

O Lord, by Your bountiful goodness release us from the bonds of our sins, which by reason of our weakness we have brought upon ourselves, that we may stand firm until the day of our Lord Jesus Christ, who lives and reigns with You and the Holy Spirit, one God, now and forever. (B86)

> B Daniel 12:1–3
> Psalm 16 (v. 11b, c)
> Hebrews 10:11–25
> Mark 13:1–13

Sunday on November 20–26 (Proper 29)

Lord Jesus Christ, so govern our hearts and minds by Your Holy Spirit that, ever mindful of Your glorious return, we may persevere in both faith and holiness of living; for You live and reign with the Father and the Holy Spirit, one God, now and forever. (B87)

B Isaiah 51:4–6
   Psalm 93 (v. 2)
   Jude 20–25
   Mark 13:24–37

   OR

   Daniel 7:9–10, 13–14
   Psalm 93 (v. 2)
   Revelation 1:4b–8
   John 18:33–37

The Time of the Church
Series C

The Holy Trinity

Almighty and everlasting God, You have given us grace to acknowledge the glory of the eternal Trinity by the confession of a true faith and to worship the Unity in the power of the Divine Majesty. Keep us steadfast in this faith and defend us from all adversities; for You, O Father, Son, and Holy Spirit, live and reign, one God, now and forever. (L52)

> C   Proverbs 8:1–4, 22–31
> Psalm 8 (v. 9)
> Acts 2:14a, 22–36
> John 8:48–59

Sunday on May 24–28 (Proper 3)

Almighty God, in Your mercy so guide the course of this world that we may forgive as we have been forgiven and joyfully serve You in godly peace and quietness; through Jesus Christ, Your Son, our Lord, who lives and reigns with You and the Holy Spirit, one God, now and forever. (C61)

> C   Genesis 50:15–21
> Psalm 112:1–9 (v. 1)
> Acts 2:14a, 36– 47
> Luke 6:(20–26) 27– 42

Sunday on May 29—June 4 (Proper 4)

O God, by Your almighty Word You set in order all things in heaven and on earth. Put away from us all things hurtful, and give us those things that are beneficial for us; through Jesus Christ, Your Son, our Lord, who lives and reigns with You and the Holy Spirit, one God, now and forever. (C62)

> C   1 Kings 8:22–24, 27–29, 41– 43
> Psalm 96:1–9 (v. 2)
> Galatians 1:1–12
> Luke 7:1–10

Sunday on June 5–11 (Proper 5)

O Lord, Father of all mercy and God of all comfort, You always go before and follow after us. Grant that we may rejoice in Your gracious presence and continually be given to all good works; through Jesus Christ, Your Son, our Lord, who lives and reigns with You and the Holy Spirit, one God, now and forever. (C63)

C   1 Kings 17:17–24
Psalm 30 (v. 5b)
Galatians 1:11–24
Luke 7:11–17

Sunday on June 12–18 (Proper 6)

Almighty and everlasting God, increase in us Your gifts of faith, hope, and love that we may receive the forgiveness You have promised and love what You have commanded; through Jesus Christ, Your Son, our Lord, who lives and reigns with You and the Holy Spirit, one God, now and forever. (C64)

C   2 Samuel 11:26—12:10, 13–14
Psalm 32:1–7 (v. 5)
Galatians 2:15–21; 3:10–14
Luke 7:36—8:3

Sunday on June 19–25 (Proper 7)

O God, You have prepared for those who love You such good things as surpass our understanding. Cast out all sins and evil desires from us, and pour into our hearts Your Holy Spirit to guide us into all blessedness; through Jesus Christ, Your Son, our Lord, who lives and reigns with You and the Holy Spirit, one God, now and forever. (C65)

C   Isaiah 65:1–9
Psalm 3 (v. 8)
Galatians 3:23— 4:7
Luke 8:26 –39

Sunday on June 26—July 2 (Proper 8)

Lord of all power and might, author and giver of all good things, graft into our hearts the love of Your name and nourish us with all goodness that we may love and serve our neighbor; through Jesus Christ, Your Son, our Lord, who lives and reigns with You and the Holy Spirit, one God, now and forever. (C66)

> C 1 Kings 19:9b –21
> Psalm 16 (v. 11)
> Galatians 5:1, 13–25
> Luke 9:51–62

Sunday on July 3–9 (Proper 9)

Almighty God, You have built Your Church on the foundation of the apostles and prophets with Christ Jesus Himself as the cornerstone. Continue to send Your messengers to preserve Your people in true peace that, by the preaching of Your Word, Your Church may be kept free from all harm and danger; through Jesus Christ, Your Son, our Lord, who lives and reigns with You and the Holy Spirit, one God, now and forever. (C67)

> C Isaiah 66:10–14
> Psalm 66:1–7 (vv. 8–9)
> Galatians 6:1–10, 14 –18
> Luke 10:1–20

Sunday on July 10–16 (Proper 10)

Lord Jesus Christ, in Your deep compassion You rescue us from whatever may hurt us. Teach us to love You above all things and to love our neighbors as ourselves; for You live and reign with the Father and the Holy Spirit, one God, now and forever. (C68)

> C Leviticus (18:1–5) 19:9–18
> Psalm 41 (v. 1)
> Colossians 1:1–14
> Luke 10:25–37

Sunday on July 17–23 (Proper 11)

O Lord, grant us the Spirit to hear Your Word and know the one thing needful that by Your Word and Spirit we may live according to Your will; through Jesus Christ, Your Son, our Lord, who lives and reigns with You and the Holy Spirit, one God, now and forever. (C69)

C Genesis 18:1–10a (10b–14)
Psalm 27:(1–6) 7–14 (v. 4)
Colossians 1:21–29
Luke 10:38–42

Sunday on July 24–30 (Proper 12)

O Lord, let Your merciful ears be attentive to the prayers of Your servants, and by Your Word and Spirit teach us how to pray that our petitions may be pleasing before You; through Jesus Christ, Your Son, our Lord, who lives and reigns with You and the Holy Spirit, one God, now and forever. (C70)

C Genesis 18:(17–19) 20 –33
Psalm 138 (v. 3)
Colossians 2:6 –15 (16 –19)
Luke 11:1–13

Sunday on July 31—August 6 (Proper 13)

O Lord, grant us wisdom to recognize the treasures You have stored up for us in heaven, that we may never despair but always rejoice and be thankful for the riches of Your grace; through Jesus Christ, Your Son, our Lord, who lives and reigns with You and the Holy Spirit, one God, now and forever. (C71)

C Ecclesiastes 1:2, 12–14; 2:18–26
Psalm 100 (v. 3)
Colossians 3:1–11
Luke 12:13–21

Sunday on August 7–13 (Proper 14)

Almighty and merciful God, it is by Your grace that we live as Your people who offer acceptable service. Grant that we may walk by faith, and not by sight, in the way that leads to eternal life; through Jesus Christ, Your Son, our Lord, who lives and reigns with You and the Holy Spirit, one God, now and forever. (C72)

> C Genesis 15:1–6
> Psalm 33:12–22 (v. 20)
> Hebrews 11:1–16
> Luke 12:22–34 (35– 40)

Sunday on August 14–20 (Proper 15)

Merciful Lord, cleanse and defend Your Church by the sacrifice of Christ. United with Him in Holy Baptism, give us grace to receive with thanksgiving the fruits of His redeeming work and daily follow in His way; through the same Jesus Christ, Your Son, our Lord, who lives and reigns with You and the Holy Spirit, one God, now and forever. (C73)

> C Jeremiah 23:16 –29
> Psalm 119:81–88 (v. 81)
> Hebrews 11:17–31 (32–40); 12:1–3
> Luke 12:49–53 (54 –56)

Sunday on August 21–27 (Proper 16)

O Lord, You have called us to enter Your kingdom through the narrow door. Guide us by Your Word and Spirit, and lead us now and always into the feast of Your Son, Jesus Christ, who lives and reigns with You and the Holy Spirit, one God, now and forever. (C74)

> C Isaiah 66:18–23
> Psalm 50:1–15 (v. 23)
> Hebrews 12:4–24 (25–29)
> Luke 13:22–30

Sunday on August 28—September 3 (Proper 17)

O Lord of grace and mercy, teach us by Your Holy Spirit to follow the example of Your Son in true humility, that we may withstand the temptations of the devil and with pure hearts and minds avoid ungodly pride; through the same Jesus Christ, our Lord, who lives and reigns with You and the Holy Spirit, one God, now and forever. (C75)

> C Proverbs 25:2–10
> Psalm 131 (v. 2)
> Hebrews 13:1–17
> Luke 14:1–14

Sunday on September 4–10 (Proper 18)

O merciful Lord, You did not spare Your only Son but delivered Him up for us all. Grant us courage and strength to take up the cross and follow Him, who lives and reigns with You and the Holy Spirit, one God, now and forever. (C76)

> C Deuteronomy 30:15–20
> Psalm 1 (v. 6)
> Philemon 1–21
> Luke 14:25–35

Sunday on September 11–17 (Proper 19)

Lord Jesus, You are the Good Shepherd, without whom nothing is secure. Rescue and preserve us that we may not be lost forever but follow You, rejoicing in the way that leads to eternal life; for You live and reign with the Father and the Holy Spirit, one God, now and forever. (C77)

> C Ezekiel 34:11–24
> Psalm 119:169–176 (v. 176)
> 1 Timothy 1:(5–11) 12–17
> Luke 15:1–10

Sunday on September 18–24 (Proper 20)

O Lord, keep Your Church in Your perpetual mercy; and because without You we cannot but fall, preserve us from all things hurtful, and lead us to all things profitable to our salvation; through Jesus Christ, Your Son, our Lord, who lives and reigns with You and the Holy Spirit, one God, now and forever. (C78)

C Amos 8:4 –7
Psalm 113 (v. 3)
1 Timothy 2:1–15
Luke 16:1–15

Sunday on September 25—October 1 (Proper 21)

O God, You are the strength of all who trust in You, and without Your aid we can do no good thing. Grant us the help of Your grace that we may please You in both will and deed; through Jesus Christ, Your Son, our Lord, who lives and reigns with You and the Holy Spirit, one God, now and forever. (C79)

C Amos 6:1–7
Psalm 146 (v. 2)
1 Timothy 3:1–13
 or 1 Timothy 6:6 –19
Luke 16:19–31

Sunday on October 2–8 (Proper 22)

O God, our refuge and strength, the author of all godliness, by Your grace hear the prayers of Your Church. Grant that those things which we ask in faith we may receive through Your bountiful mercy; through Jesus Christ, Your Son, our Lord, who lives and reigns with You and the Holy Spirit, one God, now and forever. (C80)

C Habakkuk 1:1– 4; 2:1– 4
Psalm 62 (v. 1)
2 Timothy 1:1–14
Luke 17:1–10

Sunday on October 9–15 (Proper 23)

Almighty God, You show mercy to Your people in all their troubles. Grant us always to recognize Your goodness, give thanks for Your compassion, and praise Your holy name; through Jesus Christ, Your Son, our Lord, who lives and reigns with You and the Holy Spirit, one God, now and forever. (C81)

C   Ruth 1:1–19a
Psalm 111 (v. 10)
2 Timothy 2:1–13
Luke 17:11–19

Sunday on October 16–22 (Proper 24)

O Lord, almighty and everlasting God, You have commanded us to pray and have promised to hear us. Mercifully grant that Your Holy Spirit may direct and govern our hearts in all things that we may persevere with steadfast faith in the confession of Your name; through Jesus Christ, Your Son, our Lord, who lives and reigns with You and the Holy Spirit, one God, now and forever. (C82)

C   Genesis 32:22–30
Psalm 121 (vv. 1–2)
2 Timothy 3:14 — 4:5
Luke 18:1–8

Sunday on October 23–29 (Proper 25)

Almighty and everlasting God, You are always more ready to hear than we to pray and always ready to give more than we either desire or deserve. Pour down on us the abundance of Your mercy; forgive us those things of which our conscience is afraid; and give us those good things for which we are not worthy to ask except by the merits and mediation of Jesus Christ, Your Son, our Lord, who lives and reigns with You and the Holy Spirit, one God, now and forever. (C83)

C   Genesis 4:1–15
Psalm 5 (v. 11a)
2 Timothy 4:6–8, 16 –18
Luke 18:9–17

Sunday on October 30—November 5 (Proper 26)

O Lord, stir up the hearts of Your faithful people to welcome and joyfully receive Your Son, our Savior, Jesus Christ, that He may find in us a fit dwelling place; who lives and reigns with You and the Holy Spirit, one God, now and forever. (C84)

> C Isaiah 1:10–18
> Psalm 130 (vv. 3– 4)
> 2 Thessalonians 1:1–5 (6 –10) 11–12
> Luke 19:1–10

Sunday on November 6–12 (Proper 27)

Living God, Your almighty power is made known chiefly in showing mercy and pity. Grant us the fullness of Your grace to lay hold of Your promises and live forever in Your presence; through Jesus Christ, Your Son, our Lord, who lives and reigns with You and the Holy Spirit, one God, now and forever. (C85)

> C Exodus 3:1–15
> Psalm 148 (v. 13)
> 2 Thessalonians 2:1–8, 13–17
> Luke 20:27– 40

Sunday on November 13–19 (Proper 28)

O Lord, almighty and ever-living God, You have given exceedingly great and precious promises to those who trust in You. Rule and govern our hearts and minds by Your Holy Spirit that we may live and abide forever in Your Son, who lives and reigns with You and the Holy Spirit, one God, now and forever. (C86)

> C Malachi 4:1–6
> Psalm 98 (v. 9b)
> 2 Thessalonians 3:(1–5) 6–13
> Luke 21:5–28 (29–36)

Sunday on November 20–26 (Proper 29)

Lord Jesus Christ, You reign among us by the preaching of Your cross. Forgive Your people their offenses that we, being governed by Your bountiful goodness, may enter at last into Your eternal paradise; for You live and reign with the Father and the Holy Spirit, one God, now and forever. (C87)

C   Malachi 3:13–18
Psalm 46 (v. 7)
Colossians 1:13–20
Luke 23:27– 43

The Time of the Church
ONE-YEAR LECTIONARY

The Holy Trinity

Almighty and everlasting God, You have given us grace to acknowledge the glory of the eternal Trinity by the confession of a true faith and to worship the Unity in the power of the Divine Majesty. Keep us steadfast in this faith and defend us from all adversities; for You, O Father, Son, and Holy Spirit, live and reign, one God, now and forever. (L52)

> 1Yr.   Isaiah 6:1–7
> Psalm 29 (v. 2)
> Romans 11:33–36
> John 3:1–15 (16–17)

First Sunday after Trinity

O God, the strength of all who trust in You, mercifully accept our prayers; and because through the weakness of our mortal nature we can do no good thing, grant us Your grace to keep Your commandments that we may please You in both will and deed; through Jesus Christ, our Lord, who lives and reigns with You and the Holy Spirit, one God, now and forever. (H61)

> 1Yr.   Genesis 15:1–6
> Psalm 33:12–22 (v. 20)
> 1 John 4:16–21
> Luke 16:19–31

Second Sunday after Trinity

O Lord, since You never fail to help and govern those whom You nurture in Your steadfast fear and love, work in us a perpetual fear and love of Your holy name; through Jesus Christ, our Lord, who lives and reigns with You and the Holy Spirit, one God, now and forever. (H62)

1Yr. Proverbs 9:1–10
      Psalm 34:12–22 (v. 11)
      Ephesians 2:13–22
        or 1 John 3:13–18
      Luke 14:15–24

Third Sunday after Trinity

O God, the protector of all who trust in You, without whom nothing is strong and nothing is holy, multiply Your mercy on us that, with You as our ruler and guide, we may so pass through things temporal that we lose not the things eternal; through Jesus Christ, our Lord, who lives and reigns with You and the Holy Spirit, one God, now and forever. (H63)

1Yr. Micah 7:18–20
      Psalm 103:1–13 (v. 8)
      1 Timothy 1:12–17
        or 1 Peter 5:6–11
      Luke 15:1–10
        or Luke 15:11–32

Fourth Sunday after Trinity

O Lord, grant that the course of this world may be so peaceably ordered by Your governance that Your Church may joyfully serve You in all godly quietness; through Jesus Christ, our Lord, who lives and reigns with You and the Holy Spirit, one God, now and forever. (H64)

1Yr. Genesis 50:15–21
      Psalm 138 (v. 8b)
      Romans 12:14–21
        or Romans 8:18–23
      Luke 6:36–42

Fifth Sunday after Trinity

O God, You have prepared for those who love You good things that surpass all understanding. Pour into our hearts such love toward You that we, loving You above all things, may obtain Your promises, which exceed all that we can desire; through Jesus Christ, Your Son, our Lord, who lives and reigns with You and the Holy Spirit, one God, now and forever. (H65)

1Yr. 1 Kings 19:11–21
Psalm 16 (v. 11)
1 Corinthians 1:18–25
 or 1 Peter 3:8–15
Luke 5:1–11

Sixth Sunday after Trinity

Lord of all power and might, author and giver of all good things, graft into our hearts the love of Your name, increase in us true religion, nourish us with all goodness, and of Your great mercy keep us in the same; through Jesus Christ, Your Son, our Lord, who lives and reigns with You and the Holy Spirit, one God, now and forever. (H66)

1Yr. Exodus 20:1–17
Psalm 19 (v. 8)
Romans 6:(1–2) 3–11
Matthew 5:(17–19) 20–26

Seventh Sunday after Trinity

O God, whose never-failing providence orders all things both in heaven and earth, we humbly implore You to put away from us all hurtful things and to give us those things that are profitable for us; through Jesus Christ, Your Son, our Lord, who lives and reigns with You and the Holy Spirit, one God, now and forever. (H67)

1Yr. Genesis 2:7–17
Psalm 33:1–11 (v. 6)
Romans 6:19–23
Mark 8:1–9

Eighth Sunday after Trinity

Grant to us, Lord, the Spirit to think and do always such things as are right, that we, who cannot do anything that is good without You, may be enabled by You to live according to Your will; through Jesus Christ, Your Son, our Lord, who lives and reigns with You and the Holy Spirit, one God, now and forever. (H68)

> 1Yr. Jeremiah 23:16–29
> Psalm 26 (v. 12)
> Acts 20:27–38
>   *or* Romans 8:12–17
> Matthew 7:15–23

Ninth Sunday after Trinity

Let Your merciful ears, O Lord, be open to the prayers of Your humble servants; and that they may obtain their petitions, make them to ask such things as shall please You; through Jesus Christ, Your Son, our Lord, who lives and reigns with You and the Holy Spirit, one God, now and forever. (H69)

> 1Yr. 2 Samuel 22:26–34
> Psalm 51:1–12 (v. 18)
> 1 Corinthians 10:6–13
> Luke 16:1–9 (10–13)

Tenth Sunday after Trinity

O God, You declare Your almighty power above all in showing mercy and pity. Mercifully grant us such a measure of Your grace that we may obtain Your gracious promises and be made partakers of Your heavenly treasures; through Jesus Christ, Your Son, our Lord, who lives and reigns with You and the Holy Spirit, one God, now and forever. (H70)

> 1Yr. Jeremiah 8:4–12
>   *or* Jeremiah 7:1–11
> Psalm 92 (v. 4)
> Romans 9:30—10:4
>   *or* 1 Corinthians 12:1–11
> Luke 19:41–48

Eleventh Sunday after Trinity

Almighty and everlasting God, always more ready to hear than we to pray and to give more than we either desire or deserve, pour down upon us the abundance of Your mercy, forgiving those things of which our conscience is afraid and giving us those good things that we are not worthy to ask, except through the merits and mediation of Christ, our Lord, who lives and reigns with You and the Holy Spirit, one God, now and forever. (H71)

1Yr. Genesis 4:1–15
Psalm 50:7–23 (v. 14)
Ephesians 2:1–10
 or 1 Corinthians 15:1–10
Luke 18:9–14

Twelfth Sunday after Trinity

Almighty and merciful God, by Your gift alone Your faithful people render true and laudable service. Help us steadfastly to live in this life according to Your promises and finally attain Your heavenly glory; through Jesus Christ, Your Son, our Lord, who lives and reigns with You and the Holy Spirit, one God, now and forever. (H72)

1Yr. Isaiah 29:17–24
Psalm 146 (v. 8)
2 Corinthians 3:4–11
 or Romans 10:9–17
Mark 7:31–37

Thirteenth Sunday after Trinity

Almighty and everlasting God, give us an increase of faith, hope, and charity; and that we may obtain what You have promised, make us love what You have commanded; through Jesus Christ, Your Son, our Lord, who lives and reigns with You and the Holy Spirit, one God, now and forever. (H73)

1Yr.   2 Chronicles 28:8–15
       Psalm 32 (v. 2)
       Galatians 3:15–22
       Luke 10:23–37

Fourteenth Sunday after Trinity

O Lord, keep Your Church with Your perpetual mercy; and because of our frailty we cannot but fall, keep us ever by Your help from all things hurtful and lead us to all things profitable to our salvation; through Jesus Christ, Your Son, our Lord, who lives and reigns with You and the Holy Spirit, one God, now and forever. (H74)

1Yr.   Proverbs 4:10–23
       Psalm 119:9–16 (v. 12)
       Galatians 5:16–24
       Luke 17:11–19

Fifteenth Sunday after Trinity

O Lord, we implore You, let Your continual pity cleanse and defend Your Church; and because she cannot continue in safety without Your aid, preserve her evermore by Your help and goodness; through Jesus Christ, Your Son, our Lord, who lives and reigns with You and the Holy Spirit, one God, now and forever. (H75)

1Yr.   1 Kings 17:8–16
       Psalm 146 (v. 9a)
       Galatians 5:25—6:10
       Matthew 6:24–34

Sixteenth Sunday after Trinity

O Lord, we pray that Your grace may always go before and follow after us, that we may continually be given to all good works; through Jesus Christ, Your Son, our Lord, who lives and reigns with You and the Holy Spirit, one God, now and forever. (H76)

1Yr.   1 Kings 17:17–24
       Psalm 30 (v. 5b)
       Ephesians 3:13–21
       Luke 7:11–17

Seventeenth Sunday after Trinity

Lord, we implore You, grant Your people grace to withstand the temptations of the devil and with pure hearts and minds to follow You, the only God; through Jesus Christ, Your Son, our Lord, who lives and reigns with You and the Holy Spirit, one God, now and forever. (H77)

1Yr. Proverbs 25:6–14
Psalm 2 (v. 11)
Ephesians 4:1–6
Luke 14:1–11

Eighteenth Sunday after Trinity

O God, because without You we are not able to please You, mercifully grant that Your Holy Spirit may in all things direct and rule our hearts; through Jesus Christ, Your Son, our Lord, who lives and reigns with You and the Holy Spirit, one God, now and forever. (H78)

1Yr. Deuteronomy 10:12–21
Psalm 34:8–22 (v. 19)
1 Corinthians 1:(1–3) 4–9
Matthew 22:34–46

Nineteenth Sunday after Trinity

Almighty and merciful God, of Your bountiful goodness keep from us all things that may hurt us that we, being ready in both body and soul, may cheerfully accomplish whatever You would have us do; through Jesus Christ, Your Son, our Lord, who lives and reigns with You and the Holy Spirit, one God, now and forever. (H79)

1Yr. Genesis 28:10–17
Psalm 84 (v. 8)
Ephesians 4:22–28
Matthew 9:1–8

Twentieth Sunday after Trinity

O Lord, grant to Your faithful people pardon and peace that they may be cleansed from all their sins and serve You with a quiet mind; through Jesus Christ, Your Son, our Lord, who lives and reigns with You and the Holy Spirit, one God, now and forever. (H80)

> 1 Yr. Isaiah 55:1–9
> Psalm 27:1–9 (v. 8)
> Ephesians 5:15–21
> Matthew 22:1–14
> *or* Matthew 21:33–44

Twenty-first Sunday after Trinity

O Lord, keep Your household, the Church, in continual godliness that through Your protection she may be free from all adversities and devoutly given to serve You in good works; through Jesus Christ, Your Son, our Lord, who lives and reigns with You and the Holy Spirit, one God, now and forever. (H81)

> 1 Yr. Genesis 1:1—2:3
> Psalm 8 (v. 9)
> Ephesians 6:10–17
> John 4:46–54

Twenty-second Sunday after Trinity

O God, our refuge and strength, the author of all godliness, hear the devout prayers of Your Church, especially in times of persecution, and grant that what we ask in faith we may obtain; through Jesus Christ, Your Son, our Lord, who lives and reigns with You and the Holy Spirit, one God, now and forever. (H82)

> 1 Yr. Micah 6:6–8
> Psalm 116:12–19 (v. 13)
> Philippians 1:3–11
> Matthew 18:21–35

Twenty-third Sunday after Trinity

O Lord, absolve Your people from their offenses that from the bonds of our sins, which by reason of our frailty we have brought upon ourselves, we may be delivered by Your bountiful goodness; through Jesus Christ, Your Son, our Lord, who lives and reigns with You and the Holy Spirit, one God, now and forever. (H83)

> 1Yr. Proverbs 8:11–22
> Psalm 111 (v. 10a)
> Philippians 3:17–21
> Matthew 22:15–22

Twenty-fourth Sunday after Trinity

Stir up, O Lord, the wills of Your faithful people that they, plenteously bringing forth the fruit of good works, may by You be plenteously rewarded; through Jesus Christ, Your Son, our Lord, who lives and reigns with You and the Holy Spirit, one God, now and forever. (H84)

> 1Yr. Isaiah 51:9–16
> Psalm 126 (v. 1)
> Colossians 1:9–14
> Matthew 9:18–26

Twenty-fifth Sunday after Trinity

Almighty God, we implore You, show Your mercy to Your humble servants that we, who put no trust in our own merits, may not be dealt with after the severity of Your judgment but according to Your mercy; through Jesus Christ, Your Son, our Lord, who lives and reigns with You and the Holy Spirit, one God, now and forever. (H85)

> 1Yr. Exodus 32:1–20
> *or* Job 14:1–6
> Psalm 14 (v. 7)
> *or* Psalm 102:1–13 (v. 12)
> 1 Thessalonians 4:13–18
> Matthew 24:15–28
> *or* Luke 17:20–30

Twenty-sixth Sunday after Trinity

O Lord, so rule and govern our hearts and minds by Your Holy Spirit that, ever mindful of the end of all things and the day of Your just judgment, we may be stirred up to holiness of living here and dwell with You forever hereafter; through Jesus Christ, Your Son, our Lord, who lives and reigns with You and the Holy Spirit, one God, now and forever. (H86)

> 1Yr.　Daniel 7:9–14
> 　　　 Psalm 50:1–15 (v. 15)
> 　　　 2 Peter 3:3–14
> 　　　 Matthew 25:31–46

Last Sunday of the Church Year

O Lord, absolve Your people from their offenses that, from the bonds of our sins which by reason of our frailty we have brought upon ourselves, we may be delivered by Your bountiful goodness; through Jesus Christ, Your Son, our Lord, who lives and reigns with You and the Holy Spirit, one God, now and forever. (H87)

OR

Lord God, heavenly Father, send forth Your Son, we pray, to lead home His bride, the Church, that with all the company of the redeemed we may finally enter into His eternal wedding feast; through Jesus Christ, our Lord, who lives and reigns with You and the Holy Spirit, one God, now and forever. (H88)

> 1Yr.　Isaiah 65:17–25
> 　　　 Psalm 149 (v. 2)
> 　　　 1 Thessalonians 5:1–11
> 　　　 Matthew 25:1–13

Feasts and Festivals

St. Andrew, Apostle (November 30)

Almighty God, by Your grace the apostle Andrew obeyed the call of Your Son to be a disciple. Grant us also to follow the same Lord Jesus Christ in heart and life, who lives and reigns with You and the Holy Spirit, one God, now and forever. (F01)

> ABC, 1Yr.   Ezekiel 3:16–21
> Psalm 139:1–12 (v. 17)
> Romans 10:8b–18
> John 1:35–42a

St. Thomas, Apostle (December 21)

Almighty and ever-living God, You strengthened Your apostle Thomas with firm and certain faith in the resurrection of Your Son. Grant us such faith in Jesus Christ, our Lord and our God, that we may never be found wanting in Your sight; through the same Jesus Christ, who lives and reigns with You and the Holy Spirit, one God, now and forever. (F02)

> ABC, 1Yr.   Judges 6:36–40
> Psalm 136:1–4 (v. 26)
> Ephesians 4:7, 11–16
> John 20:24–29

St. Stephen, Martyr (December 26)

Heavenly Father, in the midst of our sufferings for the sake of Christ grant us grace to follow the example of the first martyr, Stephen, that we also may look to the One who suffered and was crucified on our behalf and pray for those who do us wrong; through Jesus Christ, our Lord, who lives and reigns with You and the Holy Spirit, one God, now and forever. (F03)

> ABC, 1Yr. 2 Chronicles 24:17–22
> Psalm 119:137–144 (v. 142)
> Acts 6:8—7:2a, 51–60
> Matthew 23:34–39

St. John, Apostle and Evangelist (December 27)

Merciful Lord, cast the bright beams of Your light upon Your Church that we, being instructed in the doctrine of Your blessed apostle and evangelist John, may come to the light of everlasting life; for You live and reign with the Father and the Holy Spirit, one God, now and forever. (F04)

> ABC, 1Yr. Revelation 1:1–6
> Psalm 11 (v. 4a)
> 1 John 1:1—2:2
> John 21:20–25

The Holy Innocents, Martyrs (December 28)

Almighty God, the martyred innocents of Bethlehem showed forth Your praise not by speaking but by dying. Put to death in us all that is in conflict with Your will that our lives may bear witness to the faith we profess with our lips; through Jesus Christ, our Lord, who lives and reigns with You and the Holy Spirit, one God, now and forever. (F05)

> ABC, 1Yr. Jeremiah 31:15–17
> Psalm 54 (v. 4)
> Revelation 14:1–5
> Matthew 2:13–18

New Year's Eve (December 31)

Eternal God, we commit to Your mercy and forgiveness the year now ending and commend to Your blessing and love the times yet to come. In the new year, abide among us with Your Holy Spirit that we may always trust in the saving name of our Lord Jesus Christ, who lives and reigns with You and the Holy Spirit, one God, now and forever. (F06)

ABC, 1Yr.   Isaiah 30:(8–14) 15–17
                Psalm 90:1–12 (v. 17)
                Romans 8:31b–39
                Luke 12:35–40

Circumcision and Name of Jesus (January 1)

Lord God, You made Your beloved Son, our Savior, subject to the Law and caused Him to shed His blood on our behalf. Grant us the true circumcision of the Spirit that our hearts may be made pure from all sins; through Jesus Christ, our Lord, who lives and reigns with You and the Holy Spirit, one God, now and forever. (F07)

ABC, 1Yr.   Numbers 6:22–27
                Psalm 8 (v. 9)
                Galatians 3:23–29
                Luke 2:21

The Confession of St. Peter (January 18)

Heavenly Father, You revealed to the apostle Peter the blessed truth that Your Son Jesus is the Christ. Strengthen us by the proclamation of this truth that we too may joyfully confess that there is salvation in no one else; through the same Jesus Christ, our Lord, who lives and reigns with You and the Holy Spirit, one God, now and forever. (F08)

ABC, 1Yr.   Acts 4:8–13
                Psalm 118:19–29 (v. 26)
                2 Peter 1:1–15
                Mark 8:27–35 (36—9:1)

St. Timothy, Pastor and Confessor (January 24)

Lord Jesus Christ, You have always given to Your Church on earth faithful shepherds such as Timothy to guide and feed Your flock. Make all pastors diligent to preach Your holy Word and administer Your means of grace, and grant Your people wisdom to follow in the way that leads to life eternal; for You live and reign with the Father and the Holy Spirit, one God, now and forever. (F09)

ABC, 1Yr. Acts 16:1–5
Psalm 71:15–24 (v. 6)
1 Timothy 6:11–16
Matthew 24:42–47

The Conversion of St. Paul (January 25)

Almighty God, You turned the heart of him who persecuted the Church and by his preaching caused the light of the Gospel to shine throughout the world. Grant us ever to rejoice in the saving light of Your Gospel and, following the example of the apostle Paul, to spread it to the ends of the earth; through Jesus Christ, Your Son, our Lord, who lives and reigns with You and the Holy Spirit, one God, now and forever. (F10)

ABC, 1Yr. Acts 9:1–22
Psalm 67 (v. 5)
Galatians 1:11–24
Matthew 19:27–30

St. Titus, Pastor and Confessor (January 26)

Almighty God, You called Titus to the work of pastor and teacher. Make all shepherds of Your flock diligent in preaching Your holy Word so that the whole world may know the immeasurable riches of our Savior, Jesus Christ, who lives and reigns with You and the Holy Spirit, one God, now and forever. (F11)

ABC, 1Yr. Acts 20:28–35
Psalm 71:1–14 (v. 17)
Titus 1:1–9
Luke 10:1–9

The Purification of Mary
and the Presentation of Our Lord (February 2)

Almighty and ever-living God, as Your only-begotten Son was this day presented in the temple in the substance of our flesh, grant that we may be presented to You with pure and clean hearts; through Jesus Christ, our Lord, who lives and reigns with You and the Holy Spirit, one God, now and forever. (F12)

> ABC, 1Yr. 1 Samuel 1:21–28
> Psalm 84 (v. 4)
> Hebrews 2:14–18
> Luke 2:22–32 (33–40)

St. Matthias, Apostle (February 24)

Almighty God, You chose Your servant Matthias to be numbered among the Twelve. Grant that Your Church, ever preserved from false teachers, may be taught and guided by faithful and true pastors; through Jesus Christ, our Lord, who lives and reigns with You and the Holy Spirit, one God, now and forever. (F13)

> ABC, 1Yr. Isaiah 66:1–2
> Psalm 134 (Ps. 133:1)
> Acts 1:15–26
> Matthew 11:25–30

St. Joseph, Guardian of Jesus (March 19)

Almighty God, from the house of Your servant David You raised up Joseph to be the guardian of Your incarnate Son and the husband of His mother, Mary. Grant us grace to follow the example of this faithful workman in heeding Your counsel and obeying Your commands; through Jesus Christ, our Lord, who lives and reigns with You and the Holy Spirit, one God, now and forever. (F14)

> ABC, 1Yr. 2 Samuel 7:4–16
> Psalm 127 (v. 1a)
> Romans 4:13–18
> Matthew 2:13–15, 19–23

The Annunciation of Our Lord (March 25)

O Lord, as we have known the incarnation of Your Son, Jesus Christ, by the message of the angel to the virgin Mary, so by the message of His cross and passion bring us to the glory of His resurrection; through the same Jesus Christ, our Lord, who lives and reigns with You and the Holy Spirit, one God, now and forever. (F15)

> ABC, 1Yr. Isaiah 7:10–14
> Psalm 45:7–17 (v. 6)
> Hebrews 10:4–10
> Luke 1:26–38

St. Mark, Evangelist (April 25)

Almighty God, You have enriched Your Church with the proclamation of the Gospel through the evangelist Mark. Grant that we may firmly believe these glad tidings and daily walk according to Your Word; through Jesus Christ, our Lord, who lives and reigns with You and the Holy Spirit, one God, now and forever. (F16)

> ABC, 1Yr. Isaiah 52:7–10
> Psalm 146 (v. 5)
> 2 Timothy 4:5–18
> Mark 16:14–20

St. Philip and St. James, Apostles (May 1)

Almighty God, Your Son revealed Himself to Philip and James and gave them the knowledge of everlasting life. Grant us perfectly to know Your Son, Jesus Christ, to be the way, the truth, and the life, and steadfastly to walk in the way that leads to eternal life; through the same Jesus Christ, our Lord, who lives and reigns with You and the Holy Spirit, one God, now and forever. (F17)

> ABC, 1Yr. Isaiah 30:18–21
> Psalm 36:5–12 (v. 8)
> Ephesians 2:19–22
> John 14:1–14

The Visitation (May 31—Three-Year Lectionary)

Almighty God, You chose the virgin Mary to be the mother of Your Son and made known through her Your gracious regard for the poor and lowly and despised. Grant that we may receive Your Word in humility and faith, and so be made one with Jesus Christ, Your Son, our Lord, who lives and reigns with You and the Holy Spirit, one God, now and forever. (F18)

> ABC, 1Yr. Isaiah 11:1–5
> Psalm 138 (v. 8a)
> Romans 12:9–16
> Luke 1:39–45 (46–56)

St. Barnabas, Apostle (June 11)

Almighty God, Your faithful servant Barnabas sought not his own renown but gave generously of his life and substance for the encouragement of the apostles and their ministry. Grant that we may follow his example in lives given to charity and the proclamation of the Gospel; through Your Son, Jesus Christ, our Lord, who lives and reigns with You and the Holy Spirit, one God, now and forever. (F19)

> ABC, 1Yr. Isaiah 42:5–12
> Psalm 112 (v. 1)
> Acts 11:19–30; 13:1–3
> Mark 6:7–13

The Nativity of St. John the Baptist (June 24)

Almighty God, through John the Baptist, the forerunner of Christ, You once proclaimed salvation. Now grant that we may know this salvation and serve You in holiness and righteousness all the days of our life; through our Lord Jesus Christ, Your Son, who lives and reigns with You and the Holy Spirit, one God, now and forever. (F20)

> ABC, 1Yr. Isaiah 40:1–5
> Psalm 85:(1–6) 7–13 (v. 9)
> Acts 13:13–26
> Luke 1:57–80

St. Peter and St. Paul, Apostles (June 29)

Merciful and eternal God, Your holy apostles Peter and Paul received grace and strength to lay down their lives for the sake of Your Son. Strengthen us by Your Holy Spirit that we may confess Your truth and at all times be ready to lay down our lives for Him who laid down His life for us, even Jesus Christ, our Lord, who lives and reigns with You and the Holy Spirit, one God, now and forever. (F21)

ABC, 1Yr. Acts 15:1–12 (13–21)
Psalm 46 (v. 11)
Galatians 2:1–10
Matthew 16:13–19

The Visitation (July 2—One-Year Lectionary)

See above, page 608.

St. Mary Magdalene (July 22)

Almighty God, Your Son, Jesus Christ, restored Mary Magdalene to health and called her to be the first witness of His resurrection. Heal us from all our infirmities, and call us to know You in the power of Your Son's unending life; through the same Jesus Christ, our Lord, who lives and reigns with You and the Holy Spirit, one God, now and forever. (F22)

ABC, 1Yr. Proverbs 31:10–31
Psalm 73:23–28 (v. 1)
Acts 13:26–31
John 20:1–2, 10–18

St. James the Elder, Apostle (July 25)

O gracious God, Your servant and apostle James was the first among the Twelve to suffer martyrdom for the name of Jesus Christ. Pour out upon the leaders of Your Church that spirit of self-denying service that they may forsake all false and passing allurements and follow Christ alone, who lives and reigns with You and the Holy Spirit, one God, now and forever. (F23)

ABC, 1Yr. Acts 11:27—12:5
Psalm 56 (v. 4)
Romans 8:28–39
Mark 10:35–45

St. Mary, Mother of Our Lord (August 15)

Almighty God, You chose the virgin Mary to be the mother of Your only Son. Grant that we, who are redeemed by His blood, may share with her in the glory of Your eternal kingdom; through Jesus Christ, Your Son, our Lord, who lives and reigns with You and the Holy Spirit, one God, now and forever. (F24)

ABC, 1Yr. Isaiah 61:7–11
Psalm 45:10–17 (v. 6)
Galatians 4:4–7
Luke 1:(39–45) 46–55

St. Bartholomew, Apostle (August 24)

Almighty God, Your Son, Jesus Christ, chose Bartholomew to be an apostle to preach the blessed Gospel. Grant that Your Church may love what he believed and preach what he taught; through Jesus Christ, our Lord, who lives and reigns with You and the Holy Spirit, one God, now and forever. (F25)

ABC, 1Yr. Proverbs 3:1–8
Psalm 121 (v. 8)
2 Corinthians 4:7–10
Luke 22:24–30
or John 1:43–51

The Martyrdom of St. John the Baptist (August 29)

Almighty God, You gave Your servant John the Baptist to be the fore-runner of Your Son, Jesus Christ, in both his preaching of repentance and his innocent death. Grant that we, who have died and risen with Christ in Holy Baptism, may daily repent of our sins, patiently suffer for the sake of the truth, and fearlessly bear witness to His victory over death; through the same Jesus Christ, our Lord, who lives and reigns with You and the Holy Spirit, one God, now and forever. (F26)

ABC, 1Yr.　Revelation 6:9–11
　　　　　　Psalm 71:1–8 (v. 23)
　　　　　　Romans 6:1–5
　　　　　　Mark 6:14–29

Holy Cross Day (September 14)

Merciful God, Your Son, Jesus Christ, was lifted high upon the cross that He might bear the sins of the world and draw all people to Himself. Grant that we who glory in His death for our redemption may faithfully heed His call to bear the cross and follow Him, who lives and reigns with You and the Holy Spirit, one God, now and forever. (F27)

ABC, 1Yr.　Numbers 21:4–9
　　　　　　Psalm 40:1–11 (v. 13)
　　　　　　1 Corinthians 1:18–25
　　　　　　John 12:20–33

St. Matthew, Apostle and Evangelist (September 21)

O Son of God, our blessed Savior Jesus Christ, You called Matthew the tax collector to be an apostle and evangelist. Through his faithful and inspired witness, grant that we also may follow You, leaving behind all covetous desires and love of riches; for You live and reign with the Father and the Holy Spirit, one God, now and forever. (F28)

ABC, 1Yr.　Ezekiel 2:8—3:11
　　　　　　Psalm 119:33–40 (v. 35)
　　　　　　Ephesians 4:7–16
　　　　　　Matthew 9:9–13

St. Michael and All Angels (September 29)

Everlasting God, You have ordained and constituted the service of angels and men in a wonderful order. Mercifully grant that, as Your holy angels always serve and worship You in heaven, so by Your appointment they may also help and defend us here on earth; through Your Son, Jesus Christ, our Lord, who lives and reigns with You and the Holy Spirit, one God, now and forever. (F29)

> ABC, 1Yr. Daniel 10:10–14; 12:1–3
> Psalm 91 (v. 11)
> Revelation 12:7–12
> Matthew 18:1–11
> *or* Luke 10:17–20

St. Luke, Evangelist (October 18)

Almighty God, our Father, Your blessed Son called Luke the physician to be an evangelist and physician of the soul. Grant that the healing medicine of the Gospel and the Sacraments may put to flight the diseases of our souls that with willing hearts we may ever love and serve You; through Jesus Christ, Your Son, our Lord, who lives and reigns with You and the Holy Spirit, one God, now and forever. (F30)

> ABC, 1Yr. Isaiah 35:5–8
> Psalm 147:1–11 (v. 12)
> 2 Timothy 4:5–18
> Luke 10:1–9

St. James of Jerusalem, Brother of Jesus and Martyr (October 23)

Heavenly Father, shepherd of Your people, You raised up James the Just, brother of our Lord, to lead and guide Your Church. Grant that we may follow his example of prayer and reconciliation and be strengthened by the witness of his death; through Jesus Christ, Your Son, our Lord, who lives and reigns with You and the Holy Spirit, one God, now and forever. (F31)

ABC, 1Yr. Acts 15:12–22a
Psalm 133 (v. 1)
James 1:1–12
Matthew 13:54–58

St. Simon and St. Jude, Apostles (October 28)

Almighty God, You chose Your servants Simon and Jude to be numbered among the glorious company of the apostles. As they were faithful and zealous in their mission, so may we with ardent devotion make known the love and mercy of our Lord and Savior Jesus Christ, who lives and reigns with You and the Holy Spirit, one God, now and forever. (F32)

ABC, 1Yr. Jeremiah 26:1–16
Psalm 43 (v. 5b)
1 Peter 1:3–9
John 15:(12–16) 17–21

Reformation Day (October 31)

Almighty and gracious Lord, pour out Your Holy Spirit on Your faithful people. Keep us steadfast in Your grace and truth, protect and deliver us in times of temptation, defend us against all enemies, and grant to Your Church Your saving peace; through Jesus Christ, Your Son, our Lord, who lives and reigns with You and the Holy Spirit, one God, now and forever. (F33)

ABC, 1Yr. Revelation 14:6–7
Psalm 46 (v. 7)
Romans 3:19–28
John 8:31–36
    or Matthew 11:12–19

All Saints' Day (November 1)

Almighty and everlasting God, You knit together Your faithful people of all times and places into one holy communion, the mystical body of Your Son, Jesus Christ. Grant us so to follow Your blessed saints in all virtuous and godly living that, together with them, we may come to the unspeakable joys You have prepared for those who love You; through Jesus Christ, our Lord, who lives and reigns with You and the Holy Spirit, one God, now and forever. (F34)

ABC, 1Yr.   Revelation 7:(2–8) 9–17
Psalm 149 (v. 4)
1 John 3:1–3
Matthew 5:1–12

Occasions

Anniversary of a Congregation

Almighty God, You have promised to be with Your Church forever. We praise You for Your presence in this place of worship and ask Your ongoing blessing upon those who gather here. Dwell continually among us with Your holy Word and Sacraments, strengthen our fellowship in the bonds of love and peace, and increase our faithful witness to Your salvation; through Jesus Christ, Your Son, our Lord, who lives and reigns with You and the Holy Spirit, one God, now and forever. (F35)

ABC, 1Yr.   1 Kings 8:22–30
Psalm 84 (v. 4)
Revelation 21:1–5
Luke 19:1–10

Mission Observance

Almighty God, in Your kindness You cause the light of the Gospel to shine among us. By the working of Your Holy Spirit, help us to share the good news of Your salvation that all who hear it may rejoice in the gift of Your unending love; through Jesus Christ, Your Son, who lives and reigns with You and the Holy Spirit, one God, now and forever. (F36)

ABC, 1Yr. Isaiah 62:1–7
Psalm 96 (v. 2)
Romans 10:11–17
Luke 24:44–53

Christian Education

Lord Jesus Christ, You have entrusted to Your people the task of teaching all nations. Enlighten with the wisdom of Your Holy Spirit those who teach and those who learn that the joyous truth of the Gospel may be known in every generation; for You live and reign with the Father and the Holy Spirit, one God, now and forever. (F37)

ABC, 1Yr. Deuteronomy 6:4–15
Psalm 119:129–136 (v. 105)
Acts 2:37–41
Luke 18:15–17

Harvest Observance

Almighty God, You crown the fields with Your blessing and permit us to gather in the fruits of the earth. As stewards of Your creation, may we receive Your gifts in humble thankfulness and share Your bounty with those in need; through Jesus Christ, our Lord, who lives and reigns with You and the Holy Spirit, one God, now and forever. (F38)

ABC, 1Yr. Deuteronomy 26:1–11
Psalm 65 (v. 1)
2 Corinthians 9:6–15
Luke 12:13–21

Day of Thanksgiving

Almighty God, Your mercies are new every morning and You graciously provide for all our needs of body and soul. Grant us Your Holy Spirit that we may acknowledge Your goodness, give thanks for Your benefits, and serve You in willing obedience all our days; ▶

through Jesus Christ, our Lord, who lives and reigns with You and the Holy Spirit, one God, now and forever. (F39)

> ABC, 1Yr. Deuteronomy 8:1–10
> Psalm 67 (v. 7)
> Philippians 4:6–20
> *or* 1 Timothy 2:1–4
> Luke 17:11–19

Day of Supplication and Prayer

Almighty God, whose compassion never fails and who invites us to call upon You in prayer, hear the heartfelt confession of our sins and receive our humble supplication for Your mercy. Spare us from the just punishment of sin, which our Lord Jesus Christ has borne for us, and enable us to serve You in holiness and purity of life; through Jesus Christ, our Lord, who lives and reigns with You and the Holy Spirit, one God, now and forever. (F40)

> ABC, 1Yr. Joel 2:12–19
> Psalm 6 (v. 4)
> 1 John 1:5—2:2
> Matthew 6:16–21

Day of National or Local Tragedy

Most merciful Father, with compassion You hear the cries of Your people in great distress. Be with all who now endure affliction and calamity, bless the work of those who bring rescue and relief, and enable us to aid and comfort those who are suffering that they may find renewed hope and purpose; through Jesus Christ, our Lord, who lives and reigns with You and the Holy Spirit, one God, now and forever. (F41)

> ABC, 1Yr. Job 30:16–24
> *or* Revelation 7:13–17
> Psalm 130 (v. 5)
> Romans 8:31–39
> *or* Hebrews 12:4–13
> Luke 13:1–9
> *or* Matthew 24:32–35

PRAYERS, INTERCESSIONS, AND THANKSGIVINGS

THE CHURCH AND HER MISSION

For the Church

Merciful God, we humbly implore You to cast the bright beams of Your light upon Your Church that we, being instructed by the doctrine of the blessed apostles, may walk in the light of Your truth and finally attain to the light of everlasting life; through Jesus Christ, our Lord. (101)

Almighty God, grant to Your Church Your Holy Spirit and the wisdom that comes down from above, that Your Word may not be bound but have free course and be preached to the joy and edifying of Christ's holy people, that in steadfast faith we may serve You and, in the confession of Your name, abide unto the end; through Jesus Christ, our Lord. (102)

For the mission of the Church

Almighty God, You have called Your Church to witness that in Christ You have reconciled us to Yourself. Grant that by Your Holy Spirit we may proclaim the good news of Your salvation so that all who hear it may receive the gift of salvation; through Jesus Christ, our Lord. (104)

For the mission of the Church and her missionaries

Almighty and gracious God, You want all to be saved and to come to the knowledge of the truth. Magnify the power of the Gospel in the hearts of Your faithful people that Your Church may spread the good news of salvation. Protect, encourage, and bless all missionaries who proclaim the saving cross that Christ, being lifted up, may draw all people to Himself, who lives and reigns with You and the Holy Spirit, one God, now and forever. (105)

For those outside the Church

Almighty and everlasting God, You desire not the death of a sinner but that all would repent and live. Hear our prayers for those outside the Church. Take away their iniquity, and turn them from their false gods to You, the living and true God. Gather them into Your holy Church to the glory of Your name; through Jesus Christ, our Lord. (106)

Unity of faith

O God, Your infinite love restores to the right way those who err, seeks the scattered, and preserves those whom You have gathered. Of Your tender mercy pour out on Your faithful people the grace of unity that, all schisms being ended, Your flock may be gathered to the true Shepherd of Your Church and may serve You in all faithfulness; through Jesus Christ, our Lord. (107)

Defending the Church from error

O Christ, our defender, protect us from all those whose plans would subvert Your truth through heresy and schism that, as You are acknowledged in heaven and on earth as one and the same Lord, so Your people, gathered from all nations, may serve You in unity of faith; for You live and reign with the Father and the Holy Spirit, one God, now and forever. (108)

Those who are separated from the Church

O God, protect the tempted, the distressed, and the erring, and gently guide them. By Your great goodness bring them into the way of peace and truth. Graciously regard all who are in trouble, danger, temptation, or bondage to sin, and those to whom death draws near. In Your mercy draw them to Yourself; through Jesus Christ, our Lord. (113)

Those who have erred

Almighty God, our heavenly Father, whose nature it is always to have mercy, visit with Your fatherly correction all who have erred and gone astray from the truth of Your holy Word, and bring them to a true sense of their error that they may again receive and hold fast Your unchangeable truth; through Jesus Christ, our Lord. (114)

Teaching the faith

Almighty God, the fount of all wisdom, by Your Holy Spirit enlighten those who teach and those who learn that, rejoicing in the knowledge of Your truth, they may worship You and serve You from generation to generation; through Jesus Christ, our Lord. (115)

For the holy ministry

O almighty God, Your Son, Jesus Christ, gave to His holy apostles many excellent gifts and commanded them earnestly to feed His flock. Make all pastors diligent to preach Your holy Word and the people obedient to follow it that together they may receive the crown of everlasting glory; through Jesus Christ, our Lord. (118)

Increase of the holy ministry

Almighty and gracious God, the Father of our Lord Jesus Christ, You have commanded us to pray that You would send forth laborers into Your harvest. Of Your infinite mercy give us true teachers and ministers of Your Word who truly fulfill Your command and preach nothing contrary to Your holy Word. Grant that we, being warned, instructed, nurtured, comforted, and strengthened by Your holy Word, may do those things which are well pleasing to You and profitable for our salvation; through Jesus Christ, our Lord. (119)

O Lord, the God of all grace, You have called Your Church to minister in the name of Your Son, our great High Priest. By Your Word and Spirit inspire men to offer their lives for the sacred ministry that, ministering in the name of Christ, they may draw many to Your kingdom; through Jesus Christ, our Lord. (120)

For those who have particular responsibility in the Church

Gracious Lord and Shepherd, grant to those entrusted with special responsibilities zeal and faithfulness to perform the task of building up Your Church, bringing glory to Your saving name; for You live and reign with the Father and the Holy Spirit, one God, now and forever. (122)

For those who hold special offices in the Church

Lord of the Church, in whose name all who oversee and serve Your flock have been called, grant Your servants all the gifts necessary for the godly administration of their duties for the upbuilding of Your Church that they may bring glory to Your name; for You live and reign with the Father and the Holy Spirit, one God, now and forever. (123)

For those who minister to the armed forces

O Lord, almighty God, as You have always granted special gifts of the Holy Spirit to Your Church on earth, grant Your continual bless-

620

ing to all who minister in Your name in the armed forces, that by Your gracious working they may honor Christ and advance the good of those committed to their care; through Jesus Christ, our Lord. (126)

For church musicians and artists

God of majesty, whom saints and angels delight to worship in heaven, be with Your servants who make art and music for Your people that with joy we on earth may glimpse Your beauty. Bring us to the fulfillment of that hope of perfection that will be ours as we stand before Your unveiled glory; through Jesus Christ, our Lord. (136)

For women's organizations

Lord Jesus, in Your earthly ministry You were loved and served by devoted women, including Mary and Martha in whose home You enjoyed rest and refreshment. Give us grace to recognize and affirm the varied and singular gifts You bestow on women (and especially upon *name of women's organization*) that Your kingdom may be extended, Your Church enriched, and Your people lovingly served to the glory of Your holy name; for You live and reign with the Father and the Holy Spirit, one God, now and forever. (137)

For men's organizations

Almighty and gracious God, in every age You have inspired men to labor, with hearts united, in Your kingdom. Continue to grant to the men of this congregation (and especially *name of men's organization*) faithfulness in serving You and upholding the truth of Your Word that they, together with us all, may respond to Your redeeming love in Christ Jesus by devoting themselves to seeking and doing Your holy will and following in the footsteps of our Lord Jesus Christ, who lives and reigns with You and the Holy Spirit, one God, now and forever. (138)

To open a congregational meeting

Almighty God and Lord, as You have called us to labor in Your vineyard, so grant us now Your presence. Enlighten and guide us by Your Word that in all matters of deliberation we may always consider the best interests of Your Church and this congregation. Let Your Holy Spirit rule and direct our hearts that, in the spirit of Christian love, we may present and discuss matters and be kindly disposed toward one another, to the end that all we say and do may please You; through Jesus Christ, our Lord. (139)

To open a church council meeting

Almighty God, direct and guide us by Your Holy Spirit both to plan and to accomplish those things that will benefit Your Church and glorify Your name; through Jesus Christ, our Lord. (140)

To open a committee meeting

Almighty God, we give thanks that through the varied gifts of the members of this *committee / task force / group* You provide for the ongoing care of this congregation. Cause us to recognize and to act on every opportunity for fruitful service. Send Your Holy Spirit that everything we think, say, and do may be for the common good of the Church and the glory of Your name; through Jesus Christ, our Lord. (141)

At a retreat

Lord Jesus Christ, You withdrew Yourself for times of prayer and brought Your disciples with You that they might also rest with You. Be present with us during this time of retreat that, gathered together in Your name, we may profitably meditate on Your Word and be strengthened with a good will to serve You and Your people; for You live and reign with the Father and the Holy Spirit, one God, now and forever. (142)

AT WORSHIP

On entering a church

Lord, I love the habitation of Your house and the place where Your glory dwells. In the multitude of Your tender mercies prepare my heart that I may enter Your house to worship and confess Your holy name; through Jesus Christ, my God and Lord. (145)

Before worship

O Lord, our creator, redeemer, and comforter, as we come together to worship You in spirit and in truth, we humbly pray that You would open our hearts to the preaching of Your Word so that we may repent of our sins, believe in Jesus Christ as our only Savior, and grow in grace and holiness. Hear us for His sake. (146)

After worship

Almighty and merciful God, we have again worshiped in Your presence and received both forgiveness for our many sins and the assurance of Your love in Jesus Christ. We thank You for this undeserved grace and ask You to keep us in faith until we inherit eternal salvation; through Jesus Christ, our Lord. (147)

Grace to receive the Word

Blessed Lord, You have caused all Holy Scriptures to be written for our learning. Grant that we may so hear them, read, mark, learn, and inwardly digest them that, by patience and comfort of Your holy Word, we may embrace and ever hold fast the blessed hope of everlasting life; through Jesus Christ, our Lord. (148)

For blessing on the Word

Lord God, bless Your Word wherever it is proclaimed. Make it a word of power and peace to convert those not yet Your own and to ▶

confirm those who have come to saving faith. May Your Word pass from the ear to the heart, from the heart to the lip, and from the lip to the life that, as You have promised, Your Word may achieve the purpose for which You send it; through Jesus Christ, our Lord. (150)

For obedience to the Word

O holy and most merciful God, You have taught us the way of Your commandments. We implore You to pour out Your grace into our hearts. Cause it to bear fruit in us that, being ever mindful of Your mercies and Your laws, we may always be directed to Your will and daily increase in love toward You and one another. Enable us to resist all evil and to live a godly life. Help us to follow the example of our Lord and Savior, Jesus Christ, and to walk in His steps until we shall possess the kingdom that has been prepared for us in heaven; through Jesus Christ, our Lord. (152)

Before confession and absolution

Almighty, everlasting God, for our many sins we justly deserve eternal condemnation. In Your mercy You sent Your dear Son, our Lord Jesus Christ, who won for us forgiveness of sins and everlasting salvation. Grant us a true confession that, dead to sin, we may be raised up by Your life-giving absolution. Grant us Your Holy Spirit that we may be ever watchful and live true and godly lives in Your service; through Jesus Christ, our Lord. (153)

For right reception of the Lord's Supper

O Lord, our God, in Holy Baptism You have called us to be Christians and granted us the remission of sins. Make us ready to receive the most holy body and blood of Christ for the forgiveness of all our sins, and grant us grateful hearts that we may give thanks to You, O Father, to Your Son, and to the Holy Spirit, one God, now and forever. (154)

Lord Jesus, You invite all who are burdened with sin to come to You for rest. We now come at Your invitation to the heavenly feast, which You have provided for Your children on earth. Preserve us from impenitence and unbelief, cleanse us from our unrighteousness, and clothe us with the righteousness purchased with Your blood. Strengthen our faith, increase our love and hope, and assure us a place at Your heavenly table, where we will eat eternal manna and drink of the river of Your pleasure forever and ever. Hear us, Jesus, for Your own sake. (156)

Thanksgiving after receiving the Sacrament

Blessed Savior, Jesus Christ, You have given Yourself to us in this holy Sacrament. Keep us in Your faith and favor that we may live in You even as You live in us. May Your body and blood preserve us in the true faith to life everlasting. Hear us for the sake of Your name. (157)

General thanksgiving

Almighty God, our heavenly Father, we, Your unworthy servants, give You humble and hearty thanks for all the goodness and loving-kindness that You bestow on us. We praise You for our creation, preservation, and all the blessings of this life. But above all, we bless You for Your boundless love in the redemption of the world by our Lord and Savior Jesus Christ, for the means of grace, and for the hope of glory. We implore You to give us a right understanding of all Your mercies that our hearts may ever be deeply thankful and that we may show forth Your praise with both our lips and our lives. Direct our lives in ways of holiness and righteousness all our days that we may enjoy the testimony of a good conscience and the hope of Your favor, be sustained and comforted in every time of trouble, and finally be received into Your everlasting kingdom; through Christ Jesus, Your Son, our Lord, who lives and reigns with You and the Holy Spirit, one God, now and forever. (160)

General intercession

Lord God, heavenly Father, we offer before You our common supplications for the well-being of Your Church throughout the world. So guide and govern it by Your Holy Spirit that all who profess themselves Christians may be led into the way of truth and hold the faith in unity of spirit, in the bond of peace, and in righteousness of life. Send down upon all ministers of the Gospel and upon the congregations committed to their care the healthful spirit of Your grace that they may please You in all things.

Behold in mercy all who are in authority over us. Supply them with Your blessing that they may be inclined to Your will and walk according to Your commandments. We humbly ask Your abiding presence in every situation that You would make known Your ways among us. Preserve those who travel, satisfy the wants of Your creatures, and help those who call upon You in any need that they may have patience in the midst of suffering and, according to Your will, be released from their afflictions; through Christ Jesus, Your Son, our Lord, who lives and reigns with You and the Holy Spirit, one God, now and forever. (161)

For pardon, growth in grace, and divine protection

O Lord, our God, we acknowledge Your great goodness toward us and praise You for the mercy and grace that our eyes have seen, our ears have heard, and our hearts have known. We sincerely repent of the sins of this day and those in the past. Pardon our offenses, correct and reform what is lacking in us, and help us to grow in grace and in the knowledge of our Lord and Savior, Jesus Christ. Inscribe Your law upon our hearts, and equip us to serve You with holy and blameless lives. May each day remind us of the coming of the night when no one can work. In the emptiness of this present age keep us united by a living faith through the power of Your Holy Spirit with Him who is the resurrection and the life, that we may escape the eternal bitter pains of condemnation.

By Your Holy Spirit bless the preaching of Your Word and the administration of Your Sacraments. Preserve these gifts to us and to all Christians. Guard and protect us from all dangers to body and soul. Grant that we may with faithful perseverance receive from You our sorrows as well as our joys, knowing that health and sickness, riches and poverty, and all things come by permission of Your fatherly hand. Keep us this day under Your protective care and preserve us, securely trusting in Your everlasting goodness and love, for the sake of Your Son, Jesus Christ, our Lord, who lives and reigns with You and the Holy Spirit, one God, now and forever. (159)

Praise and supplication

Lord God, creator of heaven and earth, Father of our Lord Jesus Christ, we praise You for the abundant mercy that You this day so richly have provided us, blessing us not only with daily bread for our bodies but also with heavenly food for our souls. Grant that Your living and powerful Word may abide in our hearts, working mightily in us to Your glory and for our salvation. We commit ourselves to Your divine protection and fatherly care. Let Your holy angels be with us that the evil foe may have no power over us. Look in mercy on Your Church and deliver it from all danger and adversities. By Your Holy Spirit comfort and strengthen all who are in affliction or distress, and grant Your abiding peace to us all; through Jesus Christ, our Savior. (162)

BAPTISMAL LIFE

Morning

Faithful God, whose mercies are new to us every morning, we humbly pray that You would look upon us in mercy and renew us by Your Holy Spirit. Keep safe our going out and our coming in, and let Your blessing remain with us throughout this day. Preserve us in Your righteousness, and grant us a portion in that eternal life which is in Christ Jesus, our Lord. (168)

Thanksgiving in the morning

Almighty God, our heavenly Father, Your mercies are new unto us every morning, and though we have not deserved Your goodness, You abundantly provide for all our wants of body and soul. Grant us Your Holy Spirit that we may heartily acknowledge Your merciful goodness toward us, give thanks for all Your benefits, and serve You in willing obedience; through Jesus Christ, our Lord. (169)

Protection during the day (Collect for Grace)

O Lord, our heavenly Father, almighty and everlasting God, You have safely brought us to the beginning of this day. Defend us in the same with Your mighty power, and grant that this day we fall into no sin, neither run into any kind of danger, but that all our doings, being ordered by Your governance, may be righteous in Your sight; through Jesus Christ, our Lord. (170)

Evening

Merciful Father, whose guiding hand has brought us to the completion of this day, we humbly pray You to stay with us and shelter us in quiet hours of the night that we, who are wearied by the changes and chances of this passing world, may rest in Your changeless peace; through Jesus Christ, our Lord. (171)

O Lord God, heavenly Father, by the blessed light of Your divine Word You have led us to the knowledge of Your Son. Grant us the grace of Your Holy Spirit that we may ever walk in the light of Your truth and, rejoicing with sure confidence in Christ, our Savior, be brought unto everlasting salvation; through the same Jesus Christ, our Lord. (185)

Lord God, heavenly Father, let Your Holy Spirit dwell in us that He may enlighten and lead us into all truth and evermore defend us from all adversities; through Jesus Christ, our Lord. (186)

For divine guidance

Almighty and ever-living God, You make us both to will and to do those things that are good and acceptable in Your sight. Let Your fatherly hand ever guide us and Your Holy Spirit ever be with us to direct us in the knowledge and obedience of Your Word that we may obtain everlasting life; through Jesus Christ, our Lord. (187)

Almighty and everlasting God, direct, sanctify, and govern both our hearts and bodies in the ways of Your laws and in the works of Your commandments that through Your mighty protection we may ever be preserved in both body and soul; through our Lord and Savior Jesus Christ. (189)

Faith, hope, and love

Almighty God, grant us a steadfast faith in Jesus Christ, a cheerful hope in Your mercy, and a sincere love for You and one another; through Jesus Christ, our Lord. (190)

Thanksgiving to God

Heavenly Father, God of all grace, govern our hearts that we may never forget Your blessings but steadfastly thank and praise You for all Your goodness in this life until, with all Your saints, we praise You eternally in Your heavenly kingdom; through Jesus Christ, our Lord. (191)

Grace to use our gifts

Lord God Almighty, even as You bless Your servants with various and unique gifts of the Holy Spirit, continue to grant us the grace to use them always to Your honor and glory; through Jesus Christ, our Lord. (192)

Christian vocation

Heavenly Father, grant Your mercy and grace to Your people in their many and various callings. Give them patience, and strengthen them in their Christian vocation of witness to the world and of service to their neighbor in Christ's name; through Jesus Christ, our Lord. (194)

Against the love of money

Almighty God, heavenly Father, You have called us to be Your children and heirs of Your gracious promises in Christ Jesus. Grant us Your Holy Spirit that we may forsake all covetous desires and the inordinate love of riches. Deliver us from the pursuit of passing things that we may seek the kingdom of Your Son and trust in His righteousness and so find blessedness and peace; through Jesus Christ, our Lord. (195)

Proper use of wealth

Almighty God, all that we possess is from Your loving hand. Give us grace that we may honor You with all we own, always remembering the account we must one day give to Jesus Christ, our Lord. (196)

Proper use of leisure

O God, give us times of refreshment and peace in the course of this busy life. Grant that we may so use our leisure to rebuild our bodies and renew our minds that we may be opened to the goodness of Your creation; through Jesus Christ, our Lord. (197)

Newness of life in Christ

Almighty God, give us grace that we may cast away the works of darkness and put upon ourselves the armor of light now in the time of this mortal life in which Your Son, Jesus Christ, came to visit us in great humility, that in the Last Day, when He shall come again in glorious majesty to judge both the living and the dead, we may rise to the life immortal; through Jesus Christ, our Lord. (198)

For steadfast faith

Almighty God, our heavenly Father, because of Your tender love toward us sinners You have given us Your Son that, believing in Him, we might have everlasting life. Continue to grant us Your Holy Spirit that we may remain steadfast in this faith to the end and finally come to life everlasting; through Jesus Christ, our Lord. (200)

Thanksgiving to God

Lord God, heavenly Father, from Your hand we receive all good gifts and by Your grace we are guarded from all evil. Grant us Your Holy Spirit that, acknowledging with our whole heart Your boundless goodness, we may now and evermore thank and praise You for Your loving-kindness and tender mercy; through Jesus Christ, our Lord. (201)

For a right knowledge of Christ

Almighty God, whom to know is everlasting life, grant us perfectly to know Your Son, Jesus Christ, to be the way, the truth, and the life, that following His steps we may steadfastly walk in the way that leads to eternal life; through the same Jesus Christ, our Lord. (202)

Before the study of God's Word

Almighty God, our heavenly Father, without Your help our labor is useless, and without Your light our search is in vain. Invigorate our study of Your holy Word that, by due diligence and right discernment, we may establish ourselves and others in Your holy faith; through Jesus Christ, our Lord. (203)

For spiritual renewal

Almighty God, grant that we, who have been redeemed from the old life of sin by our Baptism into the death and resurrection of Your Son, Jesus Christ, may be renewed by Your Holy Spirit to live in righteousness and true holiness; through Jesus Christ, our Lord. (205)

For deliverance from sin

We implore You, O Lord, in Your kindness to show us Your great mercy that we may be set free from our sins and rescued from the punishments that we rightfully deserve; through Jesus Christ, our Lord. (207)

In times of temptation

Almighty and everlasting God, through Your Son You have promised us forgiveness of sins and everlasting life. Govern our hearts by Your Holy Spirit that in our daily need, and especially in all time of temptation, we may seek Your help and, by a true and lively faith in Your Word, obtain all that You have promised; through the same Jesus Christ, our Lord. (209)

For control of the tongue

We pray You, O Lord, to keep our tongues from evil and our lips from speaking deceit, that as Your holy angels continuously sing praises to You in heaven, so may we at all times glorify You on earth; through Jesus Christ, our Lord. (210)

For purity

Almighty God, unto whom all hearts are open, all desires known, and from whom no secrets are hidden, cleanse the thoughts of our hearts by the inspiration of Your Holy Spirit that we may perfectly love You and worthily magnify Your holy name; through Jesus Christ, our Lord. (211)

For faithfulness

Lord God, we thank You that You have taught us what You would have us believe and do. Help us by Your Holy Spirit, for the sake of Jesus Christ, to hold fast Your Word in hearts that You have cleansed that thereby we may be made strong in faith and perfect in holiness and be comforted in life and death; through Jesus Christ, our Lord. (212)

Innocence of life

O God, whose strength is made perfect in weakness, put to death in us all vices and so strengthen us by Your grace that by the innocence of our lives and the constancy of our faith, even unto death, we may glorify Your holy name; through Jesus Christ, our Lord. (213)

Grace to love and serve God

O God, through the grace of Your Holy Spirit You pour the gifts of love into the hearts of Your faithful people. Grant Your servants health both of mind and body that they may love You with their whole heart and with their whole strength perform those things that are pleasing to You; through Jesus Christ, our Lord. (214)

For those who care for others

Most merciful Father, You have committed to our love and care our fellow human beings and their necessities. Graciously be with and prosper all those who serve the sick and those in need. Let their service be abundantly blessed as they bring relief to the suffering, comfort to the sorrowing, and peace to the dying. Grant them the knowledge that inasmuch as they do it unto the least of the Master's brethren, they do it unto Him; through the same Jesus Christ, our Lord. (215)

For humility

O God, You resist the proud and give grace to the humble. Grant us true humility after the likeness of Your only Son that we may never be arrogant and prideful and thus provoke Your wrath, but in all lowliness be made partakers of the gifts of Your grace; through Jesus Christ, our Lord. (216)

For a blessed death

Almighty God, grant Your unworthy servants Your grace, that in the hour of our death the adversary may not prevail against us, but that we may be found worthy of everlasting life; through Jesus Christ, our Lord. (220)

Blessedness of heaven

Almighty, everlasting God, You gave Your only Son to be a High Priest of good things to come. Grant unto us, Your unworthy servants, to have our share in the company of the blessed for all eternity; through Jesus Christ, our Lord. (221)

Hope of eternal life in Christ

Almighty, everlasting God, Your Son has assured forgiveness of sins and deliverance from eternal death. Strengthen us by Your Holy Spirit that our faith in Christ may increase daily and that we may hold fast to the hope that on the Last Day we shall be raised in glory to eternal life; through Jesus Christ, our Lord. (222)

CIVIL REALM

Good government

Eternal Lord, ruler of all, graciously regard those who have been set in positions of authority among us that, guided by Your Spirit, they may be high in purpose, wise in counsel, firm in good resolution, and unwavering in duty, that under them we may be governed quietly and peaceably; through Jesus Christ, our Lord. (223)

For the nation

Almighty God, You have given us this good land as our heritage. Grant that we remember Your generosity and constantly do Your will. Bless our land with honest industry, truthful education, and an honorable way of life. Save us from violence, discord, and confusion, from pride and arrogance, and from every evil course of action. Grant that we, who came from many nations with many different languages, may become a united people. Support us in defending our liberties, and give those to whom we have entrusted the authority of government the spirit of wisdom, that there may be justice and peace in our land. When times are prosperous, may our hearts be thankful, and in troubled times do not let our trust in You fail; through Jesus Christ, our Lord. (224)

Responsible citizenship

Lord, keep this nation under Your care. Bless the leaders of our land that we may be a people at peace among ourselves and a blessing to the other nations of the earth. Grant that we may choose trustworthy leaders, contribute to wise decisions for the general welfare, and serve You faithfully in our generation; through Jesus Christ, our Lord. (225)

For responsible leaders

O merciful Father in heaven, from You comes all rule and authority over the nations of the world for the punishment of evildoers and for the praise of those who do well. Graciously regard Your servants, those who make, administer, and judge the laws of this nation, and look in mercy upon all the rulers of the earth. Grant that all who receive the sword as Your servants may bear it according to Your command. Enlighten and defend them, and grant them wisdom and understanding that under their peaceable governance Your people may be guarded and directed in righteousness, quietness, and unity. Protect and prolong their lives that we with them may show forth the praise of Your name; through Jesus Christ, our Lord. (226)

In times of war

Almighty God, You alone can establish lasting peace. Forgive our sins, we implore You, and deliver us from the hands of our enemies that we, being strengthened by Your defense, may be preserved from all danger and glorify You for the restoration of tranquility in our land; through the merits of Your Son, Jesus Christ, our Savior. (228)

For peace in the world

Heavenly Father, God of all concord, it is Your gracious will that Your children on earth live together in harmony and peace. Defeat the plans of all those who would stir up violence and strife, destroy the weapons of those who delight in war and bloodshed, and, according to Your will, end all conflicts in the world. Teach us to examine our hearts that we may recognize our own inclination toward envy, malice, hatred, and enmity. Help us, by Your Word and Spirit, to search our hearts and to root out the evil that would lead to strife and discord, so that in our lives we may be at peace with all people. Fill us with zeal for the work of Your Church and the proclamation of the Gospel of Jesus Christ, which alone can bring that peace which is beyond all understanding; through Jesus Christ, our Lord. (229)

For our enemies in times of war

Forgive, we implore You, O Lord, our enemies, and so change their hearts that they may walk with us in sincerity and peace; through Jesus Christ, our Lord. (230)

For peace in times of war

O God, the author of peace and lover of concord, defend us, Your humble servants, from all the assaults of our enemies that we, surely trusting in Your defense, may not fear the power of any adversary but may rejoice in Your abiding protection; through the might of Jesus Christ, our Lord. (231)

Following an uprising, conflict, or war

Gracious God and Father, though Your Son, Jesus Christ, came to bring us Your heavenly peace, violence and conflict still rage among Your children on earth. We thank You that in Your mercy and goodness You have caused recent violence [in _location_] to come to an end. Bring a restoration of calm and security, and heal the wounds that have been inflicted. Preserve the peace that has come so that what has been laid waste and made desolate can again be planted and built up. Open Your fatherly heart and bountiful hand to help all in need. Grant that we all may live together in unity and peace, and let all hatred and ill will be remembered no more. Give us that peace which the world cannot give, and grant us grace that, delivered from all conflict and strife, we may live in harmony and safety, and finally, having gained the eternal rest of the saints in glory, may praise and bless, worship and glorify You forever; through Jesus Christ, our Lord, who lives and reigns with You and the Holy Spirit, one God, now and forever. (232)

Armed forces of our nation

Lord God of hosts, stretch forth Your almighty arm to strengthen and protect those who serve in the armed forces of our country. Support them in times of war, and in times of peace keep them from all evil, ▶

giving them courage and loyalty. Grant that in all things they may serve with integrity and with honor; through Jesus Christ, our Lord. (233)

Industry and commerce

Lord Jesus Christ, as once You shared in our human toil and thus hallowed the work of our hands, bless and prosper those who maintain the industries and service sectors of this land. Give them a right regard for their labors, and grant them the just reward for their work that they may find joy in serving You and in supplying our needs; for You live and reign with the Father and the Holy Spirit, one God, now and forever. (234)

Agriculture

Almighty God, You bless the earth to make it fruitful, bringing forth in abundance whatever is needed for the support of our lives. Prosper the work of farmers and all those who labor to bring food to our table. Grant them seasonable weather that they may gather in the fruits of the earth in abundance and proclaim Your goodness with thanksgiving; through Jesus Christ, our Lord. (235)

Time of drought

O God, most merciful Father, without Your care and preservation all things wither and die. Open the windows of heaven and send bountiful rain on us to revive and renew the land. Graciously hear our prayer that we may praise and glorify Your name forever and ever; through Jesus Christ, our Lord. (236)

Times of unseasonable weather

Lord God, gracious and merciful Father, because You have promised that You will hear us when we bring You our cares, we implore You not to deal with us according to our sins but according to Your mercy. Send seasonable weather so that in due time the earth may yield her increase. Remind us ever to receive with thanks our daily bread, trusting You as our gracious God; through Jesus Christ, our Lord. (237)

Thanksgiving for rain

Most gracious God and Father, we thank and praise You for sending rain to water the earth, causing it to be fruitful and to bring forth food in plenteous supply. Teach us ever to remember that we do not live on bread alone in order that we may receive Your blessings with thanksgiving and Your Word with grateful hearts; through Jesus Christ, our Lord. (238)

HOME AND FAMILY

For home and family

Visit, O Lord, the homes in which Your people dwell, and keep all harm and danger far from them. Grant that we may dwell together in peace under the protection of Your holy angels, sharing eternally in Your blessings; through Jesus Christ, our Lord. (239)

For those to be joined in holy matrimony

Holy God, gracious Father, You established the marriage covenant and desire that we keep it holy. We pray Your blessing upon _name_ and _name_, who have pledged their loving commitment to each other. Help them to prepare for their exchange of vows that with You as their God they may live in marriage to Your honor and their blessing; through Jesus Christ, our Lord. (241)

For those who are married

O Lord God, at the creation of Adam and Eve You instituted and blessed marriage as the union of a man and a woman and commanded that it be held in honor by all. Grant Your blessings to all ▶

married couples (especially _ names _) that their life together may be blessed with wisdom, purity, self-sacrifice, and love; through Jesus Christ, our Lord. (242)

Most gracious God, we give thanks for the joy and blessings that You grant to husbands and wives. Assist them always by Your grace that with true fidelity and steadfast love they may honor and keep their marriage vows, grow in love toward You and for each other, and come at last to the eternal joys that You have promised; through Jesus Christ, our Lord. (243)

Adoption of children

Merciful Father, because of Your great love revealed in Christ, You called us to the household of faith in Your Son, Jesus, our Savior, and chose us to be Your own dear children. Grant Your grace to all who have adopted children that, finding in them a special blessing, they may nurture them as Your chosen ones; through Jesus Christ, our Lord. (249)

Asking a blessing at mealtime

Heavenly Father, we thank You for the gift of food You have provided and for all those whose labor brings Your blessings to our table. We pray that at this meal we may be strengthened for Your service and together may await with joy the feast You have prepared for all the faithful in Your eternal kingdom; through Jesus Christ, our Lord. (252)

IN TIMES OF NEED

For the sick

Heavenly Father, ruler of all things, Your Son, our Savior Jesus Christ, healed all manner of infirmities and cured all manner of diseases. Mercifully help Your servant _name_ in body and soul and, if it be Your will, free _him/her_ from _his/her_ sickness that, restored to health, _he/she_ may with a thankful heart bless Your holy name; through Jesus Christ, our Lord. (257)

For those undergoing surgery

Lord Jesus Christ, hear our prayers on behalf of Your servant(s) _name(s)_ as _he/she/they_ undergoes(undergo) surgery. Bless _him/her/them_ with faith in Your loving-kindness and protection. Endow the surgeon(s) and the medical team(s) with ability and skill so that, according to Your will, this surgery may bring Your servant(s) to a full restoration of health and strength; for You live and reign with the Father and the Holy Spirit, one God, forever and ever. (259 alt.)

For those who minister to the sick

Lord God, be with the doctors and nurses and all others who minister to the needs of those who are ill. Through their wise and compassionate service, grant relief to the suffering and hope to the afflicted so that all may know of Your boundless care; through Jesus Christ, our Lord. (261)

For one near death

Eternal Father, You alone make the decisions concerning life and death. We ask You to show mercy to Your servant _name_, whose death seems imminent. If it be Your gracious will, restore _him/her_ and lengthen _his/her_ earthly life; but if not, keep _him/her_ in _his/her_ baptismal grace and in Your abiding care. Give _him/her_ ▶

a repentant heart, firm faith, and a lively hope. Let not the fear of death cause _him/her_ to waver in confidence and trust. At Your chosen time, grant _him/her_ a peaceful departure and a joyous entrance into everlasting life with the glorious company of all Your saints; through Jesus Christ, our Savior. (262)

For those who mourn

Lord God, maker of heaven and earth and giver of life, we thank You for all the mercies You granted to our _brother(s)/sister(s)_ , _name(s)_ , during _his/her/their_ earthly life (lives), especially for calling _him/her/them_ to faith in Jesus Christ. Comfort the survivors who mourn _his/her/their_ death(s) with the hope of the glorious resurrection and a joyful reunion in heaven. Keep us mindful that we are mortal so that we will ever be prepared to die in the faith and finally receive the glory promised to all who trust in Your beloved Son, Jesus Christ, our Lord. (263)

Almighty God, Father of all mercies and giver of all comfort, deal graciously with all those who mourn that, casting every care on You, they may know the consolation of Your love; through Jesus Christ, our Lord. (264)

Time of bereavement

Heavenly Father, into whose keeping we entrust our loved ones, help us to look to You in our time of sorrow, remembering the cloud of faithful witnesses with which we are surrounded. Grant that we may one day share in the joys of those who now rest in Your presence; through Jesus Christ, our Lord. (265)

At a sudden death

O Lord God, by this sudden death of _name(s)_ , You have shown that Your thoughts are not our thoughts nor Your ways our ways. We thank You for the blessings of body and soul that You bestowed on the departed. Comfort the members of _his/her/their_ family who mourn _his/her/their_ death, and assist us ever to prepare for Your final summons when we will depart and be with Christ in blessedness and glory; through the same Jesus Christ, our Lord. (266)

At burial—general

O God, Your days are without end, and Your mercies cannot be numbered. Make us ever mindful of the shortness and uncertainty of life. By the working of Your Holy Spirit preserve us in faithfulness and righteousness that, when we have served You in our generation, we may finally join the saints in heaven; through Jesus Christ, our Lord. (267)

At burial—for a husband/father or a wife/mother

Eternal God, merciful Father, look graciously upon us who sorrow at the loss of a Christian _brother/sister_, a beloved _husband and father / wife and mother_. Help us call to mind the many mercies which from _his/her_ youth You bestowed on our departed _brother/sister_. Comfort us with the assurance that You will raise _him/her_ in power and glory and that we shall see _him/her_ again with You in everlasting life. Teach us all to number our days that we may gain a heart of wisdom and, when our last hour comes, be with us and grant us a blessed end; through Jesus Christ, our Lord. (270)

Death of a pastor (general)

Lord Jesus Christ, great Shepherd of Your flock, it has pleased You to call _name_, a pastor to Your people, into Your glorious presence. We thank and praise You for all the blessings and mercy You bestowed on Your departed servant, especially for the years You permitted him to be Your undershepherd. We praise You for having kept him faithful in the face of trials and difficulties, for having given success to Your Word which he proclaimed, for having built Your ►

temple in the hearts of many through his ministry, and for having given him a blessed death and reception into the kingdom of Your glory in heaven. Comfort all who mourn his departure, and help us gratefully to remember all who have spoken the Word of God to us as we await our joyful reunion in heaven, where You live and reign with the Father and the Holy Spirit, one God, now and forever. (274)

At the death of a teacher

Almighty God, eternal fountain of all wisdom, it has pleased You to take out of this life the soul of _name_, a teacher of Your flock. We thank You for having given _him/her_ the grace to devote _his/her_ life and talents to the nurture and instruction of Your people. We praise You for having blessed _his/her_ labor to show the power of Your Word in the hearts of our children. Comfort and strengthen those who mourn _his/her_ death. Grant Your grace that in the midst of sorrow they may retain a lively hope. Direct our thoughts heavenward that we may ever seek the one thing needful, the knowledge of our Lord and Savior Jesus Christ. When our last hour comes, take our hands and lead us into Your heavenly kingdom; through Jesus Christ, our Lord. (276)

In times of affliction and distress

Almighty and most merciful God, in this earthly life we endure sufferings and death before we enter into eternal glory. Grant us grace at all times to subject ourselves to Your holy will and to continue steadfast in the true faith to the end of our lives that we may know the peace and joy of the blessed hope of the resurrection of the dead and of the glory of the world to come; through Jesus Christ, our Lord. (279)

For the mentally impaired

Lord God, show forth Your heart of mercy to the mentally impaired. Grant them compassionate family members and caretakers to watch over and assist them. Help us to provide opportunities to celebrate their gifts, and grant Your Church the burning desire to share the love of Jesus with them; through the same Jesus Christ, our Lord. (284)

For those who are deaf

O Lord Jesus Christ, in Your earthly ministry You once opened the ears of one who was deaf. Bless those who are deaf that, by Your grace, their hearts may ever know Your loving voice, be filled with Your praise, and be attentive to Your Spirit; through Jesus Christ, our Lord. (286)

For those who are blind or visually impaired

O God, You sent Your Son to be the true Light of the world. Grant that those who live in a world of darkened vision or limited sight may know the light of Your presence. Enable them to find care for their physical needs so that they can joyfully fulfill their calling in this life. Grant them steadfast faith and strengthen them in Your service that in the life to come they may behold You in the fullness of Your glory; through Jesus Christ, our Lord. (287)

Those suffering from addiction

O blessed Jesus, even as You minister to all who are afflicted, look with compassion on those who through addiction have lost their health and freedom. Assure them of Your unfailing mercy, remove the fears that attack them, release them from their addiction, and grant skill, patience, and understanding love to all those who provide care for them; for Your own mercy's sake. (288)

In times of unemployment

O God, You have always been the help and comfort of Your people. Support the unemployed in the day of their trouble and need. Give them faith to cast their cares on You, and preserve them from all bitterness and resentment. According to Your goodness increase the opportunity for their employment that with thankful hearts they ►

may earn a just wage. Give to Your people everywhere a ready willingness to share their blessings with those in need. Make us merciful, even as You are merciful, O Father, through Jesus Christ, our Lord. (290)

National calamity

Look mercifully, O Lord, we implore You, on the affliction of Your people. Let not our sin destroy us, nor hopelessness overwhelm us, but let Your boundless mercy save us; through Jesus Christ, our Lord. (293)

IN TIMES OF JOY

Thanksgiving for the recovery of a sick child

Gracious God, our Father, we thank and praise You for blessing _name_ with recovery from sickness. Continue to strengthen _him/her_ in body, mind, and soul, and grant _him/her_ an increase and continuance of well-being and a full appreciation of Your gift of health; through Jesus Christ, our Lord. (299)

At the birth of a child

Almighty God, creator of all that exists, we thank You this day for the birth of _name_ . As You have added _him/her_ to the human family, so also unite _him/her_ to Your holy Church through the waters of Holy Baptism. By the gracious working of Your Holy Spirit, help _him/her_ to grow in Your nurture and admonition that _he/she_ may bring glory to You and serve others in Your name; through Jesus Christ, our Lord. (301)

For parents at the birth of a child

O God, giver of all blessings, we praise You for the gift of a new life granted to _name(s)_ in the birth of (a) _son / daughter / these children_ .

Protect mother(s) and _child/children_ and shield them from anything harmful in body or soul. May we rejoice as _this child / these children _ _is/are_ brought for reception into Your kingdom through the waters of Holy Baptism; and grant _this child / these children_ Your continued blessing; through Jesus Christ, our Lord. (302)

Anniversary of a marriage

O Lord Jesus, Your mercies are new every morning. We thank You for another year of married life together for _name_ and _name_. Open their hearts always to receive more of Your love that their love for each other may never grow weary but deepen and grow through every joy and sorrow shared; for You live and reign with the Father and the Holy Spirit, one God, now and forever. (304)

At retirement

Eternal God, You continually call Your people to new tasks and set before them new opportunities. We give thanks for Your servant _name_ and for _his/her_ years of service at tasks now completed. At this time of _his/her_ retirement, grant that _he/she_ may find joy in the new opportunities that You will provide, and grant _him/her_ a sense of worthy accomplishment in Your name; through Jesus Christ, our Lord. (310)

Commemoration of faithful departed
Anniversary of a departed Christian's death

Merciful Father, Your dear Son, our Lord Jesus Christ, rose victorious over death and the grave. We remember with thanksgiving Your servant(s) _name(s)_, who trusted in Christ and who now stand(s) in Your nearer presence where all sorrows are turned to joy. Strengthen us in the confident hope of the resurrection of the dead and the life of the world to come that we may await with joy our reunion in Your heavenly kingdom; through Jesus Christ, our Lord. (311)

Thanksgiving for light

We praise and thank You, O God, for You are without beginning and without end. Through Christ You are the creator and preserver of the whole world; but above all, You are His God and Father, the giver of the Spirit, and the ruler of all that is, seen and unseen. You made the day for the works of light and the night for the refreshment of our weakness. O loving Lord and source of all that is good, mercifully accept our evening sacrifice of praise. As You have conducted us through the day and brought us to the night's beginning, keep us now in Christ; grant us a peaceful evening and a night free from sin; and at the end bring us to everlasting life through Christ, our Lord; through Him be glory, honor, and power to You in the Holy Spirit now and always and forever and ever. (412)

We praise and thank You, O God, through Your Son, Jesus Christ, our Lord, that You have enlightened us by revealing the Light that never fades. Night _is falling / has fallen_ , and day's allotted span draws to a close. The daylight which You created for our pleasure has fully satisfied us, and yet, of Your free gift, now the evening lights do not fail us. We praise You and glorify You through Your Son, Jesus Christ, our Lord; through Him be glory, honor, and power to You in the Holy Spirit now and always and forever and ever. (413)

HYMNS AND LITURGICAL TEXTS IN GERMAN AND SPANISH

Hymns in German

So nimm denn meine Hände
Lord, Take My Hand and Lead Me

1 So nimm denn meine Hände
   Und führe mich
Bis an mein selig Ende,
   Und ewiglich.
Ich will allein nicht gehen,
   Nicht einen Schritt,
Wo du wirst gehn und stehen,
   Da nimm mich mit.

2 In dein Erbarmen hülle
   Mein schwaches Herz,
Und mach es gänzlich stille
   In Freud und Schmerz.
Wirst du in Huld und Gnaden
   Mich hüllen ein,
So werd vor allem Schaden
   Ich sicher sein.

3 Wenn ich auch gleich nichts fühle
   Von deiner Macht,
Du führst mich doch zum Ziele
   Auch durch die Nacht.
So nimm denn meine Hände
   Und führe mich
Bis an mein selig Ende,
   Und ewiglich.

651

Christi Blut und Gerechtigkeit
Jesus, Thy Blood and Righteousness

1 Christi Blut und Gerechtigkeit,
    Das ist mein Schmuck und Ehrenkleid,
    Damit will ich vor Gott bestehn,
    Wenn ich zum Himmel werd eingehn.

2 Gelobet seist du, Jesu Christ,
    Daß du ein Mensch geboren bist
    Und hast für mich und alle Welt
    Bezahlt ein ewig Lösegeld.

Lasset uns mit Jesu ziehen
Let Us Ever Walk with Jesus

1 Lasset uns mit Jesu ziehen,
    Seinem Vorbild folgen nach,
  In der Welt der Welt entfliehen,
    Auf der Bahn, die er uns brach,
  Immer fort zum Himmel reisen,
    Irdisch noch, schon himmlisch sein,
    Glauben recht und leben fein,
  In der Lieb den Glauben weisen!
    Treuer Jesu, bleib bei mir;
    Gehe vor, ich folge dir!

2 Lasset uns mit Jesu leiden,
    Seinem Vorbild werden gleich!
  Nach dem Leiden folgen Freuden,
    Armut hier macht dorten reich.
  Tränensaat, die erntet Lachen,
    Hoffnung tröstet mit Geduld.
    Es kann leichtlich Gottes Huld
  Aus dem Regen Sonne machen.
    Jesu, hier leid ich mit dir,
    Dort teil deine Freud mit mir!

3   Lasset uns mit Jesu sterben!
    Sein Tod uns vom andern Tod
Rettet und vom Seelverderben,
    Von der ewiglichen Not.
Laßt uns töten, weil wir leben,
    Unser Fleisch, ihm sterben ab,
    So wird er uns aus dem Grab
In das Himmelsleben heben.
    Jesu, sterb ich, sterb ich dir,
    Daß ich lebe für und für.

4   Lasset uns mit Jesu leben!
    Weil er auferstanden ist,
Muß das Grab uns wiedergeben.
    Jesu, unser Haupt du bist,
Wir sind deines Leibes Glieder;
    Wo du lebst, da leben wir.
    Ach, erkenn uns für und für,
Trauter Freund, für deine Brüder!
    Jesu, dir ich lebe hier,
    Dorten ewig auch bei dir.

Liturgical Texts in German

Anrufung
Invocation

Im Namen des Vaters und des ☩ Sohnes und des Heiligen Geistes.
Amen.

Apostolisches Glaubensbekenntnis
Apostles' Creed

Ich glaube an Gott den Vater, allmächtigen Schöpfer Himmels und
der Erden.   ▶

Und an Jesum Christum, seinen einigen Sohn, unsern Herrn, der empfangen ist von dem Heiligen Geist, geboren aus Maria, der Jungfrau, gelitten unter Pontio Pilato, gekreuziget, gestorben und begraben, niedergefahren zur Hölle, am dritten Tage wieder auferstanden von den Toten, aufgefahren gen Himmel, sitzend zur Rechten Gottes, des allmächtigen Vaters, von dannen er kommen wird, zu richten die Lebendigen und die Toten.

Ich glaube an den Heiligen Geist, eine heilige christliche Kirche, die Gemeinde der Heiligen, Vergebung der Sünden, Auferstehung des Fleisches und ein ewiges ✠ Leben. Amen.

Vater Unser
Lord's Prayer

Vater unser, der du bist im Himmel, geheiliget werde dein Name, dein Reich komme, dein Wille geschehe, wie im Himmel, also auch auf Erden. Unser täglich Brot gib uns heute. Und vergib uns unsere Schuld, als wir vergeben unsern Schuldigern. Und führe uns nicht in Versuchung, sondern erlöse uns von dem Übel. Denn dein ist das Reich und die Kraft und die Herrlichkeit in Ewigkeit. Amen.

Einsetzungsworte
The Words of Our Lord

Unser Herr Jesus Christus, in der Nacht, da er verraten ward, nahm er das Brot, dankte und brach's und gab's seinen Jüngern und sprach: Nehmet hin und esset; das ist mein ✠ Leib, der für euch gegeben wird. Solches tut zu meinem Gedächtnis.

Desselbigengleichen nahm er auch den Kelch nach dem Abendmahl, dankte und gab ihnen den und sprach: Nehmet hin und trinket alle daraus; dieser Kelch ist das Neue Testament in meinem ✠ Blut, das für euch vergossen wird zur Vergebung der Sünden. Solches tut, sooft ihr's trinket, zu meinem Gedächtnis.

Segen
Benediction

Der Herr segne dich und behüte dich!
Der Herr erleuchte sein Angesicht über dich und sei dir gnädig!
Der Herr erhebe sein Angesicht auf dich und gebe dir ✝ Frieden!
Amen.

Vor dem Essen
Before Meals

Komm, Herr Jesu, sei unser Gast,
Und segne, was du uns bescheret hast. Amen.

Liturgical Texts in Spanish

Invocación
Invocation

En el nombre del Padre y del ✝ Hijo y del Espíritu Santo.
Amén.

Credo Apostólico
Apostles' Creed

Creo en Dios Padre todopoderoso, creador del cielo y de la tierra.

Y en Jesucristo, su único Hijo, nuestro Señor; que fue concebido por obra del Espíritu Santo, nació de la virgen María; padeció bajo el poder de Poncio Pilato, fue crucificado, muerto, y sepultado; descendió a los infiernos; al tercer día resució de entre los muertos; subió al los cielos y está sentado en la diestra de Dios Padre todopoderoso; y desde allí ha de venir a juzgar a los vivos y a los muertos.

Creo en el Espíritu Santo; la santa iglesia cristiana, la communión de los santos; el perdón de los pecados; la resurrección de la carne y la vida ✝ perdurable. Amén.

Padrenuestro
Lord's Prayer

Padre nuestro, que estás en los cielos, santificado sea tu nombre; venga a nos tu reino; hágase tu voluntad, así en la tierra como en el cielo. El pan nuestro de cada día, dánoslo hoy; y perdónanos nuestras deudas, así como nosotros perdonamos a nuestros deudores; y no nos dejes caer en la tentación, mas líbranos del mal. Porque tuyo es el reino, el poder, y la gloria, por los siglos de los siglos. Amén.

Las palabras de nuestro Señor
The Words of Our Lord

Nuestro Señor Jesucristo, la noche en que fue entregado, tomó pan; y habiendo dado gracias, lo partió y dio a sus discípulos, diciendo: Tomen y coman; esto es mi ✝ cuerpo que por ustedes es dado. Hagan esto en memoria de mí.

Asimismo tomó la copa, después de haber cenado, y habiendo dado gracias, la dio a ellos, diciendo: Beban de ella todos; esta copa es el nuevo pacto en mi ✝ sangre, que es derramada por ustedes para perdón de los pecados. Hagan esto, todas las veces que beban, en memoria de mí.

Bendición
Benediction

El Señor te bendiga y te guarde.
El Señor haga resplandecer su rostro sobre ti y tenga de ti
    misericordia.
El Señor vuelva su rostro a ti y ✝ te conceda la paz.
Amén.

Antes de la comida
Before Meals

Cristo, nuestro pan de vida,
Ven, bendice esta comida. Amén.

PREPARATION FOR CONFESSION

"Confession has two parts: first, that we confess our sins, and second, that we receive absolution, that is, forgiveness, from the pastor as from God Himself" (Small Catechism).

Confession may be preceded by a candid examination of one's actions, motives, and nature (1 Cor. 11:28). This examination leads the penitent to speak the truth before the Lord. Like a mirror, these questions are designed to reflect the truth about one's sin in the light of the Law (James 1:22–25). They expose not merely sins, but that "by nature [we] do not possess true fear of God and true faith in God" (AC II, 2). In this way, they encourage serious, thoughtful, and truthful self-examination so that the Christian may heartily and sincerely confess, "God, be merciful to me, a sinner" (Luke 18:13). Not all questions may apply every time, nor are they exhaustive.

Absolution strengthens the faith of the penitent, comforts the conscience, and gives courage to confess sins and sinfulness. Most importantly, it declares that the Lord keeps no record of sin, that there is forgiveness with Him, that He removes our transgressions from us and remembers our sin no more (Ps. 130:3–4; 103:12; Jer. 31:34).

The following questions may be used by the pastor in his own self-examination in preparing to confess his sins. He may also adapt and use the questions to assist penitents who come to confession. He will always want to keep in mind the guidance provided in the rite of Individual Confession and Absolution that his questions and instruction are not meant to "pry or judge," but to assist the penitent in his or her own self-examination.

657

The First Commandment

You shall have no other gods.

What does this mean?
We should fear, love, and trust in God above all things.

> In what or whom do I trust above all else?

> In what or whom do I trust most for financial security, physical safety, or emotional support?

> Do I fear God's wrath, avoiding every sin?

> Is my love for and trust in God evident in my daily living?

> Do I expect only good from God in every situation, or do I worry, doubt, complain, or feel unfairly treated when things go wrong?

> Do I withhold from God what is rightfully His?

The Second Commandment

You shall not misuse the name of the Lord your God.

What does this mean?
We should fear and love God so that we do not curse, swear, use satanic arts, lie, or deceive by His name, but call upon it in every trouble, pray, praise, and give thanks.

> Is the Lord's Word evident in my daily speech and conduct, or do I curse, speak carelessly, or misuse God's name?

> Do I keep all the vows I have made in the Lord's name, such as confirmation, marriage, or legal vows, etc.?

> Am I diligent and sincere in my prayers, or have I been lazy, bored, or distracted? Do I trust that the Lord God will answer them according to His good and gracious will?

The Third Commandment

Remember the Sabbath day by keeping it holy.

What does this mean?
We should fear and love God so that we do not despise preaching and His Word, but hold it sacred and gladly hear and learn it.

> Do I despise the Word by neglect or by paying little or no attention when it is read or preached?
>
> Do I attend the Church's worship faithfully, or do I attend sporadically because I prefer to be elsewhere?
>
> Do I pray for my pastor and other church workers and support their efforts in service to the Word?

> Do I, as a pastor of God's flock, fulfill my calling through diligent preparation and faithful preaching of God's Word?

The Fourth Commandment

Honor your father and your mother.

What does this mean?
We should fear and love God so that we do not despise or anger our parents and other authorities, but honor them, serve and obey them, love and cherish them.

> Do I honor my father and mother, and other authorities, such as teachers, employers, supervisors, governmental leaders, and pastors, receiving them as gifts that God has put in authority over me?
>
> Have I been angry, stubborn, or disrespectful toward those in authority over me?

659

Do I obey all the laws of the city, state, and country?

———————

Do I faithfully represent God the Father in disciplining, caring for, and catechizing my children?

Do I exasperate my children, or do I bring them up in the training and instruction of the Lord?

Am I threatening, abusive, or overbearing to others in my household or workplace?

The Fifth Commandment

You shall not murder.

What does this mean?
We should fear and love God so that we do not hurt or harm our neighbor in his body, but help and support him in every physical need.

Have I unjustly taken the life of anyone, born or unborn?

Do I treat my own body as a temple of the Holy Spirit, or do I hurt or harm it by gluttony, chemical addiction, or other abuse?

Do I hate anyone, or am I angry with anyone?

Do I lose my temper or injure my neighbor by thoughts, words, or deeds?

Do I hold grudges or harbor resentment?

Do I ignore the plight of the helpless, or am I callous toward genuine need?

The Sixth Commandment

You shall not commit adultery.

What does this mean?
We should fear and love God so that we lead a sexually pure and decent life in what we say and do, and husband and wife love and honor each other.

> Am I in a sexual relationship with someone other than my spouse?
>
> Do I look at others lustfully and thereby commit adultery with them in my heart?
>
> Do I give myself freely and selflessly to my spouse?
>
> Do I dishonor marriage by ridicule or divorce?
>
> Do I engage in any form of sexual immorality?

The Seventh Commandment

You shall not steal.

What does this mean?
We should fear and love God so that we do not take our neighbor's money or possessions, or get them in any dishonest way, but help him to improve and protect his possessions and income.

> Do I cheat or otherwise seek to get what I have not earned?
>
> Do I take care of what I have, pay what I owe, return what I borrow, and respect other people's property?
>
> Do I give generously, or am I selfish, stingy, and greedy with my time and money?
>
> Am I unfaithful to the responsibilities of my vocation?

The Eighth Commandment

You shall not give false testimony against your neighbor.

What does this mean?
We should fear and love God so that we do not tell lies about our neighbor, betray him, slander him, or hurt his reputation, but defend him, speak well of him, and explain everything in the kindest way.

> Do I gossip, listen to rumors, or take pleasure in talking about the faults or mistakes of anyone?
>
> Do I defend others against false accusations?
>
> Do I judge others without the authority to do so?
>
> Do I speak the truth in love, trying at all times to explain everything in the best possible way?

The Ninth Commandment

You shall not covet your neighbor's house.

What does this mean?
We should fear and love God so that we do not scheme to get our neighbor's inheritance or house, or get it in a way which only appears right, but help and be of service to him in keeping it.

> Am I discontent with what belongs to me?
>
> Do I crave something better, different, or more than what God has given me?
>
> Do I seek to satisfy the desires and appetites of my flesh at the expense of the well-being of others?
>
> Do I resent or envy those who have what I do not?

The Tenth Commandment

You shall not covet your neighbor's wife, or his manservant or maid-servant, his ox or donkey, or anything that belongs to your neighbor.

What does this mean?
We should fear and love God so that we do not entice or force away our neighbor's wife, workers, or animals, or turn them against him, but urge them to stay and do their duty.

> Am I discontent with the spouse, family, vocation, job, or employees the Lord has given me?
>
> Have I done anything to break up a friendship or marriage?
>
> Have I encouraged someone to be unfaithful to spouse, family, vocation, job, or employees?
>
> Am I contentious, or have I encouraged disharmony in my congregation, family, or workplace?
>
> Am I manipulative or controlling?
>
> Have I done all I can to mend or strengthen broken relationships?

GUIDELINES FOR PASTORAL EXAMINATION OF CATECHUMENS

Before the Rite of First Communion or Before the Rite of Confirmation

Explanation of the Guidelines

Examining catechumens in the faith prior to admission to the Lord's Supper or confirmation is an important responsibility of the parish pastor. For both first communion and confirmation, candidates have learned the Ten Commandments, the Creed, and the Lord's Prayer. They have received careful instruction in the Gospel and Sacraments. Confessing their sin and trusting in their Savior, they desire to receive the Lord's Supper for the forgiveness of sins and the strengthening of their faith in Christ and in love toward others. These are the over-arching concerns for the pastor in the pastoral examination of these candidates. Concerning the worthy reception of the Lord's Supper, the Small Catechism teaches: "That person is truly worthy and well prepared who has faith in these words: 'Given and shed for you for the forgiveness of sins.' But anyone who does not believe these words or doubts them is unworthy and unprepared, for the words 'for you' require all hearts to believe." On the basis of this, baptized Christians are admitted to the Sacrament when they have been examined and absolved by their pastor in accordance with the practice outlined in the Augsburg Confession (Article XXV). When confirmation is separated from first communion, confirmation especially highlights that a catechumen has received more thorough instruction in the faith than he received prior to first communion.

The questions and answers provided in these guidelines are intended to be used conversationally, not in a rigid or formalistic manner. The pastor should feel free to adapt and adjust the questions according to the responses of the candidate and how the conversation develops. In most cases, the pastor will already be quite familiar with a candidate's confession of faith because of his contact with him in catechesis. For this reason, an examination need not cover all of Christian doctrine. As a matter of pastoral judgment, however, a pastor may wish to include additional questions that are not covered in this outline. The outline of questions in these guidelines has been shaped largely by "Christian Questions with Their Answers" from the Small Catechism. Most important to note is the recurring theme, "How do you know this?" Faith knows and confesses what is true on the basis of the Word of God. This is one of the reasons why the salutary practice of learning by heart the text of the Small Catechism has been retained.

In the case of a child, it is desirable that parents be present for the examination; as appropriate, a child's sponsors may also be present. The candidate's home or the pastor's study may be the best location to facilitate a relaxed conversation with the catechumen. When a pastor has many catechumens to examine in preparation for either first communion or confirmation, he may reserve a review of the respective rite for a time when he can gather all the candidates together. Answers are provided for each question as a general guide to the pastor as to the type of responses he should expect. Pastors should see the examination conversation as another opportunity to catechize and firmly anchor a catechumen's faith in the Word of God. Examination of one's confession does not automatically admit a person to the Lord's Table or result in confirmation. In some cases pastor and parents or sponsors might determine that further catechesis is warranted.

Prayer before beginning the examination

Lord God, heavenly Father, in Holy Baptism You began Your good work in _ name _, forgiving _ him/her _ all sin and giving _ him/her _ the gift of the Holy Spirit and faith in Your Son. You have also blessed _ his/her _ instruction in the Word of God. Be with us now in our conversation together, that _ he/she _ may faithfully confess _ his/her _ Savior Jesus Christ, who lives and reigns with You and the Holy Spirit, one God, now and forever. (881)

Examination Questions and Answers

Do you know the Ten Commandments? What are they?
You shall have no other gods.
You shall not misuse the name of the Lord your God.
Remember the Sabbath day by keeping it holy.
Honor your father and your mother.
You shall not murder.
You shall not commit adultery.
You shall not steal.
You shall not give false testimony against your neighbor.
You shall not covet your neighbor's house.
You shall not covet your neighbor's wife, or his manservant or maidservant, his ox or donkey, or anything that belongs to your neighbor.

What does God say about all these commandments?
He says: "I, the Lord your God, am a jealous God, punishing the children for the sin of the fathers to the third and fourth generation of those who hate Me, but showing love to a thousand generations of those who love Me and keep My commandments." *Exodus 20:5–6*

Do you believe that you are a sinner?
Yes, I believe it.

How do you know that you are a sinner?
From the Ten Commandments. God's Law shows me my sin.

What do you deserve from God because of your sins?
His wrath and punishment.

Do you also have the certain hope of salvation?
Yes.

Who do you trust in for your salvation?
Jesus Christ.

What has Jesus done for you that you trust in Him?
He died for me and shed His blood for me on the cross for the forgiveness of all my sins.

How do you know that Jesus died for you and shed His blood to save you from your sins?
From the Gospel, from the words of the Lord's Supper, and from the Creed.

Do you know the Apostles' Creed? How does it go?
I believe in God, the Father Almighty . . .

How many Gods are there?
Only one.

Who is the only true God?
The triune God: Father, Son, and Holy Spirit.

Do you want to receive the Lord's Supper? Why?
Yes, because . . .

What does Jesus give you in the Lord's Supper?
He gives me His true body and blood for the forgiveness of all my sins.

667

Do you believe that Jesus gives you His actual body and blood in the Lord's Supper, or are the bread and wine only symbols and not really Jesus' body and blood?
It is His true body and blood.

What are the words of Jesus that teach you that the Lord's Supper gives you the body and blood of Jesus to eat and to drink?
Take, eat; this is My body, which is given for you.
Drink of it, all of you; this cup is the new testament in My blood, which is shed for you for the forgiveness of sins.

Does the Lord's Supper strengthen your faith in Jesus?
Yes.

Does it strengthen you to love others as Christ loves you?
Yes.

We should always come to the Lord's Supper confessing our sins and desiring Jesus' body and blood for the forgiveness of our sins and the strengthening of our faith. By receiving the Lord's Supper we learn to trust in Jesus and to live in love for one another.

Do you know the Lord's Prayer? How does it go?
Our Father who art in heaven . . .

It is good to pray before and after receiving the Sacrament. In prayer we ask God for faith in what Jesus gives us in the Lord's Supper, and we give thanks for His gifts.

Here the pastor may wish to direct the candidate and his parents to prayers from the hymnal that may be used before and after receiving the Lord's Supper. He may review these prayers with the candidate at this time and ask that they be reviewed again at home before the rite of either First Communion or Confirmation, so that they may be used with understanding when receiving the Sacrament.

At this time in the examination, the pastor may also wish to review the primary texts of both the Sacrament of Holy Baptism and Confession and the Office of the Keys, using these or similar questions:

Concerning Holy Baptism, can you finish these words of Jesus? "Therefore go and make disciples of all nations . . . "
" . . . baptizing them in the name of the Father and of the Son and of the Holy Spirit." *Matthew 28:19*

"Whoever believes . . . "
" . . . and is baptized will be saved, but whoever does not believe will be condemned." *Mark 16:16*

We live in our Baptism each day when we confess our sins and trust in God's Word of forgiveness for Jesus' sake.

Concerning Confession and the Office of the Keys, can you finish these words of Jesus? "The Lord Jesus breathed on his disciples and said, 'Receive the Holy Spirit . . . "
" . . . If you forgive anyone his sins, they are forgiven; if you do not forgive them, they are not forgiven.' " *John 20:22–23*

The pastor may wish to invite the candidate to come to Individual Confession and Absolution before receiving the Sacrament for the first time, extolling the benefits of hearing the Word in its many forms: preaching, teaching, and absolution. He may briefly review the rite of Individual Confession and Absolution at this time, suggesting that when the candidate comes to confession he is not required to confess specific sins if he is uncomfortable doing so but may simply use the general confession of sins that is part of the rite.

Do you have any questions about _receiving the Lord's Supper / your confirmation_ **that you would like to ask me?**

If parents or sponsors are present, the pastor may ask if they have any questions of the pastor or candidate and if they believe that the candidate has confessed the faith and is prepared to receive the Lord's body and blood.

Review of Rites

Finally, the pastor may review the specific rite that will be used with the catechumen, explaining the rite and expanding upon various words and phrases within the rite as may be appropriate in order to aid the candidate in understanding the rite and what will take place. If the respective rite will be reviewed at a later time, the pastor may conclude with the appropriate prayer at the end of these guidelines or a similar prayer.

- **First Communion prior to Confirmation**
  (*LSB Agenda*, pages 25–27)
- **Confirmation** (*LSB*, pages 272–274)

Prayers Concluding the Examination

For the candidate for first communion

Heavenly Father, whose Son Jesus Christ loved the young and called them to Himself, we ask You to bless _name_, who is about to receive the Lord's Supper. Strengthen _him/her_ in the faith through the Sacrament of Christ's body and blood so that _he/she_ may grow spiritually and bring forth the fruits of faith in a life of love toward others to the praise and honor of Your holy name; through Jesus Christ, our Lord, who lives and reigns with You and the Holy Spirit, one God, now and forever. (512 alt.)

For the candidate for confirmation

Lord God, heavenly Father, we thank and praise You for Your great goodness in bringing _name_ to the knowledge of Your Son, our Savior, Jesus Christ, and enabling _him/her_ both with the heart to believe and with the mouth to confess His saving name. Grant that, bringing forth the fruits of faith, _he/she_ may continue steadfast and victorious to the day when all who have fought the good fight of faith shall receive the crown of righteousness; through Jesus Christ, Your Son, our Lord, who lives and reigns with You and the Holy Spirit, one God, now and forever. (513)

SINGING THE PSALMS

The psalmody in this volume is pointed for singing. Each psalm verse is divided into two parts, with an asterisk (*) indicating the point of division. Most of the text of each half verse is sung to a reciting tone (◖◗). At the point of the vertical line (|) the final two or three syllables are sung to the notes provided. Ordinarily there is one syllable of text for each note. When there are only two syllables, the first syllable is sung to two notes.

In addition to a number of single tones, three double tones are also provided. Two verses of text are sung to these tones. Double tones are especially appropriate for longer psalms and work best when sung to a psalm with an even number of verses.

Any psalm can be sung to any tone. It is best, however, that the tone, which can range from cheerful and bright to somber and austere, be appropriate to the text.

E

G

F

H

I

J

K

ACKNOWLEDGMENTS

Pastor's Prayers of Preparation (pages xviii–xxviii)

Prayers 701–708, 710–711 from *Minister's Prayer Book* by John W. Doberstein © 1986 Fortress Press; administered by Augsburg Fortress.

Prayer 709 from *Prayers for the Minister's Day* © 1946 The Pilgrim Press.

Prayers 715–727 from "A Pastor's Daily Prayer" adapted from *The Pastor's Companion (TLH)* © Concordia Publishing House.

Prayers

Prayers 297, 312, 739, 750, 763, 766, 787, 821, and 862 from *Occasional Services: A Companion to the Lutheran Book of Worship* copyright © 1982. Reproduced by permission of Augsburg Fortress.

Prayers 306, 852, and 856 from *Book of Common Prayer* (1979).

Prayer 854 by Paul Zeller Strodach from *Collects and Prayers* copyright © 1935 Board of Publication—United Lutheran Church in America. Reproduced by permission of Augsburg Fortress.

Liturgical Texts

Preface (page 44), "Holy, holy, holy" (page 44), "Lamb of God" (page 46), and "Lord, now You let Your servant" (pages 47, 93, 120, 128) from *Prayers We Have in Common* © 1970, 1971, 1975 International Consultation on English Texts (ICET).

Preparation for Confession (pages 657–663)

Portions from *Luther's Small Catechism* © 1986 Concordia Publishing House.

Psalm Tones (pages 672–673)

Tone D: Mark Bangert and tone I: Richard W. Hillert © 1978 *Lutheran Book of Worship*.

Tones A, E, F, G, H: © 1982 Concordia Publishing House.

Tone B: Henry V. Gerike © 1998 Concordia Publishing House.

Tones C and K: Paul J. Grime and tone J: Phillip Magness © 2006 Concordia Publishing House.

Hymns

"When Aimless Violence Takes Those We Love" by Joy F. Patterson © 1994, 1997 Hope Publishing Co., Carol Stream, IL 60188. All rights reserved. Used by permission.

Prayers, Intercessions, and Thanksgivings (pages 617–650)

Compiled and edited by Paul J. Grime and Gregory J. Wismar.

The Commission on Worship of The Lutheran Church—Missouri Synod serving 1998–2006

Members—Mark Bender (chairman, 2001–04), Barbara Bradfield, Stephen Everette, Ronald Feuerhahn, Daniel Q. Johnson, Reed Lessing, Allen Loesel, James Lowitzer, Mary Mountford, Janet Muth, William Otte, Roger Pittelko (chairman, 1992–98), Richard Resch (chairman, 1998–2001), Linda Stoterau, Kurt von Kampen, Elizabeth Werner, Gregory Wismar (chairman, 2004–10).

Staff—Rachel Asburry, Paul Grime (executive director and *LSB* project director), Lynda Lorenz, and Jon Vieker (assistant director).

ACKNOWLEDGMENTS

Committees and Other Contributors

Agenda—Peter Bender, John Fenton, William Otte, Frank Pies, Roger Pittelko (chairman), John Pless, David Saar.

Translations—Erik Ankerberg, Frederic Baue, David Berger, James Lowitzer, Christopher Mitchell, Gene Edward Veith (chairman), Kari Vo.

Others who served on committees for varying lengths of time include Katharine Borst, John Nunes, Harold Senkbeil, and John Stephenson.

In addition to those listed above, special thanks and acknowledgment are given to all other individuals who participated in the review of the *Pastoral Care Companion*.

Generous funding from The Marvin M. Schwan Charitable Foundation for the research and development of *Lutheran Service Book* is hereby acknowledged.

Concordia Publishing House

Editorial—David Johnson (director), Peter Reske (editor).

Leadership council—Bruce Kintz, Paul McCain, Jonathan Schultz.

Copyrights and permissions—Norma Muench.

Multiethnic consultant—Héctor Hoppe.

Art—Jackie Appelt, Chris Johnson, Ed Luhmann.

Production—Marcia Passanise.

INDEXES

SCRIPTURE INDEX

This index identifies all of the biblical texts printed in this volume and their locations according to page number.

TOPICAL INDEX OF PRAYERS

INDEX OF FEASTS, FESTIVALS, AND OCCASIONS

TOPICAL INDEX

Entries in boldface identify rites, services, and other resources in this volume. All other references are to individual topics in the Resources for Pastoral Care, pages 159–534.

Library of Congress Cataloging-in-Publication Data

Lutheran Church—Missouri Synod.
   Lutheran service book : pastoral care companion / prepared by the
Commission on Worship of the Lutheran Church—Missouri Synod.
      p. cm.
   Includes index.
   ISBN 0-7586-1225-7
   ISBN 978-0-7586-1225-0
   1. Pastoral theology—Lutheran Church—Handbooks, manuals,
etc. 2. Lutheran Church—Liturgy—Texts. 3. Lutheran Church—
Missouri Synod—Liturgy—Texts.   I. Lutheran Church—Mis-
souri Synod. Commission on Worship. II. Title.
   BX8067.L4L865 2007
   264'.041322034—dc22   2006009041

ISBN 13:   978-0-7586-1225-0
ISBN 10:   0-7586-1225-7

9 780758 612250

Church & Ministry/Worship & Liturgy
03-1178